D0961650

"Hard-core investigative reporting at its crispest. . . . The stories are exciting, the personalities border on the eccentric, and the constant turf battles among various U.S. government agencies in those often top-secret submarine activities make for intriguing reading." —*Library Journal*

"Exciting." —*Denver Post*

"Strong stuff! . . . Highly recommended. . . . A compelling testimony to the courage and ingenuity of the submariners and the intelligence wizards and operators who made use of this weapon during the cold war and up to this day."
—Roy Jonkers, AFIO Executive Director,
Weekly Intelligence Notes

"As exciting as early Tom Clancy novels . . . engrossing. . . . Highly recommended for everyone with an interest in submarines or intelligence." —*Sea Power*

"An immensely readable look at some of the blackest secrets of the cold war, as U.S. and Soviet subs engage in subterfuge as intriguing as a thriller novel." —*Providence Journal-Bulletin*

"Impressive . . . The authors managed to capture the flavor of submarine life, the innovation and ingenuity of men who have to fix complex equipment when there is no supply line, the command structure that seems casual to an outsider but which works better in an undersea environment than the more rigid arrangements on surface or shore commands."
—*New London Day* (CT)

"The most comprehensive look at the work of these intrepid sailors . . . A celebration of their ingenuity and valor."
—*Baltimore Sun*

"The authors write of top-secret operations to tap underwater Soviet cables, recover a live H-bomb mistakenly lost on the ocean floor, and steal a Russian sub. Better yet, all of it is true—and revealed on these pages for the first time."
—*Investor's Business Daily*

Blind Man's Bluff

THE UNTOLD STORY OF AMERICAN SUBMARINE ESPIONAGE

SHERRY SONTAG

AND

CHRISTOPHER DREW

WITH

ANNETTE LAWRENCE DREW

PUBLICAFFAIRS
New York

Los Angeles–class sub diagram courtesy of Norman Polmar, *Ships and Aircraft of the U.S. Fleet*, Fourteenth Edition

(Annapolis, MD: Naval Institute Press, 1987).

Published in the United States by PublicAffairs™, a Member of the Perseus Books Group

PublicAffairs books are available at special discounts for bulk purchases in the U.S. by corporations, institutions, and other organizations. For more information, please contact the Special Markets Department at the Perseus Books Group, 2300 Chestnut Street, Suite 200, Philadelphia, PA 19103, call (800) 810-4145, ext. 5000, or e-mail special.markets@perseusbooks.com.

Map Design by Michael Miller

The Library of Congress has cataloged the printed edition as follows:

Sontag, Sherry, 1960-
Blind man's bluff: the untold story of American submarine espionage I Sherry Sontag and Christopher Drew, with Annette Lawrence Drew.
    p. cm.
  Includes index.
  ISBN 978-1-89162-008-9 (hardcover)
  ISBN 978-1-58648-678-5 (e-book)
  1. Intelligence service-United States. 2. United States. Navy submarine forces. 3. Espionage, American.
  I. Drew, Christopher, 1956- . II. Drew, Annette Lawrence. ill. Title.

VB321.U54565 1998
359.9'84—dc21 98-30221

ISBN 978-1-61039-358-4 (paperback)
LSC-H
Printing 10, 2021

To the men who lived these tales,
and especially to those who shared them with us.

CONTENTS

Photo section appears between pages 198 and 199

"After all, submarining has always
been a game of blind man's bluff."

A top submarine admiral

And every man on board knew,
When the going got rough,
In this game of "Blind Man's Bluff,"
Somehow he'd pull her through.

*Lyrics from "The Ballad of Whitey Mack,"
an ode to a submarine captain by
Tommy Cox, submariner and spook*

PROLOGUE

There was something about Commander Charles R. MacVean that had a way of inspiring legend. It wasn't the way he looked: tall, a little chunky, and in his late thirties already crowned by a thatch of thinning gray hair. It was his sense of humor and his humanity. This was a man who could stand beneath a hatch after being doused with a column of water, deadpan and still chewing his dripping pipe. This was also the man who had just led the nuclear attack submarine USS *Seawolf* on one of the most dangerous operations of the cold war. She had slipped inside a Soviet sea and eavesdropped on the enemy in a way most other subs could never dare. Now, finally home, MacVean was enjoying the chance to get some sleep.

The phone rang. MacVean snapped awake and checked the time, 2:00 A.M. The call was from Navy headquarters in Washington, D.C., and the voice on the other end of the line belonged to a somewhat embarrassed and very confused Navy officer.

"There's a sailor from your ship at a bar called the Horse and Cow," he said, "and he's trying to call the president to tell him what a great job you did and how great you are. Could you go get him out of the phone booth?"

MacVean knew just where the Horse and Cow was, as did all of his men. This was the submariners' haunt in Vallejo, California, a darkened place decorated with pieces of just about every sub that ever steamed through the Pacific toward the Soviet Union, a place where men built themselves up for what they would face out at sea and where they celebrated survival when they made it home. The commander rousted his chief of the boat, and together they drove over to the spot isolated along a highway service road and pulled into a parking lot that was more potholes than pavement. Sure enough, they found a somewhat inebriated member of *Seawolf*'s crew, lodged in a phone booth, still trying to talk his way past a White House operator. MacVean got his man off the phone, then bought him a beer. MacVean was that kind of captain. Besides, he knew the guy deserved one. They all did.

This happened in the mid-1970s, but it could have occurred at almost any time during the cold war. MacVean and his men were, after all, part of an intelligence operation unlike any other in the annals of American history. For more than four decades, under the cover of classifications even higher than top-secret, the United States sent tens of thousands of men in cramped steel cylinders on spy missions off the rugged coasts of the Soviet Union. There, the job was to stay hidden, to gather information about the enemy's intentions and its abilities to wage war at sea. By their very nature, submarines were perfect for this task, designed to lurk nearly silent and unseen beneath the waves. They quickly became one of America's most crucial spy vehicles.

No other intelligence operation has embraced so many generations of a single military force, no other has consistently placed so many Americans at risk. As many as 140 men on each sub, several subs at a time, nearly every man who ever served on a U.S. attack submarine was sent to watch Soviet harbors and shipyards, monitor Soviet missile tests, or shadow Soviet subs. Several boats, such as *Seawolf,* were specially equipped to tap cables or retrieve pieces of Soviet weapons that had been fired in tests and had fallen to the bottom of the sea. No one was involved who didn't volunteer.

These submarine spies stood as lonely sentries on the frontlines of a war that was waged fiercely by both sides. Only in this war the most important weapons weren't torpedoes, but cameras, advanced sonar, and an array of complicated eavesdropping equipment. And while these men rode some of the most technologically daunting craft ever built, their goals were deceptively simple: "Know thy enemy," learn enough to forestall a surprise attack, to prevent at almost any cost a repeat of Pearl Harbor in a nuclear age.

In silence and stealth, but most importantly in secrecy, attack subs carried out as many as two thousand spy missions as they kept track of Soviet submarines. Most crucial was tracking the boomers—Soviet subs longer than football fields that carried up to twenty ballistic missiles. These missiles could launch up to ten nuclear warheads each, and a single missile sub could create a firestorm greater than the combined power of all the bombs dropped in World War II. That these arsenals were portable and hidden at sea made them much less vulnerable and much more dangerous than bombs designed to be sent on planes or launched from fixed spots on land.

There was only one good way to counter missiles carried on submarines, and that was with other subs. It was of little wonder then that learning about these missile subs and trailing them became the single biggest priority of the U.S. Navy. This was worth almost any risk, this was the reason submariners were sent out again and again. This is what motivated the decades-long game of "blind man's bluff." It was in this quest to track Soviet advances and Soviet subs that men traded their homes, the sun, and any illusion of privacy for the crowded, windowless craft and felt their way through the exotic ocean terrains that cover two-thirds of the globe. They traversed down to the Mediterranean, up to the icy hazards of the Arctic, and often straight into Soviet territorial waters. They lived with barely a view of the oceans and seas they traveled through, save for what they could glimpse through the glass of a periscope or imagine from electronic flickers playing upon sonar screens and oceans of static scratching through sonarmen's headsets.

In the cold and dark, submariners faced hazards worse than those that have traditionally confronted seafaring men, for the ocean pressures could easily crush steel hulls should they go too deep. Over the years, such catastrophes struck submarines from both sides. Just as threatening were the Soviets themselves, who were determined to stop these American spies and fought back as best they could, sometimes with depth charges, sometimes by enlisting American military and intelligence staffers to spy for them. The risk in all of this became increasingly obvious as Soviet and U.S. subs engaged in frantic chases, as misjudgments led to collisions, as U.S. submarines were detected in Soviet waters.

To the Soviets, American submariners were more than an enemy; they were ever-present pests. To other Americans, they were simply the anonymous men of the Silent Service. This book is their story, one that has gone unspoken and unheralded, until now. This is one of the last, great, untold stories of the cold war.

At its heart, the motivation for the submariners' hunt—to prevent an adversary from launching a wave of death from the oceans—seems almost timeless. In the early sixteenth century, Leonardo da Vinci sketched out a design for a proto-submarine but wrote in his notebook that he'd never reveal how one would run underwater because he feared "the evil nature of men who would use them as a means of destruction at the bottom of the sea."

Still, it was that very potential for surprise devastation that spurred on inventors who followed. During the Civil War, they tried to build bubble-shaped subs and then others that looked like short cigars, all to stick mines on the bottoms of enemy ships. The subs were powered by hand cranks and treadmills, and most of the men killed by these new weapons were members of their own tiny crews. Still, there was terror in the sheer attempt, and it was only a few years after the Civil War that Jules Verne, in his novel *Twenty Thousand Leagues Under the Sea,* depicted the submarine as a sea monster ramming ships. That his creation was powered with electricity was prophetic. The *Holland*—the U.S. Navy's first working submarine—ran on electric batteries when submerged, a gas engine on the surface. Purchased on April 11, 1900, she was only fifty feet long and held a crew of six.

Submarine technology progressed so rapidly that less than a generation later Germany's diesel-powered submarines were terrorizing Allied ships during World War I. It was one of these German "U-boats" that shattered U.S. neutrality by sinking the British passenger liner *Lusitania*, after she sailed from New York in 1915. By the time the United States entered the war two years later, German U-boats had destroyed several hundred ships.

By World War II, submarines had become so powerful they were able to go after armed surface convoys, and they had become a decisive factor. Germany sent its subs out in "Wolf Packs" that could converge for a kill, a tactic so lethal that the United States seized on it to regain control of the Pacific after Pearl Harbor. The impact on Japanese troop ships, tankers, and freighters was devastating, but it came with great cost. The United States lost fifty-two subs and thirty-five hundred men.

It is these World War II images of subs shooting torpedoes, of men trapped sweating within cramped steel cylinders as Japanese sonar pings rang through their hulls and depth charges fell around them, that remain most vivid. But there was something else going on in those days as well, the beginning of a tentative courtship between submariners and spies. A few times, subs put up simple antennas to intercept Japanese radio messages and about a dozen submarines were sent to conduct periscope beach-reconnaissance to prepare for troop landings. These experiments piqued the interest of intelligence officials and showed that submarines could have a new mission once the cold war began. Diesel subs were the first to give it a try. Then came the creation of submarines with nearly endless power and unlimited stealth—boats powered by nuclear reactors that could remain submerged for months at a time. With these, U.S. submariners would grasp the definitive edge in the cold war under the seas.

The details of all of this have been closely held by top admirals and captains within the Navy, who typically disclosed these operations only to the president, his top military and intelligence advisers, and a few congressmen who only rarely pressed for details. But ultimately, control of any mission rested in the hands of young submarine captains, who were usually about thirty-five years old and under orders to maintain complete radio silence. These men were encouraged to take risks, and some slipped right into Soviet harbors or into the middle of Soviet naval exercises to bring home the best information. Still, their prime directive remained: avoid detection and keep the Soviets unaware of just how closely they were being watched. That necessity, more than anything, was also what impelled the staunch secrecy surrounding these missions.

Still, every now and then, even a few insiders fretted. Were these missions too provocative, too dangerous? Could one failed mission or one terrible accident coax the two superpowers to the brink? Could these spy missions inadvertently spark the very war they were designed to prevent? As long as these submarine operations remained secret, the Navy was rarely faced with these questions.

It was only through six years of interviews that we were able to piece together events so long hidden, and then only with great effort and persistence. We contacted hundreds of submariners. Some responded by telephoning the Navy's investigators, and some simply declined to talk. Many others, however, agreed to meet in interviews that took place face to face throughout the United States. At times, the Naval Investigative Service visited or called these men, intoning grim reminders of secrecy oaths and legal obligations. But the details mounted nonetheless, as submarine officers, enlisted men, political figures, and intelligence officials decided the time had come to tell their stories. For the submariners especially, talking offered release. Most had never given the details of their months-long absences to their parents, wives, children, or best friends. They could never come home and just unload after hard months at work. They needed to speak to someone who understood, to find some long-overdue recognition.

And so we write about them, and for them. The people, their names, and the events in this book are real, and the tales told in each chapter are rendered as faithfully and scrupulously as possible based on extensive interviews and the few documents that have been released. Conversations are related here, as they were repeated to us by people who were involved or who were there to hear the words as they were spoken. Still, not all of the people we describe in this book talked to us. Instead, they are here because they were at the heart of some of the most critical operations of the cold war. In most cases, we had to promise our sources that they would be protected, that we would not attribute information to them or disclose even that we had met with them.

Most of the stories in *Blind Man's Bluff* have never been told publicly, and none have ever been told in this level of detail. So instead of repeatedly pointing out each time we offer new information, we have decided to flag, either in the text or in footnotes, only the details that were already available. The rest of this book is a first, even for many of the men who served full careers in the submarine service but were given only the information that the Navy deemed they had a need to know.

This is a book about submarines, espionage, and geopolitics, but it is also a book about people: the poetry-spouting deep-sea scientist who was asked to conjure up ways of recovering nuclear missiles from the ocean floor; the Naval Intelligence officer whose childhood memories led him to conjure up the idea of tapping Soviet underwater communications cables; a cowboy sub commander who couldn't resist sneaking up to within feet of Soviet subs; the men whose sub was held underwater with barely enough air to keep them alive as Soviet ships above rained down explosives. We also present new information that may solve the mystery of what happened to the USS *Scorpion,* an American spy sub that sank, all hands lost, thirty years ago.

Most books about submarines focus on one man, perhaps the single most influential officer in the modern Navy and the father of the nuclear submarine: Admiral Hyman G. Rickover. But even Rickover had to look on as other men drove his boats and led these missions. So this is not the story of one man, but the story of a force of men who served over decades. We trace their efforts through the decades in three phases: from the early fumblings, through the greatest sea hunts, to the times when technology and imagination allowed the sub force to reach straight into the Soviets' minds. And like so many great epics, this one does not end. American submariners are still being sent to keep an eye on Russia, as well as to peer at other hot spots around the globe. The stories here are not just a look in microcosm at the nation's mammoth espionage efforts. They are a lesson in how far governments will go to learn one another's secrets, no matter where they stand in time or place.

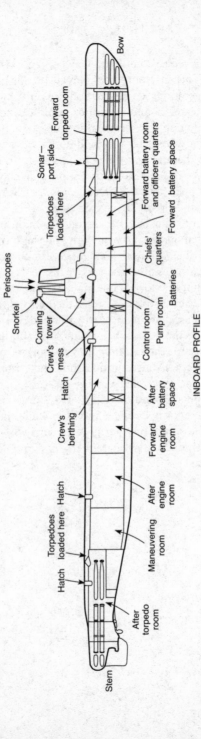

INBOARD PROFILE

GUPPY diesel submarines were the first to engage in cold war espionage.

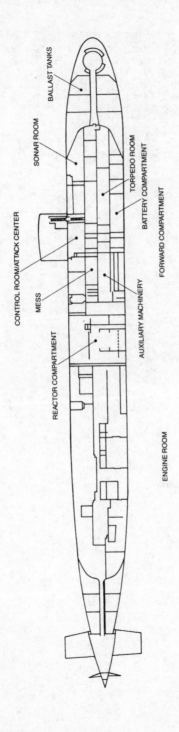

BALLAST TANKS

SONAR ROOM

TORPEDO ROOM

BATTERY COMPARTMENT

FORWARD COMPARTMENT

CONTROL ROOM/ATTACK CENTER

MESS

AUXILIARY MACHINERY

REACTOR COMPARTMENT

ENGINE ROOM

Nuclear-powered Los Angeles–class subs are the most common attack submarines used in today's espionage.

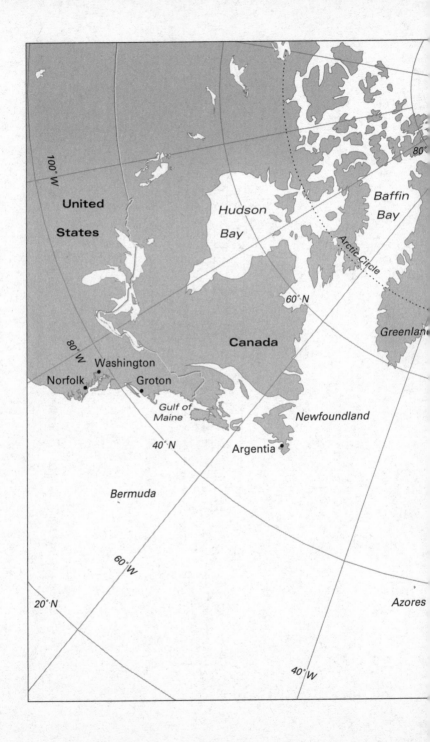

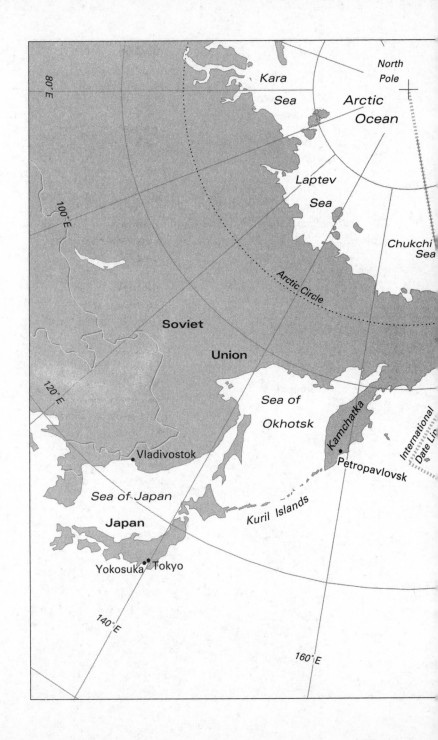

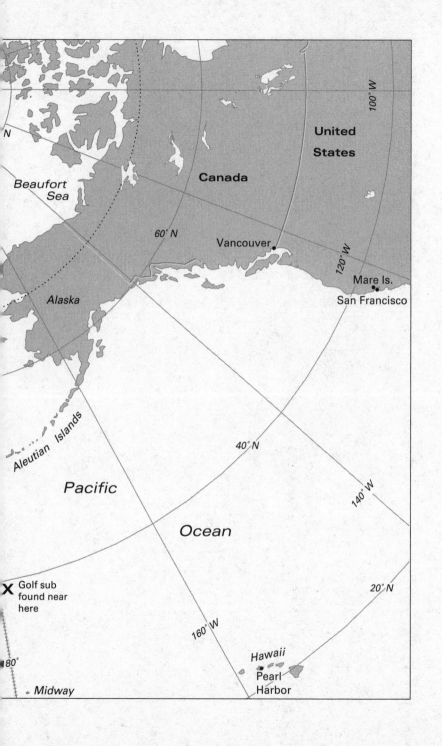

(1)

A DEADLY BEGINNING

You gotta be nuts," Harris M. Austin grumbled under his breath as he watched the ugliest-looking piece of junk he had ever seen pull into the British naval base in Londonderry, Northern Ireland. This couldn't be his sub. This couldn't be the *Cochino*.

Almost anyone else on the busy pier would have thought that he was just a twenty-eight-year-old radioman. He knew better. He was here on direct orders from the U.S. chief of Naval Operations. He had been briefed by admirals who commanded the U.S. naval forces in Europe, his background checked and double-checked. And today he was about to join the crew of this sub as one of the Navy's newest spies, a "spook," someone who had been trained to snatch Soviet military signals and electronic communications out of thin air. It was going to be his job to attempt a daring grab for some of the Soviet Union's deepest secrets.

Austin jumped down onto the pier and began pulling mooring lines along with a handful of other men. Then somebody said it, said that this was *Cochino*, U.S. submarine *SS-345*, the boat Austin had been awaiting for three days.

"Goddamn ugly piece of junk," he thought as he hoisted a sea bag stuffed with classified documents over his shoulder and lumbered down the hatch to introduce himself and his orders to *Cochino*'s commanding officer, Commander Rafael C. Benitez.

Austin had leapt to submarines from battle cruisers in a search for excitement, the same reason he had volunteered to make this latest leap, transforming himself from a radioman into a spook. That he was in the armed forces at all had been a near certainty from the day he was born. He came from a long line of Scottish warriors, a line he could trace back to the fourteenth century without breaking a sweat. His father had been a cook with an American air squadron in England before shifting to whalers and ocean freighters stateside. His Welsh mother had worked for a British ammunition company. Austin himself had been only nineteen years old when he first went to sea, his auburn hair quickly earning him the nickname "Red."

Benitez, thirty-two years old, was one of those men who had been bred to decorum. His father was a judge in Puerto Rico, and Commander Benitez had just finished law school, a perk that the Navy had awarded to hold on to him. As a submarine officer during World War II, he had survived several depth-chargings and earned a reputation for calm under fire. Now, in late July 1949, he had been back in the sub force for only three weeks, and he had his own command.

Actually, it was a command Benitez had tried to turn down, embarrassed by his sub's name. *Cochino* may have been named for an Atlantic triggerfish, but in Spanish, the language of his family and friends back home, he would be commanding the submarine *Pig*.

He had admitted as much to his mother when he wrote home, but her reply had yet to reach him as he stood in his cramped wardroom, shoulders back to make the most of his less than imposing frame. He was alone with this hulking enlisted man, this sailor turned spy, the kind of man who would still be declaring that he was "tougher than shit" when he reached his seventies.

Red Austin handed over his orders. The captain scanned them and tensed as he read that *Cochino*, his sub, was about to become an experimental spy boat.

Benitez was stunned. *Cochino*'s mission was already complex enough. She had been scheduled to embark on a training run designed to change the very nature of submarine warfare. Classic World War II fleet submarines could dive beneath the waves only long enough to attack surface ships and avoid counterattack before needing to surface themselves. But since the war ended, *Cochino* and a few other boats had been dramatically altered. They now sported new, largely untested equipment, including a snorkel pipe that was supposed to let them take in fresh air, run the diesel engines, and shoot out engine exhaust without having to surface. That would allow the boats to spend much of their time underwater, rendering them effectively invisible and making it possible for them to go after other subs as well as surface ships.

Benitez had been expecting to take his submarine out and test her new equipment, train his crew, and learn how to run her as a true underwater vehicle. But Austin's orders were adding another dimension to Benitez's mission, transforming it from one of just war games and sea trials into an operation in an unproven realm of submarine intelligence. Furthermore, all this was to take place in the frigid Barents Sea inside the Arctic Circle, near the waters around Murmansk where the Soviet Union kept its Northern Fleet.

Worse, the cables and antennas for Austin's crude eavesdropping gear had to pass directly through the sub's pressure hull. That meant drilling holes in the very steel that held the ocean back.

Benitez took one look at the plans to drill through the sub's hull, what he considered the sub's "last resort" protective shell, and became clearly upset. What happened next is a story that Austin would tell and retell.

"Drill holes in the pressure hull?" Benitez said loud enough to get the attention of his executive officer and chief of the boat, who came running. Drill holes without direct orders from the Navy's Bureau of Ships, which was supposed to oversee all submarine construction and modifications?

"You got anything from BUSHIPS?" he demanded.

"No sir, this is what they gave me," Austin replied. In a hapless gesture at conciliation, he added, "They're going to be small holes."

Austin waited for a reply. There was none. Instead Benitez turned and left the room. He was going to call London. He was going to take this to his command. At the very least, he was not going to stay and argue with Austin.

There was already little room for error in these fragile and cramped diesel boats, where fuel oil permeated the air and electrical generators had a disturbing tendency to arc. There had always been countless possibilities for disaster. Sometimes mere survival took heroic effort. That was especially true during World War II, but at least then Benitez and the others had faced a known enemy in the more familiar waters of the Pacific. Now he might have to face violent storms at the outer edge of nowhere. And on top of all of that, he was being asked to make a direct, from-the-sea grab for Soviet secrets, risk his boat and seventy-eight men on a spy mission before anyone was certain the sub could survive the ocean itself.

Benitez was back quickly, not quite contrite, but admittedly stuck. The orders had withstood his aristocratic ire. His first priority was now Austin's spy mission.

It was with this rocky start that submariners and spies began forging a relationship that would come to define the cold war under the world's oceans and seas. And from their battles would come new missions that would ultimately make these stealthy craft the most crucial and richly symbolic of the era.

Already it was clear that the United States had a dangerous new adversary and that the world was very different from the one that existed when Benitez had last emerged from the sea. Then, a nation inflated with victory had been transfixed by the image of a sailor grabbing a girl for an exuberant kiss in the middle of Times Square. Now, as Benitez prepared to return to the depths, people across the United States were terrified of the means of that victory. They had sat in stunned silence in theaters, watching newsreels of Hiroshima and Nagasaki, crying at the sight of women and children horribly burned, women and children who once were only the enemy, faceless monsters who deserved nobody's tears. People who once cheered the bomb saw it as a looming horror that could, any day now, be aimed at their homes. There were reports that the Soviet Union, the ally turned enemy, was racing to build its own atomic bomb. And there seemed no doubt that the Soviets were out to make a grab for world dominance. The Chinese Communists had just driven Chiang Kai-shek from China. A Communist takeover had occurred in Czechoslovakia. The Soviets had instituted the Berlin Blockade. And Winston Churchill had declared that an Iron Curtain had fallen over Eastern Europe. It seemed that at any moment there could be a Communist takeover within the United States. How else could the nation read the headlines pouring out of the House Committee on Un-American Activities, especially the sensational charges that a former State Department official, Alger Hiss, had spied for the Soviets?

This was the atmosphere of mistrust that gave birth to the Central Intelligence Agency (CIA) and plunged its agents into an immediate duel with Soviet spies. This was the era of fear that inspired the West to once again join forces, now as the North Atlantic Treaty Organization (NATO). And all of this was the inspiration for the blind man's challenge, the call for submariners in windowless cylinders to dive deep into a new role that would help the nation fend off this menace.

The Soviets had always used their subs, most of them small and antiquated, for coastal defense. But in dividing up Nazi war booty, the United States, Great Britain, and the Soviet Union had each come into a few experimental German U-boats, highly advanced subs with snorkels and new sophisticated types of sonar. This technology promised to make submarines more lethal than ever and raised fears that the Soviets would change their coastal strategy and design subs for the high seas. What Benitez and the other commanders wanted most was time to learn, time to practice, time to transform their submarines into the "hunter-killers" needed to meet the flood of Soviet subs that might one day head for U.S. shores.

Patterned after the Nazi technology, *Cochino*'s snorkel promised to enable her to stay underwater for days or weeks, hiding tons of bulk that stretched as long as a football field while showing only a target about as wide as a suburban garbage can. She could even stay hidden while she ran her diesel engines to recharge her batteries, her sole source of power when she needed to run silent with her engines off. Thanks to the Germans,

Cochino had batteries with greater capacity than any of the classic World War II fleet subs.

Cochino also was outfitted with a new passive sonar system: she could listen, and therefore "see," underwater without making much sound herself. World War II submarines used mainly "active" sonar, which sent out audible pings and relied on the echoing sound waves to create a picture of the surrounding waters by detecting targets and measuring distances. The result was a lot like shining a flashlight. Submarines could see what was out there, but they lit themselves up in the process. Passive sonar systems scan the entire spectrum of sound, never sending out telltale tones, and this silent sight promised to provide the crucial edge in any undersea dogfight.

The U.S. Navy was also preparing for the ultimate in undersea one-upmanship. An obscure engineer, Hyman G. Rickover, was developing a plan for nuclear-powered submarines that would be able to stay underwater indefinitely without ever having to snorkel, raising the stakes in the undersea war once again. But for now, nuclear propulsion was little more than a concept, and *Cochino* and subs like her were the best the Navy had. In a new program, aptly named "Operation Kayo," the Navy was readying *Cochino* and other World War II fleet boats to deliver a knockout punch should war come.

There was one hitch in the submarine force's plans: the nation's spies saw more immediate threats and wanted to use subs to counter them. There was still no evidence that the Soviet Navy was building snorkel subs, and the CIA and the Office of Naval Intelligence thought the submariners had plenty of time to prepare for undersea dogfights that were still far in the future. More worrisome, in the opinion of senior intelligence officers, were other bits of inherited German technology: the unpiloted V-1 "buzz bomb," a mini-airplane on autopilot with a bomb on board, and the V-2, the first rocket to pass the speed of sound. These German designs, also seized by the Allies, were the forerunners to the cruise missile and the ballistic missile, bombs with their own rocket engines to propel them. The United States was already fashioning experimental "Loon" missiles that could be fired from specially configured boats, the first crude missile subs. The Soviets also were showing signs that they were developing their own infant missiles. Reports were already coming in from defectors that the Soviets were conducting test launches from land and from old submarines stationed in the Murmansk area.

In addition, the Air Force was sending planes armed with filters designed to capture radioactive particles near Soviet territory to gauge whether the Soviets were testing atomic weapons. That was the ultimate fear, that the buzz bombs would be given nuclear warheads, that they would lead to atomic missiles.

Much of this was still conjecture. What little information the intelligence agencies had about the Soviet Navy was coming from Britain's Royal Navy, which had worked closely with the Soviets during World War II. Communications between Soviet ships and their bases were also being intercepted by U.S.-operated eaves- dropping stations in Europe and Alaska. All of this spying on a former ally was so sensitive that messengers carried reports on the intercepted Soviet communications to top admirals in locked briefcases. Any efforts to get closer, to learn more, needed to be kept a deep secret.

It was that need for stealth that, more than anything, convinced intelligence officials that submarines could be the next logical step in the creation of an eavesdropping network that would circle the Soviet Union. The effort was already under way. In 1948 the Navy had sent two fleet boats, the USS *Sea Dog* (*SS-401*) and the USS *Blackfin* (*SS-322*), into the Bering Sea to see whether they could intercept Soviet radio communications and count how quickly propeller blades turned on Soviet destroyers and merchant ships— a first step toward learning to identify them through passive sonar. But intelligence officials suspected that the new snorkel subs, like *Cochino,* could do even more. They could stay hidden off the Soviet coast and watch and monitor. Perhaps they could even find out firsthand how far along the Soviets were in developing the dangerous missile technology. With her snorkel, *Cochino* could sneak in as close as she dared. Only her periscope, antennas, and snorkel would ever have to broach into the open air. She was, in short, the perfect spy vehicle.

In fact, *Cochino* had been destined from the start for a differ- ent fight. She had been the last submarine commissioned during the war, sent to sea two weeks after the *Enola Gay* dropped the first atomic bomb. Now she and the USS *Tusk* (*SS-426*) had been remade with those snorkels and other advances, and turned into what the Navy called "GUPPYs," an acronym that stood for Greater Underwater Propulsion Power. The acronym fit far better than anyone would have liked—as hunter-killers, these subs were rank beginners, learning to swim all over again. In fact, when scientists checked the boats a few months before this trip, they had discovered that their crews and construction personnel knew so little about the passive sonar systems that crucial hydrophones had not even been hooked up. So the boats had been sent to Londonderry to practice with the British, who had gotten much further in mastering the new sonar.

It was in Londonderry that Austin caught up with *Cochino*. Also on board was a civilian sonar expert, Robert W. Philo, who was working as a consultant. The hunter-killer exercises were considered so important that the leader of Operation Kayo, Commodore Roy S. Benson, had come along and would end up on *Tusk*, commanded by Robert K. Worthington.

Like Benitez, Worthington had taken command just days before they were all to leave for this trip, and like Benitez, Worthington and Benson were skeptical of their new trek into espionage. Benson believed that, at best, it was a side mission, one that wasn't nearly as important as training in the art of true underwater warfare. Red Austin thought he knew better. But then again, this spy stuff seemed to be his calling.

"I got to have something spooky to do," Austin liked to say. "It's just the way I am."

But if all of this was second nature to Austin, it wasn't to others. His special equipment was to be installed in a shipyard in Portsmouth, England, where even the yard workers were somewhat befuddled by the new gear.

"Shit, this is just a piece of spaghetti," an impatient Austin fumed, holding onto a piece of coaxial cable that the workers just couldn't seem to install correctly. "Plain old coax, half-inch. And it looks to me like you ought to be able to get plans to do this thing. Why can't you just go by the plans?"

Austin was itching to get started. A tiny cubicle was being set up for him and his spy gear on the same deck as the control room, close to the radio room. He was ready to run the coaxial cable into what he called his "black box." Actually colored good old Navy gray, the box was one of a kind, built to capture the radio signals that the Soviets would have to use to send telemetry instructions to any missiles they were trying to test. Standing but two and a half feet tall, the box was designed to record signals on slivers of wire tape, and it was probably the most sensitive and secret device on *Cochino*.

The line from that box would run up through the hull and connect to new "ears" placed on the side of the sub's sail, the large steel piece that created the shark fin on the submarine's otherwise smooth hull. These special antennas really did look like ears. They were little wire C's sprouting about a foot from the sail, one on each side. With these extra wires added to *Cochino*'s array of the usual antennas, the sub had the look of a B-movie alien creature.

Everything was finally installed by mid-August, and *Cochino* set out from Portsmouth accompanied by *Tusk* and two standard fleet boats, the USS *Toro* (*SS-422*) and the USS *Corsair* (*SS-435*). They were operating under strict radio silence, on what the Navy called a "simulated war patrol." No one onshore was supposed to know where they were. When they left England, they were to disappear.

Within hours of their departure, the seals around Austin's cables gave way, giving Austin an unwelcome shower inside his cubicle. He managed, with a bit of tightening and some fiddling, to get his system working again. But if the seals failed again, he would have to clamp off his cables, and his part of the mission would be over.

By now, the crew knew that this mission was going to be different, just as most knew that their newest crew member was not what he seemed. Red Austin might have worn a radioman's sparks on his uniform but he really worked for the Naval Security Group, the fabled cryptological service that had intercepted and decoded crucial Japanese Navy communications during World War II. That much was secret, but even the crew realized that no common radioman would ever consult this closely with the captain.

Still, submariners are submariners, and the most popular on board are always going to be the guys with the best sea stories. That was especially true on *Cochino*, where about one-third of the crew had been through the war. Austin brought war stories from his cruiser days, and he played a mean game of acey-deucey, a sailors' take on backgammon that had been carried to sea for more than a century. Besides, it was hard not to become fast friends when everyone was "hot-bunking"—grabbing sleep when other guys woke up, moving on to make space for the next shift, time-share submarine style. The crew was divided into three groups operating according to three different time zones. One group lived by Eastern Standard Time, another by Honolulu time, and another by Indian Ocean time. There were three sets of sonar operators, of weapons techs, of cooks, of radio operators, of men for whatever job needed to be done.

Only the CO, his executive officer (XO), Lieutenant Commander Richard M. Wright, Austin, and his assistant lived across those time zones. Austin didn't mind his triple-duty load, not when he got a chance to eat some of the three breakfasts, three lunches, and three dinners served on board every day. The man loved food, even Spam, and he saw no reason to quarrel with powdered eggs.

It was after one of Austin's first or second lunches or dinners that Benitez grabbed him for duty in the conning tower, a cramped space a ladder's distance above the sub's control room, the place from which the commander or other officer in charge directed the sub.

"Man the number 2 periscope, Austin," the captain directed. It was a post where he could keep Austin busy and involved. It was also, Austin was certain, a post from which Benitez knew he could keep a wary eye on him.

Soon, the two fleet boats that had accompanied *Cochino* and *Tusk* broke off and headed toward the edge of the Arctic ice pack northeast of Greenland for exercises in those frigid waters. *Cochino* and *Tusk* continued on, heading much closer to the Soviet Union.

They spent their first few hours chugging up through the Norwegian Sea north of the Arctic Circle. Both subs had faucetlike spigots in their torpedo rooms to take in water for temperature and salinity tests, and both were charting the sea bottom. By Saturday, August 20, 1949, the boats were in the Barents. Now they too split up, *Tusk* to go off and conduct sonar tests, and *Cochino* to head toward a spot about 12 miles off the northern tip of Norway to begin Austin's mission. From here on out, Benitez would order the course changes requested by Austin, zigging the sub this way and zagging that way as the spook tried to home in on Soviet signals.

Austin tried not to let on, but he was worried. If he was to capture any signals, those special ear-shaped antennas would have to be raised above the waves. That meant that the sub would have to "plane up"—travel shallower than even snorkel depth—and expose part of her sail. This time of year, this far north, the sky was bright even at night, and the crew would have to be careful to avoid detection by the surface ships and fishing trawlers that dotted these waters. The long day also increased the danger of being spotted if *Cochino* had to surface.

"Too much daylight," Austin fretted. "This bodes evil. No place to hide." Benitez was logging similar concerns. "The night as such has disappeared," he wrote. "The best we can hope for is about two hours of semidarkness. There can be no surface running here during wartime."

Austin swept for electronic signals as *Cochino* passed by the northeastern edge of Norway. Now the sub was about 125–150 miles away from Murmansk, too far away to see land, but close enough, he hoped, to intercept Soviet missile telemetry. This was about as close as Benitez wanted to go.

On a map, Murmansk sits on what looks like the base of the thumb of a land mass shaped like an inverted glove, its fingers defined by Norway, Sweden, and Finland. The thumb is the Soviet Kola Peninsula, home to the operating bases of Vayenga (later called Severomorsk) and Polyarnyy. These were among the Soviets' most important northern ports because they could be used year-round—kept warm enough to be free of ice by a branch of the Gulf Stream. Polyarnyy was a submarine base, as well as home to the subterranean headquarters for the commander-in-chief of the Northern Fleet. Secreted beneath brick-and-stone administrative buildings were the Soviet code rooms and communications centers.

Austin was looking for telemetry signals coming from these bases or from ships nearby. Because missile telemetries were usually broadcast in the highest ranges, intelligence officials had set Austin's black box to capture the higher frequency bands of a launch in progress. If something were happening, he should be able to hear it. Or so he hoped. This spy mission was as much a guessing game as anything else. There was no way to know whether the Soviets had planned any launches at all. All Austin could do was spin the dials in his cubicle and listen for any activity. He also had taken to wandering into the radio room and tuning into Russian voice communications. Austin didn't speak Russian, and neither did the radiomen. But Austin could pick out the Cyrillic alphabet in Morse code, one of those tricks he had learned to fill the tedium during his days on surface ships. Now, as he sat clacking out Russian on *Cochino*'s manual typewriter, he imagined he could actually understand what he was typing. In his mind, one Soviet ship was making a daily report, telling its command how much rice was on board, that the fruit had all been eaten. Another was reporting the day's sick list.

Three days passed, and Austin had still collected only a few Soviet voice transmissions. Benitez decided to make one more nighttime pass to give Austin a chance to find more. Austin would have been willing to sit for weeks. He was itching to nab the grail, to record some Soviet missile telemetry.

It was on this last evening that something began to come through. It didn't sound like a launch, but Austin had also been told to look out for equipment tests. Maybe that's what was going on. Maybe the Russians were tuning up their gear, getting ready for a show. He asked Benitez to order a turn, to try to position *Cochino* for a clearer signal. Even after that, Austin was still not sure what he was hearing, or even whether it was coming from land or from sea. This wasn't voice, that much he knew.

For a moment the frequencies seemed about right for a weapons test. But there wasn't nearly enough coming through— in fact, not anywhere near the wash of sound that would have signaled the telemetry from a missile test. Intelligence officials back home might have imagined that the Soviets were engaged in endless launchings, readying to take their missiles to sea. But if that were the case, the Soviets had taken a break just as *Cochino* came near. Austin's spy mission was a failure, at least so far. He was scheduled to get another try later, but for now, *Cochino* was going back to her initial mission. She was going to play hide-and-seek with *Tusk* so the two subs could learn like any young predators how to become hunters and killers.

By now, even Benitez was disappointed as he turned *Cochino* from the area. For all of the trouble Austin's orders had caused, the commander would have liked to have been able to go back and say, "Ah, we got something," to log in his patrol report that "we intercepted this or we intercepted that." Still, as he began ordering course, west and north, he was glad to be getting on to what he considered his primary mission. In fact, he was feeling quite lighthearted. It was Wednesday, August 24, a day before *Cochino*'s fourth birthday, and Benitez had called for an early celebration.

The cooks were at work, preparing a large birthday cake and a steak dinner that even Austin had to agree was better than Spam. There were songs, jokes, and prerecorded birthday wishes set down that morning by some of the men eating in the mess. Later, Benitez would log, "It was a happy ship, and in the wardroom we expressed the wish that the next birthday would find us all together on board *Cochino*."

Early the next morning, *Cochino* spotted *Tusk* off her starboard beam. By 10:30 A.M. that Thursday, *Cochino* began moving ahead at snorkel depth. It was her turn to hide. *Tusk* had already moved away to perform the submarine version of counting to ten.

It was a gloomy day, misty and gray with rough seas. The radio room had earlier picked up a forecast of polar storms, and the winds had been blowing for hours. The waves rocked *Cochino*, and the planesmen struggled to maintain steady depth, as the crewmen braced themselves, grabbing chart tables and overhead pipes. Others lunged to catch sliding coffee cups and tools. The forward engine room got on the squawk box and told Benitez that water was pouring into the sub through the snorkel, which should have been automatically capped watertight by a valve designed to slam shut as soon as its sensors got wet.

Benitez sent Wright, his XO, back to investigate as the engines cut off for lack of air. Just about two minutes later, there was a muffled thud and the sub shuddered. Austin slammed hard against the viewer on the number 2 periscope. He was certain they had bumped a "deadhead," a log, and just as certain that he'd have two black eyes to prove it.

But what was actually happening was far worse. An electrician saw sparks coming from one of the two compartments that each held two of the massive batteries that powered *Cochino* when she was underwater. The compartments were located toward the middle of the submarine. The batteries in one of the spaces, the "after-battery" compartment, were on fire and smoke was filling the room.

"Clear the compartment," the electrician shouted, staying behind to try to find a way to put out the fire. Men began moving forward to the control room, bringing the news to Benitez.

"Fire in the after-battery!" someone gasped. Benitez answered with an order. "Surface!" Then he turned to one of the new devices they were testing, an underwater phone, and sent a message to *Tusk*. "Casualty. Surfacing."

The men blew ballast, and *Cochino* broke the surface within moments, rocking fiercely in the stormy seas, sixteen-foot waves crashing against her hull. The captain headed back to the conning tower. Then he opened the hatch and climbed out onto the weather bridge, a large protrusion off the sub's notched steel sail. From here he was well above the main deck, trying to scan for *Tusk*, his binoculars all but useless.

Calling down the ladder to the control room, Benitez sent one of the sub's youngest officers, Ensign John P. Shelton, back to report on the fire. Other men ran to try to help fight the flames, but there was a terrible delay. The emergency breathing apparatus that should have protected the lead man from the smoke and gases wouldn't work. By the time he could send for another, the watertight door leading to the room was jammed, perhaps held by the pressures building from within or melted shut by the heat of the fire.

Inside, one battery seemed to be charging another, emitting highly combustible hydrogen gas as a by-product. Unless someone could break into the fiery compartment, unless someone could push a wrench against heavy switches to break the connections between the burning batteries, the hydrogen would build to critical levels and there would be another explosion. With a large enough blast, *Cochino* could be lost.

Benitez left the bridge and headed to the control room. There he checked the hydrogen detectors. They still read zero. For a moment he was thankful, but just for a moment. Then he realized the detectors simply weren't working. He knew there was only one option. Somebody was going to have to force their way into the battery compartment from the other side, from the forward engine room. Somebody had to try again to get in to disconnect the batteries. Just then, Wright phoned forward—he was going to try to do just that. He outlined his plan tersely and without an unnecessary rendition of the risks. Both he and Benitez knew that the battery space could explode at any moment, that any attempt to enter might prove fatal. They also knew that Wright had to try.

Worried, Benitez climbed back to the bridge to look for the only help nearby, the men on *Tusk*. He was there when he felt the second explosion, a blast that ripped off a flapper that had isolated smoke from the burning compartment from the rest of the ventilation system. Smoke and toxic gases were now pouring through to the forward part of the sub. Someone called up to the bridge. The men below were in serious trouble.

Benitez ordered an evacuation, calling topside anyone who wasn't manning a critical position or fighting the fire. The men began moving forward, any instinct to panic overwhelmed by the almost unbelievable magnitude of the casualty. One after another, some gasping for air, they made their way to the bow, the very front of the sub, and climbed up the ladder leading to a topside hatch. Under captain's orders, they headed to the handrail at the lee side of the sail and lashed themselves to it.

It was bitter cold, and waves were still slamming down on the rolling boat. Some of the men had come straight out of the sack, wearing only socks, T-shirts, and skivvies. A couple were wrapped in blankets. Only a few wore foul-weather jackets. Among them, they had only a few life jackets, and no food, no water, no medical supplies. They were, for the most part, defenseless against the cold and pounding seas.

By now, there were forty-seven men lashed on deck. Another twelve had crowded onto the bridge alongside Benitez, though the space was designed to hold seven men. There were still eighteen men back aft, trying to regain propulsion and fight the fire. The captain looked down at his crew, then out at the horizon. Where was *Tusk*? The blaze had now been raging for half an hour.

Someone managed to restart *Cochino*'s engines. Benitez began to have hopes that he could drive the boat to shore when a wave came up and swallowed her stern. A cry emerged before the water receded.

"Man overboard! Man overboard!" It was Joseph Morgan, one of *Cochino*'s cooks.

"Gotta go pick him up," Benitez mumbled, now entirely focused on moving his sub closer to Morgan, who was barely visible in the turbulent seas. Just then someone spotted *Tusk* off the starboard quarter.

Austin had, by now, made his way onto the bridge beside Benitez. All of *Cochino*'s signalmen had been gassed, and Austin was the only person left standing who knew enough code to transmit a message. He hadn't used semaphores since boot camp, but now he grabbed hold of two flags and raised his hands high.

Fighting the wind, he spelled out, "M-a-n o-v-e-r-b-o-a-r-d. D-e-a-d a-h-e-a-d. X F-i-r-e i-n t-h-e a-f-t-e-r-b-a-t-t-e-r-y." It was 11:21 A.M.

Then there was a roar from within the sub that shuddered through her steel deck plating. *Tusk* was trying to move in closer, but Benitez kept his eyes on the drowning cook, aware that the man couldn't last much longer, not in waters this cold. Without prompting, Chief Hubert H. Rauch jumped in after Morgan and fought the choking seas to get to his side. By the time Rauch pulled Morgan alongside, the chief was too weakened by the 40-degree water to help lift Morgan onto the deck. Another of the ship's cooks unlashed his restraints and ran to help, leaning over the side of the ship to take Morgan from Rauch's arms. Others reached for Rauch while Morgan was carried to the bridge and laid down on a small shelf that was designed as a chart table. He was shivering uncontrollably, even as the men covered him with the few blankets they had. Two men stripped off their sodden clothes and sandwiched the freezing Morgan, trying desperately to warm him.

It was clear to Benitez that his men weren't safe out in the open, not with the seas breaking violently over the deck ready to tear his freezing crew from their lashings. He ordered his men to crowd onto the narrow bridge. They stacked themselves, creating a human pyramid. He told others to move down into the forward torpedo room at the bow, just about the only area still somewhat habitable.

As all of this was going on, Benitez learned that the same explosion that had sent smoke and gases pouring through the sub had also left serious casualties. Wright had managed to force open the door to the battery compartment, but when he did, built-up hydrogen gas exploded in a massive flash throwing him backward. He had been badly burned over his hands, chest, legs—the entire front of his body, save for his face, which was protected by his breathing mask. Now he was in severe shock. Four other men had also been seriously injured. The wounded had been dragged to the after-torpedo room, the compartment farthest astern. They were separated from their mates by the fire. They needed medical help desperately, but the medic, Hubert T. "Doc" Eason, was up front with the rest of the crew. There was no way to get through the fire and gas from inside the sub. Doc could climb outside and go over the fire, but the hatch to the after-torpedo room was more than 50 yards away—50 yards of slippery wet steel on a sub bouncing through crashing waves that were so powerful they were pushing *Tusk* around like a twig as she tried to move in to help.

One young officer offered to race a line from the sail to the back hatch, a lifeline that Doc Eason could then hang on to. When the line was set, Eason crawled, fought the violent surf, and made his way back and down the hatch that led to the wounded. Austin picked up his flags and began to signal. "C-o-m-e a-l-o-n-g-s-i-d-e, w-e m-a-y h-a-v-e t-o a-b-a-n-d-o-n s-h-i-p." As soon as Benitez received Doc Eason's first reports, Austin picked up the flags again. "R-e-q-u-i-r-e m-e-d-i-c-a-l a-s-s-i-s-t-a-n-c-e. X F-i-v-e m-e-n i-n-j-u-r-e-d. X O-n-e b-a-d-l-y b-u-r-n-e-d."

The bridge had received Eason's diagnosis. Wright was critically burned and not expected to live. Doc's reports were so dire that Benitez soon took the sound-powered phone away from the enlisted man who had been relaying messages. The news was too bad to be broadcast to the enlisted. Morale was too crucial. An officer took over.

An hour and a half had passed since the fire started, and the men huddled in the forward torpedo room began to pass out from the gases. It was clear that everyone there was going to have to come back out on the perilous deck. As many as possible would crowd onto the bridge.

One after another, men were hauled up through the conning tower, as the captain watched, thinking that some of them looked more dead than alive. One man was dragged out unconscious and not breathing. His mates began blowing air into his lungs, pumping his chest.

Back aft, Wright was in agony. Eason pumped him full of morphine, then tried to treat the other men's burns with petroleum from his first-aid kit.

Meanwhile, Captain Worthington was trying to find a way to send *Tusk*'s medic over to *Cochino,* perhaps on a rubber raft. His men began pumping diesel fuel overboard, more than sixteen thousand gallons, working to create a deliberate oil slick in an effort to calm the waves. *Tusk* shot a line over to *Cochino.* Men on both subs would try to hold on to the rope to create a lifeline through the water that could pull the raft forward. The first time out, *Tusk*'s men lost hold, but on the next try, a new line held. Watching the waves, Worthington realized that it was still too dangerous to send a man over. Instead, *Tusk* sent the raft, unmanned, filled with medical supplies, including drugs and whiskey.

Benitez also knew the dangers, knew that anyone trying to cross the rough seas on that raft could easily be lost. But by 2:00 P.M., as he counted the continuing explosions under his feet, he had come to realize that he had no choice. He needed to tell the officers on *Tusk* just how dire his situation was, that *Cochino*'s men might have to abandon ship. He needed to send more information than Austin could by fighting the wind to flag messages one letter at a time. Above all, he needed to see whether it was possible to use the raft to transfer his crew to the safety of *Tusk*.

The captain asked Shelton whether he would be willing to try to make the dangerous transit across. He was, and another man wanted to go with him. It was Robert Philo, the young civilian sonar expert who had come along for the exercises that would now never happen.

"Philo, is this something that you want to do?" Benitez said, slowly, deliberately.

"Yes."

Benitez repeated the question, word for word, just as deliberately, with perhaps a bit more emphasis on the word *want*.

Again Philo answered, "Yes."

Benitez took a breath. "Fine, you and Shelton go."

Even as he said it, he thought that he'd have a hell of a time explaining how a civilian got onto that raft if something went wrong. But there were men burned, men gassed, men freezing. The captain had no time to fight, no time to try to yell above the wind to find out whether Philo was trying to be a hero or trying to abandon ship, no time to warn that as bad as things were on *Cochino*, that trip on the raft could very well be worse. All he could do was ask Philo whether he was sure, then ask once again.

As soon as *Cochino*'s crew lowered the raft with Philo and Shelton into the water, it overturned. Now the two men were clutching straps that looped across the raft's bottom as they were dragged through the pounding waves by men aboard *Tusk*.

Benitez watched helplessly as Shelton began to drift away while trying to swim back toward the raft. Then Benitez couldn't watch any further. He had to turn his attention back to his sub. *Tusk*'s men were in a far better position to attempt a rescue. Besides, *Cochino* had no steering. Her maneuvering stations were cut off by toxic gas. It was all Benitez could do to try to keep his other men safe. There were now fifty-seven men crammed with him into *Cochino*'s sail and bridge. Below decks and aft were eighteen more men, five of them burned, including Wright. The gassed men topside were still in bad shape.

The crew's quarters and their foul-weather gear were cut off by gas. Everyone was freezing, especially Morgan, who was still shivering from his earlier immersion. Benitez took off his jacket and gave it to one man, then he took off his shoes and gave them to another.

Now Benitez stood in shirtsleeves and stocking feet, wanting more than anything to get some of his men off the boat, over to *Tusk*. If he could manage to keep a skeleton crew on board, he was certain he could get *Cochino* home, even if she had to be towed in and beached. He was still determined not to abandon ship, not when Wright couldn't be moved. Benitez was not going to leave the sub without his exec.

But *Tusk* was again out of sight. Benitez hadn't seen the end of Shelton and Philo's attempt to reach her and didn't know that Philo had been thrown by the waves hard against *Tusk*, leaving him limp, face down in the water. By the time a *Tusk* crewman jumped in and grabbed hold of him, Philo was bleeding and no longer breathing. *Tusk* officers began working on him right on deck, performing mouth-to-mouth resuscitation and administering Adrenalin. Shelton was pulled aboard three minutes later, conscious but suffering from exposure. He was taken below where, shivering violently, he managed to give Benson and Worthington their first detailed report about the catastrophe unfolding on the other sub—about the arcing batteries, the explosions, the toxic cloud that had consumed most of *Cochino*'s interior.

Outside on *Tusk*'s deck were fifteen crewmen, some administering to Philo, who had no evident pulse, others trying to keep the rescue party from being swept overboard. Suddenly, a huge wave hit *Tusk,* then another so powerful it bent four pipe stanchions that had been securing a lifeline for the men outside. All at once, twelve men were washed overboard, Philo among them.

Worthington and his crew scanned the seas. Philo and another man were out of sight altogether. One man was spotted face down in the water. Worthington began again fighting the currents, trying to reach his men.

But the horror was becoming worse. Unlike anyone on *Cochino,* two of *Tusk*'s men had time to put on foul-weather gear, and now that gear was conspiring to drown them. The gear was another Navy experiment, one-piece suits, prototypes designed to protect the crew from the Arctic cold. They were built with "Mae Wests," inflatable life preservers sewn directly into the jackets and boots that clamped tightly onto the suits with metal ankle grooves that required a special tool to unlock them.

The suits had seemed fine on deck. But on one, worn by Chief John G. Guttermuth, the attached life jacket burst when it hit the frigid water. That left only one part of the suit highly buoyant—the boots, which were sealed so tight that they retained air pockets.

Guttermuth, was desperately trying to swim toward a lifeline, towing an unconscious mate. The two men were only twenty yards away, close enough to be saved. Guttermuth's feet were coming up toward the surface, forcing his head down. Worthington watched, horrified as the chief fought his boots for his life, watched as Guttermuth let go of the other man, who sank instantly. "Guttermuth's boots then brought his feet to the surface," Worthington would write in *Tusk*'s log. "He attempted to right himself by swimming but was unable to do so and drowned with his feet still above the surface of the water."

There was no time to mourn. There were other men in the water. The rescue continued. More men jumped overboard to help. Other men already in the water tried to grab hold of mates in worse shape than they were. Lieutenant Junior Grade L. Philip Pennington was in the water an hour and twenty-five minutes before he was pulled onto the sub. Raymond T. Reardon was spotted in a life raft, but was tossed out by the waves. Another man jumped in and grabbed him.

By now, it was two hours since the men had gone overboard. Worthington was faced with a nearly unbearable reality. Seven men were still in the water, and they were almost certainly dead.

Nobody on *Cochino* knew that the disaster had logged its first deaths. But death was on everyone's mind. Austin was thinking about his wife and two kids, about sinking below the waves before he could see them again. He was comforted by the thought that he had always heard that the frigid water would knock a man out before the very end.

Benitez continued to assess and reassess their situation. He had made three attempts to vent his boat, but gas continued leaching through. He tried to send some men aft over the deck, past the damaged battery compartment to the very end of the boat, where Eason still was ministering to Wright. It was the one corner of the sub that was still gas-free, but the first two men to try to walk back were nearly washed overboard.

Two attempts were made to crack the conning tower hatch. But each time gas came rushing out, inviting disaster. The picture of the men gassed early that afternoon was still vivid in Benitez's mind. He couldn't risk exposing all the men crammed into the sail to the same fate.

There wasn't much to do now but wait, and pray a little. Six hours had passed since the first explosion. The fires still raged when *Tusk* once again broke through the fog. It would be hours more before Benitez would learn that the sub was carrying seven fewer men than before. All that was on his mind now was getting *Cochino* home.

Cochino's steering was a loss. Still, Benitez had hopes of driving his sub to calmer seas, where he could safely get the wounded over to *Tusk,* which could then race ahead and get the men to Hammerfest, Norway, and to a hospital.

Benitez tried to follow *Tusk* for nearly an hour, but *Cochino* kept turning in circles. Then one of the wounded, below at the very rear of the sub, managed to restore steering by holding his pain-wracked body against a pipe wrench he had crammed into a rudder control valve. He steered by blindly following Benitez's piped-in instructions. Finally, *Cochino* could follow *Tusk*. It was about 7:10 P.M., nearly nine hours since the first explosion.

Over the sub's internal phones, Benitez kept assuring the wounded that they were nearing Norway. Only three hours away, he had said at one point that afternoon. Then four hours later, he repeated his promise—only three more hours. Even then, he knew it would be at least twice that long before they would near land.

"We had to slow down so that the men forward would not suffer from the seas still breaking over the bridge," Benitez said, trying to sound as reassuring as he could. "I know that you will understand."

The men back aft knew he was lying. But they answered, "Of course we understand. Thank you."

Benitez choked up, amazed that this group of burned and wounded could still find concern for the men freezing out on deck, could use that concern to ease their own suffering. He wanted to get them home, all of them.

It looked as though most of the wounded would make it. Save for Wright, they were showing signs of improvement. The seas were even beginning to abate a bit. Benitez kept talking to his men, encouraging them, asking them to just hang on. The CO was calling upon every moment he had spent in the war, when he had crouched silently among another crew as their sub was depth-charged. If he was showing his aristocracy now, it was the aristocracy of sheer valor, and he was impressing even the hulking, red-headed Celt who stood at his side.

Benitez still believed he could win his battle against sub and sea when another explosion hit shortly after midnight on Friday, August 26. The boat shook violently, and the fire spread into the second engine room, moving closer to the torpedo room, where Wright and the others were. There was no longer any choice. Those men had to come topside. One by one, fifteen men climbed out the back hatch and made their way forward. Still, Wright and one of the other injured men could not be moved, and Doc Eason wasn't going to leave them. He told Benitez they could hold out.

Meanwhile, the captain knew he had to try to transfer the rest of the crew over to *Tusk*. In the nighttime haze, Austin did not want to take a chance that *Tusk*'s men would no longer see the signal flags. So he picked up a battle lantern and using its toggle switch spelled out in Morse code, "A-n-o-t-h-e-r e-x-p-l-o-s-i-o-n. C-l-o-s-e m-e."

That done, Benitez turned his attention back to getting those last three men topside. The sound-powered phones had finally gone out. There was no way to communicate. A volunteer offered to run back to the hatch. The seas were still washing over the deck, but there was a better chance now that the man could make it. Benitez gave the okay—he wanted those men topside. Still, from everything he'd been told about Wright's condition, he had little hope the exec would make it out of the sub.

Benitez made a silent declaration, "Okay, if he doesn't come out, I'm going to go down into the after-torpedo room and go down with him." The sense of clarity was almost overwhelming. A deep calm washed over him. It was the same feeling he'd had during the war when he was on the submarine *Dace* as it was being pummeled by Japanese destroyers, when he had believed there could be no escape. He had been lucky that time.

Now he thought, "Well, I'm gonna die. This is it."

He fretted for a moment that he'd be swept off the deck on his way aft—or worse, be swept off and rescued, leaving Wright to die alone. But he shook away the thought. His calm gave way to a sense of peace, a peace that seemed to pass all understanding, reaching beyond feeling to prayer.

Meanwhile, *Tusk* prepared to move closer. First, her crew fired off the warshot torpedoes loaded in her bow tubes, ensuring that there would be no explosions if the two subs crashed or if *Tusk* was too close when there was another violent explosion on *Cochino*. Then *Tusk* maneuvered alongside. Back on *Cochino*, members of the crew prepared to go back aft and carry Wright out, but as they looked back, they saw him follow another man climbing out of the after-torpedo room. He had somehow managed to claw his way off the bunk, stagger to the ladder below the hatch, and force himself to lift one foot high enough to reach the first rung. The pain was excruciating. He had to stop, and as he stood there he was aware of Doc Eason behind him, aware of the water sloshing across the compartment floor. The sub was flooding now.

Later, Wright would swear that he had no idea how he began climbing again, would swear that it felt almost as if an invisible hand—maybe it was Eason's—had grabbed him by the seat of his pants and pushed him up the ladder and onto the deck. As Benitez watched, he noticed Wright's hands in front of him, heavily bandaged. Other crewmen were watching too as Wright started moving forward. There were no cheers, no shouts. Some of the men ran to help, but there was almost no place to grab onto Wright without causing him more agony. In silence they watched him take one labored step after another.

Men on both subs were already working to secure a narrow plank between them. Nobody was left below now. Everyone was on deck. Most were near the plank, a twenty-foot-long swaying teeter-totter that reached from the side of one sub to the side of the other, with barely an inch to spare on either end. Some men grabbed lines, holding the plank in place. But as the ships rolled in the violent surf, the plank would drop from its perch, and have to be hoisted back in place. If that plank dropped while a man was making his way over, it was clear that he'd be smashed between steel hulls that were crashing together where the subs were widest, just beneath the water line. It was one of the least-inviting escape routes ever designed at sea.

Wright was the first man to walk toward the plank, the men parting before him in stunned silence. One measured, agonized step at a time, he reached the makeshift bridge and then kept going, across the plank, across to *Tusk*.

That was it. That was all the rest of the crew needed. If Wright could make it in his condition, they could too. One by one, they skittered across, the wounded first. They timed it, waiting as one boat was picked up by the waves, then the other, waiting for that short moment when the boats were level. Nobody cued them. They didn't need masterminding from the bridge now. Each man picked his own moment to rush across.

No more than two or three men would get over before the plank would drop and again need to be pulled in place. Miraculously, no one had fallen. When about one-third of the crew had made it to the *Tusk,* the waves pulled the subs apart so far that several of the lines between them parted. *Tusk* made her way back, but it was clear the remaining lines would not last long. It seemed that the rest of the men made their way across the narrow plank in a matter of seconds—all except Benitez, who still stood on *Cochino*'s deck.

Benson called across to Benitez. "Are you abandoning ship?"

"Hell no," Benitez yelled back, "I'm not abandoning ship." He wanted *Tusk* to stand by and take him in tow. He believed he could still save his boat. It was about 1:45 A.M. on Friday. *Cochino* was listing to starboard. The rear torpedo-room hatch was underwater. And the sub began to take an up angle, leaning back toward the sea.

As the angle became more pronounced, Benitez watched tensely, waiting to see whether the sub would stabilize again. A few more degrees and she would be lost.

"Now!" men shouted to him from *Tusk*'s deck. "Now!" they called out again. They saw it before he did, saw that he had no choice.

Benitez stood there, as *Cochino*'s stern slipped down, as the sea encroached further and further onto the deck. "Well, this is it," he said to himself. Then he called over to Benson, called out the worst words any captain had to speak: "Abandoning ship."

He made it across the plank bare seconds before the wood shattered.

Worthington was already calling out the orders that would take *Tusk* clear of the sinking sub as Benitez began urging his men below. Then he went to the bridge to watch *Cochino*'s final dive.

His sub was listing about 15 degrees to starboard. Water was now past her sail. She stood, almost straight up in the air, as if taking one last look at the sky before leaning back and slipping gently below the waves.

Cochino sank in 950 feet of water about 100 nautical miles off the coast of Norway. It was fifteen hours since the fire began. Benitez watched until she was gone. He didn't say a word, not then, not for nearly an hour after. It was only when he began to speak that Benson and Worthington told him that Philo and six *Tusk* crewmen were dead, their bodies lost.

Six hours later, *Tusk* pulled into Hammerfest. Some of the men were taken to the hospital. The others were given a choice. They could fly home to New London, Connecticut, or they could ride back, the rescued and the rescuers, both crews crowded aboard *Tusk*. Every man who could travel went home on *Tusk*.

Cochino's loss made headlines in the United States—and in the Soviet Union. The Soviet Navy newspaper *Red Fleet* published an article accusing the United States of undertaking "suspicious training" near Soviet waters and of sending *Cochino* near Murmansk to spy.

For its part, the U.S. Navy had gone public with the disaster, acknowledging, in effect, that its men and its fragile boats were not yet any match for the treacherous northern seas. Austin's spy gambit had failed, but the Navy had no intention of disclosing that, or even that a spook had been on board at all. When asked to comment on Soviet claims that *Cochino* had been near Murmansk, officers gave the same answer that the Navy would offer to other such questions for decades to come: "No comment."

Despite the tragedy, and the initial reluctance of some commanders and admirals, there was no question that the Navy would continue to send subs to monitor the development of the Soviet atomic threat. Just nine days after *Cochino* was lost, an Air Force reconnaissance plane picked up evidence that the Soviets had detonated a nuclear device. The other side had the bomb. The anticipated threat that had inspired the submarine spy mission in the first place was now real.

(2)

WHISKEY A-GO-GO

The USS *Gudgeon* (*SS-567*) pulled into Yokosuka, Japan, on Sunday, July 21, 1957. This was the final stop, the place where submarine crews coming from Pearl Harbor and San Diego could make preparations to sneak close to Soviet shores. This is where they would return after their missions, to celebrate, to relax, to prepare to go out again. Yokosuka had become spy sub central in the Pacific.

This base at the tip of Tokyo Bay was marked by a mix of espionage and debauchery, tension and release. It had been a Japanese Navy port and was later taken over by the Allies. Here, an enlisted man could get drunker than hell and here officers had created a "submarine sanctuary" in a walk-up flat decked out with a bar, a few bunks, and images of bare women writhing on black velvet.

It had been nearly eight years since the *Cochino* tragedy, and submarines had become central to the cold war intelligence effort. They had proven their worth once and for all during the Korean War, when snorkeling diesel subs were sent into the Sea of Japan to stand watch against any Soviet efforts to intervene. Ever since, even the submarine force's most die-hard warriors had recognized the value of hanging right off the enemy's coast, watching his comings and goings. Unless war broke out, surveillance would be the submariners' primary mission, their reason for being, the best way to gather detail about the Soviet naval buildup that was now unfolding in full force.

Spy subs already had brought back news that Soviet shipyards were churning out new long-range subs, including more than 250 Whiskey- and Zulu-class boats equipped with snorkels. The Soviet high command had made clear that it was preparing to challenge the U.S. Navy on the high seas using the submarine as the principal weapon. The Soviets were still learning how to operate their subs; for example, one of the first 30-day test runs on a Whiskey left her crew so ravaged by noxious gases that their hands and legs were swollen to twice their normal size. Despite these problems, the Soviets continued to move ahead. Indeed, the United States had received reports, albeit unconfirmed, that the Soviet Navy was modifying some of its Zulus to carry missiles, possibly with atomic warheads.

That was enough to convince even the most traditional admirals that there was more to this idea of submarine spying than feeding a bunch of egghead analysts stashed away within the bowels of Naval Intelligence and the still-mysterious CIA. Realizing they could use submarines to steal intelligence that was vitally important to the submarine force itself, the admirals leading the Atlantic and Pacific Fleets had taken control of this business of submarine spying, running the show, making the assignments. At their orders, subs were lurking underwater, periscopes peeking above the waves, watching through all but the iciest months of the year as the Soviets put their newest boats through their paces. This was also a great way for submariners to maintain readiness for battle, not just in war games with friendly forces but by driving up into Soviet waters and facing the adversary.

The top priority of any spy sub captain was what the Navy called "indications and warning." Captains were supposed to forget about caution, forget about radio silence, and flash a message home from the Barents or the Sea of Japan if they picked up any sign that the Soviet Navy was mobilizing, perhaps preparing to attack. U.S. spy subs also were now using much more sophisticated versions of Austin's "ears" to scan for Soviet missile tests. And submarines, antennas at the ready, were routinely picking up the chatter that told the U.S. Navy how many Soviet ships and subs were ready for sea and what their tactics might be in wartime.

Increasingly, fleet admirals consulted with Naval Intelligence, becoming partners in espionage. Intelligence officers invited other Navy men to train alongside them, noting in one invitation that they were engaging in the world's "second-oldest profession," one with "even fewer morals than the first."

Most top government officials were given little if any indication of the risks the sub force was taking, or of what a strange game of machismo was being played. While President Dwight D. Eisenhower had only hesitantly approved U-2 spy flights high over Russia, fearful of aggravating Soviet Premier Nikita Khrushchev, many submarine captains believed it was their job—and forget the niceties of international law—to drive straight into Soviet territorial waters. Fleet commanders graded the captains on how long they kept their "eyes and ears" up out of the water. The more daring the attempt, the higher the grade. This had become a contest of sorts, a test of bravado for the captains, their crews, and their craft. And for most of the captains, these days of unfettered risk would forever mark the high point of their careers. To be sure, there was stress and lots of it. Some veteran commanders lost twenty pounds running these long western Pacific deployments—"Westpacs," in the trade. Nobody could tell ahead of time who would be able to take the pressure and who wouldn't.

Gudgeon shoved off from Yokosuka for her turn at the Soviets with Norman G. "Buzz" Bessac at the helm. Already he had led *Gudgeon*, undetected, on a reconnaissance mission beneath a group of Soviet ships operating in icy northern waters. Now, he was leading his sub straight into enemy territory, his first command in these dangerous waters. But the thirty-four-year-old lieutenant commander was here in the first place, was on submarines at all, because he craved adventure. In the year and a half since he had taken over *Gudgeon,* he had convinced his crew that he was one of those "go to hell and back" captains, a man who wanted his sub to make her mark among the lumbering propeller planes, the U-2 jets, and the landlocked listening stations that were keeping an eye on the Soviets from all angles.

In that, he had a lot in common with the spooks on board his boat. They had their pick of assignments, these men who were the Navy's chief snoops and eavesdroppers. They could have ridden Navy spy planes and been home every night in time for dinner, sleeping with their wives instead of dozing cheek to toe with a half-dozen men and a torpedo or two. But for the spooks, just about everything about submarines seemed to signal importance and drama. They sneaked aboard with uniforms, like those of *Cochino*'s Austin, altered to bear radiomen's sparks instead of their own insignias, the telltale lightning rods and quills. Their written orders said only that they were to report to the "USS Classified."

It was the spooks' job to monitor the enemy, to bring home the intelligence, to give warning if a sub was detected by Soviet ships and coastal installations that were starting to scan the oceans with radar and sonar. Soviet patrol boats had already given chase after several U.S. subs. These were, after all, the years leading up to the Cuban Missile Crisis. It was a time when the Soviet propaganda machine found fodder even in the fairy tale "Hansel and Gretel," churning out a version in which the children of hardworking collective farmers were enslaved by a fat capitalist in a plutocratic residence in the evil West. And Soviet "pen pals" were writing Americans with offers to exchange pictures of "beautiful cathedrals" for scenes of North American coastlines—perhaps including ports and harbors. As the men of the *Gudgeon* prepared to embark, few of them doubted that they were fighters in an undeclared war. Several American spy planes had been shot down, and *Gudgeon*'s crew could only guess what the Soviets would do if they ever cornered an American submarine.

Gudgeon was one of the Navy's newest subs, one of the first diesel boats designed from the start with a snorkel and electronic eavesdropping equipment. From its fabled old shipyard in Groton, Connecticut, Electric Boat Company had already finished the Navy's first two nuclear-powered subs, the USS *Nautilus* (*SSN-571*) and the USS *Seawolf* (*SSN-575*), but Hyman Rickover, now an admiral, wasn't at all sure that he wanted to send his boats directly into the path of the Soviet Navy. He easily wielded enough power to keep them home.

Rickover was already a master at power politics. He was born in the Jewish pale of Makow, Poland, about 50 miles north of Warsaw; his family used congressional connections to get him into the Naval Academy. When he first began working on early experiments with nuclear power, he pushed the Navy to begin building nuclear subs by first getting himself appointed to a top staff job at the Atomic Energy Commission. He was so brash that the Navy twice denied him a promotion to rear admiral, but Rickover called upon a friend in Congress and got that as well.

Now he was employing his nuclear subs as public relations stars—the Navy budget seemed to get another boost every time another congressman got a nuclear-propelled ride. Indeed, *Nautilus* was preparing for the ultimate in showmanship: the Navy was trying to mark her as the first submarine to slip under the Arctic ice and reach the North Pole.

So it was the diesels that were doing all of the spying work, *Gudgeon* among them as she steamed north toward Vladivostok, the Soviets' largest naval base in the Pacific. She neared her station for this special operation, or "spec op," in early August, carrying three or four spooks, some already hard at work listening for any signs that their approach had been detected.

Extra eavesdropping equipment was crammed wherever it could fit. One communications tech, trained in Russian, scanned ship-to-shore transmissions for any Soviet cries of "submarine spotted." Another spook began working the electronic counter-measures, listening for radar sweeps that could pick up *Gudgeon* and signal her need to dive. If he could, he would record a blast of that radar so that U.S. intelligence could look for ways to jam Soviet radar sweeps in the future. A sonar specialist stood ready to help record the "sound signatures" of any passing Soviet subs and ships. Those unique fingerprints of propeller and machinery noises might later help U.S. forces identify Soviet ships and subs at sea.

As always, what the spooks would ultimately collect had as

much to do with luck as skill. There was no way to predict how the mission would unfold.

Bessac didn't allow his sub to linger long before he gave the orders that sent her creeping up to the 12-mile territorial limit claimed by the Soviets, then just inside. His orders allowed him to do that, to even go inside the 3-mile territorial limit recognized by the United States. This was the real beginning of the operation, the start of a planned one-month routine. Move in by day, get close, keep most of the sub's 287-foot-long and 27-foot-wide bulk hidden underwater, while allowing the periscopes and antennas to broach the surface.

Each night, *Gudgeon* was to move out 20 or 30 miles, just far enough so that she could run her clamoring engines and charge her batteries and snorkel, bringing in fresh air and exhaling carbon monoxide and other noxious gases through a special pipe. The exercise would provide enough air and battery power to last through another day of silent submersion in Soviet waters.

If the mission went as planned, *Gudgeon* would not run her engines anywhere near the Soviet coast, and she wouldn't surface past snorkel depth until she was well on her way back to Japan. Until then, the men would live in their cramped steel shell, working through a haze of diesel fumes that even snorkeling couldn't erase.

Her crew hardly noticed the smell anymore. Their clothes, their skin, their hair, everything was drenched in "Eau de Diesel," the trademark scent of a submariner and one that masked other insults. With the crew's shower usually filled with food, the men had, at best, a half of a basin of fresh water a day to wash with. Thanks to the new evaporators on *Gudgeon*, the water was far cleaner than the running rusted tin available on older diesel boats, but it was in short supply. So the men devised tricks for making the most of the precious commodity. To wash: begin face first, then sponge down. The men ran salt water showers from the engine room bilges and mined a few extra cups of water from inside the boat by setting up buckets to collect the ever-present condensation that left everything on board damp to dripping. There was usually enough condensation to allow the men to wash their clothes at least once on each operation. That was bonus enough so that they hardly bothered to curse the mists that rose from the bilges, transforming their bunk spaces into metallic swamps. So what if their mattresses had to be kept zipped up tight against the dank with plastic flash covers? Every submariner learned fast to quickly unzip, slide into bed, and zip back up.

Comfort was one thing, staying alive was another. And for that, the rules were simple. Stay quiet, stay submerged, and above all, avoid being detected. That was the most crucial rule and one *Gudgeon* was about to break.

It happened on Monday, August 19, 1957, sometime after 5:00 P.M., Soviet Pacific Coast time. *Gudgeon* had been submerged for about twelve hours. It would take two or three hours to travel to the isolated spot where she would snorkel, and then several more to take on enough air and create enough electricity to last through the next day. Already, the air on board had become heavy. It smelled worse than the usual diesel foul, and it tasted just as bad.

A bunch of men were in the mess watching the first reel of *Bad Day at Black Rock*. Over the whir of a 16mm projector, Spencer Tracy, Lee Marvin, and Ernest Borgnine were playing out the days just after World War II. The movie was reasonably new. What submarines lacked in water, space, and privacy the Navy tried to make up for with good movies and good food.

Then, for a moment, the sub listed sideways. Only slightly really, the sort of sway that normally happens beneath the surface in rough waters. But in the calm waters off Vladivostok, that sort of list only happened when the sail broached, catching a swell. Then *Gudgeon* began to dive. Again, it was nothing extreme, not an all-out plunge. This was gentler, just an angle that the crewmen could feel under their feet.

Suddenly the alarm rang. There was nothing subtle about the call that came out over the squawk box: "Battle stations!"

Now everyone was up and running at once, scrambling out of bunks, out of the mess, out of just about every corner, squeezing past one another through passageways not much wider than one man. They were grabbing on to the bars welded over the oval watertight doors, shooting their legs through to the next compartment, shoulders and head following. They came sliding down ladders and down stairs that weren't much more than ladders. All of them were making more noise than they could afford.

"We broached," one man shouted to anyone who was there to

hear. "The damn Russians are up there. And the old man just took her deep."

Some of the other men thought the electronic countermeasures mast had been left up too long. It was about a foot wide and 18 inches tall, and the officer of the deck was supposed to bring it down the instant it tasted radar signals that meant the Soviets might be homing in on *Gudgeon*. Normally the mast was up only as long as the scope was, say, 30 seconds at a time. But for these trips near the Soviet coast, the mast was kept up a bit longer, as other intelligence antennas had been added on as branches. Either the order to take it down came too late or *Gudgeon*'s depth controls were handled badly, perhaps leaving both the mast and part of her sail exposed.

Either way, anything sticking out of these calm waters would have made *Gudgeon* all too easy to spot, and spotted she was. Soviet ships were heading her way even as Bessac began shouting the orders for evasive action. Taking his boat down deep, he was looking for a temperature layer, a mass of cold water that could hide his sub by reflecting back to the surface any sonar pings aimed down from ships above. The Soviets would definitely be going active, sending out the deadly accurate sound beams that created the most complete picture of what was below water. They had no reason to try to listen through the static of passive sonar, no reason not to make noise. They weren't the ones being hunted.

One hundred feet, two hundred feet, Bessac wasn't finding that layer he could hide under. Three hundred feet.

Then the crew heard it. "Ping. . . . Ping. . . . Ping. . . ." The Soviet probes rang steel chills through *Gudgeon* and her crew. A ship had zeroed in on them. Bessac began taking the sub deeper and back outside the 12-mile limit. Many in the crew were convinced they had made their escape, but the Soviets were continuing to chase. Operating just on batteries and submerged, *Gudgeon* couldn't outrun them, couldn't do much better than a few knots.

By now, just about every man on board was focused on getting away. Planesmen held the sub steady through the dive. Other men kept an eye on the depth gauges. Bessac stood in the cramped control room issuing orders. Lieutenant John O. Coppedge, the southern-smooth executive officer, "Bo" to the crew, was by the captain's side.

In stations set out in a circle around the captain were the fire control officers, who sat ready to aim and fire weapons if given the order, and the quartermasters, those navigators who stood over charts plotting course changes as *Gudgeon* moved to elude her tormentors. Out one watertight door, just outside the control room, the sonar techs sat in their darkened closet watching screens and trying to count propeller sounds.

There were two ships above, then more, all joining to pin down *Gudgeon*.

Men began taking note of their status. *Gudgeon*'s batteries were at that end-of-the-day low, her air that end-of-the-day foul. There was no way to run the diesel engines and bring in fresh air or recharge, not unless Bessac could drive *Gudgeon* near enough to the surface to raise her snorkel pipe and keep it there until the air was cleared. Carbon dioxide levels were already high enough that some of the men were feeling nauseous; others had headaches, the kind where it felt as if the tops of their heads were coming off. This was the worst time of the day on any diesel sub, and the absolute worst time to get caught.

Unessential equipment was shut down to conserve power and to squelch noise. The ice machines were off. The lights were dimmed down to emergency levels, more glow than illumination. Fans and blowers were off.

Bessac gave the order to switch to relaxed battle stations, allowing many in the crew to take to their bunks to conserve oxygen. Above, a ship pinged *Gudgeon*, driving her toward another ship, which repeated the sonar assault. Every ping reminded the crew that someone on board had made a mistake, a big one.

Word came from the sonar shack. There were at least four ships above now. The men cursed "Charlie Brown," their name for the Soviets when they weren't using more colorful descriptions.

Then came another round of sonar pings. They were followed by something else, something far more terrifying.

With a series of "pops," a wave of small explosions rained down and around *Gudgeon*. She had been trying to change course again, trying to elude her captors. And they had answered. The Soviets were dropping light depth charges—they sounded like hand grenades—into the water.

The sounds came through the hull, loud. The boat was okay;

Gudgeon could withstand these small explosions. But what if the Soviets followed through with the real thing, with full-sized depth charges?

Bessac began giving orders for a new set of evasive maneuvers. In the control room, the men worked, straining to listen beyond the sub. Others lay still in their bunks, listening as well, waiting for the thunder of bigger explosions, the kind that meant *Gudgeon* might never surface again.

The younger seamen were noticeably nervous. The grizzled vets, the few who had been through World War II, could hide their fear better, but for them this moment was actually far worse. They knew what a depth charge could do. They knew that their boat's namesake, the World War II sub named *Gudgeon*, was lost in the Pacific in 1944 and was believed destroyed by enemy depth charges. They had lost comrades on subs of that era, and some of them had been on boats that just barely escaped when those charges fell. They had felt the furious shocks, been drenched as seawater spurted through the wounded pipes of their fleet boats, wondered how long they could hold out inside fragile steel.

The Soviets made another pass, then another, raining down pings and grenadelike charges.

"Stay calm, we'll get out of this," Bessac muttered to a young auxiliary man, still in his teens.

The youngster was already sporting talismans against catastrophe, tattoos of a chicken and a pig, one seared onto each foot. That was a tradition of sorts, taken from an old Hawaiian legend. Chickens and pigs, it was said, would always find something to float on and would never drown. Several of the men were marked the same way.

By now, the siege had been going on for nearly three hours. Bessac continued to look for that temperature layer, taking the sub down to test depth—about 700 feet—and then a little farther. No luck. Maybe there was a layer at around 850 feet down. *Gudgeon* should have been able to withstand the sea pressure even at that extra hundred feet or so below test depth, and Bessac probably would have risked it. But there was another problem, one that prevented the captain from testing the extremes: something had gotten caught in the outer door of the garbage ejector earlier that day. Everything that went into the ejector was supposed to be bagged and secured. Everybody on board knew that. Normally a column of water is forced through the opening, and the water, the garbage, all of it, is forced out to sea. But someone had just tossed something in there, probably thinking nothing of it, and whatever the object was had jammed.

Now there was just the inner ejector door, one piece of steel, holding the ocean back. Even at a depth of just 200 feet, enough water could be forced by sea pressure through a one-inch hole to overwhelm pumping systems and sink a sub. If the inner plate covering the trash ejector gave way now, with *Gudgeon* as deep as she was, she would be lost.

One of the sub's senior enlisted men, a chief petty officer, had carried a bad feeling about that ejector all day, long before the Soviets came. He had suggested sending someone swimming outside the sub to clear it. But Bessac decided they couldn't risk that kind of maneuver. It wouldn't have been an issue if *Gudgeon* weren't now in a position where a little more depth might save her. But there could be no going deeper.

Bessac began trying other evasive maneuvers. He called for the "noisemakers," devices that could be shot out the signal gun in the stern room. They came in cans, each about a yard long. When launched, they responded by sending a wash of sonar-befuddling bubbles into the water—an effect sort of like a giant Alka-Seltzer.

The Soviets weren't fooled. They answered *Gudgeon*'s noise-makers with another round of grenadelike charges tossed into the water. Punishment for daring an evasive attempt? A taunt to show how badly it had failed? It didn't matter. *Gudgeon* was still under assault.

Next, Bessac looked at his helmsmen, and with a "Let's try it," began directing them to drive the sub right toward the enemy, hoping that was the one move the Soviets would never expect. It didn't work. Nor did it work when he sent his boat left, then right, then straight ahead again. Each evasive maneuver was answered with a storm of explosives.

There could have been as many as eight ships above now. One ship would pass over *Gudgeon*, then the next would come in for a run. Throughout, sonarmen kept track of the Soviets, and fire control men kept her torpedoes aimed. But there was a general "no shoot" policy for spy subs: don't shoot unless shot at. So far, the small charges had not been replaced by heavier explosives.

The siege continued, twelve hours, twenty-four hours. Nobody remembers Bessac—or, for that matter, Coppedge—leaving the control room. If they were getting any sleep at all, it was in quick catnaps. Most if not all of the crew were forgoing sleep as well, even the men confined to their bunks who lay tensely listening.

It was chokingly painful just to move about, to breathe. The short trek from the chiefs' quarters to the control room left a man panting, eyes watering, as if he'd just run for miles. There was, of course, no cooking on board. Instead, the mess crew handed out cold sandwiches. Smoking was banned. It was nearly impossible to light a cigarette in the oxygen-depleted atmosphere anyway. Still, a few men found air pockets where they could light up and sneak a puff or two.

The men bled oxygen into the sub from the large canisters affixed outside the hull, two aft and two forward. But adding oxygen could do nothing to reduce the carbon dioxide and carbon monoxide that were building to dangerous levels. Nearly everyone had a pounding headache. Some men were close to passing out.

Canisters of lithium hydroxide crystals were placed around the sub to absorb some of the excess carbon dioxide. Some of the crystals were spread out on mattresses to help the process along. But the carbon dioxide levels remained way too high. The crystals could not absorb the carbon monoxide, the colorless, odorless gas that could eventually lull everyone on board into a permanent sleep. The Soviets kept *Gudgeon* cornered as they moved back and forth, sideways, diagonally, drawing spokes in a wheel, a wheel defined by enemy boats. With each pass came pings, then grenades.

Wednesday, August 21, early morning: no change. Wednesday afternoon: no change. Wednesday, early evening: *Gudgeon* had been under siege for nearly forty-eight hours and underwater without snorkeling for nearly sixty-four hours. Bessac had dutifully noted the distance traveled in his logs over these two days as zero. Something had to be done, something drastic.

Coppedge began walking through the boat, telling the men they were going to have to try to snorkel, try to "stick our nose up." For most of the siege, the men had been at relaxed battle stations. Now they were called to full battle stations. They had to get fresh air. They had to send a message for help. They had to alter the status quo or die.

"We're going to come up," Bessac announced in the control room. "As soon as we hit, start to snorkel."

As *Gudgeon* came up, some of the men tried to run the hydraulics that would raise the radio antenna. The antenna wouldn't budge. It should have shot up with a bang. But all they could hear was one bump, then another. As soon as *Gudgeon*'s snorkel broached the surface, the men started the engines. The sub took one gulp, then another.

Then one of the ships made its move, came roaring right at *Gudgeon* as if to ram her, or at least to force her down. The Soviets weren't finished with the sub. They weren't going to let her men get air, and they certainly weren't going to let them yell for help.

Someone hit the collision alarm, and Bessac gave the order to dive. The engines were shut down, and *Gudgeon* was back under. The crew hadn't been able to send an SOS. The air was just as bad as before.

Bessac ordered *Gudgeon* down to about 400 feet while he pondered his next move. He consulted with Coppedge, who talked to the engineering officer about the state of the batteries and with Doc Huntley, the corpsman, about the status of the air and crew. Bessac had few choices. It was obvious that his men couldn't survive much longer. The batteries might last another eight hours or so if the sub didn't move much, but that wasn't going to accomplish anything. The old man knew he didn't have the power to outrun his tormentors.

Within moments, the decision was made. *Gudgeon* was going to try to snorkel again, and she would probably have to surface. But one thing would not happen. She would not be boarded; she would not be taken. The captain and the crew would die first. Not a single man on board objected.

Bessac ordered all the torpedo doors opened. He knew the Soviets would be able to hear them, and he wanted to show that the Americans meant business. Then, some of the officers were handed pistols, including Doc Huntley, who went around the boat waving his .45, saying it was his job to shoot the spooks if the Soviets tried to board. "You could take a green pill, or I could shoot you," he told one spook. Doc had always been a little different.

Doc probably wasn't authorized to go around touting his death's-head mask. Maybe, the crew mused, he never should have been issued a gun. But he had the .45, and for the moment the spooks were more afraid of Doc than they were of the Soviets.

Meanwhile, the spooks and the men in the radio shack across the control room, anyone who handled any codes or other sensitive papers, began loading them into leather bags that were speckled with holes and weighted down with lead. Some documents were destroyed outright. If the Soviets tried to board, those bags would go out the upper hatch and down to the bottom of the Sea of Japan.

This was the moment that no submariner wants to experience, and it was one of the worst moments any captain could face. It was also a moment that was unavoidable. Maybe *Gudgeon* would have gotten away if she had been able to go deeper, if that garbage ejector door hadn't jammed. Whatever the reasons, Bessac had been beaten.

Dejected, he gave the order to rise.

Bessac wanted to get a message out to the U.S. base in Japan. But on the way up, the radio mast jammed again. As soon as the snorkel hit the surface, Bessac gave the order and all three of *Gudgeon*'s engines came on line, shooting exhaust fumes into the sub's fouled atmosphere as well as outside. Nobody cared about the exhaust now, not as long as the snorkel kept sucking in fresh air and venting out the worst of the poisons the men had been breathing.

The sub was at periscope depth now, and it was clear that the Soviet ships were hanging back. But for how long?

A minute passed, then two. Then five. The men still hadn't been able to send the message. But *Gudgeon* was taking in air, shooting out exhaust. The men wondered whether their CO would go through with this, and surface.

Bessac was calculating, figuring his options even at the last minute. *Gudgeon* would need at least twenty minutes of snorkel time to clear the air minimally, and that wouldn't even begin to charge her batteries. If she had to dive again, she could, at best, crawl through the water on battery power. If she stayed at snorkel depth, she could transfer one engine to charging the batteries and still move a little faster. But it was only on the surface that *Gudgeon* could make a run for Japan at her top speed of about 20 knots. There was no telling whether the Soviet ships would try to charge again, but at that speed, and with a head start, maybe, just maybe, she could outrun them.

He made the only decision he could. Bessac told his crew to surface.

No one had been wounded, no swords had been broken, and no territory had been given up. But the United States had just lost a crucial battle. For the first time in this cold war under the sea, a U.S. sub had been forced to give up, to come out from hiding and sit vulnerable on top of the waves.

After that, Bessac told his men to send out an all-too-late cry for help.

"Send the damn thing in English," he shouted, answering a question from the radioman the crew called "Bad Ass."

There was no use trying to hide who they were anymore. The message went out unencoded. Meanwhile, the captain began climbing the long ladder that led from the hatch in the control room to the sail and up to the bridge. After him climbed one of the officers, a signalman, and a crew member to man the voice-powered phones that would send Bessac's orders ringing through the ship if the Soviets moved in for a fight. If there was a destroyer out there, *Gudgeon* didn't stand a chance.

It was still daylight outside. And the men on the bridge could see the Soviets. Two ships, maybe three, were left on the surface. All of them were smallish sub-hunters. The Soviets had pulled the rest of the ships back. It didn't take a crowd to herd a sub on dying batteries.

The Soviets signaled "Able. Able."—international Morse code for "Who are you? Identify yourself."

Gudgeon sent back, "Able. Able."

The Soviets answered, "CCCP," Russian for USSR.

Gudgeon sent back, again in international Morse code, "USN. We are going to Japan."

The response came back, a directive for *Gudgeon* to get under way and away from Soviet seas. The signalman blithely interpreted for the crew: "They said, 'Thanks for the ASW exercise.'"

Thanks for helping us practice antisubmarine warfare. He unsuccessfully suppressed a grin. The rest of the crew was grinning as well. In fact, the men were elated. They were getting the hell out of there.

The celebration had already begun when, it seemed like hours later, U.S. planes flew over to see whether *Gudgeon* was okay as she raced on the surface, putting as much distance as possible between herself and the Soviet Union.

For the first time in days, the cooks heated up the ovens. There was steak for dinner that night and two cans of beer per man. The men were amazed. It had never occurred to them that there would be beer on board, certainly not cases of it. But there it was, and these men would much rather drink than quote regulations to the old man. They were moving, they were breathing, the batteries were charging. They were embarassed, even bloodied. But at that moment, they didn't care. They were safely away, and for the first time the men admitted to one another that they had never been certain they would escape. The Soviets had obviously been capable of sinking the sub. They just didn't want to. Or maybe, the crew mused, they did want to but weren't allowed.

There was no official celebration for *Gudgeon*'s return back at Yokosuka when she pulled in that Monday, August 26, eight years to the day since *Cochino* had sunk. The mood at the base was grim: the Soviets announced that day that they had conducted their first successful flight test of a land-based intercontinental ballistic missile (ICBM). In such a tense climate, the Navy wanted the *Gudgeon* incident squashed and squashed fast.

"Bad Ass," the radio tech who had sent the message in English, was promoted to chief and transferred off the boat instantly. Word was, the sub force made him send messages from then on with his left hand, lest his style, his signature of sorts, tell anyone intercepting communications that a U.S. sub was around.

Bessac was off the boat as well. Slated for transfer before the hold-down, from diesel boats to a billet in Admiral Rickover's nuclear Navy, his orders didn't change. What did change, however, was *Gudgeon*'s operating schedule. The Navy hastily announced that she was going to become the first submarine of any nation to circumnavigate the globe. It was the best way to get her out of the Pacific, where she was now well known to the

Soviets, and it was the best way to try to keep the story from spreading throughout the sub force.

Of course, the Navy offered other explanations for the trip. Deeming it designed to implement a "People to People" program, President Eisenhower personally designated each man on the boat "an Ambassador of good will to the world." Each of these ambassadors was ordered never to talk about the incident.

Meanwhile, energized by its victory, the Soviet Navy began roughing up other U.S. spy subs. Among them was the USS *Wahoo* (SS-565), which was caught near a Soviet beach early in 1958 but managed to escape even though one of her engines blew out. Perhaps because subs went about their work quietly, the Soviets showed more restraint than they did with spy planes, some of which deliberately lit up defense radars in order to measure those systems. As nasty as the underwater battles got, no subs were sunk, and the "depth charges" were usually no more powerful than the small explosives dropped on *Gudgeon*.

But submarine battles in Soviet territory were now firmly entrenched as part of the cold war, and tensions only intensified as both sides prepared to deploy their first missile subs. After the Soviets launched *Sputnik* in the fall of 1957, President Eisenhower quickly accelerated plans to build nuclear-powered subs that could fire Polaris ballistic missiles while hiding underwater. In the meantime, the Navy was refitting some diesel subs to carry Regulus guided missiles, descendants of the German buzz bombs with ranges of between 300 and 400 nautical miles. The Regulus subs would have to surface to launch, and the missiles would have to be guided by radar from launch to landing by both the sub and a second boat positioned closer to the Soviet coast, but they would still be a potent new threat to the Soviets.

The fear that the Soviets would answer by sending their own spy subs and missile boats close to U.S. waters prodded top officials in Washington to extend their grasp over this business of underwater spying. Suddenly, operations that Navy fleet commanders had become used to controlling were being reviewed by the White House and the Pentagon. The CIA and the National Security Agency—the code-breaking agency that was so supersecretive that even people who worked there joked that NSA stood for "No Such Agency" or "Never Say Anything"—also began to play a larger role in setting the priorities for what intelligence would be collected.

Hardly any of the Soviet diesel subs had made the long transit to U.S. shores yet, but that didn't stop an outbreak of "Red hysteria." One member of the House of Representatives proclaimed that nearly two hundred Soviet subs had been sighted off the Atlantic coast. Ordinary citizens began manning "submarine watchtowers," and over the next several years submarine "sightings" became more frequent. One woman identified in Navy documents only as Mrs. Gilkinson would report seeing three subs near a Florida beach, including one that she said came within ten feet of her while she was skin-diving. A man in Texas reported spotting a periscope in what turned out to be five feet of water.

The Navy was watching for Soviet subs as well, but much of the surveillance was taking place just outside the natural bottleneck created by Greenland, Iceland, and the United Kingdom. It was an enormous advantage for the United States. Soviet ships and subs had to pass through this chokepoint, the "GIUK" gap, to take the Atlantic route to the United States. A string of U.S. diesel subs were often stationed on "barrier ops" outside the gap, and British naval forces also kept watch for Soviet subs. In addition, the U.S. Navy had begun seeding both the Atlantic and Pacific coasts with underwater listening devices—creating an underwater eavesdropping net known as SOSUS, for sound surveillance system—to detect ships and subs. Still, analysts trying to decipher the SOSUS recordings needed more data to be able to pick out the sounds of Soviet warships from all the background noise made by fishing trawlers and merchant ships. They needed a library of sound signatures, and that could best be created by sending spy subs to listen and record.

There was one other thing the Navy was looking for: a chance for retribution. It wanted to get the Soviets back for *Gudgeon* and other acts of harassment against U.S. subs. Admiral Jerauld Wright, commander in chief of the Atlantic Fleet, posted a framed proclamation outside his office:

Whereas, the presence of unidentified submarines in the approaches to the United States has been frequently reported, and

Whereas, the submarines have been uncooperative in declaring either their identity or their intent as is required by the customs and usages of honorable seamen, and

Whereas, tangible evidence that these surreptitious operations are being conducted would result in appropriate embarrassment to those involved.

Therefore, I do hereby pledge to donate one case of Jack Daniels Old No. 7 Brand of Quality Tennessee Sour Mash Corn Whiskey, made as our fathers made it for seven generations at the oldest registered whiskey distillery in the United States, established 1866, to the first Scene of Action Commander in the Atlantic who produces evidence that a "non U.S. or known friendly" submarine has been worn out.

/s/ Jerauld Wright
Admiral, U.S. Navy

In May 1959, Wright declared a winner. The USS *Grenadier* (*SS-525*) chased a Soviet submarine near Iceland for nine hours before forcing it to surface, completely "worn out." *Grenadier's* skipper, Lieutenant Commander Theodore F. Davis, got the whiskey, and the Navy had surfaced its first Soviet sub.

More important, the Navy also had its first good look at a Soviet missile boat. Davis had trapped one of the Zulus that had been converted to carry missiles. He also brought home photographs and sound tapes, and the Navy quietly broadcast his success all over Washington. In fact, later that year President Eisenhower's special assistant for science and technology, George B. Kistiakowsky, noted in his diary that he had received "a very interesting account of the ways in which our Navy gets intimate information on the Soviet naval activities," a briefing that was so "hush-hush" he couldn't put it on paper. "Someday," he mused, "it will make a very exciting news story."

Something else came out of these dogfights as well. There was a growing realization on both sides that as much as the snorkel had revolutionized submarine warfare, it had massive limitations. As long as submarines could be held down and their crews choked, they were still too vulnerable. For the U.S. sub force, it was clear that Rickover's nuclear navy could no longer remain a curiosity. It was time for his submarines to move to center stage.

Rickover's revolutionary boats had a seemingly endless source of power. Reactors split atoms and turned water into steam, steam enough to power a propeller shaft and run a submarine longer and faster than any diesel boat ever could. They also could generate their own oxygen and scrub excess carbon dioxide from their air. Hold-downs would no longer be a threat. These boats would be able to stay underwater indefinitely.

Nuclear attack subs began to take on missions that closely mirrored those pioneered by diesel subs, invading Soviet waters with impunity. The orders remained similar. Drive close to Soviet craft, even closer to Soviet shores. Take any risks. Don't get caught.

For instance, in late 1960, Commander William "Bill" Behrens drove the USS *Skipjack* (*SSN-585*) into the mouth of the long ship channel that led to Murmansk. He got so close to another Soviet port that his officers could look through a periscope and see the pier only 30 or 40 yards away. That may have been closer than even the Navy would have liked—at least closer than the Navy ever wanted to admit. Indeed, just before Behrens snuck into the channel, crewmen saw one of his officers disable a mechanical tracing device that plotted the sub's movements so there would never be any written record of the incursion. Later on that same mission, Behrens also monitored the sea trials of one of the first Golf-class subs, a diesel-powered boat that was the first Soviet submarine designed from the start to carry ballistic missiles. Behrens, who initially struck some of his crew as stuffy and dull, had proven that he could play as dangerously as other captains, that he could be one man on shore and quite another at sea, especially at sea in Soviet waters.

In this sense, Behrens was not alone. This was an era of daredevil nuclear-sub captains who seemed rooted in the no-holds-barred diesel heritage. Over in the Pacific, a couple of captains briefly turned off their reactors to cut down on the background noise when they tried to get sound signatures—and suddenly found their own boats drifting way too deep. Another sub lurking at periscope depth got bumped by a Soviet sub that started to surface from below.

One of the most urgent goals was to find out where the Soviets stood in their quest to develop nuclear-powered subs. Though some top U.S. officials were reluctant to believe it, it gradually became clear that the Soviets were starting to turn out three types: "Hotels," each armed with three ballistic missiles; "Echos" carrying cruise missiles meant for use against ships; and "November" attack subs. Still, early surveillance showed that these subs were so crude and noisy that the U.S. Navy had taken to using a shorthand built on a convenient acronym, nicknaming them the "HENs." And neither the Golfs nor the Hotels were anywhere near ready to head out on patrol.

It was clear that the United States had won the race to position missile subs within range of enemy shores. Four diesel boats with the primitive Regulus missiles had led the way in the Pacific in 1959 and 1960, and the first Polaris sub, the USS *George Washington* (*SSBN-598*), ventured out into the Atlantic under way on nuclear power in November 1960. In no time, the Regulus subs were spending so much time lurking in terrible weather off the Soviet coast that their crews took to jokingly calling themselves the "Northern Pacific Yacht Club." One, the USS *Growler* (*SSG-577*), was heavily damaged when she ran into an ice floe near the Kamchatka Peninsula, just off the Soviet base at Petropavlovsk. Before long, the men designed lapel pins showing an anchor crossed by three semaphore flags, labeled "S," "M," and "F." The initials stood for the typical cry during a storm: "Shit! Man! Fuck!"

Throughout these deployments, the Polaris program was pushing on. President Eisenhower had given William F. "Red" Raborn, the garrulous rear admiral in charge of Polaris, unprecedented authority, allowing him to bypass the usual red tape and to hire anyone he decided could do the work of designing and building Polaris subs well, and fast. There were predictable snags with new technology. (Raborn's aides showed enough humor to compile a classified film of Polaris bloopers—test missiles that barely rose at all and others that just cartwheeled.) But Polaris succeeded, and timetables were met, largely because the program was given top priority. Everyone was working such ungodly hours that the submariners came to believe that the new boats were designated SSBNs not because "SS" stood for submersible ship, "N" for nuclear power, and "B" for ballistic missiles, but because the initials stood for "Saturday, Sunday, and a Bunch of Nights."

While Raborn and his team labored to ensure that the subs were built, it was up to Rickover to oversee the installation of the nuclear reactors and the crews that would run them. Rickover was looking for men who would be unflinching in a crisis, men willing to pay attention to exact detail, men who were as meticulous as he was. He was convinced that was the only way to ensure reactor safety, and he knew that reactor safety was the only way to maintain public support for his nuclear-powered submarines. With all of this, he was helping to create a submarine force that would be unparalleled. Now Rickover's men were about to drive the most lethal subs ever built, subs that would prove crucial to the balance of power in the cold war.

The first Polaris subs were 382 feet long, about 60 feet longer than nuclear attack subs, and they carried sixteen nuclear-tipped missiles that could be aimed at targets more than 1,000 nautical miles away. They also were given two crews, blue and gold, who went out on alternating 60-day cruises—keeping the subs at sea as much as possible. The duty was tough. The 1,000-mile missile range forced these boats to ride the rough waters off the northern coast of Europe to stay near targeting distance of Moscow. Their job was to "hide with pride," to be an intercontinental missile force lurking and ready to fire a second strike if the nation were attacked and land missiles destroyed.*

For their part, the Soviets had only a few nuclear-powered

---

*Although not even the president knew where the Polaris missile subs patrolled at any given time, they did have prescribed operating areas to run through, boxes made up of hundreds of miles of ocean that kept these first missile subs close to the 1,000-mile launch range of their targets.

There were also crucial safeguards to make it impossible for one madman, acting on his own, to start a nuclear war. First, any launch order had to match exactly the authenticator codes that varied by date and were kept on board the sub behind two sets of locked doors in a safe welded to a bulkhead in the control room. Two men held the combinations to open the safe and check the authenticator codes, which they showed to the CO and XO. Once the order to launch had been verified, three men had to use separate keys, also kept in safes, to actually launch a missile. The CO's key allowed him to activate the ship's fire control system. The XO's key armed the missile release mechanisms. Then, the mission control officer could use his key to fire the missiles. The process was supposed to take about fifteen minutes.

subs, and those so ill designed that men were dying. One submarine suffered such a horrible reactor accident that it was redubbed the *Hiroshima* by survivors. By the time the Soviets tried to locate missile launchers in Cuba in 1962, the United States had moved so far ahead that it was able to quickly scramble several Polaris submarines, ultimately nine in all, to points within shooting distance of the Soviet Union.*

The United States had the clear advantage, but for how long? The crisis might have taught Soviet leaders that it would be impossible to build a nuclear missile force on land near U.S. shores. But by scrambling the Polaris subs into firing position, the United States had also shown the Soviets a better way to accomplish the same thing.

---

*The U.S. public never knew just how afraid its government had become that the Soviets would escalate any naval confrontation. Just months earlier, a Soviet defector had presented what had become known as the "Ironbark Papers"—details of Soviet plans to use tactical nuclear weapons against U.S. ships and subs if a war broke out at sea. President John F. Kennedy's advisers were haunted by the thought that the Soviet Union could have engineered the first crude steps of that plan. Indeed, Kennedy was afraid that any battle at sea might intensify the crisis, with or without nuclear weapons being fired. As he instituted the U.S. naval blockade of Cuba, a Soviet sub was spotted near two Soviet freighters. When Kennedy heard that, he asked his aides: "Isn't there some way we can avoid having our first exchange with a Russian submarine? Almost anything but that!"

There were such exchanges, but none lived up to Kennedy's worst fears. U.S. surface ships and aircraft near Cuba spotted a handful of Soviet diesel subs and easily surfaced three of them.

TURN TO THE DEEP

F lying on the wild success of his Polaris program, Admiral Red Raborn began looking ahead, thinking about new, imaginative ways of furthering nuclear deterrence. He quickly turned to the dreamer within his ranks, a young civilian whom the admiral had plucked from obscurity a few years earlier and anointed the chief scientist for Polaris.

John P. Craven was only in his midthirties when Raborn found him, but it was his job to look over the shoulder of everyone involved in the development of the missile subs, to find the problems, to come up with the answers. He was, as he put it, "chief kibitzer."

The moniker fit. Talking a torrent, his ideas usually overflowing, Craven was the kind of man who could dissect a blueprint and still have time to spout a few lines of poetry, biblical verse, or one of his endless series of self-scripted maxims of the sea. Sometimes he'd mix verse with maxim and sing the result aloud.

He preached fantasy amid military discipline; he carried romance to the mechanics of nuclear war.

It was a role Craven had been bred to. He was the product of a family that reached back to Moorish pirates on his mother's side and was divided on his father's between Presbyterian ministers and Navy officers yawning in the family pew.

The Navy brass was the part of the lineage that most of the Cravens liked to boast about, the part that went back to Tunis Agustas MacDonough Craven, who skippered the Civil War Union ship *Tecumseh* and drowned at the helm when she was rammed by a Confederate mine during the Battle of Mobile Bay, inspiring Admiral David Farragut's memorable cry to the remaining fleet: "Damn the torpedoes. Full speed ahead."

But only John Craven boasted of what the rest of his family dared not even whisper: the pirate blood he inherited from his mother's side.

That John Craven was going to be different was evident from the moment he made his first appearance on the planet, landing in the Williamsburg section of Brooklyn. It was a Halloween night, a fact that his paternal relatives chose to ignore as they instantly christened him Navy, fully intending that he would live a life of rigid military discipline. That their plan was doomed to fail became clear some fifteen years later when Craven was rejected by the Naval Academy. It wasn't for lack of intelligence. He'd skipped through to high school by the time he was eleven years old. But once there, he took the rogue's route to popularity. He convinced his much older classmates that he was merely small for his age and then proceeded to win their respect by becoming the class wise guy, the kid who was too tough to do homework.

Ultimately, he fulfilled at least part of his family's expectations. He never earned a Naval Academy degree, but he did get his commission in the reserves and he became an ocean engineer. From then on, he took to sermonizing about the deep, about underwater maneuvers that most of the Navy passed off as impossible, or at least hugely improbable. He expected no easy converts. But like any minister preaching the coming of a miracle, Craven was drenched in the faith that he would ultimately be proven right.

Now Raborn was handing Craven a nearly blank check to do what he did best—come up with ideas, as many as he could. By

1963 Craven was working hard on Raborn's vision of an Advanced Sea-based Deterrent Program. As his first step, he set aside $1 million a year, thinking that would be just enough to create a small political science program to dissect the strategy of deterrence. In the process, he discovered he had hired just about every political scientist specializing in strategic defense.

With the rest of his budget and his new platform, he began to peer into an untouched realm of the deep, working with his group to scribble out ideas: missiles that could be placed miles below the surface on the ocean floor; submarines that could reach down and see through the murky depths, carry cameras into untraveled and alien waters.

Most of the Navy greeted Craven's visions with hardly a yawn. What little study of the deep there had been before had long ago been shoved into a corner, the purview of a small group of oceanographers. Admirals saw operating in deep water as more difficult than the manned outer-space launches that, at that moment, held the nation's attention hostage. The Navy's best submarines could reach down just 1,000 to 1,500 feet or so. Go deeper, and there was certain death by implosion from punishing sea pressures great enough to quickly crush even the mighty Polaris subs.

The miles below the Navy's operational slice garnered about as much respect as the average landfill. The Navy's main design branch, the Bureau of Ships, listed deep submergence as tenth on its list of top ten priorities—giving the deep number ten only because the list wasn't any longer. Even Admiral Rickover, wrapped as he was in the public mantle of Navy innovator, was uninterested in plumbing the depths.

Craven's deep-submergence group was on the fringe, but eager to work. A team of his scientists was asked to help test the USS *Thresher* (SSN-593), the first of a powerful new class of nuclear attack submarines designed to go somewhat deeper than the other subs of the day. On April 10, 1963, *Thresher* failed during a test dive to 1,300 feet. As best as anyone could tell, a piping failure and a subsequent loss of propulsion set off a series of events that caused the submarine to sink, killing all 129 men aboard, including four men from Craven's team. Craven got the news as he was sitting with Harry Jackson, an engineering officer who had helped test the sub shortly before her last dive, and who had been present for every other deep dive.

Jackson sat, repeating over and over, "I should have been there." But Craven was relieved that Jackson had missed this, the nation's first loss of a nuclear submarine, along with three of Craven's own men who had been scratched from the test for lack of space.

It was only later that Craven realized that the disaster was about to mark him among the most important players in a new and dramatic chapter in this saga of undersea spying. Craven's opportunity would spring from the almost impossible promises the Navy made in its efforts at damage control. In the wake of *Thresher*, the Navy promised a massive effort to learn about the unforgiving ocean depths. There would be a "Sub Safe" program. There would be "Deep Submergence Rescue Vehicles."

This was the Navy's chance to calm the public, a chance to erase tragedy with visions of ocean wonder, a chance to obscure submarine dangers beneath visions of safety innovations. Almost everyone involved recognized that some of the proposals were more science fiction than science, especially the prospect of deep-submergence rescue vehicles (DSRVs) for sunken subs. Anyone who was to be rescued would have to have the good fortune to go down over a continental shelf or atop an undersea mountain, in waters far more shallow than the two, three, or four miles of depth that made up much of the world's oceans. Most submariners knew that a severe casualty at sea almost always meant that they would disappear—no survivors, no rescue, nothing more to say.

Still, Congress okayed these popular proposals and offered up funding that caught the attention of the Office of Naval Intelligence. The Navy might have been promising an era that mirrored Jules Verne, but a few submarine espionage specialists now saw the means to launch a new age of spying that would be much closer to James Bond.

These intelligence officers were already crafting their plans when Craven began directing a massive post-*Thresher* study. He had also taken charge of the Deep Submergence Systems Project, a program created to design the Navy's promised deep-submergence rescue vehicles and to build an underwater laboratory, a habitat known as "SeaLab," where the Navy could study the physiological effects of deep-sea pressures on divers.

Craven saw opportunity, especially in the DSRV program. Like nearly everyone else with knowledge of the oceans, he knew that the DSRVs were largely fantasy. But he reasoned that maybe the push to build them might give him an edge in pursuing another of his dreams—a fleet of mini-submarines made of glass. Chemically, glass is a liquid, so Craven reasoned that glass submarines would be at their strongest under the most powerful deep-ocean pressures.

He wasn't the only one trying to sell the Navy on the idea of some kind of mini-submarine. Reynolds Aluminum Company was building its own boat, hoping to gain a lucrative contract. The Woods Hole Oceanographic Institute, with the Office of Naval Research, was designing the *Alvin,* a three-man submersible that could go down 6,000 feet. At this point, the only deep-submersible the Navy had in-house was the *Trieste II,* a mini-dirigible that had to be carried or towed to dive sites. It had only limited maneuverability, but it could bring a crew of three down to 20,000 feet. The first *Trieste* had been lowered nearly 7 miles in 1960 to the deepest spot in the world—the Challenger Deep in the Marianas Trench, about 200 miles from Guam. Both *Trieste I* and *II* explored *Thresher*'s wreckage.

It was just as Craven began to work out the mechanics of self-propelled, independent, deep-sea mini-subs that he was approached by a Naval Intelligence officer, one of the men who helped coordinate the submarine surveillance operations off the Soviet coasts. By now, those operations had been expanded to provide a year-round presence. Operating under the code name "Binnacle"—later "Holystone"—the Navy's growing fleet of nuclear subs and diesels were keeping constant watch on the Soviets as they aimed test launches of missiles from land silos and ships into the oceans. U.S. subs were also tracking the rapidly expanding fleet of Soviet nuclear subs as they finally began to venture out into the Atlantic and the Pacific. The Soviet Navy was beginning to enact its long-threatened plan to become a blue-water force.

With all this going on, the U.S. Navy nearly always had at least one surveillance sub in the Barents and two off the Soviets' Pacific ports, where they still had to dodge occasional Soviet depth charges. Even some of the early nuclear subs, like the USS *Scamp* (*SSN-588*), got chased with small depth charges, and more diesel subs, such as the USS *Ronquil* (*SS-396*) and the USS *Trumpetfish* (*SS-425*), got held down *Gudgeon*-style in the early 1960s. In addition to these operations off the Soviet coast, some diesel subs carried Russian émigrés back to the Soviet Union to spy for the United States, and other diesel subs were landing commandos in places like Borneo, Indonesia, and the Middle East to track the expanding Soviet influence.* Submarine spying had become so important that the chief of Naval Operations in Washington had taken charge of coordinating all operations, and a special undersea warfare office had been set up within the Office of Naval Intelligence to plan them.

Intelligence officials were so anxious to learn the latest about new Soviet subs and missiles that submarine spooks were under orders to flash off messages with mission highlights on the transit home. The Russian-language experts among them began transcribing tapes of stolen communications as soon as they left Soviet waters. Couriers met returning submarines at the dock, ready to whisk the intelligence directly to NSA headquarters in Fort Meade, Maryland. The spooks themselves were so valuable that the Navy ordered them to travel to and from ports by train rather than on commercial plane. The Navy wasn't willing to risk even a slim chance that they might be hijacked to Cuba.

Now the Naval Intelligence officer had come to Craven, asking him to help with a grander effort than any that had been tried before. The officer handed Craven a top-secret document, actually a very long wish list that Naval Intelligence had been amassing for several years, a document that had been touched by barely a dozen people before him.

Stamped across the front page were the words "Operation Sand Dollar." From there the list went on for pages. These were

---

*Shortly after the failed Bay of Pigs invasion in 1961, Navy commandos used diesel submarines to engineer the escape of prominent Cubans from Castro's regime. Over several weeks, commandos slipped from the subs and rowed to shore in inflatable rafts. The Cubans who were piloted back to the subs often had to dive 15 to 30 feet through dark waters to enter the submerged craft though special pressurized compartments. Many of those rescued likely would have been jailed or executed for plotting to overthrow Castro, according to former U.S. sailors involved in the operation.

the splashdown points for Soviet ballistic missiles painstakingly monitored and noted by Navy surface ships and Air Force radar and underwater hydrophones, as well as the locations of planes and other Soviet military hardware glimpsed or heard plunging through the waves. Only a few miles away, three at most, lay the Soviets' most sensitive defense secrets: the best in Soviet missile guidance systems, metallurgy, and electronics—all of it tantalizing trash and all of it out of reach. No wonder the Soviet Union didn't even try to guard the cache. Nobody could have imagined an undersea raid through stars of luminescent plankton to the utter blackness of the deep.

But why not, intelligence officers reasoned, use the comforting notion of deep-submergence rescue vehicles to mask an effort to reach the items catalogued in Sand Dollar? Why not use the budgets of rescue gadgets that would hardly ever be used to create some tools that might just give the United States the definitive edge?

The *Thresher* tragedy would be the excuse, the new safety programs the stuff of a complicated cover story. And all of it was dependent on Craven's answer to one question. Could he manage a deep-water treasure hunt?

It was a matter of top national security, Craven was told. Left unsaid was that it was also a matter of pride, political standing, and turf. The intelligence arm of the Navy was in a desperate game of catch-up with that of the Air Force, which had just launched a new generation of spy satellites. With their growing coverage of the Soviet Union, these new "eyes in the sky" were sending back images of sites where the Soviets were digging silos for powerful land-based missiles and dry docks where the Soviets were preparing to create their own generation of Polaris-like submarines. The Polaris program had managed to prevent Air Force bombers and rockets from monopolizing the business of nuclear deterrence. Now maybe Navy spies could compete with the satellites, diving not for mere pictures but for actual Soviet arms and craft.

This was the opportunity Craven had been looking for, a chance to tap into his most fantastic plans. There was only one thing stopping him. He had no idea how to accomplish what the intelligence officer was asking for. Even *Trieste II* couldn't manage much of a secret undersea raid—it was too small, and the surface ship needed to carry the submersible out to mid-ocean would be a dead giveaway.

"Basically, we are developing the technology, but not the assets," Craven said, calling upon his best Navy-speak. Silence. Two beats, maybe three. No matter how officiously he said it, he was still admitting he had no way to do what he was being asked.

Then, Craven had a flash of inspiration. "Hey, look, we don't have anything that could do your operation because that requires things be clandestine." One more quick inhale and he came out with the kicker. "So it's really not worth doing Sand Dollar unless you do it from a submarine."

There it was, blurted out in desperation, the idea for what would become the Navy's most daring venture yet. A full-sized submarine, big enough to navigate the high seas, would be outfitted to hover in place in the upper reaches of the ocean and dangle cameras miles down, deep enough to scout the ocean bottom for Soviet treasures. It was inspired. Make the effort from below the surface, find a way to be nearly undetectable. Never let the Soviets know the Americans were anywhere near.

Actually all Craven was doing was rehashing his long-held belief that operating from the ocean surface was its own kind of hell. He had already included the concept in his self-scripted "Ten Commandments of Deep-Ocean Engineering." The way he said it was: "Remember that the free surface is neither ocean nor air and that man cannot walk upon it nor will equipments remain stable in its presence. So design your equipments that they tarry not long and that they need neither servicing nor repair at this unseemly interface."

Now, suddenly, he had not only the means to put that commandment to the test, he also had his chance to fulfill his favorite part of his lineage and plunder buried treasure. His pulpit secure, his corsair's blood aboil, all Craven needed was a submarine.

There were twenty nuclear attack subs in the fleet now, and more being built. But Navy admirals weren't about to give up a first-rate boat so that it could sit out in mid-ocean trolling with cameras. If Craven wanted a sub, he would have to take one of the Navy's two nuclear clunkers, the two failed experiments whose designs were never replicated. There was the USS *Seawolf*, a confused boat with a bow V-shaped like a destroyer and the top of a sub built to house a touchy reactor run with liquid sodium—a reactor that had been replaced early on. Then there was the USS *Halibut,* a boat with a grander, but short-lived, past. *Halibut* (*SSGN-587*) had been the only nuclear sub to carry the Regulus guided missiles, making seven missions off the Soviet coast. But that program had ended in mid-1964 when the Navy began basing Polaris subs in the Pacific. With the Regulus era over, no one knew quite what to do with *Halibut.*

She was a marine oddball, one of the least hydrodynamic of the nuclear fleet and one of the most ridiculous-looking creations ever born in a dry dock. Unlike the flat fish she was named for, *Halibut* wore a huge hump that might have been appropriate on a gargantuan desert creature except for the fact that it opened up into a large shark's-mouth hatch, part of the original missile hangar. Perhaps in another time, *Halibut* would have been quietly scrapped. After all, this boat was not only odd, she suffered from what was a near-fatal malady for a submarine: hydromechanical cacophony. *Halibut* was loud. Submariners heard the din, saw only potential flooding when they gazed upon that hatch, and shuddered when they examined her cumbersome ballast tanks, gaping caverns originally designed to allow her to surface fast, shoot a missile, and submerge even faster.

Craven took one look at the submarine it seemed nobody could love and was transfixed. All he saw were the possibilities, the strange and wonderful things that could be done with all of that excess space. And when he caught a glimpse of that gorgeous gaping mouth, it was enough to send him, like any self-respecting mad scientist, reeling with joy. No other submarine in the fleet boasted a hatch larger than 26 inches. *Halibut*'s hatch was 22 feet.

It was settled: *Halibut* would be Craven's submarine, his laboratory, his ministry, his pirate ship. He would have $70 million to outfit her with electronic, sonic, photographic, and video gadgets. The Navy put out the word, and in February 1965 *Halibut* went into Pearl Harbor to be refitted as an oceanographic research vessel.

Less a lie than a huge omission, that was only one of several cover stories Craven would employ. The DSRV program and his other deep-sea projects would add more layers, all hiding what

Craven had proclaimed to be his "Skunk Works"—a term he borrowed for its drama from Lockheed Aircraft Corporation, the spy-plane manufacturer Craven would soon have working on the design of the DSRVs and also on a Deep Submergence Search Vehicle. The plan was that the DSSV would be able to sit on the ocean floor 20,000 feet deep and pick up objects with a mechanical arm. It was to travel to any recovery area mounted on the top of a submarine.

It would take two years to rebuild and test *Halibut,* but Craven would have little time to be impatient. From almost the moment the refit began, Craven's mass of cover stories began earning him notice outside the insular realm of Naval Intelligence. Suddenly he was being pulled into other high-profile projects.

Rickover, who had once done everything he could to limit Craven's interest in deep-diving mini-subs, now came to Craven asking him to help build the first nuclear-powered one, though one of steel, not glass. (The admiral would forever remain scathing about glass, to the point of insult.) But Craven was now working with Rickover, and the liaison would prove to be a crucial step in the scientist's education: crucial because it was through Rickover that Craven would learn how to mine the Navy's budget, deal with Congress, and handle the cadre of admirals who ran the submarine program.

It was a Faustian pact. Rickover may have been sixty-four years old, an age at which even less controversial officers have long been retired, but Craven, like just about everyone else in the Navy, could never quite learn to handle him. Rickover liked to begin their conversations in a way that showed just who was in charge: "Craven, my people are more competent than your people, but your shop is bigger, so I'm going to have to work with you." Rickover liked to try to throw men off balance just to see how they would handle themselves.

Rickover personally christened the mini-sub "*NR-1.*" It might as well have been called the USS *Rickover,* for "NR" was the designation for the Naval Reactors Branch—Rickover's realm. If the president could have Air Force One, Rickover would have his *NR-1.*

Unlike Woods Hole's *Alvin,* which was completed in 1965 and was only 22 feet long, *NR-1* was to be 137 feet, nearly half the size of an attack sub. *NR-1* would be able to go down to 3,000 feet. Equipped with underwater lights, cameras, and a grappling arm to retrieve small objects, it also would have the potential to do some spying. One of the chief design problems was finding some way to shield the nuclear reactor in the *NR-1*. Standard sub reactors were shielded with a foot of lead on either end. But that would have made the *NR-1* too heavy. Instead, Rickover, Craven, and the other designers decided it would have the standard lead shielding only in front where it faced crew compartments. The entire thirteen-foot area of the sub behind the reactor would be closed off permanently and flooded. The idea was to allow the wall of water to absorb any escaping radiation and work as a substitute for lead shielding. Craven had no doubt that environmentalists would cringe at the plan, but both he and Rickover believed it was entirely workable. Thirteen feet of water has the same molecular weight as one foot of lead. But when *NR-1* was submerged, the water would add no weight at all—when water displaces an equal amount of water, the effective weight is zero.

But before *NR-1* could be built, it had to be paid for, and right now there was little room in the budget for a mini-submarine among the plans for DSRVs and SeaLabs. The problem didn't faze Rickover, and he solved it at a meeting with Craven; Rear Admiral Levering Smith, Raborn's top deputy on Polaris; and Robert Morse, the assistant secretary of the Navy for research and development.

"You have any money we can get started with right now?" Rickover asked. Craven answered that his deep-submergence group could spare $10 million of its research and development money. Smith noted that the Polaris program had about $10 million of unused ship construction funds.

"How much is this submarine going to cost?" Morse asked.

Without hesitation, Rickover answered: $20 million. Morse went on to outline the tortuous process by which ships are normally built: contract definition, bidding, congressional approvals. Rickover cut him off before he could finish. "Just leave all that to me." Then Rickover turned to Craven and directed, "You call up Electric Boat tomorrow and tell them to get started."

Craven, Smith, and Morse exchanged looks of disbelief. Nobody believed this could be done for $20 million—the budget soon grew to $30 million. They also saw no way that Congress was going to stand for this. Less than a week later, Rickover called Craven and told him that the president was going to announce that afternoon that *NR-1* was going to be built.

Upon hearing the news, Morse moved quickly from a state of shock into a state of panic. Up until that moment, *NR-1* had been little more than an admiral's fantasy; indeed, Rickover had given only sketchy accounts of his plan to Paul H. Nitze, the secretary of the Navy, and Robert S. McNamara, the secretary of Defense. Though both had approved it, Morse knew Congress was not going to like hearing about a major project this way. As soon as the president announced the *NR-1*, the House Committee on Appropriations hastily called a hearing.

Craven, on Rickover's orders, had just a few days to come up with an official mission statement, a full-bore cost-benefit analysis, and a detailed study as to why the Navy needed the mini-sub.

"Well, you know, Admiral, that study really doesn't exist," Craven answered.

"It will exist by the time the hearing takes place," Rickover barked back.

Now the existence of *NR-1*, and perhaps his own career, rested on Craven's ability to spin visions from a black hole. He needed to prove that *NR-1* was a crucial investment, one worth $30 million.

The appropriations committee wasn't fooled, but in the end it had no choice but to give in. *NR-1* was now a presidential directive. No other submarine or ship had ever been authorized faster, or ever would be again. Later, the General Accounting Office, Congress's investigative arm, scrutinized the project and concluded that it was one of the worst managed programs its investigators had ever seen.

Rickover answered in typical form, firing off a letter to his critics that so amazed Craven that he committed it to memory. "I read the GAO report, and it reminds me of a review I read of *Lady Chatterley's Lover* in the magazine *Field and Stream*. The reviewer of that book knew as much about the real purpose of *Lady Chatterley's Lover* as the GAO knows about the design and development of submarines."

Rickover was no gentler on Craven. The admiral was infuriated that he had to share Craven with the *Halibut* refit, the DSRV program, and the other deep-ocean projects. As far as Rickover was concerned, none of those was more important than his *NR-1*.

Making the admiral even angrier was the fact that he was not cleared for the details about *Halibut*'s new mission. Little went on within the submarine force that he didn't know something about, but the intelligence programs were one of the few areas in which he had no official "in," no real say. He took out his frustrations on Craven, who began to imagine that the admiral was waiting up nights before calling, waiting until Craven fell into a deep slumber or thought about romancing his wife. He was almost convinced that his time submerged conducting tests on *Halibut* was being monitored by Rickover, who seemed to time his calls for moments when it was impossible for Craven to answer. Craven always paid dearly for being unavailable.

One Friday, Rickover was giving a speech in New York City and he sent word to *Halibut,* which was out near Hawaii, demanding that Craven meet him in New York first thing Monday morning.

Craven hopped a plane, suffered a moment of panic when the flight got socked in by fog during a layover in Los Angeles, and finally landed in New York and raced breathless to Rickover's hotel suite, where the admiral was waiting. "You were out there playing golf with the beach boys," he said, mocking the cover story Craven had crafted for his trip to Hawaii.

He then turned to the house phone. "Bring this man the biggest lunch in the hotel." Craven waited for the punch line: he knew the admiral wasn't worried that he might be hungry after the long trip.

Sure enough: "For the next hour, you are going to sit and eat lunch," Rickover announced. "And I am going to bawl you out."

Appearances to the contrary, Rickover liked Craven almost as much as he liked making him miserable. Rickover was impressed that Craven had moxie enough to withstand his worst tantrums. The admiral also loved that Craven had never attended the Naval Academy. Rickover had been a loner as a midshipman, and now he made great sport of adding a little torture to the mix when he interviewed Naval Academy graduates for his nuclear program. Those entrance interviews had become more like initiation rites, in which the admiral took young men to the psychological brink in his quest for perfection. Trying to rattle his applicants, Rickover would spout obscenities, seat them in chairs with one leg cut short, or send them off to "Siberia," a storage closet where they would be left for hours.

Perhaps the all-time Rickover classic occurred when he squared off against a candidate and said, "Piss me off, if you can." The young man answered without hesitation and without a word. He lifted his arm and with one motion swept Rickover's desk clean of books, papers, pens, everything. The candidate was accepted.

For Rickover, torturing Craven was a mere sideline.

Craven, meanwhile, was increasingly on call as the Navy's resident deep-ocean expert. But there was one call that stood out from all the rest. It came on a Saturday morning in January 1966.

"This is Jack Howard," said an assistant secretary of Defense in charge of nuclear matters. "I've lost an H-bomb."

"Why are you calling me?" Craven asked.

"This one I've lost in the water, and I want you to find it." Craven was being assigned to work with a team hastily assembled by an admiral in the Pentagon. Another group was going to the site.

A B-52 bomber had collided with an air tanker during a refueling operation 30,000 feet in the air off the coast of Palomares, Spain, losing its atomic payload. Three of four bombs were recovered almost immediately. But a fourth was lost and had presumably fallen to the bottom of the Mediterranean. President Lyndon Johnson knew the Soviets were looking for the bomb, and he refused to believe the Navy's assurances that there was a good probability that it would never be recovered by either side. Indeed, that was the belief of most of the people assigned to find the bomb—but not Craven.

Craven called in a group of mathematicians and set them to work constructing a map of the sea bottom outside Palomares. That sounded reasonable enough, but Craven intended to use that map for an analysis that seemed more reminiscent of racetrack betting than of anything ever put down in a Navy search and salvage manual.

Once the map was completed, Craven asked a group of submarine and salvage experts to place Las Vegas–style bets on the probability of each of the different scenarios that might describe the bomb's loss being considered by the search team in Spain. Each scenario left the weapon in a different location.

Then, each possible location was run through a formula that was based on the odds created by the betting round. The locations were then replotted, yards or miles away from where logic and acoustic science alone would place them.

To the uninitiated, all this sounded like the old joke about a man who loses his wallet in a dark alley. Instead of searching the alley, the man chooses to search for his wallet yards away under a street lamp because the light there is better. But as far as Craven was concerned, there was good science behind his apparent madness.

He was relying on Bayes' theorem of subjective probability, an algebraic formula crafted by Thomas Bayes, a mathematician born in 1702. Essentially, the theorem was supposed to quantify the value of the hunch, factor in the knowledge that exists in people beyond their conscious minds.

Craven applied that doctrine to the search. The bomb had been hitched to two parachutes. He took bets on whether both had opened, or one, or none. He went through the same exercise over each possible detail of the crash. His team of mathematicians wrote out possible endings to the crash story and took bets on which ending they believed most. After the betting rounds were over, they used the odds they created to assign probability quotients to several possible locations. Then they mapped those probabilities and came up with the most probable site and several other possible ones.

Without ever having gone to sea, the team now believed they knew where the bomb was. According to their calculations, the most probable site lay far from where the other three bombs had been recovered and far from where most of the plane's debris had hit the water. Worse, if Craven's calculations were correct, the bomb lay in a deep ravine and was all but unreachable.

The Navy had come across a Spaniard who was reputed to be the very best fisherman in Palomares, Francisco Simo-Orts. Simo-Orts claimed to have seen the bomb fall into the water, and he pinpointed its location right over the same ravine. With no other leads, the team in the Med had no choice but to arrange a serious search of the ravine and began contacting the companies that had tried to interest the Navy in their deep-diving submersibles.

The Bureau of Ships agreed to pay to fly two submersibles to Palomares, Reynolds's *Aluminaut* and Woods Hole's *Alvin*. After several weeks and no success, President Johnson was furious. He demanded to know where the bomb was, and he demanded to know just when it would be recovered.

In answer, a copy of Craven's latest probability hill—altered to take the weeks of failures into account—was sent to the president.

Johnson blew up at the sight of Craven's curves and graphs. If the search teams couldn't give him instant answers, the president would find scientists who could. He insisted that another group of scientists be hired from Cornell and the Massachusetts Institute of Technology. They met in an all-day session. In the end they agreed that Craven's plan was the best anyone had.

Johnson didn't have much time to react. For that same day, the crew of the *Alvin*, on its tenth dive, sighted a parachute enshrouding a cylindrical object. It was 2,550 feet underwater wedged into a 70-degree slope. The *Alvin* had found the missing H-bomb right where Craven's latest calculations put it. It would take several more weeks to recover the bomb. First the *Alvin* tried to hook it, but the bomb fell back into the water and was lost for another three weeks. Then the Navy dangled a robot, the cable-controlled underwater recovery vehicle (CURV), from a surface ship. The recovery team almost lost both the CURV and the bomb on April 7, 1966, when the robot failed to hook the bomb and instead became entangled in the parachute attached to the weapon. In desperation, the Navy decided to hoist both the CURV and the bomb up together, hoping the tangle was enough to bring both up to the surface. It was a less than elegant recovery, but it worked. More important to Craven, he had proven his theories. He was certain now that he could work miracles once he had *Halibut*.

He didn't have long to wait. *Halibut* was deemed finished just three weeks after the H-bomb recovery.

From the outside, she didn't look much changed. Her already towering sail had been raised to make room for extra masts that held periscopes and antennas to intercept communications to and from Soviet ships that might give chase. Atop her bow there was a small lump anyone could mistake for a misplaced dome of the type used to hold sonar arrays. In truth, that lump was something

Craven called a thrust/vector control. It was a gadget he had origi-nally doodled on the back of an envelope, and it allowed water to flow into *Halibut*'s front and out her sides, causing the boat to hover nearly still in the water. *Halibut* could not only scan the ocean bottom, she could hang over objects, giving the Navy time to study them, perhaps one day giving *Halibut* divers the oppor-tunity to slip outside of the sub and retrieve.

Inside, *Halibut* had been sliced, gutted, and given innards unlike any carried by other submarines. That camel-like hump with its gaping hatch had been transformed into a technological cavern now christened the "Bat Cave."

With gray, brown, and sky-blue laminates highlighting the stainless steel of its walls, the cave opened up 28 feet wide, stretched 50 feet long, climbed 30 feet high, and was divided into three levels.

There was a darkroom, a data analysis room, and a computer room stuffed with one massive computer: the Univac 1124. It was a huge machine with big tape reels and blinking lights, and it gave the cavern the feel of the science fiction–adventure realm for which it was named. (Still, Univac had only a tiny fraction of the power of the average modern laptop.) Crammed everywhere else were bunks, enough for a team of sixteen submariners and spooks.

Craven's crowning achievement was *Halibut*'s "fish," which he hoped would swim through the deepest deep. Weighing two tons each, and spanning 12 feet long, these aluminum creatures had cameras with battery-powered strobe lights for eyes, whiskers of towed sonar arrays, and rudders and bow planes for fins. Designed to be towed from the bottom of the Bat Cave on several miles of cable, they had been spawned by Westinghouse Electric Corporation for $5 million each.

As Craven and company prepared the final round of tests on *Halibut,* he was meeting with his intelligence contacts almost daily in special soundproof rooms. He made a game of juggling his myr-iad other projects, all the while keeping the clearance-deprived within the Navy completely in the dark. There were cover stories within cover stories as he was called upon to solve various prob-lems of the deep. There were the continuing demands from

Rickover, as well as concern from Congress about why his deep-submergence projects were spending tens of millions of dollars more than anticipated. The overruns were, of course, being sunk into *Halibut*. But the project was one of the most highly classified in the Navy, and Craven could no more disclose those costs than he could his own whereabouts when he was on the sub.

Other programs became his casualties as he spread *Halibut*'s costs in bogus budget items throughout the Navy. One poor captain was ordered to stash *Halibut* expenses in the accountings of a missile-warhead program, then faced weekly meetings at which he had to find some way to explain why his team was so badly over-spending its budget. Another of Craven's favorite hiding places was the DSRV program. There was a certain poetry to this, since Craven was working on a fake DSRV that would one day be welded down to the back of *Halibut* to serve as a decompression chamber for divers. By the time Craven was done, the DSRV program had gone 2,000 percent over budget.

The sum so appalled Senator William Proxmire that the Wisconsin Democrat gave the project his "Golden Fleece Award." The DSRV, he declared, had one of the worst budget records in U.S. history. The Navy was horrified at the public dressing-down. Craven was elated. How many pirates get handed a cover story written by a senator?

Of course, Rickover eventually found out what *Halibut* was doing. He pushed until he knew most of the details. When he was refused by intelligence directors, he went straight to the admirals in charge of submarine operations. He would not accept that there were operations using his submarines that would take place without him. The admirals didn't dare turn him away. But intelligence officers bristled at his interference. For one thing, Rickover refused to sign the standard secrecy oaths, believing that his loyalty should be taken for granted.

Halibut's officers did little to make the job of appeasing the admiral any easier. When one of Rickover's inspectors sought to keep the submarine docked over concerns about the way the crew was handling the boat's reactor, *Halibut*'s skipper, Commander Harold S. "Hank" Clay, refused to bow to Rickover's authority. *Halibut* operated under the highest priority code in the military, and the way the story was told on board *Halibut,* Clay barked at Rickover's man, "You want to fail me, fail me. You tell the president I can't get under way. This boat has Brick-Bat 01 authority."

Clay had enough problems without Rickover's interference. *Halibut*'s test runs weren't going well. None of the spy equipment had been built to any of the normal military specifications. The military had, in fact, never devised a set of specs for anything that would operate 20,000 feet down. And so, by trial and error, mostly error, *Halibut*'s crew tried their best to make all of her space-age equipment function. In these early days, the crew was becoming convinced that gremlins had moved into the Bat Cave. There were never-ending computer problems. The computer's "Interleaf" operating system needed more than the computer's 32 kilobytes of memory to operate. When computer components in the fish failed, new ones were secreted into Pearl Harbor in the luggage of American Airlines stewardesses.

Then there was the rest of *Halibut*'s deep-sea equipment. Her crew was discovering that systems that functioned fine at a few hundred feet underwater just didn't work the same way 15,000 feet deep, where pressures were enough to crush any slight flaw or weakness into a full-scale failure. The tiny, gold-plated rubber connectors used in the fish's wiring failed at 10,000 feet when the gold and the wire began to compress at different rates, sending the gold flaking off and breaking the circuits.

The strobe lights, so carefully designed to ride the fish and light the sea floor, worked too well. They were so bright that they blinded the cameras. Ultimately, dimmer lights were built. Unfortunately, the video signal failed to survive the climb through the coaxial cable that toted the fish, one at a time. So on *Halibut*'s early missions, the crew would have to make do with grainy sonar images of shadows, bright spots, and shapes. The crew would be able to grab hold of clearer photographs only once every six days, when a massive fish was hoisted back aboard, carrying its film to the surface.

"If something is worth doing, it's worth doing badly," Craven kept repeating, trying to ease the pain of failure. Meanwhile, he met weekly with the fish designers at the Westinghouse plant in Maryland, hoping to trade his tales of disasters for solutions.

"Okay, fellas, we are going to have a wire brushing, but I want you all to smile," he started each meeting, commanding grins at times, grimaces at others.

One day the engineers decided to answer his greeting in kind. They handed Craven a clear plastic box. Inside was a wire brush. His name was stenciled on the back of the brush which lay next to a small plate engraved with one word: "SMILE."

On one of the last runs to test the fish, a surface ship was supposed to drop an object into the ocean. The idea was for the fish to be employed in a scavenger hunt. *Halibut*'s crew would have to identify the object, which would be hidden from periscope view by a huge box. The box would open from the bottom and drop the object unseen into the depths.

The day came, the weather was good. *Halibut* and the surface ship set out to sea. A crane on the ship lifted the box and lowered it until it barely dangled above water. Then the box opened from the bottom. Moments later, the bad news came over the ship-to-sub radio: the object that the Navy had taken such pains to hide was floating.

The crew on the surface ship hauled the object back aboard and began wrapping it in canvas and heavy anchor chains, lots of them. They threw it back overboard. Soon after, the Naval Investigative Service sprang into action, sending officers on board to force promises of confidentiality from all the men on the surface ship, who now knew exactly what their secret cargo was. Judging from the size of the box and the investigators' reactions, the secret object was probably designed to resemble a missile's nose cone.

For the next few days, *Halibut* searched. Somewhere along the line, a control rod got stuck at the bottom of *Halibut*'s reactor chamber, shutting it down and forcing the boat to resort to diesel engines. Then one of the camera-toting fish was lost, joining all of the high-tech, sensitive trash it had been designed to find. Craven had expected some sort of fish disaster. He had ordered six of the contraptions, although *Halibut* was designed to carry only two at a time. As far as he was concerned, they had just dropped a spare—a very expensive spare.

Finally, the other fish was lowered and captured the images the men had been seeking. Later, and with some glee, the special projects crew proudly paraded a photograph of the object of their search around the boat.

Craven had just logged a major success, the first indication that *Halibut* might actually be able to accomplish all she had been rebuilt for. But *Halibut*'s men couldn't see that. Most of the photograph had been blacked out for security reasons. As far as the men of the sub were concerned, they had just pulled off a massive search for nothing more than a lump of tangled anchor chain.

VELVET FIST

Halibut's one success left Craven convinced that she was ready to start filling the Sand Dollar wish list. And over at Naval Intelligence, nobody was more anxious to believe him than Navy Captain James F. Bradley Jr.

Bradley, forty-six years old, had just taken over as the Navy's top underwater spy, and now he was meeting with Craven regularly in his unmarked, soundproofed suite on the fifth floor of the E Ring of the Pentagon. Three sets of locked doors barred trespassers. Guarding the entrance was a receptionist armed with a well-practiced look of confusion and a standard answer to unwanted inquiries. She always said that she knew nothing of Bradley or of his staff. His official Navy biography listed his assignment simply as "Naval Operations, Navy Department"— no specifics, nothing more.

Nothing in the public record suggested that Bradley had a hand in crafting intelligence missions for every attack submarine in the nation's fleet. And nothing suggested that he now was responsible for crafting *Halibut*'s first real missions.

Bradley and Craven knew they weren't going to be able to keep taking money from other Navy departments to support *Halibut* indefinitely, not without very high-level backing. Rickover was already gunning for them, in part because their submarine, considered a "special projects boat," was one of the few nukes he had trouble controlling. They needed results, and they needed them fast if their deep-sea search idea was going to survive.

The way Bradley saw it, all of the Soviet missiles that other spy submarines had monitored through launch and splashdowns or crash were only words on a list unless *Halibut* could prove her worth and make them into something more. Otherwise, the $70 million and thousands of hours of work poured into refurbishing her might as well have been tossed into the seas.

The Soviets had been developing missiles at a phenomenal rate ever since they were forced to back down during the Cuban Missile Crisis. Test shots fired from rocket centers deep within the Soviet Union, and others fired from submarines, had splashed down out in the Pacific. U.S. subs had been focused on trying to film these tests and capture readings that could help determine the telemetry of the weapons. These subs took great risks, sneaking into waters all but cordoned off by Soviet ships conducting at-sea launches and monitoring splashdowns of land-based missiles, the remains of which were scattered in shards over a vast sea bottom, bits of black metal strewn about by the force of splashdowns, implosions, and ocean currents. What Bradley wanted most were missile nose cones that held the guidance systems and dummy warheads that could provide a good estimate of the weapons' size, power, and yield. Finding the pieces wouldn't be easy—*Halibut* may have been able to find a test object carefully placed in the water, but how would she fare now that her destination was far less exact and her quarry was in northern Pacific waters commonly patrolled by Soviet vessels? Detection now, in the summer of 1967, would be diplomatically disastrous. Just that June, the United States and the Soviet Union had seemed close to blows when both sides sent armadas of ships and submarines to the Mediterranean Sea during the Arab-Israeli War.

Nevertheless, Bradley wanted a miracle, and not just one. He wanted *Halibut* to find so much Soviet treasure, ferret out so much intelligence, that the Pentagon would have no choice but to build a fleet of special projects subs. Craven wanted much the same and that bonded the two men as a team.

Like Craven, Bradley came from a seafaring family. Both men shared an awe for the unexplored and hazardous depths, as well as a sense of amazement at what *Halibut* was about to dare. But Craven's Brooklyn bravado was a direct contrast to Bradley's midwestern pragmatism. Bradley had no Civil War family yarns to tell. There were no skulls and crossbones in the Bradley past—only the stars tattooed with coal dust and a pocket knife on each of his father's knees and a great black and yellow tattooed tiger leaping across the old man's stomach. It was on his father's left arm that Bradley had taken his first world tour, tracing the fourteen tattooed flags that marked the ports of call of his first naval hero, his dad, who was a boatswain's mate in President Theodore Roosevelt's "Great White Fleet."

Bradley joined the Navy not to fulfill long-held family obligations, but because on the eve of World War II he believed he had to choose between images of mud-filled army trenches or valiant battles in sun-sprayed seas and pretty girls featured in the 1940 movie *Navy Blue and Gold*. Bradley found himself in battle less than a year after graduating from the bottom half of his Naval Academy class in 1944. Despite that, he had so much fun tooling through the sea in diesel submarines that he later refused Rickover's invitation to join the nuclear Navy.

It was a move tantamount to turning down the first stock offering of IBM or AT&T. It was already clear that the high-profile nukes would soon become the best route to a set of admiral's stars for most of his peers. But Bradley was not like the other white-gloved candidates coming out of the Naval Academy. He would rather down a margarita than a martini, shaken or stirred, and if anyone had ever tried to serve him a cucumber sandwich, he probably would have doused it in Tabasco sauce. He ate Tabasco with everything except cake and ice cream.

Brawny, handsome, and stubborn, he had moved into intelligence backwards and sideways. He didn't take either of the two diesel subs he commanded out on spy missions. But he had taken a turn practicing cocktail party intelligence, mainly quizzing naval attachés and diplomats from other countries in the late 1950s when he was an assistant naval attaché in Bonn. He landed that job because he had studied German at Georgetown University, adding to the already colorful vocabulary he had picked up as a twelve-year-old playing Little League for a church team in the German section of St. Louis.

When the job of director of undersea warfare opened up in the Office of Naval Intelligence in 1966, Bradley had a pal who happened to be the assistant to the director of Naval Intelligence. This was a time when Rickover was refusing to spare any of his nuclear submariners for landlocked staff jobs, so the job had to go to a diesel submariner, and it went to Bradley.

Bradley enjoyed the irony that he was now directing the spy missions for Rickover's nuclear fleet. Indeed, the captain enjoyed this almost as much as his beloved Tabasco sauce.

For his part, Rickover could never forgive Bradley his slight, his refusal to join the admiral's elite society, any more than Rickover could tolerate the ill-kempt irreverence of other diesel submariners. He thought Bradley was a "freebooter" and hated the fact that he couldn't control him. But by the late summer of 1967, Bradley was less concerned with appeasing Rickover than with proving that his spy program could come up with the goods.

Much of Bradley's beloved diesel fleet was on the sidelines now, as the Atlantic Fleet had quit sending diesels off Soviet waters. The Pacific Fleet had fewer subs and was slower to get nuclear ones, so it still made good use of its diesels, sending them both to the Soviet Union and into the shallower waters off China to monitor efforts there to develop nuclear missile subs. (The Pacific Fleet even sent diesel subs to monitor France's nuclear weapons tests in the South Pacific.) Just before Bradley got to Washington, two U.S. diesel subs had smashed into freighters while on surveillance missions off Vietnam.* But while mistakes like these were hastening the end of the diesels' reign, nuclear submarine commanders were

---

*Just as in the Korean War, little fighting took place at sea during the Vietnam conflict. Subs were sent on a few surveillance operations and diesel subs were used to land commandos. *Perch* and two former Regulus subs—*Tunny* and *Grayback*—landed SEALs on beaches for several covert raids from 1965 through 1972.

being encouraged to take as many risks as diesels ever did—or more. Indeed, as the nukes took over, most fleet commanders were still willing to overlook incursions into Soviet waters and detections that stopped short of collisions.

The commanders knew as well as Bradley that the risks were worth it if it meant catching Soviet missile subs as they came out of port. Once they hit the open waters, they were far more difficult to track; even the expanding SOSUS listening nets covered only a small portion of the oceans. This problem was becoming more urgent because after all the years of worry in Washington, the Soviets had finally begun to send missile subs—mostly Golf-class diesels—on regular patrols off of U.S. coasts. The Air Force also was desperate for help in learning the capabilities of the newest Soviet land-based missiles test fired into the oceans.

And so began "Operation Winterwind," Bradley's plan to grab one of the most important items on the old Operation Sand Dollar wish list. At the Air Force's request, he was going to send *Halibut* out to find the nose cone from a Soviet intercontinental ballistic missile. It didn't matter to Bradley that *Halibut* still had no capacity to actually retrieve anything. He figured that if *Halibut* could simply track down shards of a missile and mark where they lay with signal-emitting transponders, the Navy could figure out a way to retrieve them later. The transponders should remain active for up to seven years, time enough to come up with a plan, perhaps time enough to allow Craven's team to build one of those deep search vehicles to move in for the final grab.

This time *Halibut* was being led by Commander C. Edward Moore, a man fresh from "charm school," the training ground for prospective commanding officers (PCOs) where they were grilled in the working of nuclear reactors. Run by Rickover's minions, the reactor courses were exercises in desperation and frustration, one where candidates were hammered mercilessly. Rickover himself took delight in warning the PCOs that at least a third would fail. He and his men relentlessly interrogated candidates about the details of circuit breaker theory, physics, anything in the thick stack of reactor manuals, testing to see which third that would be.

Now Moore had inherited a boat plagued with a temperamental reactor and Rickover's rancor. Built solid like a wrestler, Moore faced his task with quiet determination. His hair, already graying, would go just a bit lighter on this command, but he rarely complained out loud, and almost never about Rickover himself—though he would periodically aim a curse at some of the admiral's more overtly sadistic subordinates.

As *Halibut* moved more than 400 miles north of Midway, only Moore and a few officers knew what she was after—not even the handpicked, specially cleared denizens of the Bat Cave had been told. Their leader, Lieutenant Commander John H. Cook III, a thirty-one-year-old electrical engineer with the dual title of operations officer and project officer, mentioned only that they were to scan the ocean bottom 17,000 feet down for any object larger than a garbage can.

Things started out well enough. The team laid a transponder grid on the ocean floor, using *Halibut*'s torpedo tubes to launch more than a dozen of the signal devices. Each had a unique sound signature that could be triggered by remote control from the sub. As each transponder hit bottom, navigators plotted its precise location using a satellite navigation system.

Craven wasn't aboard while all this was happening, but his spirit was. Most of *Halibut*'s crew believed the cover story he had crafted—that the 8-foot-long transponders were underwater mines. The transponders had even been marked with munitions codes and delivered to *Halibut* via a Navy munitions depot. To make sure the crew was convinced, Craven gravely warned the men to deny that mines were on board.

It took thirty-six hours to set the grid. After that, the men launched one of the fish. Most of the crew had been told that the mechanisms were a new type of towed sonar, but the "special projects" crew crammed inside the Bat Cave's tiny control room knew better.

The video signals still weren't coming through. Instead, the men were trying to "see" the bottom by sonar images sent up through the fish. They sat, staring into the gray shadows sent up to the screens, trying to separate one wash of shadow from another, to distinguish what might have been key objects from passing fish, from rocks. There were also panels displaying digital readouts to track the mechanical fish's altitude from the bottom as it swam along illuminating its own path, taking photographs that nobody would see until it was hauled back into the sub.

Things became even more difficult when the Univac 1124 crashed. This time, though, the Bat Cave crew was ready. Armed with a hand calculator carried on board by a Westinghouse engineer, the men did the job for which the computer had been designed. Not long after that, though, *Halibut*'s gremlins almost got the better of the mission. This time the problem was caused in part by a weakness Craven had knowingly left alone, a calculated risk. The hydraulically powered cable spool was smaller than it should have been. To fit within the seven-foot gap between the submarine's pressure hull and the top of the deck, the spool could be only six feet wide. As a result, the seven-mile-long braided steel cable had to be wound so tight that it was stressed to its limit.

Craven had calculated that the cable should stand up nonetheless. But he forgot something. Overall, the cable itself was strong enough, but it was actually made up of a bunch of separate strands wound together. The strands themselves were built of shorter lengths welded together to stretch 7 miles, and each weld was a weak point. It was one of those welds that had snapped, leaving a loose wire jamming the device designed to hoist the cable, and leaving the fish dangling aimlessly at the end of the line. In a desperate effort to prevent the loss of the second of the $5 million devices, a crowd of men began working together to hoist the two tons of aluminum and managed to get the fish back on board and through the tube that launched it. Then *Halibut* surfaced. Over the next three days, her men pulled the entire 35,000-foot cable off its spool, laid the steel out in the Bat Cave in a seemingly endless figure eight, then rewound the entire expanse—only this time in reverse. The idea was to make sure the broken section remained wrapped around the spool when a fish was sent back out. The effort worked, but the men still never found a piece of missile.

When *Halibut* slipped back to port late that October, Craven was waiting on the dock. He had already figured out that *Halibut* couldn't go out again with a welded cable. He put out word through the Secretary of the Navy's research and development office. He wanted a seven-mile-long weldless cable. The Navy began contacting contractors, explaining only that it needed seven miles of continuous cable, no welds, for a classified project. From oil-drilling companies to elevator companies, vendors came to the

Pentagon. One man couldn't bear the suspense. "You just have to tell me," he blurted out. "What building is this for?"

Not a single company could meet the Navy specification for 37,500 feet of weld-free cable. Finally, U.S. Steel agreed to modify its cable-making process. Even then, it would take three months—until January 1968—to spin the seven miles of steel. When the cable was finally finished, Bradley decreed that it was time again to try to catch a missile.

Halibut's departure came roughly at the same time the North Koreans captured and boarded the USS *Pueblo,* an intelligence ship that spied from the surface. *Pueblo* was in international waters, intercepting radar signals, when the Koreans attacked. It was an audacious move. The Koreans sprayed the ship with gunfire, and *Pueblo*'s crew, their ship only lightly armed, didn't dare fight back. When the Koreans moved to prevent the crew from destroying the ship's espionage equipment and records, one American was killed and three others were wounded. In the end, the Koreans stole some of the United States' most highly sensitive cryptographic gear, and U.S. intelligence officials were convinced that the gear would be handed over to the Soviets.

Back on *Halibut,* all started out well. She made it back to the transponder grid without incident. This time the fish swam without a snag. Grainy sonar images played continuously on the screens of the Bat Cave, a fuzzy reproduction of a far-off planet 17,000 feet below.

The submarine and her crew searched for nearly two months, but there was still no sight of a Soviet missile. Then the cable system broke down again, and the electronics that communicated with the fish shorted out. All this was nothing new. The crew had long ago figured out how to jury-rig a quick fix at sea. The entire operation should have taken less than an hour. The problem was that it had to be engineered on the surface. The men would have to brave *Halibut*'s deck, in the 3:00 A.M. dark.

Up until now, day had blurred into night for these men 300 feet below sunlight. Drifting deep in the quiet of their underwater universe, they had felt little of the big ocean swells above. But now, Commander Moore had no choice. His men would have to face the rough waters of the surface.

As he gave the order to blow ballast, a three-man repair crew began to squeeze into their uncomfortable wet suits. Among them was machinist's mate chief Charlie Hammonds. He waited until Moore gave the order. The captain had been watching the swells, waiting for a time when the deck wasn't taking on water. After a while he gave the nod.

"Flip on your light," said senior chief Skeaton Norton as Hammonds readied to climb out the hatch onto *Halibut*'s hull. Over their wet suits, the repair crew wore life jackets decorated with small, canister-shaped, battery-powered strobe lights. They had been designed for the Air Force, part of jet-fighter pilots' rescue packs.

"I'll turn it on in time," Hammonds answered in his typical hard-nosed fashion. The mechanic was gruff, 5'8" tall, balding, and muscular. He was a loner but had been dubbed "Uncle Charlie" on board.

"You'll turn it on before you step out that door," Norton answered in his toughest chief-of-the-boat voice.

Hammonds knew an order when he heard one. He answered with a simple flip of a switch.

In the night black and fog, the tiny jet-fighter light barely illuminated Hammonds's face as he stepped out and hooked a safety line through an open notch on the safety track that ran almost flush with the deck the length of the sub. He made his way down the wet, narrow black deck, then over to the front of the sail where he grabbed hold of a rail. He was in as good a position as any submariner could be, considering that he was standing outside at night, on a submarine, in the middle of the rolling ocean.

Then the ocean reached out, as if it were trying to pull the entire submarine back down into the depths where she belonged. A rogue wave rose higher than sixty feet, reaching over the conning tower, crashing gallons through the open control room hatch, washing over the deck and grabbing Hammonds along with it. He was pulled toward the front of the submarine, his safety line running the length of the track. The line should have been enough to hold him on board, and it would have been enough had the wave been less powerful, had he been pulled less far. Only Hammonds was pulled all the way forward, near the torpedo room hatch, to another notch in the safety track, there by design to allow men to hook their lines on and secure themselves.

Only now, as Hammonds zipped past, that tiny notch became his exit from the track. Suddenly unlatched, he was washed into the rough waters.

Inside the conning tower, that same wave caught a young lieutenant who sprained both arms as he desperately held on. By the time he emerged sputtering, he could see Charlie Hammonds was gone. Men on deck began shouting: "Man overboard!"

Now a lot of people were shouting that. They began to search according to drill, what would have been normal routine on a surface ship. But this was a nuclear submarine. And submarine crews had come to spend most of their time below decks and underwater. Back in the diesel days, the days of *Cochino* and *Tusk,* this kind of casualty was a constant threat. But now, few if any men serving in the nuclear Navy had ever experienced this, and the recovery drill for a man overboard was seldom practiced.

"Who's lost?"

"What happened?"

"It's Charlie. We lost Charlie."

The chorus went on as men raced to their battle stations. One of the officers jumped up to the periscope. *Halibut* continued to rock back and forth, creating a dizzying view of the waters outside.

"I see a light out there," the officer shouted.

"Stay on it," someone, probably the captain, shouted back.

Hammonds was seventy-five yards away, off the starboard beam. *Halibut* had been moving slowly forward and away from him.

"Back emergency, back emergency," Moore shouted to the engine room, fully aware that if they lost sight of Hammonds's light, he might never be found.

The engine room poured on power, kicking *Halibut* into reverse. The sub vibrated, then bucked, as her screws churned against her forward momentum. Someone shouted into the loudspeaker from the engine room that the sub's engines were overheating.

"Keep your bell on!" Moore yelled back. He knew backing at too high a speed for too long could overheat the turbines, but he was convinced *Halibut* could take it. She had been designed for emergency maneuvers. Besides, there was no choice but to take the risk. They had to get to Hammonds.

By now there were men on both periscopes, probably the executive officer and the lead quartermaster. They stared out into the black desperately trying to hang on to the distant glow of Hammonds's tiny light as other men set up a far more powerful search light.

Four divers scrambled into their wet suits and raced to the control room. Two went out on deck and into the water. Another man stood beneath the bridge hatch, sweltering in his wet suit, ready to jump into the ocean if the other divers got into trouble.

Cook scrambled toward the Bat Cave shouting that he was going to reel in the fish.

"Fuck the fish," Moore shouted after him.

Cook went on anyway.

Captain Moore climbed out and onto the sail with a pair of binoculars, and began tracking Hammonds's light himself.

Storm and ocean in his eyes and ears, Hammonds couldn't see *Halibut* bearing down on him. He was swimming frantically without any direction. Then he heard a voice in the distance, a voice saying, "Hold on chief, we're going to get you." Hammonds relaxed. It was the most important thing he could have done. In his wet suit, hypothermia wasn't going to be the problem, but panic kills. He held on to that voice, the voice of his captain, even as his tiny light blinked out. Moments later *Halibut* was alongside him. Divers leapt into the water, and tied a line under his arms. Then he was pulled aboard. He had been in the icy water fifteen minutes, and Moore knew it was only luck that the chief hadn't been lost for good. The moment he was lowered through the hatch, Hugh "Doc" Wheat, the crew's corpsman, began treating him with brandy, the most effective medicine on board.

Hammonds just kept repeating, "I couldn't see anything, I couldn't see anything." He was shivering violently. Doc Wheat prescribed more brandy. Chief Gary L. Patterson asked for brandy as well, but Doc wasn't going for it. Hammonds was brought to the showers to be warmed, then put to bed. Still, it would take hours for the shock to wear off, hours the crew spent decorating *Halibut* with signs declaring, "Welcome back, Charlie. How was liberty?"

The humor may have been lost on Hammonds. His crewmates would tell and re-tell the tale of his harrowing swim at every

Halibut reunion for years, but Hammonds would never show up to listen. Still, while they were at sea, he amazed everyone by going back out onto the deck, almost daring the ocean to try again. Nobody expected it of him. Just about any other man might have stayed below, might have been too terrified to face the rolling waves. But as long as Hammonds was on the boat—and he would be for another month—he would refuse to give in to fear.

In early April, Moore turned his boat for home. He was coming back empty-handed. He and his men never did find a missile. But he was also coming home with every single one of his men, and he didn't mind the trade-off, not one bit. Besides, he was about to get the chance of a lifetime to redeem himself and his submarine.

Halibut pulled into Pearl Harbor on April 11, 1968, the sixty-eighth anniversary of the day the Navy purchased its first submarine. The enlisted men attended the "Submarine Birthday Ball," and the officers gathered at what the locals called the "Pink Lady," the Royal Hawaiian Hotel on Waikiki Beach. There, they made their way through three or four cases of champagne that one of them had stacked under their table, as well as a case of liquor that had been swiped from an admiral's suite.

As they celebrated, an amazing detective story was unfolding. A dozen Soviet ships had poured out into the Pacific, moving slowly, banging away at the ocean with active sonar. They were obviously looking for something. Soon it became clear that the Soviets were looking for one of their own. They had lost a submarine.

The USS *Barb* (SSN-596) had been sitting off the Soviet port at Vladivostok when the frantic search began. *Barb*'s CO Bernard M. "Bud" Kauderer had never seen anything like it. Four or five Soviet submarines rushed out to sea and began beating the ocean with active sonar. The submarines would dive, come back to periscope depth, then dive again.

The Soviets made no effort to avoid detection, no effort to hide. Their cries filled airwaves, shattering the air around Vladivostok with unencoded desperation.

"Charlie, Victor, Red Star, come in."

"Red Star, come in."

"Red Star, come in, come in, come in."

Back on shore, U.S. intelligence agents gathered around electronic intercept monitors and listened in. *Barb* watched, keeping radio silence. A message flashed in from shore command: "Stay on station." Kauderer felt a flash of frustration. He had planned on turning for home, planned on arriving in time to attend his only son's bar mitzvah. But now his boy would become a man without him. Kauderer was legally forbidden from telling his son why.

As *Barb* and other U.S. surveillance craft listened, it was clear that the Soviets had no idea where to find their submarine. Back in Washington, Bradley thought that he might know better.

For some time, Bradley's Office of Undersea Warfare had been keeping a long and frustrating vigil over an obscure set of Soviet submarine communications that U.S. intelligence had never figured out how to decode. The Soviets were using sophisticated transmitters that compressed the communications into microsecond bursts. Bradley thought the key to finding the missing sub lay in these indecipherable bursts of static.

Intelligence officers had figured out that the transmissions were coming from Soviet missile submarines on their way to and from patrols within firing range of U.S. shores. The United States had been monitoring and recording them using a series of reception stations that were built upon German technology—dozens of antennas were strategically placed along the Pacific Coast and in Alaska.

After a while, it didn't matter much that the bursts couldn't be decoded. There was a wealth of information to be found just within the pops and hisses. Slight variations in frequency distinguished one Soviet submarine from another, and the Soviets were so regimented that their submarines created a running itinerary for U.S. intelligence to follow as they ran, tag-team style, through the 4,000 miles from Kamchatka to one of their main patrol stations 750 to 1,000 miles northwest of Hawaii. A burst typically was sent when the submarines hit the deep-sea marker just outside Kamchatka. Another was sent as they crossed the international dateline, about 2,000 miles away from the Soviet Union at 180 degrees longitude. A third marked their arrival on station.

It was as if they were saying, "We are leaving. . . . We have hit

180 degrees longitude. . . . We are on station." The progress reports continued as the subs headed back to Kamchatka, and Bradley's men believed they could almost hear within the static the Soviet requests for fresh milk, fresh vegetables, vodka, women.

Now Bradley's team searched the communications records and found what they were looking for almost immediately. A Golf II submarine—one of a class of diesel subs that filled in between the first Zulu subs converted to carry missiles and the coming of the first Soviet nuclear-powered missile subs—had left port on February 24, 1968. The sub had been transmitting as usual until it hit midcourse. Then the transmissions stopped. There was no message when it crossed 180 degrees longitude; none saying it had left deep water; nothing that could be construed as a request for milk or fruit or anything else that would mark a safe return.

Bradley rushed the news to the Navy's top admirals: the Soviets had indeed lost a submarine, one that carried three ballistic missiles. He believed that the sub had to have gone down between the last burst transmission and the next expected one that never came, but the Soviets weren't looking anywhere near the area Bradley had pinpointed.

What if the United States could find the sub first? There in one place would be Soviet missiles, codebooks, a wealth of technological information—and Bradley thought he had the means to find it. *Halibut* might not have been able to find a relatively small missile fragment, but a submarine was a much bigger and better target.

Halibut Commanders Moore and Cook were called to Washington. Waiting for them were Rear Admiral Philip A. Beshany, deputy chief of Naval Operations for submarine warfare, Craven, and Albert G. Beutler, who supervised *Halibut*'s work.

"We've got some intelligence that the Soviets may have lost a submarine in the Pacific," Beshany announced as soon as the men walked in. Then Beshany filled in the details and the punch line, that *Halibut* was going after the Soviet Golf.

From Beshany's office, Craven rushed Moore and Cook in to see Paul Nitze, secretary of the Navy. This time, the officers were grilled on *Halibut*'s failure to find any missile fragments. Craven held his breath while Cook offered up a spiel that rivaled the best that Craven himself could have delivered.

Failure or not, Cook said, *Halibut*'s crew had now had time to work out the kinks in their equipment. The men could, he insisted, find a submarine if given the chance. It wasn't a hard sell. There was no other craft in the Navy that could attempt this kind of a search as long as the Soviets were out in force. Cook's optimism was enough to send the secretary straight to the White House to seek the okay.

Craven, Moore, and Cook could do nothing now but pray for the final go-ahead. They barely had time to kneel. Within a few hours, Nitze telephoned Beshany, who called Moore, Cook, and Craven back into his office with the news.

"You have a new mission."*

Craven now began looking for any other evidence that might further pinpoint the location of the Golf. He was convinced that there had to be other audible signs of a sub going down, so he contacted Captain Joseph Kelly, the man chiefly responsible for expanding the SOSUS net of underwater listening devices that the Navy had been laying throughout the oceans.

Kelly's staff ran through a series of SOSUS records, looking for

---

*As Craven and company began to look for the Soviet sub, and the chance to study Soviet technology from underwater camera close-ups, other photographs had Admiral Rickover in the sub force convinced that U.S. national security had been greatly compromised. As top-secret photos go, these appeared to be pretty innocuous. A bunch of submariners off the USS *Barb*—the same sub that had monitored the Soviet search for the Golf—had created a cruise book to commemorate their months at sea on a previous mission in 1967. In some of the pictures, a few *Barb* men were photographed with either the engines or some part of the nuclear reactor in the background. When Rickover heard about that he flipped. He insisted that all photos of his reactors, of any part of his reactors, remain highly classified. By the time he was done, the rest of the Navy had flipped too. Admirals began frantically trying to recall the 112 books distributed. Calls and memos criss-crossed the Pacific from *Barb*'s captain to the commander of subs in the Pacific, to top submarine officers in Washington, back to Rickover. The FBI crime lab got involved, called in to determine if the photos could be blacked out to hide the offending reactor bits. The FBI decided chemical processes could undo the black out and make the bits visible. Finally, nearly nine months after the crisis began, the Navy determined that the classified background could be mechanically erased from the photos and the *Barb* men could have their cruise books back.

signs of death: the convulsive terror of an implosion followed by the smaller explosions that together indicate a submarine falling to the ocean bottom. But as Kelly's staff searched, they found no massive aberrations that would indicate a powerful implosion. There was, however, a tiny blip on their paper tapes, a little rise indicating a single loud pop. It was right in the area where Bradley believed the Soviet sub had gone down.

What if, Craven reasoned, the Golf had somehow flooded before hitting crush depth? She would have fallen without a searing, deafening, blinding, cataclysmic, implosive crash of steel. Her death would have been much quieter than that. Craven needed to know what a sinking submarine sounded like, one going down with hatches open, filling with ocean water, internal and external pressure equalizing long before the boat reached crush depth. There was only one way to find out.

Craven and Bradley prevailed upon the Navy to sink a submarine in sacrifice, a submarine whose death could be taped. The Navy gave him an old diesel submarine, a warhorse that had probably escaped countless Japanese torpedoes during World War II. Now she would suffer a vainglorious end.

World War II submarines had been executed before, made targets for torpedo practice. But those boats went out running, their engines on, their rudders wedged into position. There was something almost noble about that kind of death, downed with a single shot like a valiant old steed.

This submarine, on the other hand, was just given up to the waters, while SOSUS engineers recorded her descent. She died silently, which was just what Craven and Bradley had expected. Now, they reasoned, if a submarine with every hatch and watertight door carefully opened went down silently, then another boat might go down with a small pop if one of its watertight doors had remained shut. So, calling on data from other hydrophones that had also picked up the pop, Kelly and Craven triangulated what they believed was the Golf's most likely position: 40 degrees latitude and 180 degrees longitude. That put her just about 1,700 miles northwest of Hawaii, where the water was more than 3 miles deep.

Beshany still wasn't convinced. He believed there would have to have been implosions. The fact that the Soviets weren't anywhere near the area also caused him doubts. But he had nothing else to go on. So he gave the nod, and *Halibut* was sent to the spot Craven had pinpointed.*

She set out on July 15, her orders kept secret from the men on board. Even the occupants of the Bat Cave were told little. Most assumed they were going back to look for the Soviet missile that had eluded them before.

As a fish was sent out, sonar gray again replaced images from a video camera that still didn't work. Watching the monotone miles roll by on a continuous taped-together sheet was dizzying. The men's eyes stung as they forced themselves to focus, looking for shadows that seemed foreign to the Pacific bottom. Their shifts never lasted longer than ninety minutes. After that, the sky-blues in the Bat Cave began to quiver with gray ghosts.

Day and night, *Halibut* trolled back and forth. The site that Craven, Bradley, and Kelly had targeted still left five miles of sea to search. The Soviet submarine could have drifted a long way before it fell the three miles to the bottom.

Every six days or so, the fish was hauled back into the submarine so that the still film could be collected and developed. This went on for weeks. Still nothing. Then the haze was interrupted.

"Captain Moore, Captain Moore." It was the ship's photographer bursting out of the *Halibut*'s tiny darkroom, suddenly completely aware that he hadn't been looking for a missile this time. He was at once stunned and certain he had found his target.

It was a perfect picture of a submarine's sail. The photographer was shaking so hard Moore worried for a moment that he'd col-

---

*There was another subtle irony to the fact that it was *Halibut* that was going out to search for the Golf. The Soviets had, by now, become convinced that their sub was lost in a collision with the USS *Swordfish* (SSN-579), the only other sub to have been given some of *Halibut*'s special capabilities in the 1960s. The Soviets had noticed that *Swordfish* had pulled into Yokosuka with a damaged sail and periscope shortly after the time they lost contact with their sub. Decades later, when *Swordfish*'s captain, John T. Rigsbee, heard that, he was very surprised. It never occurred to him that the Soviets had even noticed that *Swordfish* had been damaged, and it especially never occurred to him that they'd add two and two and come up with thirty-six. *Swordfish*, he insists, just hit a chunk of ice in the Sea of Japan, far from where the Golf was lost. Actually, he was surprised that anyone even noticed *Swordfish*'s bent periscope, because at the time it seemed all eyes were on Mount Fuji, which looked especially magnificent the day *Swordfish* pulled into port. Soviet intelligence, it seems, had not been gazing at the horizon.

lapse. There it was, *Halibut*'s first success, a view of the steel tomb of about one hundred Soviet sailors.

At Moore's orders, the fish dove again, down to the spot captured in the photograph of the sail, down to where the Soviet Golf looked as though someone had carefully driven her 16,580 feet to the ocean bottom and parked.

Sonar and camera gobbling up everything in the area, the fish collected new detail with each dive. There was a hole blown nearly 10 feet wide, just behind the Golf's conning tower. There must have been an explosion, probably on the surface, given the quiet recorded by SOSUS, and it probably came from a hydrogen buildup that could have occurred as the Soviet crew sat charging the diesel submarine's 450-ton sulfuric acid battery. Although severely damaged, the submarine looked basically intact.

The photos also showed that small hatches had been blown off, exposing two missile silos. Inside the first was twisted pipe where a nuclear warhead had once sat calmly waiting for holocaust. Inside the second silo, the warhead was completely gone. The third silo was intact.

Then the fish's camera found something else, something that shocked even Moore. It was the skeleton of a doomed sailor, probably just an enlisted man, a kid, lying alongside his submarine, alone, his crewmates probably entombed within. One of his legs was broken and bent almost at a right angle, perhaps from the shock of the explosion that destroyed the submarine. Maybe that's what had killed him. Or maybe he had drowned as he fell the three miles to the ocean floor.

The boy had to have been out on deck when the submarine was destroyed. He was dressed in foul-weather gear, a brown sheepskin coat buttoned up to his neck, thick wool pants, and heavy black military boots. Now the clothes warmed only his stark white bones.

Bones, a bare skeleton—by all accounts, that should have been impossible. Little or nothing lived this far down in the ocean, the experts had said. But there he was, and there was something else in those photographs. Tiny, carnivorous worms wriggled around the body they had already eaten bit by horrific bit.

No one who saw the Soviet boy-submariner could forget

him, not anyone who saw the 22,000 photographs *Halibut* brought home on September 9, 1968.

Bradley code-named the pictures "Velvet Fist" after the gentle way they were snatched from the ocean. All those millions of dollars, all those hours poured into *Halibut,* had finally paid off. He rushed the plunder straight to the new director of Naval Intelligence, Frederick J. "Fritz" Harlfinger II, who had taken the post while *Halibut* was still out to sea.

This was a man who had been the Defense Intelligence Agency's assistant director of collection, a polite word in intelligence circles for theft. Working with the Syrians and the Israelis a few years earlier, his team had managed to steal a Soviet MiG fighter jet. During the Vietnam War, they handed the Pentagon a Soviet surface-to-air missile. They also managed to pilfer a Soviet missile in Indonesia and the engine from a Soviet plane that crashed near Berlin.

But the Velvet Fist photos were unprecedented. As far as Harlfinger was concerned, presenting these to the president was the perfect way to start a new job.

Under Harlfinger's direction, Bradley created a montage of forty photographs to show to the top Navy ranks and up at the White House. First stop was Beshany at submarine command.

"American technology is pretty terrific," Beshany thought as he experienced his first brush against the Velvet Fist. He would forever compare *Halibut*'s feat to a helicopter hovering 17,000 feet in the air with a small camera at the end of a line taking pictures in a dense fog.

Soon after, Harlfinger presented the photographs to President Johnson, who was so impressed that Naval Intelligence officers would congratulate themselves for months.

In January 1969, Richard Nixon was sworn in as president. Shortly after, the phone rang in Bradley's office. It was Harlfinger.

"Get your ass over to the White House, and take Velvet Fist with you."

Alexander Haig, then deputy to Nixon's National Security Adviser Henry Kissinger, wanted to see the photographs. Haig was so impressed that he demanded that he become the guardian of Velvet Fist.

Bradley called Harlfinger for help, pulling him out of a meeting. "Haig wants to keep the material," he reported.

"Fuck him," the intelligence chief answered.

But ignoring Haig was easier said than done. "He wants to show this to his boss and to his boss's boss," Bradley said.

No one needed to explain to Harlfinger that Haig's "boss's boss" just happened to be the new president of the United States. Harlfinger had played enough politics over the years to know when it was time to concede.

"Okay," he relented. The photographs could be left with Haig, but only for twenty-four hours.

That was time enough for Haig to bring the material to Kissinger. Later, it would be Kissinger who made the presentation to Nixon. Nixon was fascinated. So much so that word got back to the CIA.

While the agency's analysts had long been interested in what the regular spy subs managed to pick up, it had generally left control of the operations to the Navy. But now, the CIA and its director, Richard Helms, were suddenly and intensely interested in the ocean deep. Helms began to engineer a takeover, CIA-style. First, he created a new level of bureaucracy, a liaison agency that would supposedly pool the resources of Naval Intelligence and the CIA. It would be called the National Underwater Reconnaissance Office (NURO).

This wasn't the first time the CIA had made this kind of arrangement. In 1961 the agency decided to share control over the satellite operations with the Air Force by creating a joint venture dubbed the National Reconnaissance Office.

NURO was supposed to be divided evenly between Navy and CIA staffers. At its top ranks, it was. Its director was John Warner, Nixon's new secretary of the Navy. Bradley would be staff director. Heading up the CIA end was Carl Duckett, its deputy director for science and technology. But from the day NURO was formed, the CIA took charge. Bradley could spare only a few people for the new office. His entire staff in the undersea part of Naval Intelligence numbered only about a dozen. The CIA, however, had no such constraints. It moved in with eight permanent staffers and more consultants loyal to the agency.

Worse, it was becoming increasingly clear to Bradley and

Craven that the CIA couldn't tell a submarine from an under-water mountain. By now, the two men had come up with a plan for retrieving the best of what was on board the Soviet Golf. Their idea was to eventually send mini-subs to grab a nuclear warhead, the safe containing the Soviets' "crypto-codes," and the submarine's burst transmitters and receivers so that the Navy could finally decode all of the message traffic it had been collecting.

The two men had already proven that the Golf's hull could be opened without destroying everything inside. They had borrowed Army demolition experts to test their theory. With a large steel plate shielding various fragile and flammable objects set up in a pool of water, plastic explosives were affixed to a tiny area and detonated. The blast left a small doorway, barely singeing the articles behind the steel.

That's really all anyone needed to do: open a small doorway and reach in. The rest of the Golf could be left buried at sea. The military had watched these submarines being built in overhead photography for ten years. Naval Intelligence knew the Golf II down to nearly every nut and bolt. The rockets that the Golfs used to launch their nuclear payloads were primitive, with ranges of only 750 miles. Both the United States and the Soviet Union had already engineered rockets with 1,500-mile ranges. There was little to be gained in attempting the impossible job of pulling up thousands of tons of already antiquated gear from the bottom of the ocean. Besides, it would take years to develop the equipment for such a salvage attempt.

Carl Duckett and his CIA loyalists listened politely to the more abbreviated plan. But when they came back with their answer, Craven and Bradley were dumbstruck. The CIA recommended picking up the whole submarine and intended to build a massive crane-laden ship to reach down and grab the Golf.

Craven and Bradley couldn't believe it. The Golf may have hit bottom at 100 knots or more, accelerating 70 feet per second as it fell. It may have looked intact, but it was probably as fragile as a sand castle. Touch it hard enough, and it would disintegrate.

"You can't pick up the goddamn submarine, or it will fall apart," Bradley blurted out. "Oh, no, Jesus Christ almighty. You people are in a tank. That's a pipe dream."

Bradley may have been right, but the CIA held the power in Washington and usually got what it wanted, even when what it wanted was, in Harlfinger's opinion, crazy and impossible. (Former CIA Director Richard M. Helms says now that he never even heard of the alternative that Bradley and Craven had proposed.)

The CIA, however, wasn't alone in its enthusiasm. Chief of Naval Operations Thomas H. Moorer loved big, fascinating technological projects and was captivated by the CIA plan. Here was a chance to snatch a whole submarine and get back at the Soviets for North Korea's capture of *Pueblo*. Besides, he wasn't convinced that Bradley and Craven's method could recover all of the key gear on the Golf.

In the end, Defense Secretary Melvin R. Laird gave the final approval to the CIA plan, acknowledging that he did so despite the fact that "some people thought it was a nutty idea." Laird rationalized the exercise. Creating a ship to lift the Golf from the Pacific might also give the United States the ability to retrieve its own submarines if they were lost.

Laird consulted Howard Hughes, the billionaire recluse whose shipping company was hired by the CIA to build the ship that would try to hoist the Golf from the ocean floor. That ship would be called the *Glomar Explorer*, and the effort code-named "Project Jennifer."

Craven watched these wranglings, no longer surprised by a national intelligence program run by politics. He may have been cynical, but he was certain that the CIA was looking for a project that would funnel hundreds of millions of dollars to Hughes to pay off Nixon's heavy political debts.

Whatever the reason, Nixon quickly approved the CIA plan. And Bradley and Craven were left to whisper their dissent to themselves and to one another. No one else, it seemed, cared to listen. If anything, Craven was rewarded for his protest by being shut out of the operation. The largest deep-water undertaking ever was going to go forward without the guidance of the men who had made it possible.

It would also go forward without *Halibut*'s Commander Moore. It was time for Rickover to make his move, to crack down on this world that had tried to exclude him. The admiral had stood by when Moore's predecessor claimed higher authority for *Halibut* than Rickover's Naval Reactors Branch. Rickover had observed tens of millions being poured into *Halibut* while he himself came under fire when *NR-1*'s $30 million budget ballooned to $90 million. He had bided his time while Nixon awarded *Halibut* the Presidential Unit Citation (PUC), the highest submarine award possible. And he was unmoved when Moore won the Distinguished Service Medal for finding the Golf.

All the while, Rickover's reactor specialists at the shipyard were focused on *Halibut*. Her men became so agitated under the constant scrutiny that Moore suspected they were making mistakes just to give Rickover's men something to mark down, just enough so that the men would be satisfied and leave. Crew members weren't admitting as much, but Moore knew the tension was getting to them, just as he knew that it was only a matter of time until Rickover had the ammunition he was looking for. He was going to send a fleet-shaking salvo that no submarine, no matter its mission or its accomplishments, was beyond his reach or the reach of his safety inspectors.

He got his opening early one morning in 1969. *Halibut* had been moved to the Mare Island Naval Shipyard, just out of San Francisco. Her reactor was being refueled while her officers were distracted by yet another refit designed to enhance *Halibut*'s deep-sea capabilities. Rickover was scheduled to come to the sub that day, only nobody on board knew when. Moore was back at his shore quarters, six blocks away from *Halibut*'s dock, when the admiral arrived at Mare Island, dressed as usual in civilian clothes.

Rickover first encountered a pair of Marine guards who refused to let him past the gate. That wouldn't have been too much of a problem—these men might not have recognized Rickover in person, but they would have known his name. All he had to do was show his identification, and that, he refused to do. He was infuriated that anyone at a sub base could fail to recognize him on sight. He crashed the gate. Later, Moore would hear that the admiral raced down the causeway on foot, guards in chase. He was caught and again asked to show his identification. By the time the guards had been satisfied, Rickover stormed straight to the office of Robert Metzger, his reactor-safety chief on Mare Island.

Still infuriated, Rickover decided not to go to *Halibut* himself. Instead, he sent a representative, one of the men who had traveled with him from D.C. In doing so, Rickover set the stage for history to repeat itself.

Just about anyone on the sub would have recognized Rickover immediately and no one would have questioned him. Nobody, however, knew his representative, so the young submariner serving topside watch did what he was supposed to do. He approached the man and asked for identification, then called down to the duty officer who ended up denying Rickover's man access.

When Moore heard about all of this, he immediately sought out Rickover. The admiral didn't give him much chance to smooth things over. Instead, he barked, "Moore, you ought to worry about your career." Then he demanded, "And what are you going to do to the duty officer who denied us access?"

Rickover never did bother to inspect *Halibut*, but the sub would feel his wrath. The constant review of *Halibut* reactor operations continued. *Halibut*'s crew knew there was enough to find, if you noted every small move, a wrong wrench used, a failure to exactly follow procedures, and more.

Moore was removed from command of *Halibut* three months after his run-in with Rickover. Although the move was wrapped in the paper of a usual transfer, few people doubted that Rickover was behind it. "That to me was one of the numerous irrational personnel actions that the gentleman was capable of doing and did do," says Rear Admiral Walter L. Small Jr., then commander of submarines in the Pacific. Rickover was going to dismiss anyone he wanted to dismiss "whether he had the authority or not."

Much of Moore's wardroom chose to resign from the Navy—some in silent protest over Rickover's treatment of their captain, others simply to avoid the endless barrage. Even Doc Wheat, the corpsman who had poured the brandy that revived Charlie Hammonds, had come under fire when Rickover's crew deemed that the records of the crew's radiation exposures were a mess.

Moore was moved to the Pentagon to work with the deep-submergence group, and ironically ended up being part of the team seeking missions for Rickover's beloved *NR-1*. Rickover had engineered Moore's firing, but he hadn't gotten rid of him. And despite Rickover's ire, Moore made full captain along with the rest of his class. He had too many favorable fitness reports, had accomplished too much, for anyone to deny him, even Rickover.

But full captain or not, Moore had lost his boat. It was a bizarre reward. After leading the Navy's boldest undersea spy program, Moore would never command at sea again.

DEATH OF A SUBMARINE

t was May 27, 1968, and the end of a long day. John Craven was driving along the Potomac, on his way home, when the news came over the radio: the USS *Scorpion* (*SSN-589*) was missing; ninety-nine men were missing.

Barely two months had passed since U.S. intelligence had realized the Soviets had lost their Golf submarine. And Craven was still helping Bradley figure out where it had gone down when this latest news came. Craven listened hard for details about *Scorpion*, but there weren't any.

Nobody had any idea where *Scorpion* was or what had happened to her. All they knew was that the 3,500-ton nuclear attack submarine was due back in Norfolk, Virginia, and had failed to arrive. She hadn't been slinking off Soviet shores or even plumbing new depths, as the USS *Thresher* had been doing when she was lost five years earlier. *Scorpion* had simply been cruising through the Atlantic Ocean on a straight track for home. Just like the World War II submarine she was named for, *Scorpion* had vanished without a trace and seemingly without reason.

Craven slowed his car at the next exit and turned for the Pentagon. As Craven stepped into the controlled pandemonium of the War Room, all he knew was that, as the Navy's top deep-water scientist, he would be needed. A submarine was missing; ninety-nine men were missing.

Surveying the crowd of captains and admirals and other officers already there, Craven sensed something he had never encountered in a room full of top-ranking military men: abject fear.

The fear could be seen in the tensed faces of the men who stood scrutinizing a huge wall chart mapping *Scorpion*'s assigned track, and it could be heard in the shaken tones of others who were intently studying navigational charts strewn all over the room. Men were laying out hypotheses and search patterns. They were replotting *Scorpion*'s track, now creating a path for search planes above and looking for the sparse undersea mountains below. Just a few months before, the USS *Scamp* (*SSN-588*) was nearly lost when she rammed into an undersea mountain in the Pacific in her race to go monitor a Soviet missile test. A similar accident, and *Scorpion* might be lost forever. Then again, those mountains might also be the only places along her path where she and her crew could have sunk without meeting instant, crushing death.

Other officers were studying the positions of nearby Soviet ships and submarines, wondering whether any had crossed *Scorpion*'s path. People all over the room were trying to weigh the possibilities, wanting to believe that *Scorpion* was still intact, her crew stranded but alive.

"What can my organization do to help?" Craven said over the worried voices, the roar of competing conversations, and the rustle of the charts. Nobody looked up or even seemed to notice him speaking from the doorway. Most of these officers knew nothing of *Halibut,* of Craven's role in preparing her for deep-sea searches, or even of his success in pinpointing the atomic bomb the Air Force lost in the deep Atlantic near Palomares, Spain. To most of the rank and file here, Craven was just another skinny engineer. Those few who did know him well found him to be a man full of odd ideas and strange search methods that didn't sound like anything ever penned in a Navy manual. Few of the officers in the War Room that day would have believed that Craven might be their best and perhaps only chance of finding *Scorpion*.

Craven repeated his question. This time, someone answered: "We haven't been able to find *Scorpion* on the acoustic nets. We don't know where it is. If there's anything you can do with respect to that, do it."

With that, Craven was left on his own, left to try to figure out why and where *Scorpion* had vanished. Odds were worse than a million to one against anyone finding the boat. She could have been anywhere on a track that covered 3,000 miles of the Atlantic.

The families of the *Scorpion* crew had begun to worry as early as February 15, 1968, three months before Craven heard the news on the radio, three months before rumors began swirling through the sub force that the Soviets might have sunk her.

There, standing on the dock tossing the final mooring line to the crew as *Scorpion* departed, was Dan Rogers, an electrician's mate who had risked his career by demanding to be transferred off the boat, writing to his captain, Lieutenant Commander Francis A. Slattery, that everyone on board was "in danger." The Navy had always portrayed the 252-foot-long sub as a gleaming showpiece, but Rogers said *Scorpion* was so overdue for a thorough overhaul that the crew had taken to calling her the "USS Scrap Iron." There were oil leaks in the hydraulic systems and seawater seeping in through the propeller shaft seals. Her emergency ballast systems weren't working, and the Navy had restricted her depth to 300 feet, less than one-third of the operational depth of other boats of her class.

There had also been a frightening incident three months earlier when *Scorpion* had vibrated so violently during high-speed maneuvers that she seemed to corkscrew through the water, sending huge pieces of equipment swaying on their rubber mountings. Rogers and other crewmen feared that the problem could reappear at any time.

Most of the submarine fleet had undergone massive safety

overhauls after *Thresher* was lost. The bulk of the work on *Scorpion*, however, had been postponed due to tight budgets and the relentless pace of intelligence operations, which were growing rapidly toward a peak never before seen during the cold war. As she set out, *Scorpion* was one of only four of the Atlantic Fleet's submarines that was still waiting to be refitted with post-*Thresher* safety features.

Rogers and his mates complained to Slattery that he and his officers weren't taking their concerns seriously. Rogers wasn't even released from the boat until he agreed to Slattery's demand that he erase the Cassandra-esque warning of "danger" from his request for transfer.

One month later, *Scorpion* was assigned to join in NATO exercises in the Mediterranean. She was sent there only because the Navy needed a last-minute replacement for *Seawolf*, the same submarine that Craven had bypassed in favor of *Halibut* when it came time to pick a special projects boat. *Seawolf* had knocked herself out of the fleet rotation by ramming an undersea mountain in the Gulf of Maine, badly crushing her stern.

The Mediterranean had become the latest cold war arena. Since the Arab-Israeli War in 1967, the Soviet Union had been sending growing numbers of attack subs armed with nuclear cruise missiles to stalk U.S. aircraft carriers and to try to trail U.S. missile subs roaming from a base in Rota, Spain. U.S. surveillance subs were also watching ports in Egypt, where some of the Soviet vessels stopped. The traffic was so thick that by December the Med saw its first underwater collision, between the USS *George C. Marshall* (*SSBN-654*) and a Soviet attack sub.

Most of the time, however, the problem was simply detecting the Soviet subs. SOSUS listening nets, which helped in other areas of the world, didn't reach into the Med—or, for that matter, down the west coast of Europe, a key Soviet route to the area. The Med itself has horrible sonar conditions, with saltwater meeting fresh water, warm meeting cold, all of it sending sonar bouncing in unpredictable directions. Besides all that, nobody on the U.S. side really understood how the Soviets operated in the Med, or how many subs they were sending. Indeed, submarine analysts in London and their counterparts in

Norfolk, Virginia, were having long analytic arguments about Soviet operations, arguments that went on all the longer because there were so few facts to back them up.

On the assumption that sheer numbers would fill in the gap left by expertise, the United States began trying to train its allies' sub forces—those in southern Europe and the Middle East—in the art of sub-chasing. *Scorpion,* in fact, was sent to the Med to play rabbit, to be hunted by foreign forces as part of their training. For *Scorpion*'s men, this should have been a plum assignment, one with the rare perk of port stops in sun-sprayed Spain, Italy, and Sicily. But many would have preferred to have stayed onshore with Rogers, at least judging from their letters home.

"We have repaired, replaced, or jury-rigged every piece of equipment," twenty-four-year-old Machinist's Mate Second-class David Burton Stone wrote to his parents on April 12. Stone sent his letter two months into the trip, just before *Scorpion* got caught in a dangerous game of chicken with a Soviet destroyer. The incident was typical of operations in the Med: both sides had taken to harassing the other at sea. When *Scorpion* surfaced to exchange messages with the USS *Cutlass* (SS-478), the destroyer raced forward as if to ram the submarine. With a crash seemingly moments away, the Soviet ship backed off.

"It did it three or four times," says Herbert E. Tibbets, the commanding officer of *Cutlass,* who watched the incident from his bridge. "I kept sweating, thinking, 'I hope those guys back it down this time.'"

Reports of that incident and rumors of another mission have left many of the families convinced that the Soviets were the likely cause of *Scorpion*'s destruction. According to the most virulent story, *Scorpion* supposedly was hit by a Soviet torpedo during a final mission in which she tried to chase a Soviet attack submarine away from a U.S. Polaris boat out in the Atlantic.

There was, in fact, a final mission, but it had nothing to do with chasing Soviet attack subs. It began in late April. *Scorpion* was on her final port visit, this one to Naples, Italy. From there, her men expected to be going home. Instead, they were told they were being sent to monitor strange Soviet activity. U.S. satellites had photographed a group of Soviet surface ships, just outside the

Med, flying balloons about the size of weather balloons. The Soviet ships had been engaged in this baffling behavior for nearly a month. In the Pacific, the Soviets had been known to launch balloons equipped with electronic sensors in the vicinity of U.S. nuclear tests. Perhaps this was a new application of that spying technique.

Figuring that *Scorpion* was going to pass near the area on her way home anyway, Captain James Bradley, still the Navy's top submarine intelligence officer, ordered the sub to swing by and take a look. Slattery and the other *Scorpion* officers were distressed. After more than two months at sea, the officers wanted to go straight home, and they made that clear at a farewell cocktail party in Naples, cornering Bradley with their concerns. He was sympathetic, but the orders stood.

Scorpion set out on April 28. Slattery stopped outside the breakwater at Rota, Spain, to drop off a crewman who had become ill and another who had a family emergency, then went on. *Scorpion* lurked near the Soviet ships for two or three days before Slattery turned his sub for home. When he reached a safe distance from the Soviets, he radioed that he had collected a few photographs but little insight about the Soviet exercise.

It is not entirely clear where this group of ships was working, but declassified Navy documents cite one possibility. Air-reconnaissance planes had spotted two Soviet hydrographic survey ships—a submarine rescue ship and an Echo II–class nuclear attack submarine—conducting an unspecified "hydro-acoustic operation" southwest of the Canary Islands, which lie about 300 miles off northwest Africa. Air reconnaissance was cut off on May 19 and resumed on May 21, just about the time *Scorpion* would have left the area.

"There were no observed changes in the pattern of operations of the Soviet ships, either before or after *Scorpion*'s loss, that were evaluated as indicating involvement or interest in any way," the Navy would later report in a document prepared in 1969 by a court of inquiry into the *Scorpion* disaster and kept classified for years.

On the evening of May 21, *Scorpion*'s crew radioed in their location and reported that they had embarked upon their assigned route home, the "Great Circle Track" through the North Atlantic.

Ordered to transit at 18 knots, they said they expected to arrive in Norfolk at 1:00 P.M., Eastern Standard Time, on May 27.

Admiral Thomas Moorer, the CNO, and Vice Admiral Arnold F. Schade, commander of submarines in the Atlantic, began to worry when *Scorpion* failed to answer messages on May 23 as well as repeat messages over the next two days. They quietly asked a few Navy ships and planes to scan for signs of the submarine. No general alarm was raised. After all, Slattery and his men could be racing home underwater and out of radio contact.

Concern turned to fear on May 27, at 12:20 P.M. It was twenty minutes before *Scorpion* was supposed to arrive at Norfolk. By now, she should have been on the surface, her crew talking with the base. Schade initiated an intensive communications check. Ships and planes flooded the air with *Scorpion*'s call name.

"Brandywine. . . ."

"Brandywine. . . ."

"Brandywine!"

There was no answer.

At 3:15 P.M., *Scorpion* was declared missing.

Back at the dock, the crewmen's families waited, waited for their husbands, sons, and fathers to come back from sea, waited in a spring rain that washed the dock clean. They knew nothing about the frantic radio messages tearing through the air around them. Then the Navy told them to go home, told them that *Scorpion* had been delayed. It was only when news reporters started calling that the families learned that their sons, husbands, and fathers were missing.

By the time Craven turned for the Pentagon, intelligence officers had already been frantically scrambling for acoustic evidence or other signs of an accident, a collision, or a battle. Reconnaissance pilots placed all known Soviet and Eastern Bloc surface warships, merchant ships, and submarines at least 50 miles away from any point *Scorpion* was expected to pass. The Navy would later report that there was "no evidence of any Soviet preparations for hostilities or a crisis situation such as would be expected in the event of a premeditated attack on *Scorpion*." Indeed, by the time Craven walked into the War Room, the Navy basically had ruled out Soviet involvement in *Scorpion*'s loss.

Vice Admiral Schade set out himself to join the search on the USS *Pargo* (*SSN-650*). Rogers, the former crewman, went out looking as well, aboard his new submarine, the USS *Lapon* (*SSN-661*).

There was a moment when everyone on *Lapon* believed that *Scorpion* had been found. *Lapon*'s radiomen picked up an SOS from "Brandywine." But soon it became sickeningly apparent that the message was a fake, a sadistic joke from merchant seamen or pleasure boaters.

Meanwhile, Craven launched a search that would take so many twists, and leave him so at odds with the rest of the Navy, that he himself would begin to wonder whether he had indeed gone mad. He began routinely enough, thinking of ways to acoustically delve the ocean depths. It was clear that the SOSUS listening nets were going to be useless. While the listening system in the Pacific had picked up that one pop, the only sign of the Soviet Golf's loss, the extensive SOSUS arrays in the Atlantic could not do the same thing. The Atlantic SOSUS system was designed to filter incoming noise, allowing the sonar nets to record the consistent clatter of machinery, the whir of submarine screws, and all the other music made by submarines as they move underwater, while muffling the blasts of oil exploration, undersea earthquakes, and the calls of whales. That same filtering system would have eliminated any evidence if *Scorpion* had fallen to the ocean bottom, would have broken apart the terrible cries of a submarine imploding, rendering them nearly indistinct from the normal ocean din.

"How the hell are we going to find these poor bastards?" Craven muttered to himself. Within days, he would be named chairman of a technical advisory group convened to help find *Scorpion* by Robert A. Frosch, the assistant secretary of the Navy for research and development. Craven and the other group members were to report directly to the CNO and the commander of the Atlantic Fleet.

He began calling upon the small oceanographic research stations that dotted the Atlantic. Top on his list was Gordon Hamilton, a friend who ran an oceanographic laboratory in Bermuda that was funded by the Office of Naval Research.

"Hey, Gordon, do you have any hydrophones in the water that could have heard the *Scorpion*?" Craven asked without bothering to offer a greeting.

"Well, I don't, but part of my laboratory in the Canary Islands has a hydrophone in the water all the time," Hamilton answered.

The hydrophones generated mounds of scrawled paper, those peaks and blips that accumulated as pens moved over continuously rotating drums. There was a problem, though. Six days had passed since *Scorpion*'s last message to shore, and laboratory workers were supposed to clean up and toss the records after two or three days. Any scrawls that could have registered a final tragedy aboard *Scorpion* should have gone out with the trash.

Still, Craven firmly believed that people rarely do what they are supposed to do. Housekeeping, he reasoned, is usually the first thing to go. Within a couple of hours, Hamilton called back. Craven was right. There were piles of paper all over the lab, and buried within those piles were two weeks of acoustic records—including eight separate ocean explosions or severe disturbances during the six days *Scorpion* had been out of contact. But the disturbances could have been caused by almost anything, including blasts from illegal oil explorations, a fairly routine sound ringing through the North Atlantic. And they could have come from almost anywhere, and from any direction.

With only one set of records, Craven had no way to come up with a geographic fix on any of the blasts. To do that, he would need to triangulate three separate recordings from three different hydrophones set up in three different points. Since he didn't have the data to come up with a precise fix, Craven worked backward, charting the times of the explosions against *Scorpion*'s known path and speed. He came up with eight mid-ocean locations where he assumed the sub would have been at the time of any of the disturbances. Bathymetric charts showed all eight sites to be in waters deeper than 2,000 feet, deeper than the crush depth of a submarine.

Acting on Craven's data, the Navy sent planes to all eight spots. The pilots were looking for floating wreckage and oil slicks. They found none. The lack of debris was far from conclusive, given that the water was so deep. But Craven needed more to go on. The hunt for sonic evidence continued.

Independent of Craven's efforts, Wilton Hardy, the chief scientist of an elite acoustic team at the Naval Research Laboratory, the Navy's primary underwater testing facility in Washington, D.C., came up with the next clue. He knew that the Air Force kept two hydrophones near Newfoundland to track underwater shocks from Soviet nuclear tests. One was right off the peninsula of Argentia. The other was about 200 miles from there.

Hardy sent for the records, knowing he was playing a long shot. Both Air Force hydrophones were about as far from the Azores, and *Scorpion*'s last-known position, as any listening devices could be and still be in the North Atlantic. And sitting right between the hydrophones and *Scorpion*'s track was the largest chain of mountains on earth, the undersea Mid-Atlantic Ridge. The mountains were enough to block most sounds from the Azores.

Indeed, at first glance the Air Force records looked useless. There were none of the dramatic peaks that had been registered by the Canary Islands lab. But, to Hardy, it seemed that if he looked real hard, maybe squinted a bit, he could just possibly see something. He laid the Canary Islands recordings directly on top of the Argentia recordings.

There they were, almost entirely buried in local noise, slight blips that seemed to match the more dramatic peaks picked up by Hamilton's lab. Hardy called Craven, who was by now coordinating the Navy's entire acoustic search effort. Craven decided to convince himself that the Argentia recordings were neither coincidence nor phantoms.

If the Argentia blips were worthless noise, then the plots would probably fall hundreds of miles or thousands of miles from the relatively tiny line of ocean that made up *Scorpion*'s track. But if the new data pinpointed any one of the eight events picked up in the Canary Islands on that tiny line, the acoustic matches would almost certainly have to be valid.

Hardy found it first. There, right on *Scorpion*'s track, was an explosion strong enough to tear through a steel hull and send a submarine, flooded, toward the ocean bottom.

There was no telling what caused the explosion. But 91 seconds later, there were a series of much louder blasts and there was no mistaking what caused those. Craven and Hardy were convinced that they had to be implosions, the agonized shouts of a submarine collapsing in on itself, compartment by compartment breaking down with the force of nearly 500 pounds of TNT.

The men on the submarine could have survived the initial explosion, if that sound was indeed from *Scorpion*. They might have lived long enough to see her walls begin to quaver inward, but that would have been all. Nobody could have lived through the first implosion. That shock would have sent the tail section and the bow section plowing into the center of the submarine, like a papier-mâché model crushed in front and in back with a single, violent clap. The cataclysmic heat and the shock of that would have killed everyone on board in less than one-hundredth of a second. The men would all be dead even as the ocean pressures continued to pummel *Scorpion*: a second implosion four seconds after the first, then another five seconds later, then two seconds, then three seconds, then seven seconds, then another and another and another. Three minutes and ten seconds after the first explosion, it would have been all over. Three minutes and ten seconds of destruction before the ocean went suddenly quiet.

Recorded only eighteen hours after *Scorpion*'s crew had sent word they were heading home, the blasts meant that the sub had managed to travel less than 400 miles toward Norfolk.

It was now four days after *Scorpion* had been declared missing. Craven called the chief of Naval Operations to tell him that *Scorpion* was probably lost forever. Moorer wasn't ready to hear that. He wasn't about to tell the crewmen's families and the nation that there was no hope based on a bunch of tiny, almost indiscernible blips on paper. The fact that they occurred at a point right on *Scorpion*'s track, at a moment when she was expected to be there, was enough to convince him only to declare the spot "an area of special interest." Then he waited to see whether any of the planes, ships, and submarines turned up anything else.

Rear Admiral Beshany, commander of the submarine force, began funneling all press inquiries to Craven. But the scientist remained under strict orders to avoid the word *lost* and even the suggestion of death. It wasn't until another six days had passed with no sign of *Scorpion* that Beshany and Moorer were forced to accept that Craven and Hardy were right. On June 5, Moorer announced that the *Scorpion* was "presumed lost." Hours later, the secretary of the Navy formally declared Captain Slattery and his ninety-eight other officers and crewmen legally dead.

But *Scorpion* was still missing. Without examining the remains of the sub, the Navy would never know what had gone wrong. Without that understanding, the nuclear submarine fleet would forever operate with the fear that a fatal flaw, somehow overlooked, could cause another catastrophe. Absent proof the crewmen were dead, their families might never be able to shake the thought, against all logic and against all available information, that the men might have been captured and were alive somewhere, perhaps in a Soviet prison.

And so began the second phase of the search. Now it was up to Craven and his team to find *Scorpion* and to find out what killed her. He turned his attention back to the acoustic echoes.

The site of the first explosion—now being called "Point Oscar"—marked where his search would begin. But that still left him far from finding the sub. Thermal layers in the water could have distorted the sounds of *Scorpion*'s loss as they traveled to the Canary Islands and the Argentia hydrophones. Craven calculated that there could be ten miles of error for any of the spots mapped by the triangulated data.

Also, the water at Point Oscar was 2 miles deep. The *Scorpion* would have stopped imploding about 7,000 feet before she hit bottom, cutting off the acoustic trail. Depending on how fast she had been traveling, and in what direction, and depending on the force of implosion and the position of her stern planes as she fell, she could have been thrown miles further.

All that meant that the submarine could be anywhere within a 20-mile-wide circle, leaving a vast, unknown universe to search. And the art of deep-sea search was still in its infancy.

In starting the *Scorpion* search, Craven had far less data than he had when searching for the Soviet Golf in the Pacific. The Navy decided to send a surface ship to comb the area surrounding Point Oscar. There was no thought of sending *Halibut* on this search; *Halibut* was a boat designed for secrecy, and there was little need to shroud the fact that the search was going on since the Soviets could easily read about the missing submarine in American newspapers.

Instead, the ship the Navy employed was the USNS *Mizar*, an oceanographic survey vessel. She was a 266-foot-long former polar supply ship that had been converted to research at the start of the Navy's post-*Thresher* scramble to the deep. For this mission, she would be under the direction of Hardy's team at the Naval Research Laboratory, where she was based.

Mizar carried towed cameras, less-advanced versions of *Halibut*'s fish, and with those she would start the slow, painstaking survey of the ocean bottom. The search would be led by Chester "Buck" Buchanan, a civilian oceanographer and senior NRL scientist.

As Buchanan set out, he knew he was in for a long haul. Crawling at two knots, it would take *Mizar* months to cover the area. But Buchanan was a tracker by nature, short, stocky, and good-naturedly pugnacious. He began to grow a beard the day *Mizar* left port, a Vandyke, declaring that he would shave only when he found his quarry.

Staying in constant contact with Hardy and Craven as they sorted through the acoustic crumbs, Buchanan began directing *Mizar* in circles over Point Oscar, finding little more than what seemed to be iron-rich meteorites. Following the Navy's lead, *Mizar* then began scouring the area west of Point Oscar. The Navy reasoned that since *Scorpion* had been heading west toward Norfolk, that was the best direction to search.

Meanwhile, Craven began digging for more evidence, anything that could help direct *Mizar* from shore. He set about trying to map each implosion in the hope that he could figure out how far *Scorpion* had traveled before the final sounds of her loss subsided.

He found much more.

Craven's map showed that *Scorpion* had not been traveling west toward Norfolk during her final moments. Instead, Craven's calculations surprisingly showed that the submarine had been moving east, back toward the Mediterranean. Perhaps a submarine could turn if it were fleeing from another boat, but intelligence officials had already told Craven that they were all but certain that the Soviets were not involved. It had to be something else.

The scientist went straight to Beshany's submarine command. He had one question. "What could make a submarine go in the wrong direction?"

Craven asked the same question of several captains and admirals. Each time he got the same answer.

A submarine turns around 180 degrees when a torpedo activates while it is still on board, an event submariners call a "hot run." The boat turns because that triggers fail-safe devices on a torpedo, shutting it down. The same safety devices keep the weapons from turning and blowing up the submarines they are fired from.

Scorpion carried a load of torpedoes, armed and ready for the worst, as did all cold war attack submarines. There were fourteen Mark 37 torpedoes, seven Mark 14s, and two nuclear-tipped Mark 45 Astor torpedoes. Hot runs were particularly common with the Mark 37s, and if there had been a hot run, Slattery would have called "right full rudder," ordering a 180-degree turn the moment the torpedo room reported the problem. Any captain would have—the maneuver is one of those things that are drilled into submariners until the reaction becomes simple reflex. In fact, *Scorpion* had recovered from a hot run in December 1967, six months before she was lost, precisely because Slattery had followed the standard procedure.

That had to be it, Craven reasoned. *Scorpion* was traveling west, and that had to mean that something had gone wrong with one of the sub's torpedoes. Somehow it had activated. And somehow it had exploded.

Craven began to dig around. He learned that there was a flaw in the onboard testing equipment that could easily have triggered a hot run. And he learned that torpedoes, along with almost every other piece of equipment on board, are routinely tested as submarines make way for home.

One of Craven's favorite maxims was "If something can be installed backward, it will be." And in this case, it was true. Several submarines had reported hot runs as a result of electric leads on the test equipment being installed backward. The problem had become common enough that the commander of the Atlantic Fleet issued warnings.

With that known flaw and the acoustic data, it seemed to Craven that *Scorpion*'s fate had been determined. *Scorpion* had been battling a hot-running torpedo, probably created when somebody mistakenly reversed the leads during a test. Only her turn to the east had been too late. The logic, the evidence—it all fit. Craven was convinced.

There was only one problem: almost nobody else agreed with him. The sonic experts, the torpedo experts, the submarine commanders, all listened as Craven held forth with his theories, his evidence, and his logic, his voice rising and falling as if offering a Shakespearean soliloquy, albeit one punctuated with his own trademark maxims of the deep sea. But nobody of any rank, from the chief of Naval Operations on down, thought Craven could be right.

Hardy, the acoustic expert at the Naval Research Lab, was convinced that Craven was reading way too much into the acoustic data and was chasing ghosts. The only thing that turned east toward the Med, Hardy believed, was Craven's phantom trail. His arguments instilled some doubts within Craven. Besides, it was Hardy's lab that was guiding the *Mizar,* and Craven needed his support if the ship was going to turn around and start searching to the east. Craven's own relationship with the lab was shaky. As director of the Deep Submergence Systems Project, he had basically stolen one of the lab's prize possessions, the bathyscaphe *Trieste II,* to assist in working out features for Rickover's *NR-1* mini-sub.

The officers in charge of torpedo safety at the Ordnance Systems Command soon joined the group of naysayers. They insisted that it was impossible for a hot-running torpedo to detonate inside a submarine. For detonation to occur, the command insisted, a warhead would have to run into an object at top speed and stop moving only as it hit. Then and only then would it go off. The Ordnance Systems commanders were backed up by the Bureau of Ships. Walter N. "Buck" Dietzen Jr., a top submarine official, was also firmly in doubt. As the debate raged on, none of the men forgot that they were looking for their own dead.

Still at one point, in an effort to lighten things up a bit, Dietzen wagered Craven a bottle of Chivas Regal scotch whiskey that he would turn out to be wrong. Operational commanders were betting with Dietzen. *Mizar* had already dug up some tantalizing clues on the Norfolk side of Point Oscar. There were three items found that could have fallen from *Scorpion:* a piece of elbow pipe, what seemed to be a woman's umbrella, and a rope tied in a "monkey's fist," the ball-shaped knot that sailors tie at the end of a mooring line to make it easier to catch when it is tossed onto a pier.

There was some argument within the Navy about whether the monkey's fist *Mizar* found was tied in the U.S. style or in the style favored by the Italian Navy, but the umbrella, the operations officers believed, had to have come from *Scorpion*'s crew. They had made port stops, hadn't they? This could have been someone's souvenir or gift for a woman back home. Months would pass before Navy biologists declared that what looked like an umbrella was actually alive, one of the many odd creatures that live on the ocean floor.

Still, given the *Mizar* evidence and the strong opinions around him, even Craven began to wonder whether he was wrong, just "smoking opium," as he liked to say. But then again, maybe he was the only one who was right. Craven had no trouble believing either possibility, so he kept digging. He arranged to have a ship drop small explosive charges at Point Oscar. By comparing the acoustic signatures taken at the site with the signals that reached Norfolk, he would be able to figure out once and for all whether an explosion in the area would create echoes—sonic ghosts—as others had contended.

Gordon Hamilton flew into Norfolk from the Canary Islands for the occasion. The two men camped out in a bare cinder-block room in a Norfolk communications station. There they would wait, all day and all night and all the next day, until the calibration charges rang through to shore.

On the first and second tries, the charges were too weak, and none of the acoustic signals made it back to Norfolk at all. By now, Hamilton and Craven were tired of eating cold sandwiches, tired of the bare walls and bare room, tired of sleeping on the blockhouse floor, and more tired of one another. They had exhausted their repertoire of shop talk. Craven had even run out of maxims of the sea.

Craven began doing push-ups. He had already taken to filling in the time left over from his two submarine searches, the design of *NR-1*, and his running of the SeaLab program by putting himself through the Royal Canadian Air Force exercise program. By now, he could do eighty push-ups at a set. He proved that several times over before the explosives finally signaled through to Norfolk.

They came through with no echoes. And when Craven and

Hamilton recalibrated the *Scorpion* signals with the new data, they realized that not only had *Scorpion* been traveling east, but she was traveling east even faster than Craven had thought.

Craven was back to his torpedo theory. But he wanted more evidence.

With typical dramatic flair, Craven arranged a reenactment of the tragedy. He needed a submarine simulator, and he needed Lieutenant Commander Robert R. Fountain Jr., the former *Scorpion* XO who had been detached from the submarine just before she embarked on her final mission.

Fountain was put at the simulator's helm, and a computer was programmed to factor in the orders he gave as the simulator reenacted various possible causes of *Scorpion*'s loss. Ten different scenarios were tested this way, and ten failed to create a match with the acoustic evidence. Then, Craven's team asked Fountain to try one last time. They said nothing about a possible torpedo explosion, they simply told Fountain that he was heading home at 18 knots, leaving it to him to choose a depth. Craven then asked him to test his torpedoes. The team waited ten or fifteen minutes, giving Fountain a chance to stand calm. Then they rang an alert. "Hot-running torpedo in the torpedo room."

Without missing a beat, without waiting, without asking questions, Fountain ordered, "Right full rudder."

There it was. The turn that Craven believed had been executed on *Scorpion*.

When Fountain's simulated turn was almost complete—maybe half a minute or so after he had called out "right full rudder"—the staff called into the simulator: "Explosion in the forward torpedo room."

The same information was fed into the computer, which began to register extensive flooding in the submarine.

Fountain answered with a seemingly endless stream of orders: blow ballast, initiate watertight security, speed the boat. He did everything a submarine captain should do. Still, the mythical submarine continued to flood, and it continued to head toward the bottom. Exactly 90 seconds after Craven announced the explosion, it passed 2,000 feet—passed right through collapse depth—and the computer registered an implosion. Someone on the staff announced the event with one word: "bang."

The simulated implosion occurred just one second off the 91-second time recorded between *Scorpion*'s explosion at Point Oscar and the first implosion under crushing ocean pressures.

Chills shot through Craven when he saw the results. By now, he and several others attending this test were nearly certain they had replicated *Scorpion*'s loss. No one told that to Fountain. No one told him he had just possibly enacted the circumstances that led to the deaths of the men he had once helped to command. Maybe nobody had to tell him. He left the simulator without asking any questions, without saying a word.

Craven's compassion for Fountain and for the crew of *Scorpion* couldn't squelch the exuberance he felt. As a detective, he had come up with two new important pieces of evidence, and he now raced them to Admirals Schade and Bernard A. Clarey, the vice chief of Naval Operations. By now, even they were becoming intrigued by Craven's detective work, but they remained unconvinced. As did the Ordnance Systems Command, which continued to insist that there was no way a torpedo could explode on board a submarine.

Nobody was ready to face the specter that the Navy itself was responsible for the deaths of those ninety-nine men. Craven understood their reluctance, understood how difficult it was for the admirals to believe they might have been somehow responsible for a mistake that had caused the loss of so many people's lives. Both admirals had lived through a time when death aboard submarines was common. Both were veterans of the World War II diesel boats, but then death had come from the enemy and not from their own boats. Schade was probably the more hard-nosed of the two, and no wonder. As a young executive officer on the USS *Growler* (SS-215), Schade had gotten his first taste of command while his skipper lay wounded on the bridge of the sub. Commander Howard Gilmore shouted a final order to young Schade, an order to take *Growler* into a desperation dive to escape a Japanese gunboat while leaving Gilmore wounded up top. Schade did as he was directed.

Despite the admirals' reluctance, Craven wasn't about to give up, not now that he was convinced he had enough information to find *Scorpion* and prove what killed her. He began to mathematically construct a map of the ocean bottom, using Bayes' theorem of subjective probability, the same algebraic formula he had employed during the search for the H-bomb.

Few of the officers involved in the search for *Scorpion* had taken much note of Palomares. And by the time Craven was finished explaining that he was going to use a system of Las Vegas–style bets to factor the value of a hunch into his data, some of the operational commanders were convinced that he had gone completely over the edge. To them, it sounded like he was talking about ESP. Craven once again tried to explain that Bayes seemed to draw on the knowledge that even experts are not always consciously aware they have. The commanders remained highly skeptical.

Still, Craven pushed on, asking a group of submarine and salvage experts to bet on the probability of each of the different scenarios being considered to explain *Scorpion*'s loss. To keep the process interesting, and in line with previous wagers, the men bet bottles of Chivas Regal.

Scorpion could have glided down to the ocean bottom at speeds between 30 and 60 knots. His submarine experts bet that *Scorpion* had glided downward at between 40 and 45 knots.

Next, the experts were asked to bet on whether they believed *Scorpion* was trying to shut down a hot-running torpedo and was therefore traveling east. About 60 percent of the bets favored the torpedo theory. Craven, it seems, was winning some converts.

In a third round of betting, the experts picked a glide path. At the most, *Scorpion* could have moved 7 feet forward for every foot she descended; at the least, she could have nosedived straight down. The bets favored a glide path of about 3 or 4 feet forward for every foot down. That meant *Scorpion* would have traveled 6 to 8 miles after the first explosion.

By the time the bets were finished and Craven sat down to draw a probability map, the calculations had become so complicated that he had to rehire the group of mathematicians who had helped him with the H-bomb. They concluded that *Scorpion* was east of Point Oscar, 400 miles from the Azores, on the edge of the Sargasso Sea.

Years later, the mathematicians would write a book based on their work with Craven, entitled *Theory of Optimal Search*. The U.S. Coast Guard would adopt the method for search and rescue, and the Navy would use Craven's interpretation of Bayes to help

Egypt clear sunken ordnance from the Suez Canal. But in the *Scorpion* search, naval officers just shook their heads at Craven's acoustic evidence and his probability map. The scientist may have been convinced that *Scorpion* lay further east, but the *Mizar* had found the three scraps of debris to the west, and that's where the Navy wanted to keep searching.

Weeks passed. Craven waited, trading messages nearly every night with Buchanan. By late August, nothing new had been found and the jubilation within the Navy that had accompanied the *Mizar's* find of the supposed umbrella and the monkey's fist knot diminished. By September, all of the likely spots between Point Oscar and Norfolk were almost ruled out. By October, the weather was getting so bad that the Navy decided it would end the search by the end of the month.

But *Mizar* still hadn't really searched east. And it had never searched the site Craven had pinpointed. By now, Buchanan was sporting a fully grown Vandyke beard and was willing to point *Mizar* east one last time.

Almost as soon as *Mizar* passed east of Point Oscar, its long-range sonar registered iron, and lots of it. *Mizar* steamed ahead full speed, right past Craven's point of highest probability, and then lowered its cameras for another look. All it found was iron ore–filled rock.

That was it. The end. Schade and Clarey had had about all the disappointment they could take. The decision was made. It was time to give up. Time to call Buck Buchanan and *Mizar* home.

Buchanan, pugnacious and stubborn as ever, refused to accept their decision. He flashed a message to Craven.

"Can't you get the Navy to let us stay out another month, or a week or two weeks? Tell them I need to calibrate the area for future operations."

Craven knew that there was nothing left to "calibrate." But Craven also knew that if Buck Buchanan wanted to stay out, it could mean only one thing. The oceanographer was going to take *Mizar* to the spot Craven and his team had pinpointed. Craven went to the admirals and began mixing his rapid-fire logic with pleas. By the time he was finished, he had won two more weeks.

Exactly one week later, Craven received a one-line missive from the survey ship: "Buchanan shaved his beard."

Craven didn't need any translation. *Scorpion* had been found. It was October 29, almost five months to the day that she had been declared missing.

Mizar found *Scorpion* within 220 yards, one-eighth of a mile, of where Craven, his mathematicians, and a group of experts betting for bottles of scotch had said she would be. The sub was 11,000 feet underwater.

Dangling cameras, *Mizar* took photographs showing *Scorpion* half-buried in silt and sand and separated into two pieces that were barely held together by a small hinge of metal. The forward part of the engine room had imploded and, in a fraction of a second, collapsed like a telescope into the auxiliary machine space.

The propeller and the propeller shaft were separated from the hull altogether. So was the submarine's sail. Lying near the submarine was *Scorpion*'s sextant—an age-old symbol of navigation. No navigator, officer, or crewman was anywhere in sight. It was impossible to see inside the submarine or even the outside in much detail. Although *Mizar*'s cameras dangled only between 10 and 50 feet over *Scorpion*, the overhead pictures looked as though they'd been photographed through a deep fog.

A court of inquiry looking into the disaster was made up of seven naval officers and chaired by retired Vice Admiral Bernard L. "Count" Austin, who had also led the inquiry into *Thresher*'s sinking. In a January 1969 press release, the Navy told the public that the court of inquiry, after a six-month investigation, had concluded that the *Scorpion* disaster remained a mystery, that the cause could not be "ascertained from any evidence now available," and that "no incontrovertible proof of the exact cause" could be found.

Indeed, the Navy publicly appeared to rule out a torpedo disaster of any sort, saying, "Procedures used in handling ordnance on board were consistent with established safety precautions." Then it went on to boast that testimony "also established a long history of safety in submarine torpedoes."

Technically, the Navy told the truth, but in such a limited form that the result was a massive evasion that bordered on an outright lie. In fact, when the court's more detailed findings were finally released in 1993, they showed that it had concluded that the top three probable causes of *Scorpion*'s loss all involved torpedo accidents.

Leading the list was Craven's theory that there was a hot-running torpedo on board *Scorpion*, perhaps caused when crewmen tested torpedoes in preparation for their arrival home. But then the court veered from Craven's theory that the torpedo exploded on board *Scorpion*. Instead, it speculated, "Acting on impulse, and perhaps influenced by successful ejection of a Mark 37 exercise shot which was running hot in the tube in December 1967, the torpedo was released from the tube, became fully armed, and sought its nearest target, SCORPION."

The court acknowledged there was no evidence of an external torpedo hit but reasoned that there was also a lack of any visible torpedo-room debris near *Scorpion*, which would prove that the explosion occurred inside the sub.

Former submarine torpedomen say it is almost unthinkable that *Scorpion*'s crew would have panicked and jettisoned a warshot torpedo. The 1967 incident involved a torpedo meant for practice shots that carried only a dummy warhead and no live explosives.

The court seems to have crafted a compromise for its classified findings. Citing Craven and his acoustic evidence, the court concluded that a torpedo was at fault. But the contention of an outside explosion seemed patterned on the Ordnance Systems Command's insistence that it was impossible for a hot run to lead to an onboard explosion.

Also in the report was a list of possible submarine accidents of all types, prepared by the Bureau of Ships. The list included gas leaks, broken hydraulic lines, fires, and more. But only one item on the list showed catastrophic results: a weapons accident. That, the bureau said, would result in "loss of ship."

In mid-1969 the Navy directed a top-secret effort to try to examine more closely the submarine's wreckage and unravel the mystery. It was most interested in the torpedo room and the torpedo doors. The *Trieste II* was sent down for a closer look. The first dive was made on July 16, only days before the *Apollo 11* astronauts made the first manned landing on the moon.

"My God, what a crazy world we live in," Craven muttered to

himself as he stood on the floating dock that had launched the *Trieste.* "We think we're doing a technological feat which is every bit as difficult and every bit as meaningful to humans as this man-on-the-moon thing, and we're the only ones who will get the chance to savor this operation."

Trieste made nine dives that year. Watching the first from monitors aboard the floating dry dock were Craven and Captain Harry Jackson, the engineer who had helped test *Thresher* and never stopped being haunted by his near-miss on that sub. They could see that there was no evidence of attack, and no evidence of an external torpedo hit. But there was also no conclusive evidence to show just what had sent *Scorpion* to the ocean bottom.

Craven would always struggle with the last piece of the puzzle. He was nearly certain a torpedo blew up inside *Scorpion.* But how?

It all seemed to end there, with the question left unanswered, with the families of the *Scorpion* men left to wander in nightmares of explosions and phantom battles and disbelief.

"All we ever wanted was an explanation," said Barbara Baar Gillum, who lost her twenty-one-year-old brother, Joseph Anthony Baar Jr. "After the disaster everything was covered up."

The *Scorpion* disaster quickly faded from the greater public conscience, which was already being battered by nightly images of bullets flying, soldiers bleeding, and a seemingly endless line of body bags in Vietnam. The *Scorpion* families might have been left alone to forever struggle with their own investigations had the Navy not decided to mark the grisly quarter-century anniversary of *Scorpion*'s loss by releasing the court of inquiry's conclusions and videotapes of her sunken shell.

By then, Craven was sixty-nine years old and long gone from the Navy. He was, instead, intensely involved in developing a new form of agriculture in Hawaii. The *Chicago Tribune* printed a story about the documents and his role in using his torpedo theory to find *Scorpion.* It was only when that story ran that Craven was handed what he is convinced is the last piece of the puzzle.

It all played out in a scene reminiscent of the final chapter of a detective novel. The *Tribune* article reached the desk of Charles M. Thorne, who had been technical director of the Weapons Quality Engineering Center at the Naval Torpedo Station in

Keyport, Washington. Seeing Craven's name in print, Thorne picked up the telephone and dialed.

The two men had never met. Neither had known anything about the other during the long *Scorpion* search and all the years after. Still, they had much in common. Thorne, too, had long had reason to fear that a torpedo had been the cause of *Scorpion*'s death. Back in the spring of 1968, he had been a top engineer in the Keyport lab responsible for testing torpedoes and their components. He worked there for twenty-five years, and by the time he called Craven, he had been retired for twelve years. All that time he had held information about *Scorpion* that he felt barred by classification rules from telling anyone. Now the engineer reached out to the scientist.

Thorne asked Craven whether he had seen a classified alert that had been mailed in mid-May 1968 to the department that had been renamed the Naval Ordnance Command. The letter described a test failure of an MK-46 battery that was designed to power the Mark 37 torpedo, a fast-moving warshot that had been deemed the primary weapon for use against Soviet subs. He was referring to an alert that the testing lab had sent to Rear Admiral Arthur Gralla, who headed that command. Then Thorne went on to describe its contents. He knew them well since he had written the alert himself, although it had been reviewed and signed by Captain James L. Hunnicutt, the CO of the station and a decorated World War II submarine skipper, who has since died.

In the alert, the lab reported that a torpedo battery had exploded in flames during a vibration test because a tiny foil diaphragm, a part worth pennies, had failed. As Thorne related this to Craven, the news seemed to parallel the discovery that the failure of inexpensive rubber O-rings had caused the space shuttle *Challenger* to explode. About a yard long and 17 inches wide, the batteries on Mark 37s were bolted within about an inch of the torpedo warheads. And each warhead carried 330 pounds of HBX explosive.

The lab's alert had recommended that all batteries from that production lot "be withdrawn from service at the earliest opportunity," and it said that sufficient heat was generated in the test sample "to risk warhead cook-off and loss of a submarine."

This alert was the strongest of any ever issued by the testing lab. It was the only time in the lab's twelve years of operation that it had ever warned of the possibility of a failure that could have life-threatening consequences. It was because the engineers were so deeply concerned, that they had their commanding officer sign the alert. They wanted the added emphasis.

Scorpion was carrying fourteen Mark 37 torpedoes, and she was lost days after the letter was sent. Horrified at the possible connection, lab engineers specifically asked the Naval Ordnance Command about the torpedoes *Scorpion* was carrying. The Navy keeps records and serial numbers of all torpedo components and where they are issued. One of the lab's engineers remembers being told verbally that one of the batteries powering a torpedo on *Scorpion* did indeed come from the same production lot as the torpedo battery that had exploded at Keyport. (Other former engineers there said they did not remember hearing this.)

Over the past several years, one of the engineers made requests for the battery records under the Freedom of Information Act, hoping they might answer that question once and for all. But the answer came back twice that no such records could be found.

Still, Thorne believes that a warhead cook-off initiated by a battery fire was the likely cause of *Scorpion*'s loss, and he became all the more convinced of that when he read that Craven had concluded that *Scorpion* had suffered an internal torpedo explosion. He was stunned that Craven had never seen the lab's alert. Thorne had always assumed that the secret missive had been shown to the people involved in trying to make sense of the *Scorpion* disaster. Now it seemed that vital information had been withheld from Craven and the court of inquiry.

Thorne asked Craven for a copy of the videocassette of *Scorpion*'s wreckage and the court of inquiry report. After viewing those, he wrote to Craven with his analysis.

"I have agonized for years over what more we might have done to have averted that tragedy," Thorne said in the letter. "The people that did the testing, the workman and other engineers, we all wondered. We asked questions."

Thorne then went on to tell Craven that his worst fears were borne out by *Scorpion*'s wreckage. The videotape clearly shows that the upper hatch covers of the torpedo-loading hatch and the escape trunk hatch are gone. Both hatches lead into the torpedo room. Both, Thorne wrote, could have been blown away as a result of a violent explosion inside the torpedo room, and that could have resulted in massive and uncontrollable flooding of the submarine.

The battery failure that prompted Thorne to pen the alert was easily the most severe the lab had ever experienced. The test failure happened on a Saturday afternoon as three engineers—John Holman, John Grobler, and Robert Trieschel—subjected one of the 250-pound batteries to strong vibration. They had just walked out of the room where the tests were conducted when there was a tremendous explosion, strong enough to rattle the 2-inch solid wooden door. Holman threw the door open and ran in. The mechanism meant to shake and vibrate the battery was all but obscured by blue-green flames shooting 10 feet to the ceiling.

"Fire!" he yelled as he grabbed an extinguisher. The room began to fill with black smoke and flames. Two technicians were missing. Holman got on his hands and knees and began looking for them as fire trucks screamed up to the laboratory.

Chemical extinguishers failed to put the fire out. The men slipped rags over their faces and began unbolting the still-burning battery from the shaker. The battery exploded a second time, drenching them in the potassium hydroxide solution that served as the batteries' electrolyte. Shrapnel was embedded in the ceiling and walls.

The engineers took the burning battery out of the building. Its 16-gauge steel case was peeled open like foil and the silver plating on the battery was partially melted. As soon as they could they raced back inside to drench themselves in the laboratory's emergency showers. Then the three lab employees and three firemen were rushed to the hospital to be treated for smoke inhalation and chemical burns. The lab called for the recall within two or three days of the incident.

A similar battery failure on *Scorpion* could have been enough to cause a warhead to explode, but the alert was sent too late to save the sub and crew. The phrase "withdrawn from service at the earliest opportunity" was usually construed to mean that a recall should be conducted as each boat reached port. When the recommendation reached the ordnance command, *Scorpion* was either already lost or still en route to Norfolk, where the recall would have been implemented.

Had the alert been made available to Craven right after the accident, months might have been shaved off the search for *Scorpion*. But instead of sharing the information, the ordnance command continued to insist that such an explosion was impossible. Had the court of inquiry been given the information, it might have done much more to solve the mystery. But the court in its report clearly relied heavily on Naval Ordnance's statements about the impossibility of an onboard detonation.

That the lab's alert made it to the ordnance command is certain. It was specially coded to be routed from the mail room straight to the commander's desk. In addition, some weeks after *Scorpion*'s wreckage was found, a representative of the ordnance command showed up at the Keyport lab, called Thorne into a private office in another building, and castigated him for including warnings of warhead cook-off and loss of a submarine in the alert.

The command had good reason to be deeply concerned by what Thorne wrote—Naval Ordnance had created the potential for catastrophe by bypassing its own safety procedures. In its effort to keep up with the sub fleet's demands for the torpedoes, it had rushed the weapons into production. The fleet desperately needed torpedoes that could go fast enough to catch the new classes of Soviet nuclear subs, but manufacturers were having a terrible time building components that could pass safety tests. There was such a backlog caused by repeated battery failures that the Keyport lab was at least two months behind in its quality assurance tests. Rather than slow down production, the ordnance command had been issuing torpedoes with components from lots that had never been safety tested at all. That was a clear violation of regulations that required that three samples from every lot of one hundred batteries be tested before any battery from the lot was issued to the fleet. The samples were supposed to be subjected to two or three weeks of tests measuring their resilience to shock, heat, vibration, and any other condition that could be expected to occur on a submarine. Only after the samples passed muster was the ordnance command supposed to allow any of the components on board any submarine.

Two companies had originally contracted to manufacture the batteries and suffered so many failures that the Navy brought in a third company to try to make up for the production problems. That company never managed to produce any batteries that passed quality assurance tests, but because of the shortages, the contractor was allowed to ship as many as 250 of its batteries to the fleets. It was one of the third company's batteries that exploded in the lab.

All three companies were having problems because the basic design of the batteries was dangerously flawed. Engineers had warned of this from the first failures back in 1966, well over a year before the catastrophic explosion that resulted in that last and strongest alert. Throughout that time, they had said the batteries had no margin of safety and recommended a redesign. The ordnance command was unwilling to do that.

The problem existed in how the batteries were activated. A sliver of foil that governed the flow of electrolyte into the power cells was etched to be only one seven-thousandth of an inch thick. That was because it was supposed to break with pressure, allowing the battery to power the torpedo's propulsion motor when the weapon was activated.

In a typical hot run, the kind Craven imagined had occurred, a torpedo receives an inadvertent start-up charge, fully activating the battery and also turning on the motor. That condition is easily detected as a spinning propeller on the torpedo alerts crews to the need for an immediate 180-degree turn.

The kind of failure experienced in the lab was far more insidious because there never would have been enough power in the battery to turn on a motor, or cause the torpedo propeller to spin. Instead, what happened to the batteries in the testing lab, and what caused the explosion of the test sample, was more difficult to detect. The lab discovered that when the batteries were subjected to vibrations, the electrolyte was pushed against that thin diaphragm with enough force to only partially rupture the foil. This allowed just enough electrolyte to slowly leak into the batteries' power cells to cause them to begin to spark and overheat. It was precisely because the diaphragms broke so easily, and the overheating condition could remain hidden until a fire or explosion, that the lab determined that the design had almost no margin of safety.

During the vibration test that Thorne described in his letter, there was no hint of a problem until the battery exploded into flames. If the same thing had happened on a submarine, it was entirely possible that no one would have noticed anything was wrong unless they smelled insulation burning or touched the torpedo and felt heat. By then, the battery could have been only minutes away from exploding.

"If the hot torpedo shell is not discovered until the paint begins to blister or burn," Thorne wrote to Craven, "there may not be time to move the torpedo from a stowage rack and load it into a tube for jettison before warhead cook-off."

Such a torpedo accident could have occurred in any of the fourteen Mark 37 torpedoes on *Scorpion,* or, for that matter, on any of the submarines equipped with those torpedoes. Carrying a battery from a defective lot would have heightened the risk, but the risk existed in the design nonetheless. The diaphragm on one or several of the batteries could have ruptured as the weapons lay in torpedo tubes or in their racks. Men didn't have to be testing them or handling them in any way. Shipboard vibration could have been enough.

Scorpion may have been more at risk than any other boat. The vibration tests in the lab that led to the explosion were supposed to emulate the usual vibrations that could be expected on board a sub and when transporting torpedoes to a submarine—vibrations that were far less severe than the shaking *Scorpion* had suffered in the 1967 incident when she was sent corkscrewing through the water.

Naval Ordnance has never acknowledged that *Scorpion* could have been at risk for torpedo detonation, or even that *Scorpion*'s torpedoes were powered by batteries with a defective design. In fact, after the sub was lost, the Naval Underwater Systems Center in Newport, Rhode Island, vigorously argued against the test lab's conclusions.

Naval Ordnance also withheld the information about the flawed battery design even after another torpedo battery began to heat up on board a submarine in the western Pacific months after *Scorpion* was lost. The crew of the second boat reported that their torpedo battery reached temperatures so high they had to spray the torpedo constantly with water to cool it. The water turned to steam. They had no choice but to continue spraying until the torpedo could be loaded into a tube and jettisoned.

Finally, about a year after *Scorpion* went down, Naval Ordnance did order a new battery design. The new system replaced the thin foil diaphragm with two stronger ones. In this new design, both diaphragms could be broken only when they were mechanically punctured with a cookie-cutter device, eliminating the danger that shipboard vibration could lead to a battery fire and set off an explosion.

Any written record of the Keyport lab's alert, and the alert itself, appear to be missing. There should be copies of the engineers' alert at the main administrative offices of the Naval Undersea Warfare Engineering Center, formerly the Naval Torpedo Station at Keyport, and at the ordnance command, but another recent request made under the Freedom of Information Act for a copy of the alert at both sites came back with the answer that there was no record of it, or even of its destruction—something that also should have been logged if the alert was removed from the files.

Still, after hearing Thorne's story, Craven and some sub commanders and weapons experts are looking back at the *Scorpion* disaster. Craven is angry that the ordnance command failed to disclose the fires itself. "The public and the press and a lot of other people feel an organization is engaged in a cover-up when they so stoutly deny this kind of thing," he says.

Taking the new evidence into account, Craven theorizes that the cry that led *Scorpion*'s skipper to make that final turn could have been "Hot torpedo" instead of "Hot-running torpedo."

Chester M. Mack, who skippered *Lapon* when she searched for the downed *Scorpion*, insists that no captain would ever take the time to ask for more information before executing an immediate 180-degree turn. "'Hot torpedo'—there's only one thing it could mean. The damn thing is running in the torpedo room," Mack says.

After years of being told over and over again that he was wrong, that it was impossible for a torpedo to detonate on board *Scorpion*, Craven is now convinced that he has what is very possibly the final piece to the mystery he set out to solve more than a quarter of a century ago.

It is a mystery that continues to unfold. In 1998, almost five years after the Navy released the court of inquiry report, almost five years after Craven first spoke to Thorne, the Navy released a 1970 report by another technical advisory group—this one convened shortly after Craven retired from the Navy. It was set up to review pictures and data collected by *Trieste* during her nine dives down to *Scorpion*. The report had been completed only a year after the court of inquiry had finished its work, but the document had been held back from the public, from the *Scorpion* families, even after the court of inquiry report was released, and even though it specifically discounts many of the conclusions reached by the court of inquiry.*

This advisory group throws out the court of inquiry's conclusion that *Scorpion* was likely felled by the external explosion of an ejected torpedo that turned back on her. It also tosses out the possibility that *Scorpion* was destroyed by an internal torpedo explosion. Still, the authors of the report clearly did not have the information about the torpedo battery failures in the Keyport lab. Indeed, Craven, Thorne, and some submarine captains believe that much of the evidence used to refute the torpedo theory actually supports it.

The group's report also makes no attempt at all to explain why *Scorpion* was found just where Craven said she would be if her captain had turned to battle what he believed was a hot-running torpedo. Instead the Navy had gone back to debating the meaning of the acoustic trail Craven and his team followed to *Scorpion*'s grave. Although the details of the *Scorpion* search and the crucial role Craven played were retold in a second report the Navy declassified at the same time, the 1970 analysis instead relies heavily on Naval Ordnance assurances that *Scorpion* could not have suffered a torpedo accident. The group, in short, based its conclusions on statements made by the same Navy department that was withholding critical information that had been kept from the court of inquiry and the search teams.

By the time the second report was written, Naval Ordnance's argument had changed. Instead of insisting that a torpedo could

*The TAG report does agree with the court of inquiry findings in one profound way—both say there is no evidence that *Scorpion* was attacked. Still, lingering rumors and periodic news articles continue to place blame for *Scorpion*'s loss on an attack by the Soviets.

never explode on board a sub, Naval Ordnance had focused on the visual evidence collected by *Trieste:* from the outside, the hull of the torpedo room looked basically intact, while the ship's battery well was largely destroyed. The *Trieste* pictures did show that all three hatches leading from the torpedo room through the pressure hull—the forward escape trunk access, the escape trunk hatch, and torpedo loading hatch—were all dislodged. (*Trieste* could not get cameras inside the torpedo room to check for internal damage.*)

As the report states:

> The most logical location for an internal explosion that would cause the loss of the submarine would be the Torpedo Room. However, the evidence indicates that the Torpedo Room is essentially intact. . . . It is possible that the explosion of a single weapon could rupture the pressure hull in the keel area, and cause the loss of the submarine—thus, this possibility must be considered. However, experts from NAVORD have stated that the explosion of one weapon would cause sympathetic explosion of others. If more than one weapon exploded there would be extensive damage to the bow section, which would have the appearance of outward deformation. There is no deformation of that nature in any of the visible structure, nor is there deformation to indicate an explosion in a torpedo tube. Internal explosion in the Forward Room is considered unlikely.

Because of that argument, the technical advisory group also discounted the simulated reenactment of *Scorpion*'s loss staged by Craven and Fountain.

Still, Craven and several munitions experts say that the ordnance command's argument is deeply flawed and that if the command had told investigators about the failures of the batter-

---

*In 1986, another attempt was made to examine the wreckage. This time Woods Hole's *Alvin* submersible was sent down, toting the Jason Jr., a remote controlled, swimmer camera. The report from that expedition is still classified, but people with access to the findings say that the Jason could not enter the torpedo room. A team analyzing that expedition said as much in a letter dated January 14, 1987, that was declassified in 1998 along with the TAG report.

ies on the Mark 37 torpedoes, the analysis would have been changed considerably.

The kind of external hull damage the ordnance command insisted would have followed a torpedo explosion, weapons experts say, may not have followed a torpedo explosion caused by a fire. Rather, the damage the command was describing would likely occur during a full-triggered explosion, an explosion in which a torpedo is set off just the way it is designed to be set off, with the power of 330 pounds of HBX explosives unleashed all at once in a massive and directed forward thrust. That kind of detonation would, the experts agree, likely detonate other torpedoes. And a multiple detonation would, as Naval Ordnance said, probably crack or at least buckle the submarine's hull in a way that would be visible from the outside.

But the fact that there was a possibility of a torpedo detonation caused by fire in the torpedo battery profoundly changes the equation. A weapons explosion caused by fire will almost certainly not be the same power or predictable shape of a neatly triggered explosion. In fact, there is no way to predict the size, the shape, the properties of a blast caused by fire. Such blasts just don't follow the usual rules. It is, weapons experts say, entirely possible, even probable, that a torpedo warhead set off by a fire could go up in what is known as a low-order detonation.

A low-order detonation could be strong enough to kill anyone nearby and could be strong enough to blow the hatches in a torpedo room without setting off other torpedoes, especially if those other torpedoes were not lying directly against the torpedo that exploded. Submarines often went out without their torpedo racks full. (That's why men often bunked in the torpedo rooms. Any torpedo rack without a torpedo lying on top of it made a reasonable place for a mattress.) One low-order detonation, without subsequent detonations of other torpedoes nearby, could easily occur without the kind of external hull damage the men diving on *Trieste* had been told to look for. The Navy itself acknowledged that to be entirely possible in the 1969 court of inquiry report into *Scorpion*'s loss. The report cites a 1960 incident on the USS *Sargo* (*SSN–583*) in which an oxygen fire in the after-torpedo room spread and caused two Mark 37 torpedo warheads to detonate "low-order." The report states: "The pressure hull of the *Sargo* was not ruptured." *Sargo* was pier-side and on the surface at Pearl Harbor at the time.

Indeed, the fact that *Scorpion*'s torpedo room is intact raises the probability that she was lost to a torpedo casualty, say sub commanders and Craven. *Scorpion*'s torpedo room did not implode, which makes it very likely that it was flooded before she fell to crush depth. Since a flooded room is exposed to equal ocean pressures both inside and out, it does not collapse at crush depth and it does not implode. It is left intact.

The technical advisory group does say that the torpedo room hatches "probably failed" when "pressure inside the torpedo room increased," or when the bulkhead leading to the operations compartment gave way. The idea seems to be that the hatches were forced open by the violent implosions going on right outside the torpedo room. The advisory group offers no theory about why the torpedo room would have lost only its hatches, when the group's own experts say compartments just outside were completely destroyed in the same violent instant. *Trieste*'s pictures show that *Scorpion*'s operations compartment, which is right next to the torpedo room, is squashed flat and that just beyond operations, *Scorpion*'s tail has telescoped completely into her auxiliary machine space.

The *Trieste* photos also show that the massive battery that powered *Scorpion* was torn apart. The advisory group theorizes that this is what destroyed *Scorpion*—echoing the theory about what destroyed the Soviet Golf. The sub's battery could have exploded as it was being charged if ventilators failed and the concentration of highly combustible hydrogen gas was allowed to build up. The battery, however, could also have been torn apart by the same forces that destroyed the rest of the submarine.

Admiral Schade, Fountain, and others have guessed that perhaps *Scorpion*'s trash disposal unit failed, allowing tons of seawater to pour into the sub and into the battery well. Seawater can cause a battery to emit a number of gases, including hydrogen gas. The trash disposal theory is based on the fact that a trash disposal unit failed on the USS *Shark* (SSN–591), *Scorpion*'s sister ship. (*Shark* survived.) Again, many of these observers had discounted that the first flooding could have been caused by a torpedo, because they were told that there was no way for a torpedo to explode on board *Scorpion*, certainly not without blowing up the rest of the weapons as well.

"I think we are all guessing," says Ross E. Saxon, who went down on *Trieste* and took some of the photographs studied by the technical advisory group. "We who were out there, who dove down on the thing, are guessing."*

Offered the new information about the flawed torpedo batteries, some people close to the investigation who had discounted a torpedo explosion after the 1970 report now say that a torpedo explosion has to be put back on the list of possible causes of *Scorpion*'s loss.

"If a room blows up and there was a hand grenade there, but then I call up and say I took the hand grenade out of the room, you would discount the hand grenade," says an active-duty Navy official familiar with the case through its latest developments. "If I didn't tell you there were two hand grenades though, if someone was being less than fully truthful, providing less than all of the information, maybe there would be cause to go back and look at it again. Based on the information on file now, the two most likely causes are a ship's battery explosion and a weapons cook-off. Based on the information we had, I'd say battery explosion. Now there is a good way for a weapon to cook-off. Any information about specific engineering problems in a weapon ought to be tossed into the fore, ought to be discussed."

The officer, as well as Craven and many others, agrees that there

---

*Saxon and two others aboard *Trieste* also believe that they saw an object that looked like a body wearing an orange life-jacket near *Scorpion*'s wreckage. They saw it in passing and could not go back immediately because the *Trieste* is not very maneuverable. Later, nobody could find the object. Craven says it's entirely possible that someone could have attempted to get out at the last minute through an escape hatch. If there was a torpedo explosion, it would have had to have occurred reasonably close to the surface or the acoustic sounds would have been lost. However, he also says that objects are sighted on the ocean floor all the time and often don't turn out to be what they appear. Saxon says he can't be certain one way or the other, but he agrees that there is reason to believe *Scorpion* was close to the surface when she suffered her fatal mishap—her masts appear to be in the upright position, as if her commander tried to send out a last-minute message. It is also possible, however, that the masts were thrown up by mechanical shock or the explosive forces tearing apart the submarine.

needs to be more investigation, perhaps another effort to take a look inside *Scorpion*'s torpedo room. For now, Craven remains convinced that a torpedo was the most likely cause of the sub's loss. He is not alone. In June 1998, Craven stood before a throng of Navy officers when he became the first man to be given the distinguished civilian service award by the Naval Submarine League for his work on *Scorpion*, Polaris, and other projects. When the ceremony was over, an officer approached him. His voice lowered so it wouldn't carry through the crowded room, the officer began talking about *Scorpion* and told Craven that he had been convinced for years that she was lost after a torpedo accident.

Without knowing about the alert sent from Keyport, without knowing that there were known problems with the batteries powering the Mark 37 torpedoes, the officer told Craven: "I know it was a torpedo because I had a torpedo battery cook-off on me."

"THE BALLAD OF WHITEY MACK"

Commander Chester M. Mack, a 6'6" maverick known as "Whitey," after his pure blond pate, looked through his periscope out onto the Barents Sea. He was here in search of a new and lethal Soviet ballistic missile submarine that NATO had dubbed, without mirth, the "Yankee."

It was March 1969, and in one terrifying technological leap, the Soviets had finally come out with a nuclear-powered missile sub with a design that seemed borrowed from Polaris and that might be capable of striking the White House or the Pentagon from more than 1,000 miles offshore. It was Mack's job to learn more about it.

Mack had driven his sub straight through the Barents, the zealously guarded training area for the Northern Fleet, the Soviet Navy's most advanced and powerful. He was traveling with the arrogance of somebody who knew he was at the helm of one of the Navy's newest subs, a Sturgeon-class attack boat armed with the latest sonar and eavesdropping equipment. He was also traveling with a lot more luck than most, because in this game of hit and miss, he had just found what he was looking for.

There in front of his scope was a Yankee, 429 feet long, 39 feet across, weighing in at 9,600 tons. Mack sidled *Lapon* up to within 300 yards and stared.

"Holy Christ, that son-of-a-bitch looks like a Mattel model," he blurted out. The submarine was indeed a Polaris look-alike, from the shape of its hull down to its sail-mounted diving planes. The image might have been broadcast down in the crew's mess on a television wired to the periscope—what submariners called "periviz"—but on this early run nobody could get the periviz to work properly. So, only Mack could see the amazing feat his men and his sub were pulling off.

A Hasselblad single-lens reflex camera was hooked onto the periscope and Mack pulled the trigger on the pistol-grip device. Film advanced on a motorized drive, several shots for each pull on the trigger, as *Lapon* moved slowly forward, Mack lifting her scope out of the water for only seven seconds at a time in an effort to avoid detection. With each peek of the periscope, he grabbed a few photos, each time capturing another small portion of the massive boat. It would take seven of the photos pasted together to show the entire Yankee.

During the years the first Yankees were under construction, U.S. intelligence had collected little more than fuzzy images captured by spy satellites showing the Soviets were preparing to mass-produce the new weapon. But over the last year, as the Yankees ventured out on sea trials, U.S. surveillance subs had been moving in for a closer look at this nuclear monster decorated with sixteen doors hiding sixteen portable missile silos. The Yankee seemed a huge advance over the other ballistic missile subs the Soviets had put to sea, the diesel-powered Zulus and Golfs and the first nuclear-powered missile boats, the Hotels. None of those boats had inspired the same fear the Yankee inspired now. The earlier subs were loud and easy for SOSUS and sonar to spot. Now the U.S. sub force was faced with a crucial question: Did the Yankee mimic more than Polaris's shape? Was it possible that, just six years after the

Cuban Missile Crisis, the Soviets were positioned to launch a first strike with little or no warning? If the subs were as silent and deadly as they seemed, then, at the very least, the Soviets would have matched the United States in creating a second-strike capability, a way to punch back if all their land missiles and bombers were destroyed.

Captain James Bradley knew his spy program had already produced a lot of critical information about the development of Soviet subs and missiles. Photographing the sunken Golf had been a technological coup. But the Golfs posed little threat compared to the Yankees, and nothing was more important now than learning how to find these new subs, how to destroy them.

Photos of a Yankee did only so much good. The U.S. Navy and its NATO allies needed to see these boats in action, see just where they carried their missiles, needed to collect sound signatures to ensure that the subs could never pass SOSUS listening nets unheard, and so that surveillance subs and sonar buoys dropped by P-3 Orion sub-hunter planes could recognize the threat as it passed.

Someone had to get close to a Yankee in action, and he would have to stay close enough for long enough to give the United States ammunition to counter the new threat. For this, almost any risks were warranted.

As pumped up as Mack was from his photographic feat, he knew that the real star of the sub force would be the man who accomplished a long trail. Other commanders knew it too, and even the loss of *Scorpion* was not enough to kill the fighter-jock bravado that the new mission was sparking within the ranks. But Mack was feeling quite proprietary about the Yankees now, and he was certain he could be the guy to get in close and stay there. He was sure of that even though nobody else had been able to. Mack had that kind of an ego.

In fact, everything about this thirty-seven-year-old commander was big. His towering, 240-pound frame didn't quite fit through *Lapon*'s low hatches and narrow passageways, and he was almost always bent over in the control room, littered overhead with a maze of piping and wire. Submarines were just too small to contain Whitey Mack. He was a larger-than-life renegade, much like the heroes in the novels he devoured by the basketful. He saw himself as the hero in a story he was writing as he went along, a story ruled by his own tactics and sometimes by his own rules.

He had never attended the Naval Academy. Instead, he was recruited into Officer's Candidate School by a brash ROTC XO at Pennsylvania State University who bragged that he won his wife in a poker game. Mack himself was the son of a Pennsylvania coal miner, and he held up this lack of official polish as a badge of honor. Mack labeled himself a "smart-ass kind of guy," and he faced down his superiors with piercing blue eyes and a brand of brass that had nothing to do with epaulet stars. With wry irony, he sported a homemade pair of Russian dolphins alongside his standard American dolphins—the emblem of the U.S. submarine fleet—and he liked nothing better than to rush about his submarine shouting obscenities in Russian.

"A faint heart never fucked a pig." That was *Lapon*'s motto and it had been ever since Mack's first voyage on the sub when he used the phrase to announce his decision to follow a new Soviet sub close to her territorial waters. (The line was recorded on a continuous tape running in *Lapon*'s control room.) Although, when the subject came up once in front of an admiral, Mack delicately altered the phrase to "A faint heart never won a fair maiden."

Mack had plunged into command of *Lapon* in late 1967, first by horse-trading with other commanders for the men he believed would create an all-star crew, then by installing all manner of experimental, and often unauthorized, equipment on his submarine. He alternately inspired and mercilessly drove his men. He alternately impressed and badgered senior admirals, until he was allowed to skip the usual months of U.S.-based shakedown training and head straight into the action.

To a large degree, Mack was emblematic of his era. Throughout the sub force, captains who avoided risks were branded with nicknames such as "Charlie Tuna" or "Chicken of the Sea." Still, Mack left his superiors—not to mention other commanders who prided themselves on their own daring—debating whether he was dangerously blurring the line between valor and recklessness. To be sure, those close-up photos of the Yankee were as valuable as any intelligence anyone had gotten lately, but Mack had also taken other immense risks for limited intelligence return.

Lapon had already been detected in the Barents once under

Mack's watch. It may have been a glint of sunlight off her periscope, no one was sure, but suddenly the men in *Lapon*'s radio shack heard a Soviet pilot sending out an alert in Russian: "I see a submarine."

When *Lapon*'s officer of the deck pointed his periscope toward the sky, he saw a helicopter pilot who seemed to be looking right at him. "He's got the biggest fucking red mustache I ever saw!" the officer exclaimed.

"That's close enough," Mack said, breathless, as he raced from his personal quarters into the control room, still in his skivvies. "We better get the hell out of here." With that, he got his boat out of Dodge before the Soviets had a chance to mount a full search.

Mack also had driven so close to two Soviet subs conducting approach and attack runs that *Lapon* ended up in the path of one of their torpedoes. Mack knew that, for an exercise like this, the Soviets were shooting duds. But he had no intention of proving his point by letting the torpedo hit. Instead, he sent the order to the engine room that kicked *Lapon* into high speed. Flying "balls to the wall," as submariners say, Mack outraced the weapon. (The incident occurred just after he had taken *Lapon* out searching for *Scorpion*, though well before anyone realized that a torpedo might have killed that boat.)

Two spooks on board, George T. "Tommy" Cox and Joseph "Jesse" James, were so shaken by the incident that when they later tried to grab a smoke in the radio room, neither man could steady himself long enough to light up. Cox wanted to be a country-western singer, had once taken first place at the Gene Hooper Country Western Show Talent Contest in Caribou, Maine, and had worked his way through high school playing backup at a place called Cindy's Bar. After this trip on *Lapon*, he recorded a ballad called "Torpedo in the Water" on his first and only collection of submarine greatest hits, *Take Her Deep*. The song was an ode to a close call:

> *There's a 400 pounder of TNT*
> *'Bout to blow us to eternity.*
> *Gee, I hate to see a grown man cry,*
> *But goodness knows that I'm too young to die.*
> *Torpedo in the water, and it's closing fast.*

From her encounter with the torpedo, *Lapon* carried back transcripts and photographs of the initial part of the test, as well as rolls of film filled with other Soviet activities—all of it interesting, none of it crucial, none of it enough to make Whitey a star—*the* star—of the Atlantic Fleet.

Instead, it was another man who was so heralded, Kinnaird R. McKee, a lithe southern gentleman with bushy eyebrows and a showman's flair. He had set the standard for surveillance operations when he was on the USS *Dace* (*SSN-607*), and even though McKee's stellar command was nearly over by the time Mack photographed the Yankee in March 1969, he stood as an icon in the sub force. In 1967, McKee had not only photographed a Soviet nuclear-powered icebreaker as it was being towed, but he grabbed radioactive air samples that proved the ship had suffered a reactor accident. The next year, in one breathtaking mission, McKee collected the first close-up photographs and sound signatures of not one but two of the second generation of Soviet nuclear-powered subs: an attack sub and a cruise missile sub that NATO had named the "Victor" and the "Charlie." He had found one of the new subs in the waters off Novaya Zemlya, a large island between the Barents and Kara Seas that was one of the Soviets' main nuclear test areas.

Like Mack, McKee had been detected. Indeed, he had snapped a photograph of a Soviet crew member standing on the deck of one of the subs and pointing right at the *Dace*'s periscope just before the Soviets began to chase. McKee had to outrace a group of Soviet surface patrols pinging wildly with active sonar. He finally managed his escape by driving *Dace* straight under the hazardous reaches of the Arctic ice. When it was safe to emerge, he continued his mission, locating the second new Soviet sub within a week.

"Gentlemen, the price of poker has just gone up in the Barents Sea," McKee announced on his return at a session with the Joint Chiefs of Staff and members of the Defense Department. With typical flair, he captured his audience with a briefing no less dramatic for his exclusion of the detection and his omission of the shot of the Soviet crewman pointing at *Dace*. McKee's presentation and his slide show of other photographs shot through his scope went over so well that his immediate superiors never thought to criticize him for allowing his sub to be detected. Instead, for McKee, the mission was marred only by the fact that the Navy had refused to let him name the Soviet submarines he had found.

His manner, as much as anything, was what separated McKee from the likes of Whitey Mack. McKee was everybody's idea of a hero. While Mack bullied his way through the system, McKee was one of those officers pegged early on for the fast track to the top. This was a man who courted his sweetheart, Betty Ann, by spinning her through a winter's night in a Jaguar convertible with the top down and then spun her about with a marriage proposal thirteen days later. On *Dace,* he courted the vigilance of his junior officers by promising cases of Dewar's scotch and Jack Daniels to any who helped him spot the new Soviet subs. He won over admirals with the same flair, conjuring up such amazing tales of his exploits that the men who reigned over the U.S. submarine force never thought to question the risks he took.

Mack also had other competition in the Atlantic Fleet. There was Alfred L. Kelln, the commanding officer of the USS *Ray* (SSN-653), who had shot the very first pictures of a Yankee. Then there was Commander Guy H. B. Shaffer of the USS *Greenling* (SSN-614), who had slipped his sub directly beneath both a Charlie and a Yankee a few months before Mack spotted one. That gave *Greenling*'s crew a chance to record the noise levels and the harmonics that the Soviet boats created in the water and the chance to film the hull and propeller, underwater through the periscope, with a new low-light television camera. Indeed, *Greenling* got so close to the underside of the Yankee that had the Soviets checked their fathometer, the ocean would have seemed very shallow, perhaps not more than 12 feet deep.

The job, known as "underhulling," was enormously dangerous. At any time, one of the Soviet submarines could have moved to submerge right on top of *Greenling,* but the payoff was enormous as well. The United States had the first acoustic fingerprint of a Yankee submarine, and the sounds from *Greenling*'s tapes were quickly plugged into the SOSUS computers.

Now one question remained: Would the data collected by *Greenling* be enough to make the Yankees stand out as they moved into the open ocean din of fishing boats, marine life, and currents? Nobody would know that until somebody accomplished the longer trail through an actual deployment.

The race was on. Mack and the other commanders took their turns, steaming again out past 50 degrees north latitude, out of U.S. waters, and out of touch with fleet leaders back home, toward the Barents Sea and the Yankees' home ports.*

Mack's chance came in September 1969. As *Lapon* pulled out of Norfolk, she was stocked with a mountain of eggs, meat, and syrupy drink mixes known as "bug juice"—typical fare for a long mission. There was, however, one major exception: her mess held three months' worth of frozen blueberries. Mack had a voracious appetite for blueberries and blueberry muffins, and he shared his passion with his crew. On board were also ingredients enough to fuel weekly pizza nights and a one-armed bandit to stave off boredom.

There never would have been room for a slot machine on *Gudgeon* or any of the other diesel boats that went out on the first spec ops. That's not to say *Lapon* wasn't cramped, but at least each man had his own rack—no hot-bunking, no sharing. The racks were still stacked one atop another—shelves with mattresses on them—and some mattresses were still crammed in among the torpedoes, but there was some relief in having 15 square feet or so of private space that could be curtained off from the rest of the crew. The shorter guys even had room to stow a few books so long as they didn't mind designating the bottom square of their beds a bookshelf. And just about everyone had a single drawer, although that was all the space they had to store three months' worth of

---

*Tightly coordinating their efforts with U.S. submariners, British subs sometimes helped fill in what had become a nearly seamless round-robin surveillance of the Soviet ports in the Barents. There were only a couple of British subs trained for the task, and they went near Soviet shores only during spring and fall, but those subs were dedicated to the spy mission, and that's what their commanders and crews specialized in. They were good at it, and they were aggressive. The British Royal Navy just didn't mind confronting the Soviets.

Once, a Soviet surface ship tried lining the Strait of Sicily near Italy with twin-cylinder buoys, and it seemed to U.S. intelligence that it was an effort to create an acoustic barrier—a sort of floating SOSUS net. There was great hand-wringing from the U.S. State Department to the Navy, debates about whether the United States should just go in and grab the buoys, when suddenly somebody noticed they had vanished. It turns out the British had a squadron of destroyers in Malta that went in and sank each and every one of the devices with naval gunfire.

skivvies, uniforms, and anything else they believed they couldn't live without.

The diesel stench was gone with these nukes, as was the condensation that had plagued the diesel submarines. *Lapon* was downright comfortable, practically climate-controlled for anyone who didn't mind the constant clouds of cigarette smoke that massed despite the advanced air-filtering system. Nobody expected much more from life in their "closed sewer pipe." For most of the guys, contact with the outside would be pretty much limited to periviz and "family grams": the three- or four-line messages that wives and parents were allowed to send a few times each deployment.

Beyond that, the men's existence was charted out in a rhythm that amounted to six hours of watch, followed by twelve hours of equipment repair, endless paperwork, and qualifying exams. Nobody was handed his dolphins, the mark of an official submariner, until he had qualified on nearly every system on the boat.

Still, sanity finds a way, and on this sub Mack was determined to help it. Mack had managed to dig up about a dozen guitar players among his handpicked crew, and now they played in nightly sing-alongs. Tommy Cox was among them, back on board, carrying his guitar and a three-month supply of strings and picks. Cox, who had become one of the first spooks to bother with all of the standard submariners' qualifying exams and earn his dolphins, now entertained his true crewmates with performances of "Torpedo in the Water" and a new song about *Scorpion*, as well as standard covers of Johnny Cash, Ricky Nelson, Jerry Lee Lewis, and Elvis Presley tunes.

It was no accident that Cox was back on *Lapon*. While most spooks were assigned to subs by the Naval Security Group and almost never rode the same boat twice, Mack had managed to handpick his spook team just like he had the rest of his crew. He fought to keep his favorites, his core team, together. Along with Cox, there was Lieutenant Donald R. Fallon, the spook team leader. Mack decided Fallon would be a permanent member of the crew about ten seconds after the spook first boarded *Lapon*. He had spent his first nine seconds staring Mack down. The tenth second was the kicker. That's when he came up with a description of Mack that was never topped. Borrowing from the sub force's love of acronyms, he dubbed Mack "NOMFWIC," or, in non-naval parlance, "Number One Mother Fucker What's In Charge."

Mack liked men who were bright, inventive, just odd enough to appreciate his own eccentricities, and as willing as he was to bend the rules. One of Mack's favorite acquisitions was a chief machinist's mate with the unlikely name of Donald Duck. He was a self-proclaimed hillbilly, raised in a log house in Shelby County, Alabama. Mechanics was the family business. Duck's dad worked on buses, Duck on submarines. He never finished grade school. In fact, he had enlisted in the Navy under an illiteracy program, but he could fix anything on *Lapon,* and he was an even better scrounger than Mack. That, in particular, was an especially useful art now that the Vietnam War made materials scarce. Duck would find or steal whatever *Lapon* needed, keeping his cache of spare parts in a place only he believed to be secret.

Duck's lack of formal schooling didn't matter on *Lapon,* where most of the enlisted men had little more than a high school education anyway. This was a blue-collar crowd, but they were, as a whole, a bit brighter, a bit more inventive, and a lot more willing to put up with long months of confinement than just about anyone in the regular Navy. The officers mostly came out of the Naval Academy. In the end, the differences blurred. Rank, station, pedigree—on the best subs none of that mattered much. Maybe it was the confinement; maybe there was no other good way to run a submarine. After all, one of the first lessons any college-educated lieutenant learned was that he wasn't going to get very far without the help of his grizzled chiefs and a bunch of enlisted guys willing to engineer imaginative fixes to all of the unimaginable problems that were likely to crop up month after month at sea.

Now the crew that Mack built was about to be put to the test. One week into the trip, *Lapon* got a message, the one Mack had been hoping for: on September 16, SOSUS had detected a Yankee north of Norway. It was heading out of the Barents Sea toward the GIUK gap. A second SOSUS array then picked up the Yankee as it passed just north of Norway's Jan Mayen Island at the mouth of the Denmark Strait, which separates Greenland and Iceland. If Mack could intercept the Yankee before it made it past the gap into the open ocean, where she would be far more difficult to find, *Lapon* would be able to attempt a trail. Whenever *Lapon* dared to come to periscope depth, his crew would also get a glimpse of the waters they hunted. The periscope television, periviz, was finally working.

As Mack raced *Lapon* toward the Denmark Strait, an Allied P-3 Orion airborne submarine-hunter confirmed the Yankee's heading. *Lapon* arrived the next day and began a patrol moving slowly back and forth at the southernmost tip of the Denmark Strait, just southwest of Iceland.

Donnie Ray Bolling, the chief of the boat, hung a map in the crew's mess. From now on, the quartermaster would go below periodically to give the crew a look at *Lapon*'s position. If they caught up to the Yankee, he'd chart her position as well. Sharing such details with the crew was against regulation. But Mack wanted his men enthusiastic. He believed that knowing what they were attempting would make up for the lack of sleep that was about to become the rule on the boat.

Mack called for modified battle stations. Around him the control room was packed with men crammed in between charting tables, computer equipment, and weapon controls, with all their corresponding oscilloscopes, dials, gauges, and plotting gear. The pipes that hung from nearly every inch overhead and all around made the compartment seem all the more crowded. In the center of it all was the periscope stand. Two scopes sprouted out of the foot-high pedestal. Just in front of the stand, the diving officer and two planesmen sat tightly tiered in a pyramid, staring at depth gauges. From here on out, the fire control party, the sonar crews, the navigators, and the diving watch would have two imperatives: finding the Yankee and keeping the Yankee from finding the *Lapon*.

Only one day went by before the Yankee passed to the east of *Lapon*. The sound of the submarine was so faint that the sonarmen almost failed to pick it up over the clamor of nearby fishing trawlers and teeming marine life. But there it was, a slight flicker on the oscilloscope, the electronic image of the Soviet submarine. This wasn't going to be easy. In the noisy waters off of Greenland, the submarine was audible in the din only when it ventured within 1,400 yards of *Lapon*.

Mack ordered *Lapon* southeast. He was going to try a "sprint and drift." The plan was to race *Lapon* at 20 knots for half an hour or so to a point where the Yankee would soon pass if she maintained her track. Then *Lapon* would slow down to 3–5 knots, drift back and forth, and listen.

The Yankee showed up, but then disappeared again. Mack was worried. The Soviets weren't keeping to their expected course. Each time the sounds from the Yankee came through, they were lost almost immediately, drowned out by the living Atlantic made even louder now by violent currents caused by a raging storm above. Mack paced about the control room, frustrated at having to crawl blindly around the ocean knowing that the Yankee was so close.

Lapon found and lost the Yankee several times over the next few days. Then, on the fourth day, the Yankee showed up again. This time *Lapon* followed, first for an hour, then for two, then for three. The Yankee's propellers spun a steady rhythm through the sonar team's headsets. Six hours, twelve hours, the Yankee was still on a steady course in front of *Lapon*. But at eighteen hours, the Yankee disappeared from the sonar screens, lost again. Mack's burgeoning underwater drama had fallen flat.

By now, most of the officers and some of the crew had gone several days with little sleep. Mack had only dozed, minutes at a time, mostly while still standing in the control room. And now, for these men, grave disappointment replaced the adrenaline rush that had already sustained itself far too long.

No one spoke the obvious. No one wanted to say that maybe it was impossible to keep track of this new, quieter generation of Soviet submarine as it rode through the cacophonous ocean. No one wanted to give up.

Sharing Mack's disappointment back in Norfolk and in Washington, D.C., were Captain Bradley; Vice Admiral Arnold Schade, who was still commander of submarines in the Atlantic; and Admiral Moorer, the CNO. They had been in constant touch as Mack flashed UHF progress messages to U.S. aircraft flying overhead. The Navy, in turn, kept aides to the president up to date. Nixon was following the trail in real time.

The admirals ordered all SOSUS installations in the area to listen for the Yankee. P-3 Orions also were on the lookout. But in both instances, the efforts were futile.

Mack decided to take a huge gamble. Calling his navigators and officers into the wardroom, he announced that they were going to give up trying to pick up the Yankee near the Denmark Strait. Instead, Mack was going to try to guess where the Yankee was headed next, and he wanted to try to beat her to her destination. Now Mack, his XO Charles H. Brickell Jr., the engineer officer Ralph L. Tindal, and others bent over charts and began an intense game of "what if," putting themselves in the place of the Yankee's commander. Desperation weighed in as much as logic when they finally decided to attempt to pick up the Yankee's track several hundred miles south, near Portugal's Azores Islands.

Lapon hurried down there and then trolled about the appointed spot for three days. Too much time, Mack fretted. He made another guess and moved the sub west. Almost as soon as *Lapon* settled into her new patrol, her hull began to reverberate with the grinding of metal on metal. Mack came running into the control room. The diving officer reported that *Lapon* was losing depth.

The 4,800-ton *Lapon* had been caught in the net of a deep-sea fishing trawler, tangled in the net's metal weights and thick metal cable. The Yankee could pass by at any moment, and *Lapon* was dangling along with Sunday brunch.

It didn't take long for the fishermen to give up, or maybe they cut their net. Either way, they left the area with the greatest one-that-got-away story of their lives. But a piece of the trawler's cable had worked its way around a sonar device on the front of the submarine. There was no way *Lapon* could effect a silent trail with the dangling cable clicking across her bow.

Mack had no choice. He waited for dark, then ordered *Lapon* to the surface. Now praying that the Yankee would *not* pass, at least not now, he sent a man out onto the sail with a large pair of bolt cutters. His gamble worked—the cable was away and *Lapon* was ready when the Yankee showed up twelve hours later.

This time Mack was determined not to lose the Soviet submarine. This more southern portion of the Atlantic wasn't as loud as the waters off Greenland, but the Yankee was still quieter than any submarine a U.S. boat had ever tried to follow. It was time for a new tactic that Mack dubbed on the spot the "close-in trail." *Lapon* would tailgate the Yankee, moving no further than 3,000 yards away. More than 4,000 or 5,000 yards away, and the Yankee would be lost.

Mack's strategy was risky. Hurtling 4,800 tons that close to the massive Yankee was dangerous. Normally even surface ships try to stay about two miles apart for fear of collision. And *Lapon* had the added worry of detection. Mack just hoped that this new submarine didn't have better sonar than her predecessors. *Lapon* was so close that all someone had to do was drop a piece of equipment or slam a watertight door at the wrong time and even the Soviets' outdated equipment could register an American shadow.

Just about everyone on board realized the risk they were taking, but nobody dared question Mack. Nobody had time to. It had become crucial now to figure out what the Soviet vessel sounded like when she slowed down, or turned. Until *Lapon*'s sonar team could figure out what combination of clicks or tones matched which maneuvers, both submarines were in grave danger of colliding.

Mack ordered *Lapon* to slip side to side behind the Yankee as his men set about finding answers to a matrix of questions. Once again, Mack engaged himself in a game of "what if," trying to put himself in the Soviet captain's place, wondering what he would do, and when. It was like working on a very large, very difficult crossword puzzle. One answer led to others. One blank created several avenues of confusion. All *Lapon*'s crew could do was keep collecting information. The sonar teams began listening for any flaws in the Yankee's construction, anything that would give them clues to help them "see" the other submarine as it maneuvered.

Standard sonar would never have been enough. The Yankee was simply too quiet. But *Lapon* wasn't relying on just standard sonar. Mack had slipped aboard an added edge, an experimental sonar device designed to capitalize on some discoveries that Kelln's USS *Ray* had made in 1967 and 1968 when she trailed the November-class attack sub into the Mediterranean and then tracked a Charlie in the North Atlantic. The device worked by upgrading the way the standard system registered noise levels in the ocean. It zeroed in on certain tones, those made by the Yankee as she moved through the water, almost the way notes of music sound from a bottle when somebody blows over the top. After a fair amount of trial and error, *Lapon*'s crew realized that one particular frequency changed each time the Yankee turned. A shift to the left, and the tone was slightly higher. When the Yankee moved away, the tone lowered. If the tone changed quickly, it meant the Yankee was making a swift course change.

The one place *Lapon* couldn't follow from was directly behind. Unlike other Soviet submarines that offered an easy-to-follow din from their propellers, the Yankee was quiet enough from behind that she was rendered effectively invisible. Indeed, the Yankee might have been able to slip away entirely, even with *Lapon*'s extra sonar gadget, if not for what must have been a structural flaw. To the left, the Yankee's machinery was making more noise than any other portion of the boat.

From now on, *Lapon* was going to follow that machinery noise. If it got louder, Mack would know that the Yankee had made a left turn. If the Yankee seemed to vanish, she probably had turned right.

Ultimately the best vantage point turned out to be a little off to the side of the Yankee's stern, in either direction—with the left side being a little louder. From there the new sonar device picked up strong tones, and standard sonar registered steam noises coming from the Yankee's turbines and the clicks made by the Yankee's propeller each time it made a revolution. Counting those clicks and logging turn counts was how Mack and his crew determined the Yankee's speed.

All this took four or five days to figure out—longer than the entire length of most trailings attempted so far against the noisy Soviet Hotel, Echo, and November subs, the HENs. But Mack wasn't going to break off. Instead, he was going to keep following, and he would figure out the mechanics as he went along. The process of trial and error spanned several watch stations, leaving it up to Mack and his engineer officer to teach each succeeding team what had been discovered over the past twelve hours.

Mack was determined not to lose the Yankee again, especially when he realized that she was headed on a track toward the U.S. Atlantic coast. He again began to forgo sleep, although he slipped in 15-minute catnaps at the helm, a trick he picked up in college from an article in *Reader's Digest.*

Days later, *Lapon* was still tracking the Yankee. Mack began to map out the Yankee's operating area, one of the most crucial pieces of intelligence he could carry home. The Soviets had settled into a holding pattern that covered about 200,000 square miles.

They moved back and forth, staying between 1,500 and 2,000 miles off the United States.

Up until now, the Navy had been convinced that the Soviet Union would send its Yankees as close as 700 miles from U.S. shores. But Mack's discovery would help Naval Intelligence determine that the Yankee's new SS-N-6 missiles actually had a range of 1,200–1,300 miles.

If *Lapon* had not followed the Yankee this far, it would have been difficult for the United States to keep track of the new Soviet nuclear threat, even though the Yankee plowed through what appeared to be a well-defined box. The United States would have been searching 800 miles too close to shore.

Now Mack mapped the Yankee's exact course. Choosing one area, she meandered at about 6 knots before racing to another area at 12–16 knots. Then she slowed again. Every 90 minutes, almost to the second, the Yankee changed course. Sometimes by 60 degrees, sometimes by far more.

A few times a day the Yankee went to communications depth, presumably to receive radio messages, and every night, at the stroke of midnight, she rose to periscope depth to ventilate. Between ten and sixteen times a day she turned completely around to clear her baffles, listening to see whether anyone was following. Each time the Yankee turned, *Lapon* turned with her, trying to stay behind, just off to one side, shielded in the backwash of the Yankee's own noise. (U.S. submariners also clear their baffles regularly when they are out on operations, only never according to schedule. The delicate question of timing those maneuvers was left to a pair of dice kept in the *Lapon*'s control room for just that purpose.)

Once a day the Yankee kicked out with a wild, high-speed move that *Lapon*'s crew called the "Yankee doodle" because it resembled the twisted designs on someone's desktop notepad. The Yankee would curl about, usually in a figure eight or some version of that, ending up facing 180 degrees from where she had started. Shifting to port, she would then make a 180-degree turn, then a second 180-degree turn, then a 90-degree turn, then a 270-degree turn, and end with two more 90-degree turns.

The first set of turns seemed designed to catch an intruder following close in, and the second set to catch another submarine following from farther away. All this was usually done at high speed, sometimes twice, back to back. The entire process took about an hour.

Had the Yankee's sonar been any better, the maneuver might have been effective. But the Soviets seemed to have made one key miscalculation. *Lapon* could hear the turns and get out of the way long before the Soviets could hear *Lapon*. In fact, *Lapon* sonar techs realized that their sonar seemed to have more than twice the range of Soviet sonar. In good conditions, *Lapon* could spot a surface ship from 20,000 yards away. But the Yankee would pass within 10,000 yards of the same ship before showing any reaction.

As *Lapon*'s trail fell into a routine, Mack was finally able to give up his standing catnaps. He actually went to his stateroom to lie down and sleep, though never longer than 90 minutes. He never missed a course change or a Yankee doodle. It was during one of his naps, however, that Mack made the biggest mistake of the mission, perhaps the biggest mistake of his career. The mess cook awakened Mack on the advice of a junior officer who decided Mack would rather give up sleep than his nightly order of blueberry muffins. Startled, Mack let out a roar, the cook went running and the muffins and coffee went flying. In that one moment, Mack had destroyed possibly the best perk ever offered a submarine captain: his beloved fresh blueberry muffins, split and drenched with butter. Nobody would again dare delivery, not then, not as the third week of the trail gave way to a fourth, and then an unheard-of fifth week.

By that time, *Lapon*'s three rotating officers of the deck realized they had each fallen into sync with their Soviet counterparts. Indeed, each American could identify his Soviet "partner" by slight stylistic differences in the Yankee doodles and other course changes. They named these Soviets—"Terrible Terence" and "Wild Willy" were the two most memorable—and they began to take bets on how well they could predict the Yankee's next move. Tindal won most often. The sonar crew also got into the act, interpreting the sounds they picked up from inside the Yankee. Sounds of drilling, pumps running, and other noise led to some crude jokes, mostly bathroom humor. A quick clank was automatically recorded as a toilet lid being slammed, and every time *Lapon* sonarmen heard the rushing of air over their headsets that could have been sanitary tanks being blown, they reported, quite formally, "Conn. Sonar. We just got shit on."

Every man in the crew, down to the youngest seaman and the lowliest mess cook, was getting into the act. Mack let each of them take a turn at manually plotting the unfolding course. It was heady stuff for the young crewmen. Here they were on a trail longer than any other, trailing one of the most crucial pieces of hardware the Soviets had put to sea, and they were integrally involved in the process. The excitement was extending from sub to shore. Mack had gotten to know the Yankee captain's habits well enough to be able to predict when the Soviets would go deep, and he used those moments to bring *Lapon* to periscope depth and flash a quick message to the P-3 Orions that were flying high over the Yankee's patrol area.

All continued to go well until one of the Orions almost ended the entire effort. The pilot must have come lower than he should have, because when the Yankee came to periscope depth, her crew spotted the plane and made an immediate dive. The Orion sped away. The men on *Lapon* listened to the entire drama, their sub undetected. They realized that, although the Orion had been spotted, the Soviets didn't seem to know that they were being trailed through water as well as air. That seemed true, in fact, until someone back in Washington made a big mistake.

Rumors in the sub force say it was an admiral in naval aviation who leaked information to a newspaper that could threaten the mission. The leak didn't specify that *Lapon* was out following a Yankee, and it didn't even say that a Soviet ballistic missile submarine was, at that very moment, wandering 1,500 to 2,000 nautical miles off the United States. But on October 9, 1969, the *New York Times* ran a front-page story headlined "New Soviet Subs Noisier Than Expected."

Whoever leaked the story was either unaware of *Lapon*'s findings or distorted them, because what the *Times* reported was far more reassuring than the truth. As Mack had found out, the Yankees were by far the quietest subs the Soviets had put to sea— although U.S. subs were still quieter.

Word of the story must have made it back to the Soviet Navy and to the Yankee's captain. Either that, or he had become suddenly psychic. Within hours of the story's publication, moments after the Yankee made its midnight trip to communications depth, she broke all of her patterns. In fact, she went wild. The Yankee made a sudden 180-degree turn and came roaring back down her former path full-out at 20 knots, heading almost straight for *Lapon*. This did not at all resemble the calculated set of turns that made up the Yankee doodle. Nor did it have the calm routine of the Yankee's usual slow turns, those baffle-clearing maneuvers.

This was a desperation ploy, an all-out search by the Soviets to see if they were being followed. This was the ultimate game of chicken. This was what the U.S. sub force called a "Crazy Ivan."

The Yankee came flying through the water, her image filling the screens in *Lapon*'s control room and the noise of her flight screaming through sonarmen's headsets. It sounded like a freight train running through a tunnel: "Kerchutka, Kerchutka, Kerchutka . . ."

"That bastard is coming down," someone in the control room blurted out. The men tensed, although they knew *Lapon* was still 300 feet below the Yankee as she blindly passed to starboard. Nobody missed the irony, that the Yankee, in her noisy high-speed flight, had missed her chance to detect *Lapon*. The Yankee continued to search, moving in circles for hours, but Mack countered with his own evasive maneuvers enacted by a crew who had been standing at battle stations throughout the drama. Mack refused to break off the chase. Instead, he waited for the Yankee to calm down. Then he continued the mission.

On October 13, nearly a month after the trail began, Admiral Schade sent a top-secret message to the *Lapon:* "ADMIRAL MOORER STATES THAT SECDEF AND ALL IN WASHINGTON WATCHING OPERATION WITH SPECIAL INTEREST AND NOTES WITH GREAT PLEASURE AND PRIDE SUPERB PERFORMANCE OF ALL PARTICIPANTS. I SHARE HIS THOUGHTS."

Lapon continued on, through the rest of the Yankee's patrol and then some as the Soviets took an almost straight track back home. There were no more Yankee doodles, no more Crazy Ivans. The Yankee beat a path to the GIUK gap, where *Lapon* left her on November 9.

Lapon had followed the Yankee for an amazing forty-seven days.

Tommy Cox again was moved to write, this time coming up with "The Ballad of Whitey Mack":

Whitey's got the deck and the conn.
Now he had quite a job to do,
And every man on board knew,
When the going got rough,
In this game of "Blind Man's Bluff,"
Somehow he'd pull her through.

Cox's lyrics were right on target. It really was Blind Man's Bluff, a game far more dangerous than mere hide-and-spy operations. Mack's success marked the beginning of a new mission for the submarine force. From here on out, the fleet would be focused on trailing Soviet ballistic missile submarines at sea. U.S. attack submarines were suddenly elevated to critical participants in the nation's strategic nuclear defense. And they would lead the greatest sea hunt in maritime history. For now, as he drove *Lapon* back to Norfolk, Mack was basking in the glory that was finally his. Messages of congratulations flooded the radio channels.*

Months later, *Lapon* would receive the highest award ever given to submarines, the Presidential Unit Citation. Whitey Mack would win a Distinguished Service Medal, the highest personal honor the Navy awarded its officers in peacetime.

But it was one of the messages sent out when *Lapon* was still on her way home that pleased Mack more than any other accolade. It wasn't addressed to Mack or to his crew. Instead, this message was sent out to every other submarine out on operations in the Atlantic: "Get out of the way. Whitey's coming through." The order was clear. Everyone was to make way and give the *Lapon* a clear track home.

When Mack heard that, he slapped his fist in his hand, shook his head and said: "Eat your heart out, suckers. Whitey's coming through."

---

* Mack was told by an admiral that his men would get their presidential thank you, PUC certificates, and ribbons, in a ceremony as secret as their mission: wives and children cordially not invited. In answer, Mack kindly informed the admiral what he could do with his PUC. As far as Mack was concerned, there would be no award and no ceremony, unless the men's families could be there. He stood his ground, and in the end, the awards were made in the steel bowels of a Navy ship, families present, without a single word spoken about how or why the men had earned awards signed by the president.

"HERE SHE COMES . . ."

Whitey Mack had set the new standard, one that other commanders were itching to match—indeed, itching to beat. Trailing Soviet missile subs was fast becoming the Navy's most critical mission, though not all of the men leading these dangerous hunts were as skilled as Mack, or as lucky.

At least two subs put the United States on the verge of nuclear alert when they radioed that the Yankees they were following had opened their missile doors and seemed ready to launch. In both cases, the U.S. subs quickly radioed again to say that the Soviets were engaged in simple drills.

Within months of *Lapon*'s feat, there were also several collisions between American subs and Soviet subs, accidents that threatened U.S.-Soviet moves toward détente. When the USS *Gato* (SSN-615) slammed into an old Soviet Hotel-class missile sub in November 1969, Sergei Georgievich Gorshkov, the long-time commander in chief of the Soviet Navy, sent warships into the Barents in search of the intruder. He was hoping to find proof that *Gato* had been sunk. Gorshkov wasn't a bloodthirsty man, but the collision came just two days before arms control talks were scheduled to begin in Helsinki, Finland. It stunned him that President Richard Nixon and his national security adviser, Henry Kissinger, could proffer arms negotiations as though they were simple handshakes, while letting their submarines invade Soviet waters.

Evidence of *Gato's* steel corpse would have given Gorshkov one knockout of a handshake to proffer back. But his forces never did find *Gato,* which had hightailed it out of there, weapons armed and ready. At the orders of the Atlantic Fleet commanders, *Gato's* captain prepared false mission reports showing that his boat had broken off her patrol two days before the accident.

Close calls, especially those that stopped short of major incident, were almost always omitted when Navy intelligence officers went to brief Nixon and his aides. Thus, there was no pressure on the submarine force to curtail its brazen operations, even after two more minor collisions in 1970, one in the Barents and one in the Mediterranean.

There was, however, a third accident that year, one that was so violent and so severe that the Navy had no choice but to immediately tell top Pentagon officials and Nixon.

It happened in late June. The USS *Tautog* (*SSN-639*) was heading for waters filled with Soviet traffic outside of Petropavlovsk, the big missile sub base on the Kamchatka Peninsula in the northern Pacific. Little rattled *Tautog's* thirty-nine-year-old captain, Commander Buele G. Balderston, who had already overcome childhood rheumatic fever to grow to a 6'4" all-American in swimming and track. He had studied desert scorpions at the University of Nebraska and then enlisted in the Navy during the Korean War, where he was promptly assigned responsibility for the disposal of unexploded ordnance left over from World War II. Ultimately he switched to diesel submarines because he and his wife, Irene, both thought the job would be safer. He had later thought of giving up the filthy, cramped life of a diesel submariner to study medicine, but before he could apply to medical school, Rickover tapped him for the nuclear sub force. Balderston decided that maybe it was a sign, that maybe he was destined to remain on submarines. He believed that, even after all of his illusions of safety were shattered with *Scorpion*'s loss. He had been the engineer officer during her construction, and after her disappearance, accident investigators trying to unravel the mystery frequently called him away from *Tautog*.

On *Tautog*, Balderston was known as much for his idiosyncrasies as anything else. This man who could drink any of his crew under the table during port stops was also something of a health nut. He drank Sanka in lieu of the full-powered brew that kept most of the crew fueled, and he demanded that his sub be stocked with copious supplies of chopped walnuts—he ate them after every meal, save breakfast, because they were full of lecithin. He also had a peculiar dexterity: he could raise his large, gray, bushy eyebrows one at a time. Right or left, it didn't seem to matter, both could make the singular crawl up the side of his face. It was a talent he used for emphasis. When crew members scrambled answers during qualifying exams, an eyebrow would levitate. When a mistake was especially stupid, one of those great brows would leap. One young seaman was especially unnerved by the gesture and could never deliver a message to his commander without stuttering as soon as Balderston sent a brow on its ascent.

For the crew, those brows were almost as memorable as the ingenuity Balderston displayed during their first mission together in the summer of 1969—a mission that earned their sub the nickname "The Terrible T."

They were sent to monitor a test of a new Soviet cruise missile from start to finish. Unlike the Yankees' ballistic missiles, cruise missiles posed little threat to U.S. shores. But these smaller weapons could destroy a massive U.S. aircraft carrier from as far as 250 nautical miles away, and carriers were still one of the primary platforms being used for U.S. bombing missions over Vietnam. Indeed, Echo II submarines—each toting eight cruise missiles that could hold either nuclear or conventional warheads—had been spotted trailing U.S. aircraft carriers near Southeast Asia. If the Soviets got directly involved in the war there, Naval Intelligence would need to know as much as possible about the missiles and the subs that carried them. It was Balderston's job to learn how many missiles the Soviets could fire in rapid succession, to capture electronic pulses that might indicate trajectories, and to grab communications that might help to assess weaknesses. He would also try to snap photographs of the launches so analysts back home could measure the flames as the missile shot skyward and maybe figure out what type of propellant the Soviets were using.

Brazenly, Balderston led his sub through the Soviets' sonar net and right beneath a group of Soviet ships and a submarine, keeping *Tautog* hidden, hovering at just 70 feet below the surface. Most of the time, the tips of *Tautog*'s intercept antennas and periscope barely broached the waves. The scope's small, cup-shaped eye was so low in the water that every third wave washed over. Balderston took to counting, "One, two, under; one, two, under; one, two, under. . . ."

Perhaps the most critical trick to all of this was keeping the 4,800-ton *Tautog* level despite the fact that she was constantly taking on water and getting heavier. Subs take on water in part to cool their reactors, and pumps usually recycle it back to the ocean, but the pumps were too loud to use this mechanism close to the Soviets. Michael J. Coy, one of the diving officers on watch, somehow had to keep *Tautog*'s scope at just the right height without the pumps.

It was nerve-racking business. Coy had been on *Tautog* for only three months, and he knew he was not one of Balderston's favorites. It irked the captain that Coy had enlisted in the sub force only as an honorable alternative to fighting in Vietnam, just as it irked Coy that Balderston kept talking up the advantages of military life. But now the two of them worked together as Balderston employed a solution that was ingenious and amazingly low-tech. He called upon an old submariner's trick and ordered all off-duty men out of their bunks, out of the crew's mess, and on a march: first to the forward half of the boat, next to the engine room in the stern. Back and forth they went for hours, living counterweights, keeping *Tautog*'s nose up and the submarine buoyant. There were no breaks for Coy, not even to go to the head. Instead, when it came time to adjust Coy's buoyancy, Balderston sent for an empty coffee can.

In the end, *Tautog* watched the Soviets for two days—capturing the entire missile test from start to finish. Balderston brought home so much data that the Navy awarded him one of its highest personal honors, the Legion of Merit. Now, in the summer of 1970, as

Balderston drove *Tautog* toward Petropavlovsk, captain and crew were convinced they could do just about anything. One thing high on their list was trailing an Echo II sub. This sort of trail might prove crucial to safeguarding the U.S. carriers off Vietnam, and it was one of the most important roles a sub could play in the war effort.

As luck would have it, it was an Echo II that registered on *Tautog*'s sonar almost as soon as she reached Soviet waters. There was no mistaking it—sonar showed the Echo's trademark pair of four-bladed propellers. The sub was moving south from Petropavlovsk, and *Tautog*'s crew had visions of following the sub through an entire patrol.

The Echo was noisy and seemed as though she would be an easy target, but no trail was ever really easy. Relying on passive sonar, *Tautog*'s men essentially had little more to interpret than textured static (the muffled whir buried within that static was their only "view" of the Soviet sub), and the flickering oscilloscope that transformed some of that static into a light display.

It helped that the Soviet commander seemed to be taking no precautions against a hunter. Instead, as *Tautog* followed behind, he motored noisily, spending five hours maneuvering through an odd undersea dance that submariners call "angles and dangles." It was almost an undersea "cossack." Submariners on both sides do this awkward dance, a series of random figure eights, sharp turns, and changes in depth meant to shake things out, to see what kind of noise a submarine is making, and to find out whether anything is stowed where it shouldn't be. The dance has little of the offensive fury of a Crazy Ivan, but the steps are tempestuous. And it is impossible to outguess a commander who might order his submarine up or down, right or left, simply as the mood strikes him.

The trick to trailing a submarine tripping through angles and dangles is to back off. But aboard *Tautog*, the order to back off never came. In fact, as the hours passed, the Soviet sub's angles and dangles had begun to seem routine, and Balderston and others left their stations to their seconds-in-command. The captain went down to his quarters to get some sleep, a marked departure from the past year's missile-test mission when he had stood awake at the helm for nearly forty-eight hours.

On this mission, *Tautog* had an unusual complement of two

sonar chiefs instead of one. But, as it turned out, neither of those chiefs was in the sonar shack while the captain was in his bunk. One of them had been assigned as chief of the watch and was overseeing the enlisted men in the control room. The other was off duty. That left the sonar operations supervised by a more junior man, Sonarman First-Class David T. Lindsay.

Before this mission, Lindsay's biggest claim to fame was accidentally being photographed with Pat Nixon. The first lady had been visiting wounded Vietnam veterans at a Honolulu military hospital. Lindsay was there because of an accident on his motorcycle, a super-souped-up machine that he lovingly called "Betsy." When the first lady came to the submariner, no one had the courage to tell her how he had been hurt. It was a photograph of the two of them that made the local papers.

Lindsay had lost an inch off one leg in the accident, and on *Tautog* he was dubbed "Step-and-a-Half." Now Step-and-a-Half was listening for the Echo, relaying information to the helm, manned by *Tautog*'s executive officer, who was holding to a track set by the captain. As *Tautog* cut through depths of 120–200 feet at a moderate 12–13 knots, her path was leading her dangerously close to the Echo. Finally, the XO sent for Balderston.

Balderston showed up in the control room wearing a dark blue and maroon bathrobe and slippers. He walked directly over to Scott A. Van Hoften, the officer of the deck who had won minor celebrity among the crew for being the boat's best ship handler and for winning the onboard Coca-Cola consumption record. Now Van Hoften gave the captain a tactical update.

Meanwhile, Paul S. Waters, one of the sonar chiefs, returned to the sonar shack, taking over operations there. Putting on a headset, Waters listened for the Soviet Echo.

"Son-of-a-bitch, it's close," Waters murmured just before he got up to brief the captain.

"Captain, to the best of my knowledge, this is an Echo II. It is close aboard."

Balderston towered over the short sonar chief, staring at him from beneath those famous eyebrows. As the two men spoke, Balderston settled into a small foldout seat just behind the periscope stand. With that one move, he took over. He made no dramatic pronouncements. He didn't have to say a word.

Van Hoften remained officer of the deck and continued to yell the orders, but everyone knew they came from Balderston. He would not leave the bridge again—not to return to his bunk, not to change out of his bathrobe. At his side was Michael Coy. By now, the all-Navy captain and the decidedly nonmilitary Coy had struck an uneasy peace. Coy had learned to refrain from repeating that he had no intentions of staying in the Navy, and Balderston had stopped talking up the advantages of military life. Besides, Coy also was the boat's supply officer and kept the health-conscious commander in vitamins, Sanka, and enough walnuts to keep his body swimming in lecithin.

Balderston began to scrutinize the oscilloscope. On its nine-inch-wide screen a single electronic amber arc offered a sonar-generated image of the Echo. Usually, ten or more faint arcs flickered on the sonar screen, computer depictions of the noise generated by distant boats, land masses, even whales. But the image created by the Soviet sub was large and bright, and it was jumping back and forth across the screen. There was only one interpretation possible. The Echo was very, very close.

"Here . . . she . . . comes. . . . There . . . she . . . goes," the captain commented, drawing out the sentence to add emphasis to anyone and no one in particular as he watched the Echo's athletics. He would repeat that comment a few minutes later, and a third time after that.

The XO stood to Balderston's left, studying the navigators' plots. About five feet away, Van Hoften bent his 6'5" frame over the fire control station, monitoring the weapons computers, which were also tracking the Echo's direction, speed, and distance from *Tautog*. Just outside the conn, in the sonar shack, men crowded shoulder to shoulder and continued to track the Echo.

Mentally they sifted the soft, rhythmic *shw-shw-shw* sounds of the Echo's propellers from the blanket of ocean noise coming through their headsets. But nothing they heard or could see on their display read the Echo's depth. For that, the men could only listen and guess. Every few minutes the distance between the subs registered zero. At one point, sonar operators guessed that the Echo had risen near the surface, which would have placed her directly above *Tautog*. Then it seemed that the Echo was descending again.

This all could have been much easier. *Tautog* had been scheduled to receive a newly engineered device designed to measure another submarine's depth by measuring the disturbances in the water it created. The device consisted of four hydrophones, which were supposed to have been mounted on *Tautog*'s sail. But the shipyard had been behind schedule, and the submarine left port with the new technology sitting in Pearl Harbor.

One officer muttered that it was too bad about those missing hydrophones, and others began to talk about trying to open up the distance between the two subs. Just then, the image on the oscilloscope leapt again, this time violently.

"Here she comes. . . ," the captain began. He never finished the sentence.

The image on the oscilloscope disappeared. At that instant, the sonar operators lost all track of the Echo. No one knew whether the Echo had gone to the right or to the left. She was just gone.

Then, the Echo announced herself in the worst possible way. The 6,000-ton sub slammed belly first into the top of *Tautog*'s sail with an impact that sounded like two cars colliding at 40 miles an hour. With a horrible screech, the Echo's propellers ground through *Tautog*'s metal with a din that forced Chief Waters to recoil from his headset.

Tautog flipped on her right side, rolling nearly 30 degrees as she was forced backward and down. Men went grabbing for a handhold on rails and tables. Coffee mugs, pencils, rulers, charts, and erasers went flying through the control room. Maraschino cherries and pickle relish splattered all over the mess area. Tools popped out of wall lockers and littered the floor of the engine room. Step-and-a-Half Lindsay was thrown down a ladder. Down in the torpedo room, three men who had been sleeping, curled up against the long, green weapons, were tossed from their "bedpans," those mattresses on top of empty torpedo racks. Around them the massive weapons strained at their canvas straps.

One man jumped up to close the watertight door nearest the torpedo room. He didn't check to see whether anyone was inside, didn't realize that he had just locked in Greg Greeley—an eighteen-year-old recruit who had boarded *Tautog* just three weeks earlier. All that man knew was that the bow compartment might be among the first to flood and as the one closest to the hatch, it was his job to seal it off. Then, as he was trained, he turned his back, never looking in the small round window to see Greeley frightened inside. It would be several minutes before anyone could be sure the hull was intact, several minutes before anyone let Greeley out.

Meanwhile, other officers jumped out of their bunks, raced out of the wardroom and to the control room, scrambling to assume their preassigned collision stations. One man ran frantically, back and forth, unsure of what to do. Coy took over the diving station and began struggling to level the sub. Van Hoften gave his last order as officer of the deck before formally turning the boat over to the captain.

"Do not sound the collision alarm."

It was awfully late to try to stay quiet and avoid detection and just as unnecessary to announce the collision. Still, according to rote, the crew quietly passed a collision alert from man to man, compartment by compartment. Compartment by compartment, the men reported back that each area of *Tautog* was essentially intact. The watertight doors were opened.

"They build them well at Ingalls," Waters finally said, referring to the sub's shipyard in Mississippi. His comment would be caught on an audiotape that was running in the sonar shack, recording the drama.

Step-and-a-Half hustled back, grabbed hold of a headset, and shouted, "Fuck you, God, nothing gets through HY-80." HY-80 was the steel that *Tautog*'s hull was made of, so named because it could withstand 80,000 pounds of ocean pressure per square inch.

Then the two men sat back to listen. What they heard, and what was recorded on the running tape, seemed to confirm the worst. It sounded as if one of the Echo's propellers had been torn off and, with nothing to resist the water, its turbine was spinning wildly. If that were true, and the Echo's pressure hull was gashed through, she would likely sink into the ocean. At 2,000 feet down, she would implode. There would be no survivors.

Then the men heard noises like an engine starting up and sputtering, followed by banging, perhaps watertight doors being slammed shut on the Echo. Finally sonar picked up something that sounded like popcorn popping, what Lindsay interpreted as the sound of steel cracking apart.

After that, the ocean seemed to go silent, a blanket of uninterrupted static through the sonarmen's headsets. They listened for anything that could be the Echo racing away, or blowing ballast tanks and surfacing. But everything, the spinning, the banging, the popping, had just stopped.

Someone in the sonar shack jumped up and turned off the recorder. The tape normally ran on a continuous loop, and had the recorder been left on, the sounds of the crash would have been lost.

Stunned, the operators continued to search, looking for any sign that the Soviet sub had recovered. The silence seemed to mean only one thing: that as many as ninety submariners were helplessly sinking into the crushing depths below. It didn't seem to matter now that they were Soviet submariners.

Within minutes of the collision, Balderston gave the order that sent *Tautog* steaming away, fast. There was no thought of surfacing or even of going to periscope depth. This was, in fact, an undersea hit and run. *Tautog*'s crew would not mount a search for survivors or wreckage, normal procedure for a collision at sea. Balderston's prime directive was to avoid any further encounter with the Soviets.

Tautog headed due east, moving at only about 12 knots and listing at least 10 degrees to her starboard side. Every time Balderston tried to drive the submarine faster, she leaned over more sharply. One by one, metal plates that had been welded to *Tautog*'s sail were torn off by the force of the water. Each slammed onto the submarine's hull with a resounding crash. The crew started a pool, betting on how much of the sail would be left when they got back to Pearl Harbor.

Water leaked into the control room from the gash left by the Echo's propeller, but it would be hours before *Tautog* surfaced, hours before a small team of officers could, under the cover of darkness, inspect the damage outside.

Men rushed around, trying to clean up evidence of the debacle. The sugar bowl looked like it had exploded as the captain and his officers gathered in the wardroom to make sense of what had happened. Scott Laidig, one of *Tautog*'s spooks, greeted the senior officers as they arrived. Laidig was a U.S. Marine. He had been assigned to work with the Naval Security Group, which decided that his fluency in Russian qualified him for submarines. Still, he knew he could offer no help during a collision, so he had done the next best thing. He had gotten out of everyone else's way, slipping down to the wardroom to wait out the adventure.

"I don't know how you guys do this," he said now. "You sit out here in the middle of nowhere, and you let somebody run right through you."

"Gee, I hope we didn't ruin your cup of coffee," Balderston countered.

Laidig was a veteran of two tours in Vietnam and was well known on *Tautog* for his ability to spin a yarn. Now it seemed as if he and Balderston were conspiring to divert the other officers, at least for a few moments.

Balderston asked Laidig whether he'd ever been afraid, really afraid. That was Laidig's cue. He launched into a harrowing tale about the time he had led a platoon after a sniper who had been firing on Americans from across a rice paddy. When the Americans were surprised by a second gunman, Laidig sought the only shelter available, a skinny tree. As he pressed against it, a barrage of bullets sawed his pack off his back.

The officers listened, their hands still quaking from the crash. They decided that as bad as their day had been, Laidig had been through worse. He said he wasn't so sure. The men concluded that they were probably all more comfortable dealing with the devil they knew. With that, the officers turned their attention to the devil at hand.

For more than two hours, they tried to reconstruct the accident, and came to a single conclusion. *Tautog* should have been traveling at a different depth. No one talked about what might have happened to the Soviet sub or her crew.

For the first time, Balderston's officers saw him almost humble. At one point he just shook his head, saying, "You take care of things that need to be taken care of, the safety of the ship, the safety of the crew, and of course, nondetection . . ."

Balderston didn't finish. He didn't have to. His men understood what he meant. Later he would say what everyone was thinking, but not for several hours. Not until *Tautog* had surfaced and his officers had assessed the damage. Not until he was sure his submarine could make it back to Pearl Harbor.

"Well, there goes my career," Balderston finally said. "I can forget about stars." He had lost his chance to make admiral.

When they were 150–200 miles away from the Soviet Union, Balderston gave the order to surface. Several officers climbed out the forward hatch into the darkness. They couldn't take the usual route out to the sail and up to the bridge. The hatch leading to the bridge had been breached and the sail flooded.

When the officers climbed on deck, they saw that their sail had been dished in one-third of the way back, maybe more. It was almost as if the massive structure had been made of cardboard. A fist-sized chunk of the Echo's propeller was lodged in the tower's upper hatch, which was bent and crammed back into its housing. One of the sub's two periscopes was hopelessly bent. Most of *Tautog*'s antenna and electronic masts were jammed inside the damaged sail and useless. That was going to make it tough to send a message back home, but it was very definitely time to let Pacific command know what had happened.

The crew strung a makeshift antenna—little more than a wire—across the top of the submarine. Then they flashed the bad news: there had been a severe collision; a Soviet submarine was involved; and *Tautog* was ending her operations two months early.

Commanders onshore flashed back: *Tautog* was to bypass all closer ports and return directly to Pearl Harbor. Later, the instructions would become more detailed. The submarine was to remain away from port until the dead of night. Then she was to creep in, all lights out.

On the way back, Balderston ordered the crew to gather, in shifts, on the mess deck. As if anyone really needed to be reminded, he told them that any discussion of the collision outside of an official inquiry was definitely out.

Tautog's arrival at Pearl Harbor was logged late on July 1. She was maneuvered into a shipyard dry dock where a huge shroud was draped over her sail. No one without authorization would be able to see the damage, not even her crew. The men were to be kept aboard for another twenty-four hours, until the damage was well hidden and they had signed formal secrecy oaths. One man tried to hold on to a piece of the Echo's hull as a souvenir, stashing it in a locker on board behind some cleaning fluids and alcohol. Some months later, he was discovered, and security officials insisted that he turn the piece over.

Rear Admiral Walter Small, commander of submarines in the Pacific, met *Tautog* at the pier and was among the first to learn the details. Also briefed was Admiral Moorer, who was just being promoted from CNO to chairman of the Joint Chiefs of Staff. It was either Moorer or a top Pentagon intelligence official who carried the bad news to Melvin Laird, Nixon's secretary of Defense. These reports were made verbally. No one wanted to leave a paper trail.

Laird briefed Nixon himself, telling the president that there had been a collision and it looked like the Soviet sub had sunk. Nixon's reaction, Laird recalls, was inscrutable.

It was clear that the United States would not tell the Soviet Union about the unmarked, underwater grave officials believed existed perhaps only 50 miles off the coast of the Kamchatka Peninsula. Given the secrecy that surrounded all submarine operations, it went without saying that the White House was not going to announce that two nuclear-powered submarines, both carrying nuclear weapons, had met in one violent, possibly fatal, moment. Besides, the Soviets were suffering so many at-sea accidents at the time, Nixon and his advisers decided the Soviets would likely blame another lost submarine on their own jinxed technology.

A court of inquiry was convened, although just about everyone involved was already certain that the Soviet boat was lost. Indeed, Small, Moorer, and Laird all say they remember specifically being told that the Echo had sunk. Other former senior Navy officers, including one who heard the sonar tapes, say that conclusion was based largely on the terrifying sounds captured on the recordings. But officials say that, without more definitive evidence, a formal declaration that a Soviet sub had sunk would not have been made part of the Navy's official records.

Shortly after the accident, James Bradley rushed out to Pearl Harbor to try to determine a cause. As best as anyone could guess, the Echo's captain had just made an unlucky and sudden maneuver. That in itself raised another issue. Bradley realized that U.S. captains were going to have to alter their techniques. As things stood now, the danger was too great that two subs would meet head-on at flank speed. If that happened, both subs would be lost.

So Bradley wrote some new rules for trailing, one institutionalizing a favorite Whitey Mack technique: subs would now trail slightly to port or starboard of the enemy. That would leave the Americans more maneuvering room, while still allowing them to hide in the wash of noise coming from the hunted sub. There was another rule, however, that ran directly counter to Mack's style: subs would now try to trail from safer distances.

Bradley didn't blame Balderston for the incident, and Balderston, who had already been scheduled to leave *Tautog*, became commander of a division of four submarines that included her. Still, he had been right about making admiral. It would never happen. He retired seven years later and became a Baptist minister. His heart weakened by his childhood rheumatic fever, he died in 1984. He never told his wife or children about the collision.

Balderston's silence was typical. Bound to secrecy, submariners could not seek the kind of emotional solace that most men get from their wives and children when something goes wrong on the job. "It was not for him to tell," Irene L. Balderston says. "And I would never have dreamed of questioning him or of prying anything out of him."

Just about the only ongoing discourse about the incident took place among members of *Tautog*'s crew, who passed the story on to new members as they joined the boat. They whispered to one another about what had bent their crooked sail, and crew after crew of sonarmen passed along a hidden bootleg recording—the sonar tapes made during the collision. Off the boat, the tapes were played in sonar school as an anonymous example of a Soviet sub sinking. Then two decades later the fate of the Echo II came surprisingly into question.

After the collapse of the Soviet Union, Boris Bagdasaryan, a former Soviet submarine commander, stepped forward to say that he was the captain of the Echo II that collided with *Tautog* and that he was very much alive. With so few people in either the Soviet Union or the United States aware that their governments had long hidden a terrible accident, his account got little attention. But Bagdasaryan tells a story that has been supported by high officials of the Russian Navy, and his tale meshes with many of the details provided by *Tautog* crew members, although there are a few small discrepancies.

Sitting in his Moscow apartment, cigarette in hand, Bagdasaryan's slight build and graying hair make him look more like an aging professor than a Soviet sea captain. But he had been a commander for more than a decade before he took the Echo II submarine the Soviets called the *Black Lila* out on a three-day training run in June 1970.

Bagdasaryan had survived early experiments on Soviet diesel subs, staying underwater on one of the boats the Americans called "Whiskey" for thirty days despite a design flaw that allowed exhaust gas to be sucked back into the sub through its snorkel. By the end of the month, the crew was so poisoned that their legs and hands were swollen to nearly twice their normal size. The Soviet Union chalked up the voyage as proof of the superiority of Soviet manhood.

No wonder Bagdasaryan had such a well-developed sense of political cynicism and was so willing to speak out. He especially despised the *zampolits,* the Kremlin's political officers who were assigned to every submarine. Ostensibly, they were there to ensure that crews remained Communistically correct, but Bagdasaryan thought them drunks, pests, and inept nags and let them know it. He roared at one, "You have been as useful as a suitcase on my submarine for two months," after the man accused Bagdasaryan of playing "outlaw's music" when he put on a tape of a new popular singer to inspire his men.

Nor was Bagdasaryan afraid of the Americans. As he put it, he had once "attacked" the American battleship USS *New Jersey,* stalking her as she headed full speed for Vietnam's Gulf of Tonkin. Had he been given the order, he could have sunk her. He also had gone inside U.S. waters to try to trail an American ballistic missile submarine as it left Guam, later falsifying his patrol reports, as some U.S. commanders did. He never did manage to keep tail on a U.S. sub longer than eighteen hours—a mere wink in comparison to the feats of Whitey Mack—but that was long enough to win him a reputation as one of the most daring commanders in the Soviet fleet.

Yet through all this, he always remained superstitious and fearful of disaster. He once delayed deployment rather than leave without his crew's lucky mascot, Mashka the rat. To buy time, he told an admiral that much of the meat in the ship's refrigerator was dated 1939. "Rat flight is a well-known sign," Bagdasaryan says. "It was necessary to delay our departure." *Black Lila*, however, had no such good-luck charm on that fateful day in 1970. Perhaps she should have.

Bagdasaryan says that he was moving *Black Lila*, formally identified as K-108, through a series of exercises, a set of planned revolutions through the water similar to angles and dangles, much as *Tautog*'s crew had guessed. By early in the morning of June 24, his submarine was running circles at a depth of 40 meters and a constant speed of 5 knots.

She came to periscope depth to scan for messages from shore. Then she went back to 40 meters and began to turn 90 degrees to her right. The idea was to practice checking for sounds in the area that had been shielded by the din of *Black Lila*'s own propellers—just as the Americans had thought.

As Bagdasaryan tells it, his sonarmen soon heard sounds that they identified, not as an American submarine, but as a "submarine imitator," an exercise device that looks like a torpedo and creates the same kinds of noises as a trailing submarine. Four minutes later, they lost the contact. Two minutes later, there was a crash.

What happened next inside *Black Lila* was very much like what *Tautog* sailors say they heard, and very much like what they say they imagined.

Black Lila's deck began to slant forward. First by 20 degrees, then by 30 degrees. The submarine was starting to slide out of control.

"We had 2,500 meters below us," Bagdasaryan says. "I announced the emergency alarm. Ordered to blow the main ballast bow part. No change. We started to blow the entire ballast. Useless again. The sub kept sinking. Gave an order, 'Lock in compartments!'" Silence in response. His crew was apparently in shock.

"Truth to tell, I began to doubt at that moment a possibility of successful surfacing," Bagdasaryan says.

He shouted at his stunned men. Finally they began to report in. "I hear air being slackened," sonar said.

By then, the commander realized that they had collided with another submarine. The noise of slackened air could have meant that the other sub was sinking along with the Soviets, or it might have been surfacing.

Bagdasaryan's chief engineer, Volodya Dybsky, crawled into the control room, literally pulling himself by his arms. His legs were paralyzed with fear and shock. The engineer continued to give orders, lying down.

Meanwhile, *Black Lila* continued to fall, for what seemed like several minutes. Bagdasaryan shouted what he thought would be his last order ever: "Reverse!"

It was a desperation move. If his crew could reverse the engines, their sub just might drive herself to the surface. But descending this steeply, Bagdasaryan knew the reverse clutch was likely to fail.

Black Lila began to vibrate. Inside the sub, "the depthometer's hand shook, then stopped, near 70 meters, then it moved back to 50 meters, to 25 meters. From the depth of about 25 meters, we went like a shot from the gun to the surface," he said. "Suddenly we appeared on the surface, like a cork from the champagne bottle." After that dive, he added, referring to his men, "they have a toast to the engines."

As soon as *Black Lila* hit the surface, her men opened a hatch. The sun was shining. They could see no other boat for miles around, and they feared the worst for the American sub. "I thought for a second, 'I have sunk a brother submariner,'" Bagdasaryan says. "It was hard to have realized it."

The Soviets were reporting the incident to their shore commanders when they caught the sound of what Bagdasaryan now believes was *Tautog,* moving away from the scene of the accident at 15 knots.

Bagdasaryan says his submarine limped back to port with only one propeller still working. Her right propeller shaft was hopelessly bent, and there was a large hole in her outer hull. The sounds of that outer hull cracking up could have created the popcorn effect recorded in *Tautog's* sonar room.

But the Echo had a second reinforced inner hull. American submariners used to joke that the Soviets used a two-hull design because their metallurgy was, well, Soviet metallurgy. But it was very likely that the second layer of steel held back the crushing ocean and kept *Black Lila's* men alive.

The hole in the outer hull "was so big that a trolley bus with antennas up could drive into it," Bagdasaryan recalls. "Truth to tell, if the *Tautog* had run into our sub a few meters closer to the center, we would have been very unlucky. The American submarine's speed was fairly high. And she would undoubtedly thrash both the light hull and the pressure hull of our sub."

Crammed into the hole between the inner and outer hulls, Bagdasaryan believes, were pieces of *Tautog*. He says he was certain that the crash had completely sheared off *Tautog*'s sail. Like the men on *Tautog*, who had tried to hold on to pieces of the Echo, *Black Lila* crew members tried to keep pieces of the American sub for themselves, but the chunks of HY-80 were confiscated by the KGB. Only Bagdasaryan, who refused to give his up, still has a souvenir.

After that, Bagdasaryan's story departs from the tale told by *Tautog*'s crew. He insists that it was *Tautog* that rammed *Black Lila*, not the other way around. And he says that the Soviets tracked *Tautog* heading back to Japan. He also says Soviet intelligence sources reported that once there, *Tautog* remained to undergo a long overhaul. But *Tautog* never went to Japan—she returned directly to Pearl Harbor.

When Bagdasaryan returned to the Soviet Union, he faced a torturous hearing before a Communist Party commission. He says his squadron commander gave him advice: "Don't fly into a rage. Drop some tears on dusty boots."

A severe reprimand was registered on his service card. The transgression meant that he would no longer be allowed to teach at the naval academy. Instead, his boat was overhauled, then sent to spend two and a half months hiding outside of San Francisco. This "combat service," Bagdasaryan says, was meant to make amends for his failure, to "wash out the fault with blood."

After the crash, a new joke began to make the rounds among Soviet submariners, although the facts it was based on were altered somewhat, as no one wanted to be caught referring directly to a classified incident. With such constraints, it's little wonder that the humor is somewhat strained.

The joke went like this: "An American nuclear sub collided with an iceberg in the ocean. The iceberg's crew had no casualties."

After about six months, Bagdasaryan's superiors decided to rescind the reprimand. Somehow, it wasn't erased from party documents until many years later, and by then, Bagdasaryan wanted to hold on to his unique blemish.

His reason: "It would be hard to find a Communist whose service card would say 'Severely reprimanded by the party for the collision with an American nuclear-powered submarine in underwater position.'"

As Bagdasaryan spoke, he paused and wondered aloud whether he might meet Commander Balderston, perhaps to "have a drink and think together how to avoid similar collisions in the future." Told that Balderston had died, the former Soviet commander seemed crestfallen.

"It's too bad about the commander," he said. "I guess this incident did not pass easily for him."

(8)

"OSHKOSH B'GOSH"

t was after 3:00 A.M., and even the Pentagon seemed almost still. Official Washington wouldn't start to churn for hours, not until the sun began baking the asphalt-and-concrete moat that surrounded the 34 acres taken up by the building.

James Bradley sat beyond that moat, deep within the long cream-colored corridors, still on the fifth floor of the Pentagon's E Ring behind three sets of locked doors, his suite of offices empty but for him. It was late 1970, Bradley's fourth year as the director of undersea warfare at the Office of Naval Intelligence, and it was in these early morning hours that he could dream best, immersed in the quiet of his office and in the deep oceans beyond.

He was preoccupied with notions bordering on the fantastic, plans for a new mission for *Halibut,* one that would shake the intelligence community even more than the photographs of the Soviet Golf submarine that had so caught the imagination of President Nixon and, unfortunately for the Navy, the CIA.

Bradley wanted to send *Halibut* into the heart of a Soviet-claimed sea after a quarry that was living—practically breathing—and beyond almost anything U.S. intelligence had attempted to grab before. Closing his eyes for a moment, he could almost see his target. It was a telephone cable, a bundle of wires no wider than five inches.

But what a bundle of wires. Bradley imagined the cable as it ran from the Soviet Union's missile submarine base at Petropavlovsk, under the Sea of Okhotsk, and then on to join land cables going to Pacific Fleet headquarters near Vladivostok and then to Moscow. If *Halibut*'s camera-toting fish could find that cable, if her crew could tap it, then the United States would violate the very soul of Soviet secrecy. Here could be an open ear to the plans and frustrations of Soviet leaders, intelligence unmatched by any human spy or even the newest surveillance satellites floating high over the Kremlin.

Bradley could almost hear the words flowing through the line, technical analysis clear of propaganda, measures of the abilities and problems of Soviet submarines, information that might make them easier to trail, tactical plans for patrols that would take those submarines and their missiles near U.S. shores. If he was right, maybe the Americans could even grab the Soviets' own assessments of the test flights of ICBMs and sea-based missiles that smacked down on the Kamchatka Peninsula and in the northern Pacific. That cable might provide entry inside the minds of Soviet commanders themselves.

Of course, the Soviets would probably see *Halibut*'s intrusion into Okhotsk as an act of piracy. If she were detected, they might try to board or destroy her, forcing an international incident that might end the delicate dance toward détente.

And there was another hitch, a big one. Bradley had no proof that this cable existed at all. Even if it did, there was no way to tell where it lay beneath the 611,000-square-mile expanse of Okhotsk. Even Bradley could see the humor in his predicament. How could he present this idea to the cadre of White House, military, intelligence, and State Department officials who were supposed to have final say over an operation as dangerous as this one? How could he say that he wanted to send *Halibut* out on a hunch in search of an ethereal strand?

Still, as far as Bradley was concerned, it was a pretty good hunch. After all these years of watching the Soviets, American intelligence knew that Soviet defense officials insisted on constant reports from the men in the field and that the Soviets painstakingly coded most communications sent through the air to thwart interception. If Bradley's intuition was right, Soviet admirals and generals would be far too imperious and impatient to suffer an ocean of cryptographers already overwhelmed by the sheer bulk of their work. Top Soviet officers would want, would insist upon, an immediate and simple communications method, and the only simple and secure way to talk was through a hardwired telephone system.

Any telephone line the Soviets set up between the mainland and the submarine base at Petropavlovsk would have to run beneath the Sea of Okhotsk. Petropavlovsk was, after all, a tiny, desolate port across that sea, isolated on the Kamchatka Peninsula and nearly hidden among ancient volcanoes and primeval birch forests. Okhotsk itself was almost empty, save for a few fishing trawlers and occasional submarines engaged in missile tests.

The Soviets had to consider the sea secure, given that it was nestled into the crook of Kamchatka and the east coast of the Soviet Union as neatly as the Chesapeake Bay fits into the U.S. eastern seaboard. The way in for an enemy submarine or ship was through narrow, shallow channels that sliced through the Soviet-controlled Kuril Islands. Those channels could be easily blocked in an alert.

But even if the cable was out there, where was it? Where in all those miles and miles of water lay a strand that couldn't be more than five inches wide?

Bradley cleared his mind of charts and maps, freed himself from official assessments, from the meetings, memos, and briefings that swamped the business of intelligence in Washington. He let his eyes close and his thoughts wandered to simpler journeys taken in simpler times, before the cold war, before World War II, back to the waters of his childhood.

There he found an answer that was beguilingly simple and just strange enough to be true. It was buried in his memories of St. Louis in the 1930s when he was a boy and his mother packed him up to escape the summer's heat on riverboat rides along the Mississippi River. From the point where the Mississippi meets the

Missouri River through Alton, Illinois, the boats steamed through water dyed with brown silt and banked by miles of flood plains painted with wild upward strokes of grasses until the green gave itself up abruptly to towering gray barrier bluffs. Eagles traced circles above, while sand cranes left leggy tracks along the shore. It was this scenery that captured most people riding the river—that and the riverboat orchestra and social scene on board.

But for a boy, there were other sights that marked the trip. The young Bradley had taken to passing time with the steamer captains in the pilothouse, and from there he could see a series of black-and-white signs placed discreetly along the shore. Most of the signs marked mileage and location. But there were a few, he remembered now, that declared: "Cable Crossing. Do Not Anchor." These signs were there to keep some idiot in a boat from snaring and snapping a phone or utility cable in the shallows.

Bradley's eyes snapped open as he realized that what was true of the Mississippi just might be true of Okhotsk. That's how they would find the cable, he thought. That's how they would engineer one of the most daring acts of tele-piracy of the cold war. *Halibut* would be led directly to her quarry by signs placed somewhere on a lonesome beach in the Soviet Union, declaring: "Watch Out! Cable Here."

This wasn't the way intelligence operations were normally crafted in Washington, but Bradley's imagination had always been vast, sometimes too vast for the rigidity that often ruled much of the military crowd. He had been dreaming about a possible cable tap almost from the moment he had gotten the job and control of *Halibut*. He and his staff had spent hours talking about the possibilities for *Halibut* and that mythical communications cable. They scanned maps and pored over charts of Soviet seas and bases, and they soon came to realize that there were three spots that held special promise, three places on the maps where Soviet naval bases were separated from Moscow by miles of water: the Baltic Sea, the Barents Sea, and the Sea of Okhotsk.

Of these, only Okhotsk was truly desolate. Covered with a layer of ice nine months of the year, the sea was as dreary and cold as Petropavlovsk, where nuclear submarines and missile arsenals were secreted among buildings that had been decaying for a century or more. Soviet naval officers made dingy homes in these cheap squares of concrete built among civil defense shelters and radar receivers.

The more Bradley thought about Okhotsk and the sub base on Kamchatka, the more he knew that *Halibut* was destined to go there. But throughout his first three, even four years directing her missions, there had been no safe way to allow men to leave a submarine, walk the sand 300 to 400 feet under the sea, and reach out and tap a cable. Bradley had to wait for the technology to catch up with his vision. And that had finally happened.

The same post-*Thresher* panic that had prompted the Navy to put money into underwater research, the same push that had given birth to a redesigned *Halibut,* had also paid for a program to create new ways for divers to survive in the deep. Bradley's old friend John Craven had overseen much of this work until he retired from the Navy. Under Craven's direction, the ability of divers to work in the depths had progressed at an incredible pace.

The problem had been daunting. What is life-giving air on the surface can kill divers down deep. By 300 feet down, air compresses so much that a single lungful contains about ten times the surface amounts of oxygen and nitrogen. At these concentrations, oxygen becomes poisonous and nitrogen has a druglike effect— nitrogen narcosis—that makes divers go squirrelly.

Specially trained Navy divers and scientists had been experimenting with recipes for a new underwater atmosphere that replaced much of the oxygen and all of the nitrogen with helium, which is nontoxic. On ascent, those gases could be remixed to fulfill the divers' increasing need for oxygen in shallower waters. Animal experiments had given way to human underwater habitats called SeaLabs. Placed 200 feet down off La Jolla, California, the living was dangerous and uncomfortable. At one point, the plumbing failed on one and the habitat tilted, but four divers inside survived on the new gas mixtures.

Everything was progressing well until one of the SeaLabs developed leaks in 1969. A diver was killed while trying to make repairs—not at all the kind of publicity the Navy was looking for just a year after *Scorpion* had been lost. The SeaLab program was unceremoniously canceled, and to outsiders, it seemed as though the Navy had abandoned the effort altogether. But development quietly continued, and Bradley and Craven prepared to put the new gas mixture and the new "saturation diving" techniques to use for divers on *Halibut.*

The sub was now at the Mare Island Naval Shipyard outside San Francisco being fitted with a portable version of SeaLab, a pressurized chamber to support the divers as they acclimated to the water pressures they would find if they walked the seafloor to tap the Soviet cable. But before *Halibut* could navigate the bottom of Okhotsk, Bradley had to win the funding and political support that the mission would require.

Bradley's office was still the clearinghouse for all submarine spy missions. He and his staff collected wish lists from top policy-makers within the National Security Agency, the Pentagon, and the White House. It was up to Bradley to come up with the operations that could fulfill those requests—the submarine trailings, the observations of missile tests, the gathering of electronic signals.* After that, Bradley had to sell those missions to the fleet commanders, who still had the final word on whether any of their submarines went out and where. Bradley had already made dozens of trips to Pearl Harbor, Norfolk, and Yokosuka, Japan, to brief and debrief submarine captains, and he had earned their respect and trust. Besides, the daring of the cable-tap mission would make it an easy sell to these men.

Navigating through Washington required more finesse. Still, Bradley knew how to court the crowd in this town where information was currency and was jealously distributed under the amorphous guideline of "need to know." This was a place where power was measured by access, and Bradley traded access for

---

*Some of those missions were almost as far off the usual track as Bradley's imagined underwater cable, and not all of them were successful. In the early 1970s, a series of subs were sent to the Strait of Sicily to investigate what U.S. intelligence believed was a Soviet effort to plant an underwater system that would operate like SOSUS—one that seemed even more sophisticated than the sonobuoys that the British had destroyed a few years before. First the USS *Tullibee* (SSN-597) was sent in and found a suspicious cable, suspended high above the seabed. Then *Lapon* was sent in to try to snag the cable, but failed. After that, the USS *Seahorse* (SSN-669) and Rickover's *NR-1* were sent in. *Seahorse* used her sonar to find the cable, then guided the small crew of *NR-1* to the spot for what may well have been the first intelligence mission for the mini-sub. Finally, *NR-1* got close enough to discover the Navy had been turning underwater backflips to check out a sunken Italian telephone cable left over from World War II.

approvals, packaging facts within a romantic haze of deep-ocean wonders. His briefings drew on the storyteller's art that he had picked up decades earlier listening to his father weave wondrous yarns of wine, women, and sea.

In fact, Bradley's idea to search for a Soviet cable was inspired almost as much by its dramatic impact as it was by its potential intelligence value. If that cable did exist, finding it and tapping it would do more to bring his office high-level exposure and funding than just about any mission he could think of. Bradley was already counting his successes in dollars and in enemies. His bounty usually came straight from the zipped pockets of other Navy departments. After he nearly decimated one project headed by a naval aviator, the man was ready to punch Bradley in the nose right there in the Pentagon. "You son-of-a-bitch," swore the burly aviator, pouncing on the captain in the corridor. Bradley didn't blame him, didn't blame him a bit. But Bradley also was unapologetic. He felt completely sincere in believing that his group was doing better work than anyone else.

As long as his program had money, Bradley had power, and more of it than any four-stripe Navy captain had a right to expect. He still reported to Rear Admiral Fritz Harlfinger, the director of Naval Intelligence, and through him to Admiral Elmo R. Zumwalt Jr., who was now the chief of Naval Operations. But power or not, Bradley was still a captain in a town full of admirals, and a mere Naval Intelligence officer in a town where the top spooks reported to the president. There also were more than a few admirals who resented his refusal to take them into his confidence. One man, especially powerful within the Pentagon, insisted that he had to approve every operation before Bradley could send a spy submarine out. It was a directive Bradley found impossible to comply with. "You gave me an order that was not legal," Bradley answered when the irate admiral confronted him. Then he added, "By the way, I don't work for you."

The admiral stared Bradley down for what seemed like a long time. Finally he intoned, "All right. You can get away with this, this time. But I'll tell you one thing, Bradley. You're never going to make admiral."

"So be it," Bradley stood his ground. "So be it." Then with a soldier's flourish, he did an about-face and walked away, the drama of his departure filling him with satisfaction. There would be time enough later to realize that the admiral might just make good on his threat.

At the moment, Bradley was more concerned with his battle with the CIA over control of *Halibut*. The agency had already snatched command of all salvage operations surrounding the sunken Golf and was still waiting for Howard Hughes to finish building the monolithic salvage craft that would attempt to tear the entire sub from its ocean grave. Most of that was being engineered through the National Underwater Reconnaissance Office, the top-secret Navy-CIA office that was still being run mainly by the CIA. Worse, the CIA seemed hell-bent on broadcasting news of all of the Navy's best submarine missions and taking credit for them.

When those missions were still entirely under Bradley's watch, fewer than a dozen top officials in Washington knew of the Soviets' lost submarine and *Halibut*'s find. Now Bradley saw CIA officers assigned to NURO handing out clearances like candy corn on Halloween. The Velvet Fist photographs, *Halibut*'s abilities, and even other submarine spying missions were fast becoming the main attraction in a circus where having a ticket to the show was more important than the performance, where the labels "top-secret" and "need to know" made the spectacle irresistible.

Bradley saw every briefing as a potential leak. He wanted to be the one to go to Kissinger or his top deputy, General Alexander Haig (Kissinger's chief liaison to the military), and then only when the time was right. Bradley had worked hard to earn his access to the two powerful men. The captain played on his realization that Kissinger was the ultimate bureaucratic infighter, someone who wanted to control everything about foreign policy and covert actions affecting foreign policy. Bradley knew that, more than anything else, Kissinger wanted to choose what would be presented to Nixon and wanted to make those presentations personally. As long as Bradley's missions reaped key intelligence, he knew the door would be open to Kissinger and to Haig. That had been clear the last time Bradley went to see Kissinger about *Halibut*'s exploits.

Kissinger was half an hour late. He walked in, leaned back in a chair, put one foot on a table in front of him, and pointed the other foot at Bradley. "Vell," he began, his trademark German accent evident in every word. "You have got ten minutes. Go ahead and start."

Bradley knew better than to cower.

"Dr. Kissinger, I can't do this in ten minutes. If ten minutes is all you've got, we ought to go away and come back and do this another time. Because with ten minutes, we're just going to waste your time and mine."

"Vell, vell. You start, and I'll tell you when to stop."

More than forty-five minutes later, they were still talking. It seemed a crucial victory to Bradley.

Now, the captain knew that news of the hunt for a sunken Soviet communications cable would be just the sort of exclusive that Haig would want to bring to Kissinger, and that the national security adviser would relish bringing to Nixon. Bradley had no intention of being scooped before he was ready to present his plan, so he told only the people who absolutely had to know: the Pacific submarine fleet commander and Harlfinger.

Normally Bradley also would have marched his plan before a national oversight group known as the "40 Committee." Chaired by Kissinger, its ranks were filled with the country's highest national security officials, including the chairman of the Joint Chiefs of Staff and the director of the CIA. It was the committee's job to evaluate all international covert operations, everything from CIA interventions in Third World countries to eavesdropping operations aimed at the Kremlin. Other presidents had had similar oversight committees, and since the *Pueblo* incident, routine missions, such as the usual submarine forays into Soviet coastal waters or sorties flown by spy planes, were included in a monthly list for review. Committee members usually just provided a final glance before checking off boxes marked "approved."

But more dangerous operations—presumably any effort that carried as much risk as a plan to tap into a crucial Soviet communications line—were, in theory, subject to far more detailed hearings where the operations were supposed to pass the most basic of all tests: Are the potential payoffs worth the risk? The riskiest missions were then supposed to be presented to the president for final approval. That was the primary job of the 40 Committee: to provide a test of common sense, a dispassionate analysis of what otherwise might be a no-holds-barred quest to gather intelligence. The committee was, in short, a layer of oversight designed to rise above parochial concerns, interagency rivalries, machismo, and the ever-present temptation to venture from the daring into the stupid.

But that ideal was often little more than fantasy. The committee almost never marked any mission "disapproved," and members of the intelligence agencies and the armed forces knew they could bypass the rest of the group as long as they didn't bypass Kissinger, who treated the committee as something to be utilized or ignored as he saw fit. Sometimes, after he okayed missions on his own authority, he would poll the committee by telephone, seeking back-door approvals. Sometimes he didn't even bother to do that.

The message Kissinger sent was clear: the only oversight that mattered was his. That suited Bradley and Harlfinger, who in the spring of 1971 were happy to avoid a formal committee hearing. It wasn't hard for them to imagine what such a hearing would be like.

"Where were those signs? Along the Mississippi, you say?"

"So, Captain Bradley, you say you came up with this sitting alone in your office at 3:00 A.M.?"

No, no, no. It would make so much more sense, Bradley reasoned, to try to get quiet approvals from the top and to wait to tell the full committee about the plan once he knew for sure that the cable was there, to come in saying, "Look what we've done."

Any step into Okhotsk, from the Soviets' point of view, was blatantly illegal, although the United States considered most of that sea to be open to international traffic. And a search for signs on a Soviet beach would have to take place at least partly inside the Soviets' 3-mile coastal limit, recognized internationally as sovereign territory. No one would see *Halibut*'s jaunt inside as anything less than trespassing.

Bradley hoped Kissinger would look past that, as much as he hoped Kissinger would ignore the fact that the timing for this kind of risk was just awful. *Halibut* would be trespassing when Nixon was publicly painting himself as a peacemaker and statesman. The president had just gone on national television to declare that he personally had rescued flagging arms control talks in secret communications with Soviet General Secretary Leonid Brezhnev.

All this left the captain apprehensive when he went to see Haig. With as few details as he could manage, Bradley outlined his plan to search out the cable. "If we can find it, we think we've worked out a way to tap it," he told Haig. There was also, Bradley said, a secondary mission—an underwater search for parts of a new kind of cruise missile being supplied to Soviet subs that stalked U.S. aircraft carriers.

Haig asked no questions, offered no words of caution. He didn't even bother to bring Bradley before Kissinger. Instead, he said, "Keep us informed."

Bradley realized he had just gotten all the official approval he would need. Haig would surely let Kissinger know, but the Navy's diciest plan had passed with the simplest approval process possible. *Halibut* was going to Okhotsk.

By the end of the summer of 1971, *Halibut*'s refit was almost complete. In addition to the huge hump—the Bat Cave—that had inspired her conversion to a so-called special projects boat, she also sported an extra lump, a secret and crucial piece of equipment that was so ingeniously hidden atop her deck that the Navy proudly advertised its presence with no fear of a security breach.

Local newspaper headlines heralded the accomplishment of this new addition, while intoning that the Navy had relaxed its secrecy surrounding *Halibut*. *Halibut*, the papers declared, was to be the mother ship for the Navy's first post-*Thresher* deep-submergence rescue vehicle. In fact, the lump wasn't a DSRV at all, but a divers' decompression and lockout chamber. Welded in place, it was where they would begin breathing the mixed gases developed at SeaLab, and it was where they would get ready to go out and work underwater.

In these final weeks before *Halibut* was to leave, Bradley's team began making frequent anonymous visits to Mare Island. Most of the sub's officers and crew knew them only as the men from Washington. *Halibut*'s captain, Commander John E. McNish, wasn't revealing much more.

Even in the final days before their October departure for Okhotsk, the crew still didn't know their destination. They knew only that they were leaving home for three months. That in itself was inspiration enough for the enlisted men to fill the submarine bars around San Francisco. Some of these boys were only months past their high school proms. Others were salted chiefs, veterans of smelly diesel boats or the first nuclear submarines. Together, they spent their final night onshore, in an era when being a hard-drinking, chain-smoking man of the sea was not yet an anachronism.

With their wives and girlfriends looking on, they drank themselves under the tables at Helen's. They drank until they danced buck-naked on top of the tables at the Horse and Cow. This was their favorite place, the "Whinny and Moo" to the initiated, with its darkened rooms, walls lined with photos of submarines, a Klaxon cutting through the air to announce each new round, and stolen pieces of equipment crammed onto every free surface: submarine commodes, plaques, dishes, ceremonial pennants, a torpedo casing, an anchor, enough contraband to drive naval investigators mad.

Snorkel Patty was probably there: she almost always was at these last-night events. For a decade, she had been mother, big sister, and lover to scores of submariners. She was the woman who knew what they would face on patrol without needing to be told, and she taught other young women braving the brash bar not to ask where or how or why. She was the woman who would make the men feel safe when they got home. A tender Mae West—Mary Magdalene of the submarine set.

In return, these men and boys gave her their hard-won silver dolphins, hundreds over the years. They gave her a volcano's worth of lighters decorated with their submarine insignias. And they gave her their undying adoration.

The Klaxon blew, an air-driven howl, a wolf's song mated with the bray of a sick mule. The men drank some more and hooted, then hooted louder when some innocent knob walked into the place still wearing underwear—just about everyone was checked, and anyone found wearing was unceremoniously stripped.

Inspired, the veterans dropped their pants, stood on the bar, and turned around to show off the screws tattooed in twin sets, making sterns of their rears. Legend has it that those inked propellers would ensure a safe and speedy passage. The especially brash powered their screws with a long trail of paper from the head planted in the only place possible on their naked bottoms. With the paper set afire, they raced smoky circles around the bar in what had become the ritual "Dance of the Flaming Asshole."

This was their celebration for finally getting out of the shipyard. This was a wake for their lost freedom. This was how the men of the *Halibut* launched one of the most critical submarine spy operations of the cold war.

The party wouldn't end until just a few hours before "Smiling Jack" McNish gave the final order to embark. Smiling Jack was the name the men had given their hulking commander, a testament to the tight grin that took the place of a growl or gritted teeth. It widened only with trouble. Few crew members remembered ever seeing the thirty-eight-year-old redheaded captain actually laugh—not now, and not on *Halibut* five years or so earlier when he had served as her executive officer.

That grin would be there, unchanging, through most of the month *Halibut* spent transiting to Okhotsk. Any other attack submarine would have made the distance in less than two weeks. But *Halibut*'s 1950s vintage reactor could not kick up past 13 knots, and she was further slowed by the drag of the fake DSRV on her back. Most of the trip progressed at an infuriating crawl of 10 knots as *Halibut* traveled a long arc, matching the curvature of the earth. Moving north to the Aleutian Islands, then down past the icy Bering Strait, past Soviet surface ships, she reached the Sea of Okhotsk.

Getting inside the sea was tense business. The crew took several hours to maneuver through a shallow channel, probably at the northernmost part of the Kuril Islands chain just below the southern tip of Kamchatka. From here, the men had a periscope view of an active volcano, but they feared sunlight more. A single glint off the periscope and any nearby submarine-hunting plane or ship would find them.

By now, they knew where they were. McNish had told them that much, and he told them the divers were going out on this mission. But he omitted any talk about Soviet cables. The commander instead declared that *Halibut* was there to find pieces of the new and deadly Soviet ship-to-ship missile. Only McNish, his officers, the divers, and a few men among those knighted as the "special projects team" knew what they were really up to as he ordered *Halibut* to move slowly up along the Soviet coastline, periscope up.

Every three hours, *Halibut* moved along an "S" path, or cut a figure eight, or shifted from one side or the other, or circled around. Anything to give a peek into that blind spot in her baffles, to make sure no other sub followed from behind.

The search continued for longer than a week. The men found nothing, but continued to look, to hope. Then they saw it, sitting along the beach, far up on the northernmost half of the Sea of Okhotsk: one of Bradley's signs proclaiming a warning to the careless—"Do Not Anchor. Cable Here"—or something to that effect in Russian.

At McNish's order, a fish was sent swimming out of the Bat Cave. By now, the problems with the video feed had been fixed. The pictures that came flying up into the submarine's monitors were still grainy and tinged with gray, but they were far clearer than the sonar images the men had to rely on while searching for the Golf. Now, the men staring at the monitors could even see vague shapes of Okhotsk's giant crabs, though only photographs would show the smaller fish, the clouds of luminescent plankton, the teeny jellyfish dancing diamonds as they were lit up by the mechanical fish's incandescent mechanical lights. Anything, no matter how large, that was more than a few feet from the cameras and lights was lost in the murky water—dark greenish brown from silt runoffs, it showed up dark gray on the video monitors. Only a few men were cleared to look at any of this, but the novelty wore off quickly and their shifts seemed to take forever as they stared at the screens for hours at a time.

Then the sand seemed to rise slightly, a bump on the bottom a foot or two long. The bump disappeared, then returned, a dash in the sand, followed by other dashes in the sand. At first, the men wondered whether they were imagining a broken line within the gray. But there it was again, and again, periodic gray rises and a more occasional glimpse of black. There was something there, something almost entirely buried in the sandy silt.

Halibut began to follow the line. As the video images flickered on *Halibut*'s monitor, the fish snapped twenty-four photographs a second. Later, the fish would be hauled up and gutted, refilled, and sent out again. The film promised images much clearer than this grainy video, but the ship's photographer wouldn't be able to develop any of the rolls until later, when *Halibut* could move high enough to the surface to snorkel and vent the toxic darkroom fumes.

Finally, McNish gave the order, and *Halibut* came up in the privacy of a black night. The photographer began unraveling the rolls of film taken from the fish, working with the officer in charge of special projects. In the cramped darkroom, the two men watched the images emerge. There, in the color photographs, lay the Soviet cable.

Now *Halibut*'s crew had to find a flat strip on the sea bottom, a place to lower the two huge mushroom-shaped anchors at her bow and stern. McNish was looking for a spot well outside the 3-mile limit. There was nothing to be gained by tempting fate now. Ultimately he settled on a place in the northern part of Okhotsk, about 40 miles off the western face of Kamchatka. His men maneuvered the boat gently down to a place just above the cable. It took almost a day to move into position and anchor.

The divers had been waiting in the fake DSRV, breathing the helium and oxygen mixture for some time, and their bodies were acclimated to the increased pressure. Now they climbed into rubber wet suits that fit loosely, leaving enough room for tubes that ran down their legs, their arms, into their hands, and around their bodies. A pump in the submarine would push hot water through the tubes as soon as they left the chamber, transforming the suits into something like rubbery, wet electric blankets. The water would come through tiny holes in the tubing, seeping warmth against the chill of Okhotsk. It was November, and the water was at near-freezing temperatures.

The divers also wrapped insulation against their gas jets; there was no point in warming their bodies if they were going to breathe cold gas. Several times they checked their umbilical cords, the two-inch-thick bundle of tubes and wires that provided the mixed gases for breathing, the hot-water sluices, and the links for communication, power, and lighting.

Running through the cord was one strong wire that had nothing to do with breathing, talking, or seeing. This was the emergency line, which would be used to yank them back into *Halibut* should something go wrong. Their only other margin for error was latched onto their belts—small bottles containing three or four minutes of emergency air, their "come-home bottles."

Finally the men were ready to crawl out the outer hatch. In the control room, McNish could see them walking what seemed a space walk. Only barely lit by their handheld lights, they cut a ghostly path through the murky water to the communications cable. Once there, they began using pneumatic airguns to blow debris and sand away from the wire. As soon as it was clear, the men started to attach the tap, a device about three feet long that held a recorder filled with big rolls of tape. Off the main box was a cylinder that contained a lithium-powered battery. A separate connector wrapped around the cable and would draw out the words and data that ran through. The tap worked through induction. There would be no cutting into the cable, no risking an electrical short from seeping seawater.

Inside the boat, men monitored the water currents, taking readings every fifteen minutes or so. *Halibut* swayed against her anchors, while planesmen struggled to keep her level through the hours that the divers worked to attach the recording device to the cable. After that connection was made, the spooks collected what seemed like an adequate sample of the Soviet voice and data transmissions running through the cable.

Nothing in *Halibut*'s history suggested that this would ever be so easy. The cable had been found without a single snag in the line towing the fish. The mission had gone so smoothly that much of the crew would remain firmly convinced that their submarine had happened upon the cable by sheer accident. They had, after all, been told that the target on this trip to Okhotsk was pieces of Soviet missiles. Now, true to his word, McNish turned *Halibut* and headed for a Soviet test range.

The water there was somewhat deeper than the waters over the cable. Still, *Halibut*'s fish quickly found a spot where the whitish-gray grains carpeting the ocean bottom became speckled with the steel gray and black of electronics and small shards of casing. *Halibut* had found a place where Soviet missiles went to die.

This mission also was important, for these new Soviet cruise missiles posed a terrible threat to U.S. aircraft carriers. The weapons had a new kind of infrared guidance system that the U.S.

Navy had been unable to counter. Bradley had already sent three standard U.S. attack submarines to Okhotsk with orders to try to get close enough to missile tests to record the frequencies of the infrared devices as well as the frequencies of the new kind of radar altimeters that let the missiles skim close to the water surface and out of range of conventional U.S. countermeasures. The idea had been for the standard attack subs to use bulky devices attached to their periscopes to squirt bits of heat at the missiles and see what frequencies reflected back. The task proved impossible. (At this point, the Navy was so desperate to learn whatever it could about any kind of Soviet cruise missiles that it had sent *Swordfish* with sonar developed for *Halibut*, side lit and mounted on her hull, out to scour seabeds in shallow waters. The sonar worked so well that *Swordfish* could skim the shallows not more than twenty-five feet off the bottom practically at flank speed.)

Only *Halibut* could actually send men out to retrieve anything, and now her divers were out again, this time to pick up piece after piece. The hope was to find one of the infrared devices or one of the radar altimeters. The divers stowed the pieces in a huge gondola-like basket hooked to *Halibut*'s steel underbelly. When the gondola was filled with hundreds of missile bits, the divers climbed back into the fake DSRV to wait out the long decompression process.

They were there much of the time it took *Halibut* to travel back to Mare Island. She docked about a month after she left Okhotsk.

Before the crew could disembark, tapes from the cable tap were on their way to the huge National Security Agency complex at Fort George G. Meade. That complex, located halfway between Washington and Baltimore, was where the Defense Department sent most of the electronics intelligence picked up by submarines and other spy vehicles to be decoded and analyzed. Protected by three layers of barbed wire and fences, one layer electrified, were five and a half subterranean acres of computers. These were used by some of the nation's top mathematicians and scientists to break Soviet codes. There were also thousands of Russian linguists and analysts poring over decoded communications. The massive operations building was nicknamed the "Anagram Inn," and it was behind its 70,000 square feet of permanently sealed windows that the *Halibut*'s tapes would be played, replayed, and judged for content.

Meanwhile, the missile fragments were sent to a Department of Energy lab secreted away in the Pacific Northwest, a so-called black installation with no outward signs of the work that went on inside. There, in a large, empty room, sat the basketfuls of junked missile pieces. Bit by tiny bit, engineers sorted through the baskets, laying out pieces on a long board. They were at it for months, but finally they had a board filled, 20 feet of junk transformed into a flattened, shattered version of nearly an entire missile, a 20-foot-long jigsaw puzzle with few pieces larger than 6 inches.

Still, in all those heaps and baskets, engineers never found the infrared homing device the Navy so desperately wanted to study. (It was assumed that the devices must have shattered when the missiles careened headlong into their targets at speeds of Mach 1 or Mach 1.5.) But the radar altimeter and other crucial parts of that device were found, allowing U.S. engineers to try to build a countermeasure, one that would hopefully send the Soviet cruise missiles plunging harmlessly into the ocean.

Meanwhile, word about the cable recordings came back to Bradley from the NSA. His guess had been right. Flowing through that cable was pure military gold: conversations between the submarine base and high-level Soviet Navy officials, some of them unencrypted or coded in fairly rudimentary ways.

The find separated the cable tap from most of the communications intelligence available to the United States. The growing network of spy satellites, planes, listening stations, and subs had watched and listened as the Soviets moved troops, built bases, and sent their fleets swimming through exercises. But even the most advanced eavesdropping system, the prototype of the Rhyolite satellite launched in 1970, could not penetrate a hardwired phone line. And the few eavesdropping satellites the United States had were focused on Moscow and the Soviets' northern coast. None pointed toward the Pacific bases, the bases that were linked by the cable through Okhotsk.

To be sure, Soviet agents provided occasional insights into the Soviet psyche. But for all the drama in dead drops and late-night forays through dark Moscow streets, finding a way to consistently intercept conversations among Soviet military leaders was something that the United States had been trying to do for decades with only limited success. A set of antennas placed atop the U.S. embassy in Moscow had captured Brezhnev complaining about his health and other Politburo members talking about the traffic or their sex lives, but no Soviet leader was going to make a habit of talking about state secrets over something as vulnerable as a car phone.

Now the cable tap was providing the first inside look at the Soviet Navy's fears and frustrations, its assessments of its own successes and failures, and its intentions. And the full potential for the Okhotsk cable tap had yet to be measured. These first recordings were only samples, an ear to conversations and reports that took place over a few days on a few of the dozens of lines that ran through the cable under the sea.

Bradley saw the next step, and he saw it clearly. He wanted to tap as many of the lines as possible, and he wanted to plant a device that could record for several months or even a year, a device that would keep working in Okhotsk even when *Halibut* was docked at Mare Island. His staff contacted Bell Laboratories, whose engineers were familiar with commercial undersea phone cables and began designing a much larger tap pod. Just like the smaller recorder *Halibut* carried on her first trip, the new device worked through induction, but this tap pod was huge. Nearly 20 feet long and more than 3 feet wide, it weighed about 6 tons and utilized a form of nuclear power. It would be able to pick up electronic frequencies from dozens of lines for months at a time, and record them on 3-inch tape that ran along a wheel nearly 3 feet in diameter. *Halibut* could plant the tap one year, then go back and retrieve it the next.

Leaving behind proof of intrusion was risky, but Bradley's group reasoned that even if the Soviets found the tap, the United States could argue that the induction device was legal. Under U.S. law, the Constitution's prohibition against illegal search and seizure had already been ruled not to apply to currents emanating from buildings, homes, or cables.

Navy lawyers wrote up highly classified papers to that effect. These legal contortions might seem disingenuous, but they accompanied almost all covert operations. It was, after all, the United States that kept insisting that other countries operate on high moral ground and within the bounds of international law.

When the new tap was finished, it looked like a giant tube that had been squashed some from the top and welded shut at the ends. The device was crammed with miniature electronics circuits and had the capacity to record for weeks at a time. The device was so huge, *Halibut*'s spooks would later come to call it "The Beast."

Finally it was time for Bradley to wade through the formal approval process that he had avoided when the cable was still only a Mississippi River hunch. If *Halibut* was going to leave evidence of intrusion sitting in Okhotsk, the project would need more than a quiet nod from Haig and Kissinger. Despite Bradley's tensions with the CIA, it had been easy to get the agency officials he worked with to go along. They were so busy building the *Glomar Explorer* they didn't mind leaving the cable-tap operation to him. So Bradley presented *Halibut* to the 40 Committee in early 1972, while the American public was being presented with details about Nixon and Kissinger's peace initiatives with Vietnam and their historic trip to China.

Given the timing, approval for the tap mission was anything but certain. For one thing, the Strategic Arms Limitation Talks (SALT) were at a make-or-break stage. For another, Kissinger and Zumwalt, the CNO, were engaged in an open feud. Kissinger had made a glaring mistake during arms negotiations that threatened to leave the Soviets with a dangerous lead in submarine-based ballistic missiles. In secret talks away from his military advisers, he had agreed, offhandedly, not to ask for limits on the Soviets' massive effort to build the Deltas, a new class of submarines that would far surpass the Yankees and carry ballistic missiles with ranges of 4,000 miles. Zumwalt was furious, convinced that Kissinger and Nixon had given away the barn in their zeal to get SALT completed before the year's elections. Zumwalt, who passed off words of caution from State Department officials—calling them "bed-wetters"—was trying to force Kissinger to pay for his negotiating mistake by pressuring him to approve an even more powerful new class of U.S. missile subs: the Tridents. It was a battle he would win.*

---

*Zumwalt did have another edge. Submarine spying had received a boost in Kissinger's and Nixon's eyes in mid-1972, when U.S. surveillance subs detected one of the rare overt Soviet moves to intervene in the Vietnam War. Shortly after Nixon announced the mining of Haiphong Harbor, the Soviet Navy sent three Echo II subs toward Vietnam. After they were detected by U.S. subs, Washington sent a message to Moscow, essentially saying, send them back home, or they're history. The subs left.

Now that the CNO had thrown his considerable weight behind *Halibut* and her return to Okhotsk, and damn the risk, it seemed that the cable tap could easily become a pawn in the battle between the White House and the Navy. Bradley did what he could to play down the risks, making his presentation without reference to a what-if-*Halibut*-were-caught scenario. Beyond that, much of what he offered the 40 Committee was pure drama. The captain pulled out a map of Okhotsk. He pointed to where the signs were found on the beach and drew a path over the sea to indicate the cable. Then he boldly stated what had once been only a guess—that this was a cable that carried crucial information about the operations and development of Soviet ballistic missile submarines. His discussion of the dangers was limited to the harrowing undersea walks facing *Halibut*'s divers.

What Bradley didn't tell the committee was just how he knew there was a cable in the first place. He left out the fact that *Halibut,* on Haig's nod, had already visited the wire. He only assured the committee that the Navy was certainly not going to draft the operations orders until it was convinced that it could engineer a cable tap.

By the time he was finished, Bradley had won over the room. If the arms control negotiations or political machinations gave these officials pause, they didn't show it. The cable-tap mission was approved, and *Halibut* left for her second trip to Okhotsk on August 4, 1972. Two months after the break-in at Democratic Party headquarters at the Watergate complex, *Halibut* was on her way to perform the ultimate wiretapping exercise for an administration that was about to be crushed under its own tapes and covert operations.

This time McNish decided to brief his men about their true mission and the risks they would encounter. He called them into the crew's mess, one-third of the men at a time. Characteristically solemn, his grin a tight wire across his face, he stood against the bulkhead and told them where they were going, told them about the cable, told them about the tap. Then McNish told his men something else: he told them about black boxes strategically placed at bow, stern, and midship. They were filled with explosives, and they were wired for self-destruct. The boxes were not carried by regular attack subs, but on *Halibut* every torpedoman's mate had been trained to crimp the explosive caps attached to fuses to ready the demolition boxes for detonation. Should *Halibut* become trapped in Okhotsk, McNish told his men, she would not be boarded, and her crew would not be taken alive.

This briefing was, presumably, at odds with general Navy security rules. Most of the crew had no "need to know" where they were going or why. But McNish was asking his crew to go out for six months and take a risk unmatched in peacetime. Need or not, his men had a right to know.

On the way to the place her men were now calling "Oshkosh," *Halibut* was stranded—her clutch blew, sending the shaft to her screws spinning uncontrollably. A *Halibut* newcomer devised a jury-rig involving a series of braces and a hydraulic jack attached to the motor. The fix held.

The men were by now affectionately referring to their usually ailing, most of the time moving, underwater nuclear-powered habitat as the "Bat Boat." The moniker stuck when somebody noticed that the huge bump created by the Bat Cave hangar made the sub look like a giant rendering of Bruce Wayne's comic-book super car.

Back in Okhotsk, *Halibut* found the cable easily. McNish gave the order, and the two huge anchors descended from bow and stern. The divers climbed out of the DSRV lockout. In a matter of hours, spooks were listening to voices coming from the cable.

"Get in here, you have to hear this," one of the spooks called to some of the chiefs.

As he listened, one chief's eyes opened wide. He understood "nyet" Russian, but that didn't seem to matter.

"Jeeesus, this is great!" the chief said, shaking his head. "Jeeesus!" Then he began to laugh, a deep-throated, gut-shaking laugh built at once of pure bravado and the realization that they could all be caught listening to a conversation they were never meant to hear. With an adolescent conspirator's sense of occasion, the chief took off his headphones and slipped them to the next man in line.

A fortunate few were these chiefs, these men on the inside track who had the good luck to be pals with the spooks. One after another, they took their turns meeting the enemy they had tracked, pointed weapons at, harangued, and forsaken their families for. They were taking part in history. They were meeting the Soviets ear to ear, with one side deaf to the transaction.

None of this, of course, concerned the two Soviets yammering happily away on the telephone in unscrambled, uncoded Russian. They had no idea that 3,850 tons of steel and more than 120 men had conspired together to listen in to their conversation, or that soon their words would be weighted with layers of classification and given points for intelligence value in Washington.

A celebration was in order, and the divers provided one. Plucking a giant spider crab from the seafloor, they sent it into *Halibut* through the DSRV lockout. One of the chiefs grabbed hold of a spindly leg, then a huge body. Someone else found a platter, a big one, the biggest one on the boat. It wasn't big enough. With legs dangling, its brownish-gray body hanging off the steel plate, the crab moved slowly as it was paraded through the engine room toward a massive pot of boiling water on its way to becoming the only casualty of the mission.

McNish kept *Halibut* hovering over the line for at least a week. Then *Halibut* made her way out of Okhotsk, leaving the tap planted and the internal recorders running. The submarine would come back to pick the recordings up in about a month. For now, the men were going to Guam. They would stay there long enough to let the tapes fill some more and long enough to patch whatever had broken on their Bat Boat.

It was a routine port stop, at least until their final night. The officers, the enlisted men, the chiefs, most everybody who was not on watch went out drinking. Then talk among the chiefs in the noncommissioned officers' club turned to the cable tap.

No one remembers who was the first to blurt out what was probably on most everyone's mind, but somebody, whether moved by fear or made courageous by beer, cracked the veneer and asked the question: Had they crossed a crucial line? This wasn't like going up against another sub or a ship and watching from afar. This was eavesdropping. What the hell were they doing crawling into the Soviet Union's backyard and tapping a military cable in peacetime? Why were they risking their lives for a mission they were all sure the United States would never acknowledge? Why were they riding a boat with a captain who had made clear that his hand was on the self-destruct button? Why were they riding a boat that could disappear without a word to their families of how or why?

Once it began, there was no stopping it. Fear, anger, concern, poured across the table. This had been building from the first moment the spooks pulled the chiefs into the radio shack and handed them the headphones. Listening to those words they didn't understand coming from a tap they weren't supposed to have planted didn't seem funny anymore. What once struck them as exciting and daring now seemed just plain illegal and dangerous.

Few of the men suffered qualms of morality or politics. As far as they were concerned, détente and diplomacy were public shows put on by both sides to hide true intentions. Still, what they were doing, the men told themselves, could be construed as an act of war. Worse, what they were doing could start the war they feared most.

For perhaps the first time since they had joined the submarine service and faced the power of the oceans and the threat of Soviet depth charges and torpedoes, some of these men were suddenly, deeply certain that what they were doing could kill them.

Then one man said it, said that they ought to tell the old man to stuff it, that they ought to tell him they didn't want to go back. Then others said the same thing in different ways.

More beers were ordered and downed. Then together, they made their way to the dock. Together, they stood in front of their submarine. Then, one by one, they climbed down the hatch, realizing that they weren't going to go tell McNish to stuff it after all. They were going to their bunks or their posts, and they were going back out to the Sea of Okhotsk.

Soon everyone was on board, except Auxiliarymen's Chief John White. He stood on the pier and announced that he was not going down the hatch. As far as he was concerned, the submarine service was a volunteer service, and he was devolunteering.

Nobody expected this. White had served more than nineteen years. He was the kind of man who always worked harder than his crew, the kind who rewarded their hard work by sending them out on the town on his tab. Maybe it was the beer talking, only White didn't seem drunk enough to throw away his career when he was only one year away from a full pension.

Still, something had made White decide to do just that, something that he refused to talk about, that day on the pier or since. In the end, he would say only that he wasn't reacting to the mission or to the self-destruct charges on board; that it was all "more personal than that." Whatever his reason, *Halibut* pulled from port without him. White was flown back from Guam to California, where he was given an honorable discharge with a normal twenty-year pension.

For the rest of the trip, it was White the chiefs talked about. Soon they were back in the spook shack listening to the Soviets. This time they even understood a little of what they heard, as one Soviet sailor used the telephone line to practice wooing his girlfriend in English. The chiefs listened and laughed, but the joy of conspiracy had left the boat with John White.

This was to be the final leg of their trip. Their orders were to collect every last bit of information they could, then leave behind the tap to silently record the Soviets through the months that would pass before *Halibut* could again make the long trip back to Okhotsk. They hovered over the cable for a week, maybe more, long enough for even White's dramatic exit to become blurred into the general monotony of watch, meals, poker, sleep, watch, meals, poker, sleep. By now, the sub had been out for nearly five months, and most of the men just wanted to start their crawl home.

Then, abruptly, their routine was broken. A storm above began boiling beneath the surface. The divers were trapped outside, unable to climb back into the DSRV chamber as *Halibut* strained against her anchors one moment and slammed into the seafloor the next. All the men could do was try to keep a safe distance and watch.

There was no way the officers and crew manning the diving planes could keep *Halibut* level. The gauge measuring anchor tension moved from 10,000 pounds to 50,000 pounds to zero to 20,000 pounds to 50,000 pounds and back to zero again. An hour passed, then another. Then there was a loud crunch. Both steel anchors snapped at once, broke so easily that they could have been rubber bands.

Outside, the divers watched as *Halibut* began to drift upward. The men were still linked to the submarine through their air hoses. They knew that they would die if *Halibut* pulled them up before they could decompress. If they cut themselves loose, they would suffocate. Inside, the officer of the deck was well aware of the danger when he shouted a desperate order: "Flood it!"

He said it a second time. Valves were rolled wide open, and *Halibut* began to take in tons of water, filling her ballast tanks in a matter of seconds. Belly first, she crashed into the sand. The divers scrambled into the DSRV chamber.

The horrendous ride was over. But there was no guarantee the submarine would ever be able to break free of the muddy sand. Rocks scraped against and past the hull, an ongoing crunch, until the men on board were certain the barrage would wreck their boat, that they would never leave Okhotsk.

"Christ, we're here forever," one mechanic said through gritted teeth.

"Hell, we weren't supposed to be here in the first place," another man muttered.

Halibut sat, one day leading into another. The storm passed, but McNish wouldn't try to raise the boat until he had milked the cable for everything he could record. He and his crew were going to go home with their tapes full, if they went home at all.

Finally, McNish gave the word, it was time to leave, it was time to see if McNish's desperate order to throw *Halibut* belly down into the sand had saved the mission, or killed them all. *Halibut* couldn't just power up and drive out—submarines were designed to be free floating, to draw in water for crucial cooling systems from sea-water intake valves that were now pressed down by a submarine's weight in the sand. Tensely, at McNish's word, the men blew a bit of ballast. It wasn't enough. *Halibut* was mired, and would need a full emergency blow to get out. But in water just 400 feet deep, she might end up blowing herself to the surface and to exposure.

The crew decided to try to engineer an emergency blow to free their sub, and then to almost instantly take on enough water to remain submerged—sort of like trying to exhale and inhale water nearly at the same time—to leave their sub bobbing mid-depth. The men also knew they had to get it right the first time. *Halibut* had enough compressed air to attempt the move only once. They would be freed, or they would be stuck and there would be no argument either way.

Halibut was freed.

She had an entirely uneventful trip across the Pacific. The response to her return, however, was anything but uneventful. Bradley got the word from the NSA almost immediately. The tap had recorded as many as twenty lines at once. The NSA had been able to separate all of them electronically. *Halibut* had hit the mother lode. There were conversations between Soviet field commanders covering operational tactics and plans and maintenance problems, including defects that could cause missile submarines—like the Yankees, which were now beginning to patrol in the Pacific—to make noises that might help U.S. submarines in their efforts to track the enemy. Logistical business was conducted through the line, reports that ships couldn't get under way for lack of spare parts. There was also other high-level reporting of command and control, decisions made about when and if patrols would get under way, and which submarines would be sent to lurk off of U.S. shores.

There were discussions of personnel problems, training problems, requests for more men, complaints when those men failed to arrive at Petropavlovsk. Then there were the intangibles: the dreaded political officers on Soviet submarines revealing their own private views about party leaders. The Soviet command also allowed young submariners to use the lines, patching their calls through to local stations where the men could wish Mama a happy birthday or ask their sweetheart to wait. All this put a human face on the massive enemy across the ocean.

This second effort to tap the cable confirmed one disappointment. There seemed to be little if any information about missile tests running through the line—Bradley had had great hopes that there would be information about the success of splashdowns of land- and sea-based intercontinental ballistic missiles. But overall, the tap was an intelligence gold mine.

Nevertheless, there would have to be a few changes. Bell Laboratories was asked to find a way to program the next tap pod so that it could home in on what were deemed the most crucial lines, and so the recorders could turn on and shut off to conserve tape. The idea was to program the tap for prime time, although at this stage no one at the NSA was really sure what constituted prime time, any more than they knew for certain which lines were best.

Bradley's office also had to let Rickover in on the program, at least in a limited way, despite his rancor toward the boat and her previous commander. Bradley needed Rickover's permission to make an important structural change. The captain didn't want to risk another incident like the one that had almost killed *Halibut*'s divers. She was going to get a pair of sleighlike feet. From now on, she would not anchor over the tap site. She'd be equipped to sit on the bottom when she went back to Okhotsk again in 1974 and 1975.

The details of *Halibut*'s mechanics didn't interest the greater intelligence community, but the recordings did. The Navy had pulled the ultimate in one-upmanship. No human agent or standard spy boat could have collected the wealth of information that *Halibut* brought home.

The NSA bestowed a code name on what was now an ongoing operation: "Ivy Bells." Bradley would plan more of these missions, and other submarines would be refitted to follow *Halibut*'s path to Okhotsk.

But Bradley would never know firsthand what his efforts had wrought. The NSA would give Naval Intelligence detailed summaries of the take, but unlike *Halibut*'s chiefs, he would never hear a single minute of the tapes. The NSA decided that Bradley, who had imagined the cable, envisioned the signs pointing it out, and labored to get funding and clearances for the mission, hadn't earned this bit of currency. Bradley, it was deemed, simply had no need to listen, no need to know.

In 1900, the Navy purchased its first submarine, the USS *Holland*. She could carry six men.

Almost one hundred years later, the Navy floated a monolith, the USS *Seawolf* (*SSN-21*), the largest attack sub ever built.

The last picture of *Cochino* was taken as she was leaving England in 1949 for the first U.S. submarine spy mission in the Barents Sea. *Cochino*'s commander Rafael Benitez had to speak the worst words any captain could utter: "Abandoning ship."

Tusk traveled with *Cochino* and saved most of her men. Seven men were washed off *Tusk* and were lost during the rescue operation.

Cochino's men survived explosions, poisonous gas and stormy seas. Refugees from submariners' hell, they gathered in Norway before leaving for home on board *Tusk*.

Red Austin may have avoided the group photo, but he penned *Cochino*'s epitaph on the back. He joined the Navy at nineteen looking for action and became a spy on *Cochino* because he had to have something "spooky" to do.

TROMSÖE, NORWAY

How did I miss getting in the picture of the survivors? It was feared the Russian might somehow have recognized me and thus proven that the Cochino was not on a "routine mission" but was in reality on a spy mission.

J. M. Austin

Only about 1/2 the crew here anyway

Gudgeon and diesel boats like her drove the spy program until the Soviets proved beyond any doubt that diesel boats could be too vulnerable.

With the undying belief that nuclear power should and could move submarines, Admiral Hyman Rickover changed the sub force, the Navy, and the course of the cold war.

Nautilus was the first U.S. nuclear powered submarine and the first sub ever to travel submerged to the North Pole.

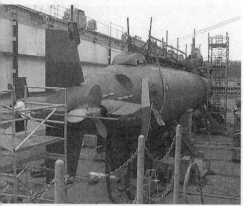

If the president could have Air Force One, then Rickover would have NR-1, the only mini-submarine powered by a nuclear reactor.

John Craven dreamed fantastic dreams of deep ocean exploration and a new kind of warfare. Here he stands with his wife, Dorothy, his son David, and Secretary of the Navy John H. Chafee (far right).

Even before the Navy sent a submersible to photograph the undersea wreckage of *Thresher*, her loss inspired the Navy to declare a new era of sub safe programs. What emerged, however, was modeled more after James Bond than Jacques Cousteau.

Halibut had a mammoth shark's mouth hatch that screamed flood to most submariners. It screamed potential to Craven.

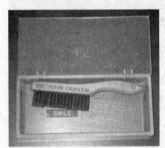

As he pushed Westinghouse engineers to build camera-toting "fish" that could withstand punishing ocean pressures and find sunken Soviet hardware, Craven loved to announce a daily wire-brushing. One day the engineers answered in kind.

Commander C. Edward Moore brought *Halibut* out to sea, found a Soviet submarine buried in the deep, and returned to stand before Admiral John Hyland (left) to receive the highest award possible for any sub: the Presidential Unit Citation.

Scorpion was outside of Naples when a photographer shot what might be the last picture ever taken of her. She was lost only a few weeks later.

Craven (left), Harry Jackson and project coordinator Robert H. Gautier stood on a floating drydock, while deep below, three men on the *Trieste II* examined and photographed *Scorpion*'s wreckage.

Scorpion's shattered hull offered no conclusive answers—only a lingering mystery. Now, evidence has emerged that *Scorpion* may have been primed for disaster before she ever left port.

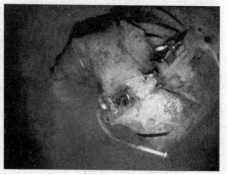

Commander Whitey Mack was just arrogant enough to believe that he could drive *Lapon* on a mission unmatched by any other sub. He believed he could trail a Soviet Yankee missile boat throughout a patrol.

When *Lapon* rode home after her feat, her men pulled down their standard and rose their own flag: Snoopy had given his doghouse up for a submarine and had beaten a new red baron.

Lapon and Mack were immortalized by Tommy Cox, the spook who really wanted to be a country and western star, in his album of submarine greatest hits.

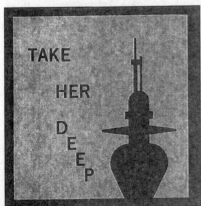

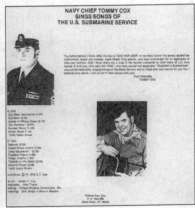

After *Tautog* crashed with a Soviet Echo II sub, *Tautog* fled from the scene, leaving her men and the U.S. government convinced that as many as ninety Soviet submariners were dead.

Commander Buele Balderston had been a rising star, but he knew the underwater crash would also crash his career.

Boris Bagdasaryan was commander of the Echo II that met *Tautog*. He called his sub the *Black Lila*.

To Capt Jim Bradley —
A celebrated submariner who
made his mark in Naval history —
Warner
June 1973   Secretary of Navy

Captain James Bradley reached back to boyhood trips down the Mississippi to find a telephone cable deep beneath the Soviet Sea of Okhotsk. He is congratulated by Secretary of the Navy John Warner (right).

The Navy announced that *Halibut* was carrying the first deep submergence rescue vehicle. But that DSRV was a welded-down fake, a disguised decompression chamber for deep sea divers who would tap Bradley's cable.

Fritz Harlfinger, director of Naval Intelligence, knew if Bradley could convince Henry Kissinger and Alexander Haig to okay *Halibut*'s search for the cable, no other approvals would be necessary.

Crammed full of stolen sub banners and parts—enough contraband to drive naval investigators mad—the Horse and Cow was where men readied to launch some of the most daring operations of the cold war.

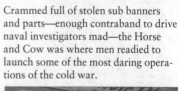

The CIA commissioned the mammoth *Glomar Explorer* to do what key Navy officials believed too difficult and absolutely unnecessary: to reach down and steal an entire Soviet submarine off the ocean floor.

One of the oldest and most broken subs in the fleet, *Seawolf* took over cable tapping operations in Okhotsk. She was nearly moored there forever.

When the Soviets discovered recording devices attached to a cable beneath Okhotsk, there was no mistake who had put them there. Inside one of the 20-foot-long pods were the words: "Property of the United States Government." One tap pod ended up in a museum in Moscow.

The Navy feared the tap's discovery in Okhotsk might signal that the Soviets also knew about an even more daring operation being carried out by *Parche* in another sea.

When Richard Buchanan led *Parche* on a mission that earned her one of her seven Presidential Unit Citations, President Ronald Reagan compared him to John Wayne.

Waldo Lyon's decades-long adventures and study of the Arctic led him early on to ride with Commander William Anderson (right) on the *Nautilus* to the North Pole. More than twenty-five years later, Lyon would still be trying to discover how U.S. subs could fight effectively under the sonar-muddling ice.

The Soviets had also been going up to the Arctic for decades. By the 1980s, it looked as though they had found a way to use the ice to steal a crucial nuclear advantage.

U.S. subs traveled to the Arctic one at a time and in groups almost every year since *Nautilus*, but the frigid waters remained a mystery—the one place where the prey had the distinct advantage over the hunter.

Danielle Petersen-Dixon hugs her aunt Gerry, as they remember Petersen-Dixon's father, Daniel Petersen, a chief petty officer who also died on *Scorpion*.

Susan Nesbitt sits with her husband Bob in Norfolk, Virginia, at the 30th anniversary memorial ceremony for the men who died on *Scorpion*. They mourn her lost brother, Richard Shaffer, petty officer second class on *Scorpion*.

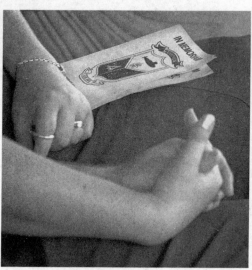

Throughout the United States and in Russia, families are asking, was the secret submarine spy war worth the risks? Was it worth the cost?

THE $500 MILLION
SAND CASTLE

I t was October 22, 1973, and journalist Seymour M. Hersh
was taking notes in a reporter's staccato, partial sentences—
partial secrets that he ingested along with dinner as he sat in
a suburban restaurant with a source whose name he was bound
by ethics and bargain never to reveal.

At the moment, anyone would have expected this thirty-six-
year-old Pulitzer Prize winner to have been entirely embroiled in
Watergate. He was, after all, the top investigative reporter for
the *New York Times,* albeit one who was rumpled and stubborn
and given to bursts of profanity. And he was running a frustrated
second to Bob Woodward and Carl Bernstein of the *Washington
Post* in the race to uncover the story that would make legends of
these unknown, scruffy reporters and felons of their more pol-
ished and powerful targets.

Watergate scoops, however, were not what Hersh had come to this dinner for, and the man he was dining with did not belong to the group that soon would be branded "All the President's Men." This man ran in different company, in the company of spies, perhaps in "The Company," as the CIA was known. He had only recently stepped down from his post as a high-ranking national security official. He was, as Hersh put it, "somebody who sat at the cat-bird's seat for a long time," somebody who "knew everything."

More than that, Hersh would forever refuse to reveal. Indeed, he was taking considerable trouble to meet this man in secret, slipping out of the Washington, D.C., bureau of the *Times* to catch up with him in another city.

Hersh was making this trip because there was a story he wanted almost as much as the epic of a collapsing presidency. He had been getting tips for years about costly wastes and excessive dangers in U.S. intelligence operations, including some of the Navy's most secret submarine spy missions. Now he wanted to shine a light on this pitch-black world that had always been left to operate under a peculiar type of political immunity that could only be imparted by the words "top-secret" and "highly classified."

These phrases had once been read by journalists and lawmakers as signals to back off and stop asking questions. But these days, the Watergate saga was emboldening the press and Congress, encouraging them to be more skeptical, and Hersh was at the forefront of a drive to hold the intelligence community accountable for what it had been doing behind the veil.

Much of what he had been hearing dealt with cost overruns on spy satellites and the risks being taken in undersea spy programs. He also had learned about the Holystone surveillance submarines that were darting into Soviet waters. And just recently, Hersh had started picking up scattered rumors about a CIA operation designed to steal something that the Soviets had lost or discarded at the bottom of an ocean. Three times he had been told that the agency was constructing an enormous barge that could reach down through miles of raging currents, crushing pressures, and unending darkness. He knew the plan only by its code name, "Project Jennifer."

The references were tantalizing, but oblique. None of his sources had been able or willing to tell Hersh just what the CIA was after. One government official had hinted that the agency was seeking pieces of spent ballistic missiles that had been fired in tests from the Tyuratam test center deep inside the Soviet Union into the Pacific, but Hersh didn't trust the information. He feared that the official was either offering up a guess or dangling deliberate misinformation.

Now, however, Hersh was meeting with a man he knew he could trust.

Appetizers were put on the table as new leads passed across. But it wasn't until the meal was ending that Hersh tossed out two words: as if offering up dessert, he repeated the code name that he had been unable to decipher: Project Jennifer.

Hersh waited, for a heartbeat, maybe ten, trying to look nonchalant. Then all at once he began scribbling, catching facts along with concern and skepticism as they poured from the man sitting across the dinner table.

"Russian sub went down in Atlantic," Hersh wrote. "Jennifer is designed to find it. We know where it is." Next came the words that revealed what may have been this source's reason for telling Hersh anything at all. "Don't you think the Russians know why there's a U.S. trawler with exotic gear out there in the middle of the ocean?"

Copying it all down, Hersh knew he now held the heart of what could be one of the most exotic undertakings of the cold war, an operation known to perhaps only a few dozen people in the government. The source didn't say how the CIA had found the submarine, and Hersh didn't realize until much later that his companion had placed the Soviet boat in the wrong ocean. But he had outlined what seemed to Hersh to be the perfect allegory, the perfect way to question what was wrong with U.S. intelligence. Here was a tale of an agency spinning a seemingly impossible dream that might antagonize the Soviets just as détente was starting to ease the worst of the cold war tensions. In fact, that very day the United States and the Soviet Union had jointly issued a call for a ceasefire in the Middle East war that had started on Yom Kippur.

Hersh went back to his other sources, pushing and pleading.

But his efforts still hadn't netted much information. Then, four months after the clandestine dinner, on a Saturday evening late in January 1974, Hersh got a break. He was at a Washington dinner party, one of those affairs where officials hobnob with journalists, both thinly disguising questions and evasions as small talk. This night Hersh was parrying with a newly retired CIA officer when his tendency toward swagger overwhelmed caution.

Smiling wryly, casting his voice with just the right amount of scorn, Hersh asked with the certainty of an insider why anyone would care about retrieving some old submarine from the bottom of the ocean. He made sure that he worked the name *Jennifer* into the sentence. Later, he would admit that he was probably showing off.

The former officer seemed not to react, offering not the slightest sign of annoyance, concern, or recognition. But Hersh had hit a nerve. He must have, because as soon as the party was over, the officer was on the telephone with William E. Colby, who had been director of the CIA for only five months.

The news that Hersh had gotten hold of Project Jennifer hit the CIA with megaton force. Colby knew that Hersh had won his Pulitzer for breaking the story of the My Lai massacre in Vietnam, and the director considered him "a good ferreter-outer." Colby also knew that after six years of planning and preparation, his secret was about to get out.

Contrary to what Hersh's source had said, the huge ship that had been commissioned for the project was not yet out to sea. But it had been completed, built by Howard Hughes's Summa Corporation. Christened the *Glomar Explorer,* she was the length of three football fields, with decks crammed with computer-operated equipment, pulleys, and cranes all designed to send a giant clawed arm diving through nearly 17,000 feet of ocean, down to the bottom where it was supposed to grab hold of the lost Soviet submarine and pull her to the surface. Only a few final tests remained before *Glomar* would be ready to set out on Project Jennifer. Five more months, and the CIA would be able to try its salvage attempt.

The idea had already survived the opposition of the men most responsible for finding the Golf in the first place, Captain James

Bradley, who would be retiring in a month, and John Craven, who was already retired. Bradley and Craven still believed that the late 1950s–era Soviet boat was of little intelligence value and certainly not worth the cost and dubious chance of success involved in trying to pull her out of the ocean. Instead, they had proposed a far simpler and less dangerous plan to recover the Golf's most valuable treasures: develop unmanned submersibles equipped to blow holes in the Golf's hull and grab the missile warheads, communications gear, and decoding machines, just about the only things of any real value on the sub.

The wisdom behind their caution seemed even clearer now. The Soviets barely relied on the Golfs anymore. They were nearly finished building a fleet of thirty-four Yankees, and they were about to introduce the even more lethal Delta missile subs. The first Deltas, already on sea trials, were slated to head out on patrol in 1974—and two to three dozen more were planned. The Deltas carried missiles that could travel 4,200 nautical miles, or nearly six times as far as the antiquated ones sitting in the Golf's wreckage.

Bradley and other Naval Intelligence officials also felt that the sub force was finally starting to get a handle on tracking Soviet subs at sea, and they saw no need for any desperate moves. Two or three Yankees were always in the Atlantic now, and SOSUS had been calibrated well enough to pick them up as they moved in round-robin fashion through patrol zones, known as the "Yankee boxes," southeast of Bermuda and west of the Azores. Indeed, more SOSUS stations were being set up, and U.S. warships were now towing portable sonar arrays to cover areas where SOSUS was deaf. Naval Intelligence also had created "operational intelligence" centers on both coasts and in Europe and Japan, which were correlating all the data coming in on Soviet sub movements and disseminating daily updates. During the Arab-Israeli Yom Kippur War, the United States had managed to keep close tabs on twenty-six Soviet missile and attack subs in the Mediterranean, one U.S. attack sub handing off responsibility to another as they kept constant track of individual Soviet subs in the crowd.

But the CIA's elaborate plan to completely recover the Golf still appealed to Nixon and Kissinger, who was now secretary of

State. They were so firmly behind the decision to grab the entire sub that final approvals were coming in right on schedule. Several top congressional leaders also had been briefed.

It was somewhat remarkable that the secret ever had survived the years it had taken to build the massive *Glomar Explorer*. Now the ship was well hidden in plain sight, shrouded by a cover story the CIA considered perfect: the country's most famous and wealthy eccentric was building *Glomar* to corner the market on manganese nodules, golfball-sized clumps of minerals that sat on the ocean floor. The venture, as promoted, was expensive, and there were far simpler ways to obtain manganese. But nobody questioned that Hughes would take huge risks to control a new market. Nor did anyone seemed surprised about the secrecy surrounding the project. Hughes was a well-known paranoid, and secrecy had marked his huge empires in aviation, oil-drilling, and hotels.

But Hersh had never heard the cover story, had leapfrogged it altogether with one crucial interview. Colby, who was known for a near-legendary calm under pressure, was becoming very nervous. A story in the papers could kill the entire mission before the *Glomar Explorer* ever embarked.

CIA lawyers had, of course, crafted legal briefs outlining why the United States had every right in the world to try to salvage Soviet property in the middle of the ocean. But those briefs—like those crafted to adorn nearly every covert mission—were useful only for public deniability. With or without supporting legal arguments, Colby knew that international law made clear that sunken warships always belonged to the country that had sailed them.

Colby couldn't muzzle Hersh, not legally. But he could cajole. And that's just what he planned to do when he went to visit Hersh at the *Times'* Washington bureau.

Hersh and Colby were a generation and a war apart, and at this time, that was a gap galaxies wide. The fifty-four-year-old Colby had walked into the intelligence services during World War II, an era when journalists and novelists vied to craft the most romantic portraits of the nation's spies, of their daring and panache. Hersh, on the other hand, had been practically thrown out of the Pentagon as an Associated Press reporter during the

Vietnam War for continuously and hostilely questioning the military's line.

Now Colby stood before Hersh, hoping to make a bargain. He had come to believe that the only way to maintain public support for intelligence efforts was by, as he would say, "bringing intelligence out of the shadows." For his part, Hersh thought Colby "essentially honest." He also believed that was probably a bad thing for a CIA director who had to deal with more hard-line agency veterans.

And so the two men sat down to talk. The director wanted Hersh to hold his story, to stop digging, to not even talk about Project Jennifer. Hersh listened to Colby knowing full well that he was far from ready to go to press. Nonetheless, there was an opportunity here: so Hersh said that he expected Watergate to keep him too occupied to go after Project Jennifer, at least for the next several months. After a bit of bluffing that suggested he knew more about Project Jennifer than he did, Hersh redirected the conversation. Hersh wanted to know about CIA ties to Watergate.

Colby happily answered Hersh's questions, and he left the *Times* convinced that he had bought at least two or three months of quiet. Indeed, Hersh was still absorbed in the president's scandal when *Glomar* left port five months later, and the reporter was still writing about Watergate when she hovered over the Soviet submarine that July in a spot in the Pacific about 1,700 miles northwest of Hawaii.

It seemed obvious to Colby that his secret was holding. Over the next weeks, he received reports that the only Soviet ships that passed anywhere near *Glomar* were commercial vessels. Still, many of *Glomar*'s crew members feared the Soviets would figure out what was going on. Most of *Glomar*'s men were roughnecks, recruited from U.S. oil fields, chosen because they could handle *Glomar*'s massive crane and other equipment. None of the men wanted an encounter with the Soviets. The men wanted to get the job done and go home.

New photographs, taken by cameras dangled by *Glomar*, showed that the Golf was still in much the same condition as when *Halibut* had found her six years earlier. The Soviet sub was listing toward starboard. Photos taken through missing and damaged hatches made it clear that there was still one intact nuclear missile. The other two had been damaged when the submarine went down.

Except for a hole blown nearly 10 feet wide just behind the conning tower, probably from the explosion that had sunk her, the Golf appeared to be in one piece. Still, there was a good possibility she was fragile. The Navy had estimated that the Golf had slammed to the ocean bottom at more than 100 knots. That kind of impact could easily have left her broken beneath the steel outer plating. That was one of the key reasons Bradley and Craven had pushed for a more limited recovery effort.

But at that moment, the biggest hurdle was reaching the submarine in the first place. It was a task that one man who recruited *Glomar*'s crew compared to lifting a 25-foot-long steel tube off the ground with a cable lowered from the top of the 110-story World Trade Center, on a pitch-black night haunted by swirling winds.

Computers in the *Glomar*'s control room began flashing information as the giant claw was slowly lowered into the depths. The claw and its steel arm had been nicknamed "Clementine," after the classic miner's lament. Indeed, at least the Soviets believed their boat to be "lost and gone forever."

The arm resembled a huge octopus that would ultimately dangle on a miles-long tether. It had eight grasping claws, three of which supported a huge steel net. The tether itself was being built a piece at a time by *Glomar*'s men, who linked sections of pipe, each 60 feet long, one by one, giant tinker toys, creating an ever-lengthening leash dangling ever lower into the ocean. Later, when it was time to try to raise the submarine, crewmen would hoist the claw and the sub by pulling the pieces of pipe from the ocean, dismantling the tether one section at a time.

It took days to lower Clementine to the bottom, days before the grasping claws were hovering directly over the submarine. Then, when the tether was three miles long, *Glomar*'s men and computers labored to compensate for the swirling current so that they could drape the steel net held by three of the claws over the Golf's conning tower. Finally, when cameras showed one of the grasping claws in contact with the sub, the men tried to maneuver the arm closer so the remaining claws could reach around and grab.

But the men miscalculated, sending Clementine crashing into the seabed. They backed the arm partway up, studying the images sent back to the ship. In the murky, partially lit ocean, the arm looked amazingly intact, as though it could still grab. They decided to send Clementine back for another try.

Again they aimed, and again they sent the steel net falling over the conning tower. This time all five claws were in position. It seemed as though *Glomar* was going to be able to reel in its catch after all.

Six feet a minute. That was how fast the Golf was pulled toward the surface, 5,000 tons of waterlogged steel. *Glomar* began to sink deeper into the water against the pull, and then began bucking under the strain. Conversation among the crew shifted from talk of capture to capsizing.

Nine hours passed, and the Golf was 3,000 feet off the seabed. More time, and the submarine was 5,000 feet off the ocean floor, 2 miles away from the surface. Another minute promised to bring another 6 feet of progress. Instead, it brought the wrenching realization that the Golf would never rise any higher.

With one jerk, three of the grasping claws cracked and fell away. They had probably been damaged by the crash into the ocean floor so many hours ago. Now, there were only two claws and the net left holding the forward section of the Golf. The rest of the submarine was dangling mid-ocean, and within moments proved itself just as fragile as Bradley and Craven had predicted six years earlier. The steel of the Golf began to tear at its seams, until the bulk of the sub ripped free from the small section still in Clementine's grasp and fell back into the depths. Back to the ocean floor went the intact nuclear missile, the codebooks, the decoding machines, the burst transmitters. Everything the CIA most wanted to reclaim.

There were no celebrations as *Glomar* headed home, no sense of victory that she carried back about 10 percent of a Soviet submarine. Most of this portion was nearly useless from an intelligence standpoint.

Glomar was still out at sea on August 8 when a report came over the radio: Richard Nixon had resigned in disgrace. Air Force One flew Nixon back to San Clemente, California, for the last time, and much of the crew of this, what was perhaps the last top-secret mission he had sanctioned, blamed his demise on the "damned media."

Back in Washington, the political storm that had so engulfed Hersh abated with Nixon's departure. Hersh had heard nothing of *Glomar*'s attempt, nor of her failure. Nor was he alerted when the CIA's underwater experts began plotting a second try for the sunken Golf. But with Nixon out of the White House, Hersh was back on the intelligence beat. That December, he published a huge exposé on the front page of the *Times*, charging that the CIA had conducted "a massive illegal domestic intelligence operation," compiling dossiers on ten thousand or more American citizens. CIA operatives, the story said, had been shadowing war protesters and infiltrating antiwar organizations.

The CIA would never fully recover from the charges. Hersh's story set off a wave of public and congressional condemnation and scrutiny. In an effort to keep the inevitable investigations in friendly hands, the new president, Gerald Ford, created a blue ribbon commission to examine Hersh's charges. This time, however, younger members of Congress pushed past the old guard who had always shielded the CIA and insisted that the House and the Senate conduct investigations of their own.

Colby and Hersh were still enmeshed with the fallout from the domestic spying story when Project Jennifer popped back to the surface. It happened on Friday afternoon, February 7, 1975. The early edition of the next day's *Los Angeles Times* hit the streets screaming news of the recovery attempt in a banner headline splayed across page 1: "U.S. Reported After Russian Submarine/Sunken Ship Deal by CIA, Hughes Told."

After holding on to the story for nearly a year, Hersh had been scooped. The *Los Angeles Times* story had mistakes—it said the sunken sub was in the Atlantic—and gave only limited details. Still, as far as Hersh was concerned, the story was out, and he saw no reason not to step in and finally publish a full account. Colby was just as determined to stop him.

For Colby, the stakes were still huge. Unknown to Hersh,

Project Jennifer was far from over. The CIA was moving ahead with plans for a second recovery attempt. After the first awful failure, CIA technical experts had convinced Colby that the *Glomar Explorer* could still reach down and steal crucial pieces of the Golf. The Hughes ship was already being refitted and repaired, and the second try was scheduled for that summer. To Colby, it seemed as if he were right back where he had started with Hersh a year earlier.

Colby believed that if the matter died quickly, the Soviets might miss the *Los Angeles Times* story altogether. But if the article began to get attention, or if Hersh stepped in now with a better rendition of the facts, perhaps with the actual location of the Golf, Colby would have to halt the operation and the agency would have to shoulder another fiasco, one with a huge price tag.

The CIA immediately sent two agents to see the editor of the *Los Angeles Times*. Their message was simple: Jennifer was not over and publicity could make it impossible for the CIA to bring home the big catch. Neither agent said that there had already been one dismal failure. Nor did they specifically say that plans were afoot for a second attempt. But the editor wasn't asking too many questions—he just agreed to bury the *Glomar* story on page 18 in the paper's final editions and promised not to run any follow-ups, at least not for the time being.

Colby then called the *New York Times* publisher and asked him to have Hersh "cool it down a little" on Jennifer. He also returned another call from Hersh, telling him, "You've been first-class about this for a long time."

But the flattery wasn't going to stop Hersh from digging into the story now, and other reporters were jumping on it as well. So Colby crafted a desperate plan, one that was unprecedented in the annals of agency history. He decided to tell dozens of editors and publishers, broadcasters and producers, about Project Jennifer, to give them some details. But his offering carried a price. The editors in turn were being asked to hold the story back. Colby made one last concession: if it looked as though anyone was going to break the embargo, he would call all the others and give them the go-ahead to publish.

He knew full well that keeping Jennifer out of the papers would be about as easy as forcing a lid on a boiling pot. He began describing himself as the center of "the weirdest conspiracy in town."

That's not to say Colby trusted his co-conspirators. The CIA began to monitor some of the reporters who were working on the story. Agents secretly recorded their conversations with journalists, investigated their backgrounds, and rated their performances. There were dozens of secret files. One unidentified West Coast reporter—code-named E-14—was deemed a "journalistic prostitute" and "a heavy drinker."

But above all others, Colby and crew were watching Hersh. They tracked who he talked to on a trip to the West Coast, helped by the fact that many of the people he tried to interview reported straight back to Colby. Among the people Hersh contacted was John Craven, who was now teaching at the University of Hawaii. Although Craven's dreams of building a fleet of small deep-submergence search vehicles had been swamped by the enormous cost of the *Glomar Explorer,* he wasn't about to cough up the secret. "Project what?" Craven answered when Hersh told him what he was chasing.

Still, Craven agreed to meet Hersh a week later at the ornate Cosmos Club in Washington, D.C. The undersecretary of the Navy urged Craven to try to find out who Hersh's sources were, but by the time they got together, fencing and blustering over cocktails, neither man gave up much. It was clear that Hersh had the story in hand whether Craven gave him any help or not.

Finally, on March 18, syndicated investigative columnist Jack Anderson declared an end to the intrigue and prepared to air the story during his show on the Mutual Radio Network. Colby rushed in, but Anderson refused to reconsider.

"I don't think the government has a right to cover up a boondoggle," he said later. "I have withheld other stories at the behest of the CIA, but this was simply a cover-up of a $350 million failure—$350 million literally went down into the ocean." (Government officials later put the cost at more than $500 million.)

The story was out, and Hersh finally got to publish his much-fuller account of Project Jennifer in the next day's *New York Times.* It ran with a five-column, three-line headline: "C.I.A. Salvage Ship Brought Up Part of Soviet Sub Lost in 1968, Failed to Raise Atom Missiles." The banner treatment of the word

Failed was enough to make Colby cringe, and the story's lead probably didn't make him feel any better: "The Central Intelligence Agency financed the construction of a multi-million-dollar deep-sea salvage vessel and used it in an unsuccessful effort last summer to recover hydrogen-warhead missiles and codes from a sunken Soviet submarine in the Pacific Ocean, according to high Government officials." Hersh went on to note that the CIA recovered only an insignificant forward chunk of the Golf, and he summed up the assessment of unnamed critics, saying that the possibility of retrieving "outmoded code books and outmoded missiles did not justify either the high cost of the operation or its potential for jeopardizing the United States–Soviet détente."

Overall, the story was a picture of waste, not heroics, and one that some naval officers quietly applauded. The CIA had, after all, been trying to swim in their waters, had stolen their prized find, and had sunk hundreds of millions of dollars in the process. Project Jennifer was a bust, and in the Navy's eyes, it was also a downright foolish mission to begin with.

Hersh mistakenly wrote that as many as seventy bodies had been recovered in the wreckage, when only six were recovered. But he did also echo one of the points that Colby had been most intent on making, that the CIA had held a burial service for the Soviet dead and videotaped it in case the Soviet Union ever found out about the recovery attempt and demanded information.

Colby himself had stopped talking altogether, rationalizing his belated silence as the only way to prevent the Soviets from being forced into a public reaction. He made that point at a visit to the White House. Toting a copy of Nikita Khrushchev's *Memoirs,* he showed President Ford where Khrushchev wrote that he had been forced to feign public outrage and cancel a summit meeting in 1960 when Eisenhower openly admitted that the U-2s flying over the Soviet Union were spy planes and not simply weather planes blown off course.

Not wanting to repeat Eisenhower's "error," the Ford administration met all further queries about *Glomar* with a strict "no comment." That was exactly what the Soviets wanted. They began sending frantic back-channel messages through any contacts they had, begging for U.S. silence—anything to keep the story from Soviet citizens who were still in the dark.* One Soviet naval attaché approached a U.S. Navy captain at a party and offered a deal: if the U.S. didn't raise the issue again publicly, the Soviets wouldn't either. Kissinger was having similar conversations as he quietly arranged damage control, among other things promising Soviet Ambassador Anatoly Dobrynin that the CIA would drop its plans for a second recovery attempt. Kissinger also gave Dobrynin the names of three young submariners

---

*The Soviets had good reason to want the story quashed. Losing a sub and failing to find it was bad enough. It was even worse that the Americans had found it and tried to wrench it from the ocean, and worse still that the best Soviet intelligence officers had read about that in American newspapers. But making the whole matter even more humiliating was the fact that the Soviets had been forewarned about Project Jennifer—and ignored the warning. When *Glomar* went out on sea trials in early 1974, Anatoliy Shtyrov, a young Soviet officer, had tried to warn his boss, Admiral N. Smirnov, commander and chief of the Pacific Fleet. As far as Shtyrov could tell, the lost Soviet submarine was the only item of value in the region where *Glomar Explorer* was sighted. By then, the Soviets had mapped out a general area where they believed their sub was lost.

Despite Colby's intelligence that no hostile vessels had come near *Glomar*, Smirnov had responded instantly. He sent a high-speed surveillance ship to the area. It got there months too soon, months before the actual recovery attempt. The surveillance crew reported back to Moscow only that they saw a U.S. ship of "incomprehensible design the size of a soccer field" with "trusses resembling oil derricks" keeping station in the area. Three days later, *Glomar* left for the Hawaiian Islands and the surveillance ship headed for home.

When *Glomar* returned to the site on another test run in March 1974, Shtyrov convinced his superiors to send out another ship. But this time, the admirals refused to risk one of their best-equipped ships to the storm-racked winter waters of the northern Pacific and agreed only to send a hydrographic expedition ship that was already out at sea. That ship's commander decided *Glomar* was on a quest for oil and he soon left the scene. An old tug-boat took over surveillance, but stayed only ten days. When *Glomar* finally began the recovery attempt in July, Shtyrov again begged for a surveillance ship. By now, however, he had lost his audience. Besides, his boss just didn't believe the Americans had the technology to go after a sunken sub. Smirnov refused to suffer the subject again, deciding he had no extra ships. Shtyrov, trying to go over his commander's head, was rebuffed with one line: "I direct your attention to the more qualitative performance of scheduled tasks."

Shtyrov never knew that his boss had crucial corroborating evidence sitting in his office. A note had been passed beneath the door of the Soviet embassy in Washington. It read: "Certain special services are taking steps to raise the Soviet submarine which sank in the Pacific." It was signed, "A well-wisher." The embassy sent a coded copy of the note to Moscow, where officials forwarded it to none other than Admiral Smirnov, who stashed it unheeded in his safe.

The story remained safe until the Soviet newspaper *Izvestia* published an account on July 6, 1992.

whose metal dog tags had been recovered amid parts of the six bodies in the salvage attempt.

With that, the Soviets seemed to let the matter drop, and in the end Colby's silence left so much mystery surrounding Project Jennifer that myth and reality blurred. The U.S. government had given the Soviets more detailed information than it gave the American public, leaving the press to fill the gap with wildly inaccurate accounts of *Glomar*'s expedition.

Nearly every newspaper and magazine reported that the United States had recovered the forward third of the 300-foot-long sub. But former Navy officials say that only a 38-foot piece was brought to the surface. Among the initial newspaper accounts, there was also confusion about what type of submarine had been lost. The CIA and other government sources had been unwilling to admit that the target of the whole venture was an antiquated diesel boat. The CIA also clearly leaked misinformation about the Golf's location, telling reporters that the operation had taken place 750 miles northwest of Hawaii when it was really about 1,700 miles away. This probably was done in an effort to throw the Soviets off track.

Ultimately, it seems the agency even convinced some reporters that Project Jennifer had been at least moderately successful, at least judging from some later articles.

Still, the episode created a huge debate among journalists over whether Colby's efforts to quash the story marked one of those moments when the phrase "national security" was used not to save national secrets, but national embarrassment. If anything, Colby's gambit left most journalists increasingly skeptical about acquiescing to requests by intelligence officials to hold back on such stories. Indeed, most reporters wrote that Project Jennifer was a huge failure and that the CIA had gone to great lengths to hide that.

Had the press known the full truth, it would have lambasted the CIA even more. In recent interviews with former top Navy officials, it has become clear that the CIA got away with its most glaring omission of all: the fact that Colby's much-touted plan for a second recovery attempt had been ludicrous from its inception.

In late 1974, several months before Colby's scramble to save the *Glomar* secret for a second try, the Navy had sent the USS

Seawolf back to the Golf's grave site. *Seawolf* had just been converted to join *Halibut* as a second "special projects" submarine. Using electronic "fish" to carry cameras down to the lost sub, *Seawolf* had collected photographs that showed the Golf had shattered after *Glomar* dropped it and lay in tiny unidentifiable pieces, a vast mosaic decorating the sand.

"It dissolved just like that, like an Alka-Seltzer in water," one former high-ranking naval officer says. "It spread all over acres on the ocean floor." Said another former Navy official: "It shattered. The judgment was made that there was no possibility to recover anything more."

These men say that there was almost no chance of finding relatively small items like warheads, code machines, and antennas. And the officers were amazed that the CIA didn't seem to recognize that. Among the Navy men who stood out as critics of the second recovery effort were Captain Bradley, who, though retired, was a consultant to NURO, and Rear Admiral Bobby Ray Inman, who had become the director of Naval Intelligence in September 1974.

But the CIA had pushed the project forward nonetheless. The agency's only apparent concession to the Golf's condition was to replace some of *Glomar*'s grasping claws with a huge scoop. The CIA was hoping to blindly sweep up something significant among the broken pieces.

Colby told none of this to the newspaper editors. All he said was that, given a second chance, the CIA could have recovered the submarine, or at least important chunks of the conning tower and missile bay. Later, Colby said that he didn't remember ever examining the *Seawolf* photographs himself and that he was relying instead on the analysis of his technical experts.

"We were all very convinced that if we could get back we could get something," Colby said. "Otherwise, why the hell go for it? It wouldn't have made any sense."

What he may have failed to take into account was that his experts were far from objective. They had spent years on Project Jennifer, had been responsible for its huge cost, and in the end they could easily have been more concerned about their professional lives than the lives of the *Glomar* crewmen. Colby himself knew that the CIA couldn't afford another embarrassment, not when it was suffering politically from other disclosures.

Carl Duckett, the CIA's chief official on the *Glomar* project, has died, leaving his views on the odds of success for the second phase of Project Jennifer a mystery. CIA records on Project Jennifer are still classified. And Duckett's top deputy, Zeke Zelmer, has refused to discuss the matter. Colby died in 1996, but insisted to the end that a second recovery attempt could have been profitable.

But the former Navy officers believe that the CIA officials were desperate to believe their own myth, desperate to believe that victory was still possible and they had not wasted so much money.

Craven's theory is far more blunt. "It was just a big, fat plum that looked juicy," he says. "And they turned loose some guys who as far as the ocean was concerned were a bunch of amateurs."

About that, Hersh agreed with Craven. His already well-honed cynicism sharpened, Hersh began digging into the Navy's regular submarine operations, and in May 1975 he published an account of Holystone, of submarine trailing and surveillance missions taking place in or near Soviet waters.

Hersh also revealed that there had been a number of collisions between U.S. and Soviet subs, that a U.S. spy sub had once grounded briefly in the approaches to Vladivostok harbor and that some White House and CIA officials were questioning whether the flood of U.S. submarines in Soviet waters made sense in the age of détente. After his story appeared, he received a call from a man who had been on *Gato* during her collision with the Soviet Hotel in 1969, and Hersh published an account of that in early July. By this time, Congress was looking into intelligence abuses. The Senate, led by Frank Church, a Democrat from Idaho, was investigating incidents included in a CIA document that catalogued its own abuses—from domestic spying to international assassination attempts. Church had already unnerved the once-proud and untouchable agency, calling it "a rogue elephant."

But the intelligence community was more worried about an investigation in the House, where a New York Democrat, Otis

G. Pike, was leading his own broader investigation, looking at Kissinger, the NSA, the CIA, the FBI, and the Navy. He also was setting out to gauge the value of the Navy's submarine spying efforts—something no other congressman had attempted in the thirty years since the cold war began.

Pike, fifty-three, was a maverick and a jokester, but more important, he was cheap. He always wore old suits in various stages of disrepair, usually serious disrepair. And he was a man who years earlier had speared the Navy for gross overspending in cartoonish depictions of admirals collecting hazard flight pay for the dangers they encountered sitting at their desks. It was Pike's investigating that led to the running jokes about toilet seats and wrenches that cost the military hundreds of dollars. When he took over the House investigation into intelligence activities, the press touted him as the consummate outsider, despite the fact that he was a product of Princeton University and Columbia University School of Law, a longtime member of the House Armed Services Committee, and a Marine war hero.

Pike was now promising that in just six months he would scrutinize cold war spying. For the submarine force, that meant Pike was threatening to poke into trailings, incursions into foreign territorial waters, and collisions. The Navy was worried that he would publicize its most classified missions. After all, he had led the House investigation into the *Pueblo* fiasco, determining that a gross lack of analysis and oversight was responsible for placing the spy ship in harm's way off the coast of North Korea.

Perhaps another congressman would have planned such an ambitious investigation in oak-lined conference rooms or over scotch in one of Washington's private clubs, the kind that don't bother to put the prices on their menus. But Pike planned his investigation sitting in his skivvies over supermarket beer with Aaron B. Donner, his longtime campaign manager, in the small apartment near Capitol Hill that they shared as a Washington, D.C., residence since their families were still living in Long Island. They plotted strategy with the enthusiasm of students plotting their first campus demonstration. True to Pike's character, they decided that he would attack the nation's most powerful intelligence agencies with a cost-benefit analysis.

Pike's congressional committee was backed by a young staff, several of them fresh from the Watergate inquiry. They brought with them a deep distrust for the political establishment, for authority, and especially for anything stamped "secret." These staffers were irreverent. They were brazen. They were Pike's marauders.

They began asking questions: What do the intelligence agencies do? What do they cost taxpayers? How much use do they get out of the massive amount of information they collect? And weren't a lot of their risky and expensive ventures just plain redundant?

One of the most obvious places to start was Project Jennifer, which struck Pike as a massive failure at best, or an all-out boondoggle, a blank check written to the Howard Hughes corporations, perhaps even a political payoff. Had Craven been privy to Pike's hunches, he would have cheered. As Pike began digging, Colby tried the approach that had seemed to work so well with newspaper editors and that seemed to be working with the Senate. He offered up some details, enough, he hoped, to win over his critics. At a Pike hearing on Project Jennifer, Colby and company put on their best cloak and dagger for the occasion, insisting on a closed room for what was arguably the nation's worst-kept secret.

The congressmen were already in session in the Armed Services Committee hearing room when the CIA contingent arrived. First in was a small army of dour young men wearing dark suits and what looked like buttons in their ears—earphones for their walkie-talkies. They swept the room with electronic gear, searching for bugs in corners and under tables and chairs. Pike and the other congressmen watched transfixed by the living theater.

Then a second, smaller contingent of agents came in, carrying big black suitcases, the sort that museums use for transporting priceless figurines. These men also began to scout the room, though none of the congressmen could figure out what the agents were looking for. It was as though two acts had been staged to make the committee feel a sense of occasion. The effect was working.

Finally, in walked Colby and some of his deputies, triggering

Act 3. The cases snapped open, and CIA men began gingerly to lift out large plastic bags, gently placing them on a long table set up before the congressmen. The committee members leaned forward and looked down, peering through the clear plastic at these top-secret items that had been carried here under guard.

A throat might have been cleared here and there, but for the most part the members were silent. Actually, nobody knew quite what to say. The objects laid out so ceremoniously on the table seemed to be nothing more than a collection of metal chunks that looked suspiciously like rusty iron.

The lawmakers examined the chunks, feigning reverence. Despite themselves, they had an overwhelming sense that something momentous was taking place as Colby solemnly announced that they were hefting pieces of a Russian submarine. It was only later that they admitted to one another that they could have been looking at anything, even refuse from a construction site down the street, and the CIA's presentation of charts and ocean diagrams seemed to hold just about as much significance. As for questions of cost and benefit, these Colby deftly evaded with vague explanations that totals were unavailable with most of the funding hidden in other, more mundane budgets. Colby's performance was masterful. By the time the show was over, not a single member of the committee had remembered to raise the question of Howard Hughes.

But the CIA's show left the congressmen with a lingering sense that they had been had. The feeling didn't go away when Colby later tried to impress the committee with a show of secret-agent gear, including what agents called a "micro-bio-inoculator," a device that looked like a gun but shot needles dipped in a drug that attacked the central nervous system. Pike's rebellious staff became outraged by the CIA's antics. If anything, the show put on to justify the *Glomar Explorer* left the staff more determined than ever to dig into a broad spectrum of submarine missions, and Pike's marauders began looking into the issues Hersh had raised in his stories about Holystone and the *Gato* collision.

Word quickly got around the Navy that Pike wasn't playing by the old rules, or any rules—that he was trying to take a hard look at the most secret operations. Some admirals were recommending that the Navy simply stonewall him. But a few submariners, veteran enlisted men, phoned the committee with stories about submarine groundings, falsified patrol reports, and news of another collision in which a Soviet submarine had been struck and was presumed lost.

The disclosures were unprecedented. Nothing in Pike's tenure on the Armed Services Committee had prepared him for any of this. Most members of that committee were told little about submarines, even about the basic surveillance ops. Before Watergate wrecked the old congressional seniority system and elevated some younger firebrands like Pike, the submarine community had been allowed to run past Congress. When a nod was needed, well, there was always a senator or two who could be counted on to push a program through—especially the late Senator Richard B. Russell of Georgia, who single-handedly oversaw most intelligence programs in the 1960s. (Or as Admiral Moorer, who supported the *Glomar* operation as CNO and then as chairman of the Joint Chiefs from 1967 to 1974, put it: "Generally speaking, in the sixties, it was sufficient simply to tell Senator Russell that you were doing it, and no one else, and it never leaked.")

Things got really interesting when somebody phoned with a description of a submarine that could search deep, a submarine able to sit on a seafloor. It wasn't long before Pike's crew heard about the cable taps recording away beneath the Sea of Okhotsk.

The source was one of the Navy's handpicked elite, one of the men of *Halibut,* and he was frightened. He was still in the Navy. He was still bound to secrecy. He was not supposed to be talking to anyone, certainly not a congressman known not only for kicking military tires but for pricing them, scrutinizing them, and complaining loudly and publicly when he found them to be flat. This was, for any submariner, a potentially career-crashing move.

Pike's staffers did what they could to reassure the man. They just asked him to point out what they should explore. The exploration, they promised, would occur through other means. They would confront the Pentagon directly. They saw no reason to haul some low-level guy up before a public committee, no reason to destroy an informant.

And so the submariner talked—of the Bat Cave, of Okhotsk. Then another man from special projects called. In the end, both submariners were actually looking for answers, much as

Halibut's chiefs had been when White refused to get back on the sub in Guam. They wanted to know how invading Soviet waters and planting the telephone tap to end all telephone taps during talk of détente was going to accomplish anything. They wanted to know why they were being asked to sit as targets in a Soviet sea. They wanted to know whether the submarine command had become overzealous and reckless, whether their lives were being risked in patently illegal operations. They were sworn to go in harm's way. This they accepted. But they wanted to know, why these risks, why this mission? They especially wanted to know why they were being sent to a Soviet sea in two of the oldest and loudest submarines in the fleet. By this point in late 1975, *Halibut* had completed her last mission and was going to be taken out of service entirely. *Seawolf*, the boat taking *Halibut*'s place, was turning out to be even more of a clunker.

As Pike's team began to follow up on these concerns, one of his most driven young staffers, Edward Roeder III, was assigned to take the lead. Admiral James L. Holloway III, who was now the chief of Naval Operations, countered with Inman, the director of Naval Intelligence.

Roeder was all of twenty-five years old, a former freelance journalist who was seen by the rest of Pike's staff as demanding and cantankerous and somewhat overzealous in his attempts at gaining information. Other staffers were appalled when he tried to date a secretary at the National Security Agency, hoping to get her to spill secrets over dinner or coffee—a maneuver that turned out to be a complete failure.

Still, Roeder was able to put a very human face on much of the mystery surrounding the high-tech undersea spy war, and even his critics believed he had come up with a shrewd explanation of how the secrets of decades had survived most of those moments when the United States and the Soviet Union caught one another in action. The way Roeder saw it, the United States and the Soviet Union were behaving much like two men in a smoke-filled room endlessly playing cards. Both of them were cheating, but neither was able to accuse the other because that would end the game.

Now Roeder had to figure out how to break through to a world where the U.S. Navy was protecting not only its own methods but its enemy's as well. What Roeder didn't figure on, however, was Bobby Inman. Inman had already decided to shock Pike and his staff with facts.

Inman was ignoring the pointed suggestions inside the Navy that he should remain silent, certain that wouldn't work. Just a couple of years before, he had served as an executive assistant to Holloway when he was the vice chief of Naval Operations. It was Inman's job to monitor Congress and the press. While there were few challenges to the sanctity of naval secrecy in those days, even the Navy had to suffer through budget hearings. He had watched as budgets were slashed after Hollywood-handsome admirals marched into hearings armed with cadres of assistants but few answers. On the other hand, he had also watched programs survive after being represented by overweight, unkempt, and gruff officers facing Congress sans entourages but with information and courtesy.

Now he approached Roeder and the rest of Pike's staff with little of the expected burnish of his brass. He didn't look or speak like any other admiral. Instead, he was plain, skinny, and decked out in horn-rimmed glasses and a uniform with a collar so worn and oversized that the admiral's stars on his shoulders seemed out of place. Pike's staffers saw him as "kind of scary smart." But what surprised them more was that the head of Naval Intelligence seemed willing to cooperate. Inman had decided to head off any criticism or unwanted attention by giving Pike what he wanted, at least some of what he wanted. Inman wanted to hand Pike enough information to swing him around to the Navy's basic point of view: that submarine operations were providing critical information that could be obtained in no other way, and that they were actually saving lots of money by helping the Navy tailor its own construction programs to a well-defined Soviet threat.

With the CNO's blessings, Inman met Roeder with promises to research submarine collisions and groundings. Inman also said that he would look into the cable-tapping. There was a condition, though. Inman wanted guarantees that none of the information would leak. He insisted that the most sensitive documents be held in a safe, a so-called 20-minute safe, one that took that long to burn open with an acetylene torch. Roeder promised to use the safe and promised that only he would have the combination. But when he brought that demand to his bosses on Pike's staff, they told him that no such safe was available. They also quickly determined that Roeder had become a little full of himself. In a grand gesture, perhaps out of honor, perhaps out of self-importance, Roeder quit over the issue, certain that Inman would know he had walked out in the name of national security.

The gesture did impress the admiral, but not enough for him to give up his effort to win over Pike and crew. Instead, Inman simply turned his brand of open and honest charm on Pike and the rest of his staff. They met several times in the committee's inner sanctum, a windowless room that staffers called the "Cone of Silence" in salute to *Get Smart,* the popular comedy series about spies. Actually it was more like a horrible little closet, with barely space for chairs around the 18-inch-wide conference table. Within the room hung a seemingly permanent cloud of stale smoke. Inman ignored his dingy surroundings and just talked. There was, he admitted, too little coordination between submarine operations and the more statesmanlike mission of détente. By offering all this without doublespeak and without excuses, he separated himself from the larger intelligence community and endeared himself to Pike's staff.

As time went on, Inman had his aides provide Pike with a detailed study of submarine mishaps. It revealed that there had been at least nine collisions with hostile vessels in the previous ten years and more than 110 possible detections of U.S. surveillance subs. Inman admitted that some sub captains were fudging patrol reports to hide the risks they took and the moments when they were detected. He had even assigned Naval Intelligence officials to look into incidents when either reports made by the spooks on board or intercepted Soviet communications contradicted U.S. sub captains' official reports. Inman also briefed Pike personally about the cable-tapping operation.

In the end, this frank, skinny intellectual with the crooked smile ensured that he wasn't nearly as attractive a target as the likes of Colby and Kissinger. Pike's marauders moved on, spending much of their time looking into the imperious ways in which Kissinger had run the 40 Committee and conducted foreign policy. But when Pike's report was finished in early 1976, the intel-

ligence community and the Ford administration convinced
Congress to vote to suppress it. A copy was leaked, though, and
the *Village Voice* printed the lengthy report in its entirety. But, as
it turned out, only eight paragraphs were devoted to submarine
spying, and not a word was said about the cable taps. Instead,
general references were made to the basic submarine surveillance
programs now deemed valuable by Pike, and the Navy came in
for only a gentle scolding: "The Navy's own justification of the
program as a 'low risk' venture is inaccurate," Pike's crew wrote.
They went on to say that the committee was troubled by risk
assessments that were "ritualistic and pro forma" and never varied from "low." It also complained that none of the captains of
subs involved in collisions had ever been disciplined.

The public had lost its first real opportunity to assess the value
of the ongoing undersea grab for intelligence. The Navy's spymas-
ters were rolling right along, just as they always had, and within
the submarine ranks it was business, and silence, as usual. All
operations would continue. Holystone surveillance operations
would now be referred to as "Navy Specials," short for Special
Navy Control Program. And Inman and Vice Admiral Robert L.
J. Long, the Navy's top submariner, decided to pour even more
money into cable-tapping. They decided to get Rickover's okay to
finally convert a modern, frontline sub for the work. NURO—the
joint CIA/Navy office—had survived the *Glomar* fiasco, though
the CIA would never again have that kind of day-to-day control
over any of the Navy spy missions. Instead, NURO had become a
funding vehicle for the special projects subs, and Congress quickly
approved the money for the latest refit, though it would take a
couple of years to ready the new boat.

In the meantime, it was up to the poor and nearly broken
Seawolf to carry on with the cable-tapping operation. Although
a few submariners had risked everything to talk to Pike, little
had changed. Nothing was going to stop these missions, even if
they were now to be conducted by a sub that was loud and had
been ill-fated from the start.*

**Seawolf was so noisy that the Navy took to sending a second sub to meet her as
she approached the Sea of Okhotsk. The other boat would make sure no one was
tailing *Seawolf* and create a noisier distraction when needed.

Seawolf had missed her champagne baptism when a congressman's wife missed her aim. This was the same sub that Craven had rejected in the mid-1960s for special projects. She ended up being converted anyway only because Rickover had little use for her, especially after she ran into an undersea mountain in training exercises in 1968. Even after the Navy equipped her with the high-tech deep-sea gear, *Seawolf* was most notable for her 1950s technology. Her barely working reactor was so antiquated that her crew joked that if the Soviets ever captured the sub, it would set their nuclear program back 50 years. Just as memorable was the alarm system that the men were calling "the Bitch in the Box," because it rang with a woman's voice—a 1950s telephone operator actually, who was chosen because someone in the Navy decided that she sounded soothing. She announced fires, floods, and other catastrophes, and as far as *Seawolf*'s crew was concerned, she talked far too much.

Together, *Seawolf*'s mishaps and her missions left her men torn between abject disillusionment and abject pride. One rare diary, kept by a young *Seawolf* crew member, often reads like a catalogue of complaints. He was well aware that it was patently illegal for anyone in the crew to keep an account about the Navy's most secret missions. But despite everything, *Seawolf* was making history, the country's history and his, and he was determined to write it.

He describes successful cable-tapping missions in both 1976 and 1977. Indeed, the diary starts off like a techno-thriller: "JUNE 20, 1976—Somewhere off San Francisco, destination: Russia. No doubt about it though we aren't supposed to know—strange things have happened and stranger things I've seen—that book next to the QM stand—Russian sea coast and charting and piloting showing their buoys . . ."

In some ways *Seawolf* was just like any other sub. Her crewmen played the same virulent game of "pinging" that existed throughout the fleet, as they took delight in attacking one another with inelegant phrases such as "I wouldn't piss in your mouth if your teeth were on fire." And many of the diarist's entries chronicle the boredom and loneliness of life on a sub where the outside world was represented mainly by stockpiles of girlie magazines and "crotch novels" with titles like *Cocksure*

Girls hidden on board. On *Seawolf*, there was a twist: the sub's top-secret camera-toting fish had been dubbed "Happy" and "Linda" after the Happy Hooker and Linda Lovelace, the porn queen.*

By now, even the spooks were fighting boredom. A team of them had come together on *Halibut* and had become the starring troupe on these cable-tapping missions. They called themselves "Arnold's Act V," for their five members: "Head Wheel," "Suzi Clean," "Cold Joint," "One Up," and their director J. P. Arnold. Unlike most of the crew, the cast of Act V knew all the details. They knew where they were and why, how important their mission was, and how dangerous. Even all that blurred through 40 days of 12-hour shifts. Six hours at a time, half the team scanned the cable for the best channels and for repeater signals, those electronic boosts that kept the voice and data clear through the miles of wire. The rest of the spooks spent the first six hours making recordings. Then the men traded seats, and tasks. The switch was designed to offer a break, designed to provide respite as the Russian they couldn't translate, the goblin-garble of encrypted speech and the static noise of even tighter encryption and data transfers, left the spooks ready to babble themselves.

As on *Halibut*, the spooks called the chiefs in to listen when anyone caught a Soviet seaman practicing English on some girl—hearing English on these wires always seemed like an event and a relief. Act V, without authorization and without question, had also declared it the right of each diver to listen to some of the recorded chatter as well. The spooks knew they were breaking the rules, but they decided that these divers were the ones most directly risking their lives, walking 400 feet down in frigid waters and punishing sea pressures, and they had a right to know why.

Monotony for the rest of the crew was interrupted by mechanical breakdowns, made even more dangerous because many of

---

*Happy and Linda were both used for relatively shallow searches, but *Seawolf* was also equipped with two other fish designed for deep-ocean search. There was "Hawkeye," so named by the spooks because it was the fish that found the scatterings of the Golf wreckage in 1974. The other fish was named "Short Time," because it kept shorting out under ocean pressures and never spent much time searching.

those breakdowns were taking place in the middle of Soviet waters. There were fires and reactor scrams. Nuclear technicians were so wearied by their faulty reactor that they were popping speed to keep themselves going. Problems with *Seawolf*'s air-conditioning systems got so bad that, while she was on the tap site, the crew was forced to relive the days of the *Gudgeon*—lighting oxygen-generating candles and then snorkeling to ventilate while they were still in the Soviet Sea of Okhotsk.

Soon after that incident the diarist gave up his crotch novels for *Alive*, a true account of survivors of a plane crash who turned to cannibalism to survive the desperate month when they were lost in the frigid Andes Mountains. He mused about "rum and fresh fruit dreams" as he scribbled, hiding behind the curtain covering his rack, the only place where he had a shadow of privacy. Despite the publicity surrounding the *Glomar* fiasco, despite the congressional hearings, secrecy reigned within the sub force and especially on board *Seawolf*.

So he kept his diary hidden, from his commanders, from most of his crewmates. And in the end, he showed that despite the fires and the reactor scrams, he was just as impressed by his sub's exploits as Pike had been: "Found out what we do—the mission of ship—unbelievable—we are ON THE MOOR—finally—really gotta hand it to the USA—not as dumb as let on to be—the country still has balls."

(1 0)

TRIUMPH AND CRISIS

Richard L. Haver could spin a tale and craft a briefing better than just about anyone in town. He was only thirty-three years old, one of many department heads at Naval Intelligence and a civilian at that, but he was also a prized protégé of Bobby Inman's, the man who had singlehandedly shielded the sub force from its one close encounter with congressional criticism. Haver had that same ability to mesmerize.

Admiral Stansfield Turner, the director of the CIA, knew that. So did Harold Brown, the secretary of Defense. That's why they had brought Haver with them on this spring day in 1978 to brief President Jimmy Carter in the White House Situation Room.

Turner made the introductions, while Haver looked around at the men assembled: the president, Secretary of State Cyrus Vance, and White House Chief of Staff Hamilton Jordan. Vice President Walter Mondale was there as well, though he had just gotten back from a twelve-day trip to Southeast Asia and seemed to be nodding off. Haver wasn't worried.

He knew it was Carter's attention he had to hold and that Carter was a former nuclear engineer and a Rickover acolyte. He had been chosen for the nuclear submarine program in the early 1950s, but before the first nukes ever went out to sea, his father died and he was called home to run the family peanut farm. Still, Carter had never stopped viewing Rickover as a mentor. Indeed, the title of his campaign biography, *Why Not the Best?*, was taken from a phrase that Rickover used to grill him and other officers. As for Haver, he had been an intelligence officer, a spook who went out on Navy air reconnaissance flights during the Vietnam War. That's how he met Inman, who had overseen some of the Navy's wartime intelligence efforts. When Haver decided to resign his commission, it was Inman who had helped persuade him to become a civilian intelligence analyst rather than go to law school.

What Haver wanted to do now was bring Carter up to date on the Soviet nuclear threat and also lay the groundwork to win Carter's okay to begin planning a mission more daring than any that had been tried before. Naval Intelligence had learned that the Soviets were taking advantage of the 4,200-mile range of their new Delta ballistic missile subs, driving them out of reach of U.S. SOSUS nets below the Azores in the South Atlantic or holding the subs back in the Barents Sea. The subs in the Barents were being protected by surface ships and attack submarines— and they were just a shot across the Arctic from Washington, D.C., or any other target within an arc drawn from about South Carolina through Oklahoma to Oregon.

Haver assured Carter that intelligence networks and spy subs were working hard at collecting and analyzing the new information. Within Naval Intelligence, however, there was a raging debate about whether the Soviets' decision to hold missile subs back in the Barents marked a true change in strategy or a momentary flux. Haver was among those who believed it likely that the Soviets were positioning to take a crucial nuclear edge away from the United States.

When the Yankee subs were the best the Soviet Union had, nearly every one sent within range of the United States had been in the line of fire of U.S. subs shadowing behind. If war had broken out, those subs could have sunk the Soviet boomers before they ever fired. Then, if both sides ever launched their land-based ICBMs, only the United States would have been left with a second-strike capability tucked away in the oceans. This was the edge the Navy had been preparing for ever since Whitey Mack first rode bronc on the *Lapon*. But the strategy relied on three things: that Soviet subs remained relatively noisy; that they never realized how often they were being followed; and that they continued to patrol in open seas where they could be trailed in the first place.

But when the Deltas were moved into the Barents, Haver and others started to seriously question some fundamental assumptions behind U.S. strategy. After all, practically since the cold war began, American planners had believed that the Soviet Navy was bent on challenging the United States on the high seas, that in a war Soviet attack subs would mainly try to sink U.S. ships resupplying Europe, just as the Germans had done in World War II. Now it seemed the Soviets might be doing a strategic about-face and, in the process, knocking over a cornerstone of U.S. nuclear strategy.

After giving a sense of these concerns, Haver reminded the president that the Navy had one other extraordinary way to keep tabs on the Soviets—the critical cable-tapping operation in the Sea of Okhotsk that Carter himself had approved just the year before. Then Haver went on to describe what Naval Intelligence was considering as a next, bold step.

What if the United States could tap cables in the Atlantic arena? What if a submarine could be sent to put a tap right in the Barents Sea, the very location of the Soviets' missile-sub bastions?

Halibut never could have done that, and neither could *Seawolf*. Both subs had been castoffs when they were given to the tapping operation, too old and too loud to sneak into these active waters. (As this briefing took place, *Seawolf* was out in the Pacific searching for missile fragments, looking for a chance to use a special retrieving claw that had been added to one of her camera-toting fish.) But the Navy finally had a boat that could do the job, a new sub just converted to hold deep-sea divers and the gear that could let spooks listen in on a new tap. She was the USS

Parche (SSN-683), the sub that Inman and Vice Admiral Bob Long had pushed for after the Pike inquiry. She was a four-year-old Sturgeon attack sub, and she was quieter, faster, and much newer than any boat that had been given over to "special projects" before.* *Parche* had new eavesdropping equipment that could support a modernized tap pod with far more recording capacity, and she was quiet enough to sneak right beneath the Soviets' powerful Northern Fleet to plant tap pods in the Barents.

As Haver talked, what had begun as a typical briefing turned into a dialogue, Navy vet to Navy vet. Carter began leaning so far forward in his chair that some of the men in the room began to wonder whether the president would wind up in Haver's lap. It was certainly clear that Carter was intrigued, and for now that was enough. Haver and his bosses weren't looking for formal approvals for the mission, not yet. They just needed to know that Carter was interested, that they could keep planning.

Getting this kind of early read was a good tactic in dealing with any president, but in Carter's case there was even more reason to move slowly, to sound him out. Despite his Navy background, Carter had been looking for ways to trim defense programs. He had spoken out against the new weapons systems being pushed by the Pentagon, and he was so forceful about the need to make peace with the Soviets that some in the military thought he was soft on communism.

Everyone in the room knew that sending *Parche* on such a mission, into crowded waters, carried far greater risk of detection and of antagonizing the Soviets than anything tried in the desolate Okhotsk. *Parche* would have to elude the dozens of Soviet warships and submarines that were constantly moving about the Barents. Not only that, but because any cable in the area probably ran alongshore, a geographical necessity, *Parche*

Parche was one of the last nine Sturgeon-class subs ever built—all of them ten feet longer than their predecessors and filled with all manner of extra eavesdropping gear. This small group of subs is considered the best the Navy ever put to sea for any espionage operation. Among these legendary surveillance boats were the USS *Archerfish* (SSN-678), the USS *William H. Bates* (SSN-680), and the USS *Batfish* (SSN-681). *Parche* did cable-tapping, but the others won awards for picking up crucial intelligence through more usual means—by creeping near the Soviet coast with antennas and periscopes breaking the waves.

would almost certainly have to plant the pod inside the Soviet's 12-mile territorial limit, and probably within the 3-mile limit recognized internationally.

But Haver had invoked Carter's fascination more than his caution. Turner was nothing less than ecstatic when the president finally thanked them all for the briefing and asked to be kept informed. It seemed that Haver had not only sold Carter on a new mission but had probably guaranteed the success of the cable-tapping program for the next decade.

Still, as jubilant as everyone felt, there was one nagging concern that Haver hadn't mentioned to Carter. Haver couldn't help but feel that there was something eerie about the Soviets' shift in strategy and other recent moves. It was almost as if the Soviets had found their own way to read the Americans' minds. Only there wasn't enough evidence to be certain, no clear patterns, just glimmers within a series of curious changes in the way the Soviets were operating.

First, the Soviets were increasingly sending attack subs to escort the Yankees and Deltas still heading for the Atlantic. Along the way, the attack boats were circling the boomers as if looking for NATO subs that might be trying to trail. Second, Soviet subs seemed to be waiting to monitor U.S. naval exercises even before U.S. ships and subs arrived on site. A few times, Soviet subs had shown up in waters where U.S. exercises had been scheduled, then canceled. Other times, Soviet subs barreled right into the middle of exercises almost as if they were trying to see how the U.S. forces would react. Finally, the latest subs the Soviets had sent out on sea trials—Victor III attack boats—were much quieter than any of their predecessors, almost as quiet as U.S. subs. It was as if somehow the Soviets had caught on to the idea that silence could be crucial. Before, they had always seemed more focused on sheer quantity.

Was this all coincidence? Or was there a glitch in U.S. communications security? Could there be a spy? Inman had sent Haver and another intelligence officer, William O. Studeman, to the fleet admirals, seeking their help in searching for any possible communications leaks. But the admirals would have none of it. How could their coded communications, the most sophisticated in the world, have been compromised?

All Haver could do now was keep digging. Maybe some of those answers would be uncovered by *Parche*, if she could manage to find and tap a Barents cable. But Haver would have to wait to find out. The Navy, with strong input from the NSA, was first sending *Parche* to Okhotsk to plant a second recording pod right next to the first to greatly increase capacity at the tap site. She was being sent, in part, to prove herself before anyone dared to send her to that other, far more dangerous sea.

Prove herself she did. *Parche* accomplished something that *Seawolf* never could. When *Parche* arrived back at Okhotsk in 1978, her spooks discovered the Soviets had changed the format of the data passing through their cable. For a brief moment the men feared the tap had been discovered, but soon they realized the format had been altered to add capacity. It might have been enough to kill the mission, and would have been had *Seawolf* been on station. Her eavesdropping equipment could have only gotten something like half of each channel. *Parche*, however, was carrying wide-band recorders, in anticipation of her 1979 trip to the Barents, and the unknown properties of the cable there. The spooks set their recorders to grab all of the data from the Okhotsk cable. The haul would be far less directed than the refined methods of cable-tapping that directly grabbed the best data at the best times, but the information would not be lost. The NSA could sort it all out later.

After a near-perfect run *Parche*'s crew came back with more than a bit of a swagger. The 140 men assigned to this new boat taunted the crew of *Seawolf,* now in dry dock and in pieces. They called her the "Pier Puppy" and joked that her men were assigned to "Building 575," after *Seawolf*'s hull number. *Seawolf*'s crew had already struck back though. In 1977, *Seawolf*'s divers had planted a cow's skull next to the cable tap, just to give *Parche*'s divers a good scare.

Both submarines were stationed at Mare Island, and their crews lived as neighbors, in wood-framed barracks on the east end at the edge of an old munitions depot, away from everyone else. Neither their proximity nor their shared status, however, prevented their intense rivalry, especially now that *Parche* was moving ahead, going out to sea, while *Seawolf*'s men were stuck with the most thankless duty a crew can pull: overhaul. They were working hours almost as long as those of sea duty, and they were stuck, hot and sweaty, in a shipyard handling tasks that seemed more fitted to construction laborers than submariners. Their wives, children, and girlfriends were nearby, but there was infuriatingly little time to see them as the men toiled relentlessly at the three R's of shipyard life: "Remove, Repair, Reinstall."

The nukes had it worst of all. Wearing canary-yellow antiradiation suits, they were saddled with the task of cutting their boat in half in order to remove and replace the spent reactor core. There was so much paperwork involved that they had taken to chanting, "Cut down another tree for nuclear power."

Rickover's reactor inspectors, the men the crew called "snakes," were everywhere, their special helmets sign enough to trigger a man-to-man alert. The sign for "snakes on board" was passed with a quick flash of a two-fingered V.

There was just no glory in overhaul. Indeed, with the country's backlash against Vietnam, there was little glory in being in the military. It seemed that not even the government had respect for its armed forces. Navy pay wasn't keeping up with soaring inflation and interest rates that had skyrocketed into double digits. Longtime submariners were making about $15,000 a year in base and supplemental pay. There were news stories of Navy men on food stamps.* It seemed there was no refuge. Even the Horse and Cow was turning into a bikers' bar.

So *Seawolf*'s crew watched with envy in 1979 as *Parche* pre-

---

*The morale problems caused by all of this were taking their toll on the rest of the sub force as well. Men were retiring in record numbers, leaving many crews bottom-heavy with new recruits. That along with cutbacks that strained maintenance schedules created an unprecedented spate of accidents. In September 1977, Commander E. J. "Buzz" Galbraith of the USS *Ray* (SSN-653) knew he was operating at a disadvantage. His navigation equipment was in need of repair, his crew was green, and *Ray* was going to the Mediterranean, where shallow waters, tricky currents and changing temperature layers made it difficult to navigate even with the most experienced men. Still, as they left port, Galbraith believed he could carry the crew. He realized his mistake on September 20, when his sub drifted 14 miles off course and slammed into an undersea coral mountain off the Strait of Sicily. It hit so hard that men were hurled into bulkheads, the auxiliary diesel engine shifted on its mounts, and the steel cone covering *Ray*'s sonar system was crushed. All told, seamanship error contributed to fourteen major incidents or accidents in the Atlantic sub fleet in the late 1970s—so many that the fleet's top sub admiral had to send out a cautionary note.

pared to shove off a second time toward a mission shrouded in mystery, the mission that had so fascinated President Carter. This time she was headed for the Barents.

She'd travel a route that had probably never been taken before, the one path that would bypass all of the Soviet choke points, just about the most difficult and dangerous way possible. *Parche* was going to travel north, due north from San Francisco, past Alaska, and through the narrow and shallow Bering Strait, where the U.S. and Soviet borders almost touch and where the ice could sink a sub faster than an enemy. From there, she would travel past the North Pole and back south into the Barents Sea. All told, *Parche* would have to transit farther than 5,500 nautical miles, much of it treacherous. There was good reason the Soviets would never expect *Parche* to slip into the Barents from this route.

There was one more precaution. *Parche* would not leave for the Barents until late summer, well after Carter's summit with Brezhnev. The two leaders met on June 18 and signed the SALT II Treaty, in which both sides agreed to limit the number of their nuclear-missile launchers.

Two weeks after the superpower summit, *Parche*'s CO, John H. Maurer Jr., held a summit of his own—with the wives of his crew. The captain provided baby-sitters, light refreshments, and a description of the men's "extended deployment" that pretty much began and ended with dates of departure and return. He gave the women "Family-Gram" forms, so that they could wire quick messages to their husbands a few times over the three months *Parche* would be gone, and a two-page list of emergency numbers, starting with that of his wife, Carol, and going down through a litany of Mare Island doctors, dentists, firemen, and police. He also gave the women a checklist of all the tasks the Navy imagined would fall to them. Know when to tune up the car. Find the telephone numbers of the plumber and the electrician. Make sure your husband leaves a will. In return, the women were asked to give up their husbands for the duration.

There were the usual tears dockside as *Parche* shoved off that August. The magnetic white hull numbers denoting her as submarine number *683* had been taken down, leaving her anonymous as she passed beneath the Golden Gate Bridge and dove.

The crew was now in the hands of the man they called "Captain Jack." He was built thick and strong, and his crew thought him a bulldog, at once determined and playful. There was something about this captain who could walk into the torpedo room and wrestle with his men. There were some, among the torpedo crew especially, who were just crazy enough to beat the captain regularly. The wrestling matches fast became ritual— "the Tag Team Follies."

Maurer was to the Navy born, his father an admiral. In fact, John H. Maurer Sr. had been commander of submarines in the Pacific in the late 1960s when *Halibut* was sent looking for missile pieces and before she set out after fantasy cables. Now his son was leading a crew top-heavy with senior chiefs, senior enlisted, and spooks on the most dangerous special projects mission yet.

Secrecy had been tight on *Seawolf,* far tighter than it had ever been on *Halibut.* But on *Parche,* the secrecy was nearly paranoiac. The crew itself had little idea of where they were going. The men were told only that they were being sent to see whether *Parche* could find her way beneath the frozen expanse and back, perhaps detecting a few Soviet subs along the way.

As *Parche* neared Alaska, Maurer began preparing to move through the narrow Bering Strait submerged. Here, the waters were only 150 feet deep and the going was hazardous. Indeed, in a few months the passage would be impossible without the help of an icebreaker. Navigators and the captain were shrouded by curtains as they tensely plotted *Parche*'s 2–3-knot crawl.

Once through the strait, *Parche* had to navigate farther north through the Chukchi Sea. Here the water was just as shallow, and the ice didn't melt even in summer. From outer space, this and other seas surrounding the pole look like a kaleidoscope as temperature and salinity patterns alter the very color of the water mile by mile. *Parche*'s sonar bounced off the layers much as it bounced off solid objects, leaving Maurer and his crew nearly blind, much like a plane flying through thick cloud cover.

The crew maneuvered *Parche* forward slowly, cursing as they tried to decipher sonar echoes, never entirely certain whether something that sounded as if it were directly ahead was at their depth or some feet above. There was no way to really tell, not until they passed closer, close enough to risk collision. But *Parche* wasn't totally helpless. The Navy had been sending at least one submarine a year up under the ice since the 1950s. A special lab had been created to study sea ice to try to make it easier to operate in the strange and difficult environment. And the entire Sturgeon class of subs had been made "ice-capable": given upward- and forward-looking sonar that could help avoid ramming into the ice, special buoyancy controls, and hull modifications that allowed the subs to break through thin ice for emergency surfacings.

During these early Arctic operations, the Navy discovered that sonar pings sounded an awful lot like the mating call of the area's ring-necked seals. When the seals heard the submarine ping—a sweet tone that sounded like a singer moving across octaves—they answered: one seal calling back to the submarine, the next seal answering that seal, and another seal answering the one before. Blasting the sea, the seals inspired walruses to join in with their bell-like barks. On the early transits, the din went on for hours, seals answering subs and other seals, walruses answering seals, and walruses answering one another. Now *Parche* was using sonar designed to avoid courtship with the local mammals.

The passage was noisy, nonetheless. Around the sub were chunks of ice that had broken off from large bergs farther north. Those chunks had a disturbing tendency to pack themselves against one another or against land, creating heavy pressure ridges that reached down deep into the sea. *Parche* could easily encounter an area with less than five feet of clearance from bottom. It was almost impossible to move through without scraping some ice, sending a screech through the hull, nails across the chalkboard amplified. The ice chunks were heavy enough to snap a submarine's screws and leave a boat helpless.

The crew also had to be on the lookout for larger bergs that often floated south, creating huge obstacles between Greenland and Canada as well as on the other side of the pole, between Greenland and Iceland. It was an iceberg that had stopped USS *Nautilus* on an attempt to cross under the North Pole in June 1958. (*Nautilus* made the Pole, and history, a few months later.)

When *Parche* finally hit deep water, she could move ahead without obstacles. This 1,500-mile swim beneath the North Pole itself would be easy—depths of 1,000 to 12,000 feet left plenty of room to maneuver beneath the most massive icebergs. After that, *Parche* again had to maneuver through a tapestry of marginal ice before finally breaking through to the Barents.

Now it was time for the crew to begin readying the fish to drag along the sea bottom in search of communications cables. Given the surrounding terrain and the location of Soviet bases, it made sense that any underwater telephone cable would run from Murmansk and along the coast of the Kola Peninsula, which pointed down from the Arctic, forming the thumb of the glove-shaped piece of land that marked Sweden and Finland as its fingers. The cable would probably stretch about 250 miles east to the tip, before it took a 40-mile hop across what the Soviets called the throat of the White Sea and looped into the Severodvinsk shipyard.

It made little sense to lay a tap in that bit of the White Sea where boats moved continuously from the shipyard out to the Barents. Instead, *Parche* would look for the cable in an area where it might be a little easier for her to hover for a while and not be discovered, such as along the granite cliffs on the northernmost coast of the Kola in that 250-mile run after Murmansk. The search inevitably would bring *Parche* within the Soviets' 12-mile territorial limit, and probably even inside the 3-mile limit recognized by the United States.

As *Parche* searched, men monitored the video images captured by the fish, looking for that vague line in the sand that could be a communications cable. They found it just about where operation planners had suspected it would be, farther out than 12 miles at some points, but a lot closer in at others. It was clear that this cable had to run from Severodvinsk to the major bases of the Northern Fleet, and on into fleet headquarters near Murmansk.

Finally, Maurer picked a spot for the tap. In Okhotsk, the cable stretched across an entire sea, and *Halibut* had been able to plant that tap about 40 miles offshore. It is not clear exactly how far from the coast this tap site was, but it clearly was a lot closer in than the Okhotsk tap had been.

Nobody had to be told that the closer *Parche* moved in, the more she risked discovery. Sonar crews monitored the constant traffic above as *Parche*'s divers began their work. The water was deeper here than in Okhotsk. Divers were now working at least 500 feet under.* Still, nothing but luck could keep *Parche* safe from a direct hit by a Soviet sonar ping. Standing in the control room, it seemed to the men that they could count the turn count of the propeller blades as Soviet destroyers and cruisers moved overhead in a near constant march in and out of port. The contacts caught by *Parche*'s sonar were played over a speaker in her conn, and it was here that the men were most acutely aware of the 150 pounds of HBX explosives on board, those self-destruct charges that had become required equipment on cable-tapping subs.

The spooks were crammed into a tiny compartment, just to the port side behind the torpedo room. Directly below, an auxiliary ballast tank had been emptied and transformed into storage space for the huge reels of tape and for spare parts. The tank was so cold that any tapes retrieved had to sit for 12 hours before they came back to room temperature and could be used. While *Halibut* had the Bat Cave, *Parche* had no more space than any other late-generation Sturgeon sub. In fact, most of *Parche*'s torpedoes had been ditched for space. Now she carried just four live warshots, the minimum number any attack sub was allowed to carry on a mission.

It would take the spooks at least two weeks to sift electronically through the hundreds of lines running through the cable and choose which lines to record—and at what times—over the next year. The process relied on educated guesses and luck. Certain channels would probably be best in the summer months when the ice cleared from the Barents and the Soviets conducted naval exercises. Missile tests tended to be seasonal as well. But lines connected directly to headquarters could be active and profitably tapped year-round.

A few of the lines were unencoded, or rang clear because whatever encryption the Soviets had tried to use had failed. Most, however, were encrypted to some degree. The NSA wanted even those lines that seemed burdened by the heaviest

---

*On later missions to the Barents some of the divers would work 600 feet deep as the tap was repositioned.

encryption, the lines that might have been hardest to decode. Intelligence analysts had learned from the first taps that those deeply scrambled lines were often running fleet to fleet, admiral to admiral, carrying crucial information. It also helped that the tap had evolved over the years. It weighed several tons, but miniaturization of the electronics and advances in recording technology now provided a greater recording capacity and some room for error.*

As all this was going on, a steady stream of Soviet ships and submarines continued to fill *Parche*'s sonar screens. The activity got the crew members to talking. One man whispered that *Parche* was "very, very near Murmansk" and "really up against the Soviet coast." One chief found a more colorful way of describing their position to a young seaman. "This is so close you could look through a periscope and see people's faces on the beach if you came to the surface."

As they sat there, some of the men began to realize that no one had ever leveled with them about the dangers of this operation. As one man put it, "Here you've got one hundred some-odd guys willing to die, and they don't even know they're truly in a situation where they might."

Finally, the job was done. All Maurer had to do now was get his men out of there and get them home. The plan was to leave the immediate area of the tap and signal "mission accomplished" to a second U.S. submarine, which had been skulking nearby throughout *Parche*'s operation. Had there been any indication that *Parche* was detected, it would have been this second sub's job to make a racket, become a decoy, and draw the heat.

Parche, of course, was maintaining strict radio silence, but she had been equipped with a special horn to send her signal. U.S. subs usually were wired for 60 kilohertz, but *Parche* would signal at 50 kilohertz, the Soviet standard. To the Soviets, it was hoped, the signal would sound like one of their own. To the men on board, the blast sounded like bongo drums. One quick beat

---

*The CIA also adapted the miniaturized recording technology in the cable-tap pods for land use and bribed a Russian construction worker to implant one against an important underground telephone cable in Moscow itself. Intelligence officials say this prized source of high-level communications was compromised in the mid-1980s by Aldrich Ames, the worst turncoat in CIA history.

on the bongos, and the message was sent. *Parche* waited for a reply, then headed for home.

For her feat, *Parche* received the Presidential Unit Citation, the highest award possible. Each man was given a certificate, with the presidential seal at the top and Jimmy Carter's signature on the bottom. It was an award that *Halibut* had won twice, *Seawolf* never.

"By virtue of the authority vested in me as President of the United States and as Commander-in-Chief of the Armed Forces of the United States, I have today awarded THE PRESIDENTIAL UNIT CITATION (NAVY) FOR EXTRAORDINARY HEROISM TO USS PARCHE (SSN 683) for extraordinary heroism and outstanding performance in the conduct of a mission of vital importance to the National Security of the United States as a unit of the U.S. Pacific Fleet in 1979," the award read.

Buried in the bureaucratese that followed was one telling line. It praised *Parche* for operating "in the hostile environment of poorly charted ocean areas."

In 1980, *Parche* was scheduled to go back to the Barents tap, and *Seawolf* was scheduled to return to Okhotsk. But in February, a fire broke out on *Seawolf* during sea trials. A turbine generator blew up and began tossing balls of flame into the engine room while the sub was submerged. By the time *Seawolf*'s crew could perform an emergency blow and surface, ten men had been overcome by black thick smoke. They were carried up to the deck and fresh air, and it was there they were photographed by a passerby. Instead of having a chance to win a PUC, to show the guys on *Parche* that *Seawolf*'s men were just as good, they were awarded with a page 1 photo in a local newspaper captioned, "*Seawolf* Sons Basking in the Sun After Rigorous Sea Trials."

Seawolf went back to dry dock for another year, and *Parche* again took her place on a run to Okhotsk in the summer. *Parche* also went back to the Barents that fall to plant a new tap and retrieve the first year's worth of recordings.

By now, Ronald Reagan was scoring big in the presidential campaign. Carter had been plagued by the hostage crisis in Iran. He also was hurt by the Soviet invasion of Afghanistan, which killed any chance for ratification of the arms treaty he had just reached with Brezhnev. (Both of these events also led the U.S. sub force to step up surveillance of Soviet naval forces in the Indian Ocean.) Reagan was promising to get tough with the Soviets. To that end, he pledged to pour billions of dollars into rebuilding the military, and he put the Navy front and center in his plans. Painting the conventional picture of the Soviet Navy as increasingly bent on challenging the West in any sea—pretty much the opposite of what Haver believed might be happening when he briefed Carter—Reagan said he would expand the U.S. Navy to 600 ships from 450 ships to prevent the Soviets from snatching maritime superiority.

In fact, the Soviet fleet was growing. In November a U.S. satellite captured images of an enormous pile of steel and a newly enlarged dock at a Soviet shipyard. That and other evidence suggested that the Soviets might be building their first full-sized aircraft carrier. To many top Navy officials, the satellite images seemed to be proof that Rich Haver and other young analysts were wrong about the Soviet Navy pulling back, and that in fact the Soviets were still gearing up for battle in the open oceans. They might finally be ready to pour money into the kind of huge surface ships and supply vessels that they would need to create a true blue-water Navy. After all, aircraft carriers had always been used to project power outward, to sail to distant places and launch planes.

After his election, Reagan appointed John F. Lehman Jr., the campaign aide who had come up with the plan for the 600-ship fleet, as his Navy secretary. At only thirty-eight years old, Lehman was the youngest man in this century to hold the post. He was smart, quick, and outspoken about his hard-line stance.

"I believe that our former narrow margin of superiority is gone," Lehman warned Congress on February 6, 1981, just one day after he was sworn in. It didn't take long for him to earn a reputation as *l'enfant terrible* as he took control of the Navy in a way that no secretary had attempted in decades. Lehman's plans included a radically new and aggressive naval strategy. He didn't talk much about what he expected the Soviets to do in a war. Instead, he wanted U.S. submarines, battleships, cruisers, and aircraft carriers to drive en masse right into the Barents and go after the Soviet surface and submarine fleets in their own waters.

He was making, he declared, "a firm commitment to go into the highest-threat areas and defeat the Soviet naval threat." Lehman became fond of describing Murmansk and the rest of the Kola Peninsula as "the most valuable piece of real estate on earth."

Soon, top admirals were grumbling that Lehman was a torpedo without a guidance system. Most liked his idea of a more aggressive strategy, but Lehman dismissed out of hand the protests of some admirals that it was suicide to drive aircraft carriers into the Barents where the Soviets could easily sink them with cruise missiles. He also shrugged off outside critics—academics and congressional staff members among them—who warned that threatening Soviet sea-based missiles too early in a war could backfire, prompting them to "use 'em or lose 'em."

This was the backdrop as Pentagon officials prepared to give Reagan his first briefing about submarine spy operations. It was scheduled for Friday, March 6, at 9:15 A.M., and was set to run 20 minutes. The luminaries who gathered in the wood-paneled Situation Room in the West Wing of the White House included Vice President George Bush, Chief of Staff James A. Baker III, Counselor Edwin Meese II, and Richard V. Allen, the new national security adviser. Attending from the Pentagon were Defense Secretary Caspar Weinberger; Admiral James D. Watkins, the vice chief of Naval Operations; Lehman; Haver; and Rear Admiral John L. Butts, now director of Naval Intelligence.

Weinberger and Watkins got things rolling by sketching the basics of the surveillance missions being run by regular attack subs. Then Butts stepped in to introduce Reagan to *Seawolf*, *Parche*, and cable-tapping. He made his presentation with a dramatic video and slide show that Lehman had told him would appeal to Reagan.

The president was, by all reports, mesmerized. Finally, he leaned over and asked his vice president, a former director of central intelligence, "Did you have something to do with this, George?"

Bush answered that some of these programs had run during his tenure at the CIA.

Then Rich Haver stepped in and, just as he had with Carter, began to describe how Naval Intelligence used the information the spy subs were collecting. Haver had slides too, but by now

Reagan was itching for answers. He wanted to know if Haver thought the Soviets would be less willing to wage nuclear war now that they were facing him and his hard line in the White House. He also asked some of the same questions the analysts had been grappling with: How do the Soviets plan nuclear war? How do they train for it? How do they intend to fight it? Would a naval war go nuclear from day one, with Soviets using cruise missiles against aircraft carriers? And if it did, could it be contained at sea before anyone fired strategic ballistic missiles at the United States?

Again Haver succeeded in drawing a president into a dialogue. In a question and answer session that went on for nearly 15 minutes with Bush and Watkins fielding questions also, Haver explained the conventional view of war on the high seas and the long-held assumption that the Soviets would probably turn to tactical, short-range nukes early in those battles. He added that such a move had seemed likely to set off a broader nuclear war.

Then he offered some of the conclusions that his team of analysts had reached—that the Soviets appeared to be turning away from the conventional strategy and dedicating the bulk of their ships, attack subs, and planes to protecting their missile subs in safe bastions close to home.

From here, Haver went on to plug Lehman's aggressive plan to confront those forces in Soviet waters. When Reagan seemed satisfied, Haver began to pack up the projector as Weinberger stepped in to carefully explain to the president what his role in the process would be, how he needed to sign off on all the sensitive espionage operations in advance. Weinberger took his time, talking slowly and very deliberately. He wanted to make sure that Reagan appreciated what was being asked of him.

Weinberger needn't have worried. Reagan was already hooked. Nobody had told him any of this when he was merely governor of California, home to the nation's most crucial spy subs. He had come to Washington still holding on to a view of the Navy built from equal parts of World War II fact and of World War II myth, the image of heroic men facing off against Japanese ships, their torpedoes sinking the enemy, dodging depth charges as they went along. This was an image dear to Reagan, and he loved to talk about how he played a submarine captain in the 1958 film *Hellcats of the Navy*.

Reagan had a favorite story about those days, and he told it now—albeit with only the details fit for screen. In Reagan's version, he effortlessly echoed commands whispered by a Navy officer and, with cameras rolling, set one of the nation's subs steaming out of San Diego in a Pacific sunset.*

As Bush and Baker began trying to hustle Reagan along, the president was still talking about his experiences on the *Hellcats* set and his admiration for the submariners he met there. This briefing had already gone on for 45 minutes, more than twice as long as it had been scheduled to run. Reagan, however, was in no rush. Turning to Haver, the president asked, "Where do you get guys like this?"

"Sir, they're just Americans," Haver answered in his best for-the-gipper style.

On that note, Reagan finally seemed ready to leave. It was clear he wanted Haver to keep trying to puzzle out Soviet strategy and that he had given his tacit approval for the next round of submarine spying missions.

All this occurred as *Seawolf* was ready to go to sea again. For the first time, the Navy could send both special projects boats out at the same time, in different directions to different seas.

Before *Parche* could leave for her 1981 run, however, Commander Peter John Graef, her new captain, ordered what he thought would be a routine drug screening. The last thing he

---

*Reagan's tale was missing some rather pertinent facts. What actually happened was that he virtually brought the house down, though not by virtue of his acting. The crew, told to treat Reagan's orders as they would their captain's, accidentally overheard the actor practicing his lines, and they responded.

"Answer all bells," he said, giving the code for get under way, practicing to get just the right inflection.

"All back full."

"All ahead two-thirds."

"Starboard stop."

"Starboard ahead standard."

"Left full rudder."

The submarine began to jerk in every direction, back, forward, stopped, forward, left. The bow lines began to stretch, then pull until the aging pier that had moored the sub snapped into pieces of cracked wood and rusted iron, just as the sub's captain raced to the bridge, yelling, "All stop, for God's sake, all stop!"

expected was to nail nearly 15 percent of his crew for marijuana use—twenty-two crew members, including three officers. There was no debate. They were off the boat, and replacements were rushed in.

This was definitely not what Reagan had in mind during the briefing when he had asked Rich Haver where the Navy found "these guys," these superheroes of the cold war. Although, in retrospect, Haver's answer seemed far less corny. They were "just Americans" after all.

Staffing these boats had never been easy. Navy recruiters went through bizarre contortions to keep their secret and at the same time find men who wouldn't mind trespassing in Soviet seas for the purpose of cable-tapping. As one young submariner described it, the recruitment process was more like an interrogation. Men in leisure suits brought potential projects men into smoky rooms and began demanding to know: Did the recruit ever use drugs? Ever get in trouble with the law? The questions were peppered with promises that the government had ways of learning every dirty detail. "If you ever jacked off behind the barn, we will find out about it," one kid was told.

Parche wasn't unique in her personnel problems, and the drug bust had intelligence officials worried. *Seawolf*'s crew was disintegrating under the mounting frustrations of serving on a broken-down and cursed boat. The pressure inspired some of her crew to lose themselves in a marijuana haze. Some even proclaimed their drug use openly and loudly, just to get off of *Seawolf*. Then there were *Seawolf*'s isolationists, who were readying for the day when they would take singular stands against communism in mountaintop homes transformed into forts. These men had taken to going out to the mud flats near the base to practice with their non-Navy-issue assault rifles, blasting apart cans and at least one truck. One man sent a live round into his television. The rest of the crew, leery, sweaty, and exhausted, just looked on at the dopers and the gun fanatics.

Such tensions remained as *Seawolf* finally headed out toward Okhotsk. By now, Michael C. Tiernan had been the CO through three years of overhaul and tests. This was to be the first time he commanded the boat through an actual operation. A *Seawolf* crew that had once compared his predecessor, Charles R.

MacVean, to Captain James T. Kirk on the starship *Enterprise* now nicknamed Tiernan "Milquetoast." The men had tried to take him out to the Horse and Cow to loosen him up, but they didn't think it had helped.

Tiernan, in fact, was only slightly more popular than his new executive officer, J. Ashton Dare, whom the men referred to as "Jashton." If the men found Tiernan aloof, they found Jashton downright irritating. His father was an admiral, and it seemed to the men that he wasn't going to let anyone forget that. Worse for Jashton, he had replaced a crew favorite, Robert S. Holbrook, an officer who could chastise a man in the morning and redeem himself later that night by taking him out for a beer. Holbrook also had been the crew's good-luck charm. He had already survived an 85-degree dive on the diesel sub USS *Chopper* (SS-342), saved only when an enlisted man thought to throw her into reverse, driving her back up toward the surface. Thereafter, Holbrook always wore a brass belt buckle adorned with *Chopper*'s image, certain that it made him unsinkable. He had his men just as convinced.

As far as they were concerned, Dare had neither the mythology nor the charm to redeem himself. He was their favorite target as they looked for ways to fight boredom. On one test run, some of the men stole Dare's mattress and flushed it through the garbage chute and out of the boat. The XO somehow missed the joke.

In fact, humor was more than a little strained on this boat full of men who felt that they were being sent to Soviet waters in the equivalent of a Model T. By the time ice began forming on *Seawolf*'s deck plates, morale was at an all-time low.

Things only got worse on station. Tiernan directed his crew to plant the sub next to the Soviet cable. The plan was to let *Seawolf* sit secure on bottom, balancing her bulk on two ski-like legs that the crew had taken to calling skegs. The skegs were a gift of imagination and technology, a safety device designed after that first terrible storm that had torn *Halibut* from her anchors. But as *Seawolf* tried to land with those skegs now, she came down hard right on the Soviet cable.

There was every chance that the fall had interrupted Soviet communications or sent a shot of static through the line, and there was every chance that the Soviets would send surface ships, blasting sonar, or repair crews to come and investigate. But there was no sign of a Soviet search. By the time the tapping operation was completed, Tiernan decided to go ahead and finish a secondary operation. *Seawolf* was going to move further into Okhotsk, and she was going on another search for Soviet missile fragments. But just as it seemed certain that the Americans were going to survive their mistake, they came under assault—not from the Soviets, but from the sea itself.

Twin storms that had started hundreds of miles away, their winds swirling, were nearing Okhotsk. Beneath the sea, *Seawolf* sat too deep to put up an antenna, and the crew was unaware of the warnings flooding the airwaves about the cyclones moving up toward the Kuril Islands. The men didn't hear when naval command centers reported winds of 55 knots and swells leaping toward the sky. They didn't know when other craft were warned that the two storms had become one, a single, lethal typhoon.

Within days of the first warnings, thrashed air, bullet rains, and massive waves were combining to force their wrath below the surface, pounding down until *Seawolf* began to shudder. At first, the men believed they could easily weather the squall. Unlike surface mariners, submarine crews are trained to fear detection, depth charges, and torpedoes, but there is usually little to fear from storms. Run deep. That was the standard procedure. Submariners are indoctrinated from the start with the faith that the skies could open up all they like, winds could gust threatening all who skim the surface, but below, where dark and calm hold court, submarines reign.

Indeed, the 400 feet of water overhead, though shallow by submarine standards, would have been enough to frustrate most storms. But this typhoon was roiling even the depths. And for *Seawolf*, there was no going deeper. She would have to weather this out on the seabed.

Seawolf began rocking from side to side. Three divers were out, and they were being tossed. The rest of the crewmen, safer inside, were trying to act nonchalant. Squeezing past one another within *Seawolf*'s cramped corridors, they offered comments about the storm as if they were discussing the weather back home. Still, the currents that were hitting *Seawolf* every twenty or thirty seconds were so violent that her skegs were lifting from the seabed. At first, the submarine rolled only a few degrees, then more. Objects inside went flying—with the submarine on bottom, nobody had thought to secure for heavy seas. Beauregard was knocked from his high perch in the torpedo room and fell to the deck with a resounding crash. For a moment the torpedomen feared their mascot, their favorite ceramic frog, would be erased from their ranks in an instant. With great relief they realized that only his stand was destroyed.

Outside the boat, the divers were losing their fight against the pull of the currents. One diver was sucked toward the rocking submarine and found himself beneath one of *Seawolf*'s skegs. Something grabbed hold of him an instant later. Another diver? A lash of the current? Just as this man was about to be pinned, he was free.

Finally the divers were able to scramble into the unsteady shelter of the submarine. That was what Tiernan was waiting for. He signaled the end of the operation. He wanted his submarine in deep water. He wanted out of Okhotsk.

But Okhotsk was holding on. "Buddha," a reactor specialist who had earned his nickname for his size and despite his thick thatch of black hair, signaled the alarm first. He had been standing at a gauge for one of the heat exchangers that cycled cooled water before it went into the submarine's nuclear reactor. The temperature was not reading anywhere near correct levels. Something was clogging the system.

Checking valves, moving equipment, Buddha started yelling: "I've got sand in there, Jesus Christ!"

The nukes, those men who worked the reactor, came running, followed by Dare and Tiernan. They stood looking at a pile of sand. *Seawolf*'s vents were sucking in muck, salt, the sea, and the seafloor into the cooling system. The storm began taking on new and terrible significance as they realized that the reactor was in danger of shutting down. *Seawolf* was at risk of losing all power.

Crewmen began checking other points where the submarine borrowed water from outside, cycled it through the boat, and cycled it back outside. Sand, little animals, snails, coral, and sea creatures had gotten into the generators, the main engines, the turbines, and a half-dozen or so critical areas on board. There were piles and heaps of the wet, partially living mass around the boat. No one was sure how much weight they had taken on as the wet mass was sucked in from Okhotsk's bottom. Worse, the sand was coming in because the seawater intake valves that should have been several feet above sea bottom were resting practically flat against it. Each time the storm rocked *Seawolf*, a little more sand was pumped over the skegs. The currents were forcing the sub to dig herself in. Somehow the engineers who designed those legs as safety devices had ignored the properties of currents that children learn about when they stand in the surf at the beach. Now, *Seawolf*'s skegs were almost entirely buried. She was stuck.

Compartment by compartment, men began to fret. The machinist's mates knew that if the steam plant shut down, it could take days to restart, if it restarted at all. The nukes worried that a loss of power from the steam plant would shut down their troubled reactor, which might not start back up. *Seawolf* was just not strong enough for this kind of test.

No one, it seemed, was immune to the growing tension. An electrician's mate lost control and began yelling, screaming, crying. A medic was ordered to sedate him and send him to his rack. Others began to have chilling visions of blank epitaphs: somewhere lies this seaman, sent to do something in an unknown place and killed somehow in a war that didn't exist.

Seawolf was mired for nearly two days as the chiefs, the old salts who had ridden submarines for twenty years, joined forces with the junior officers. With Tiernan's approval they began trying anything they could think of. First they attempted to rev *Seawolf*'s engines to see whether that would get her to pull up. That failed. Next they tried a controlled emergency blow, hoping the sudden loss of weight would send them floating out of the sand. It was dangerous—*Seawolf* might pull free, but she might also broach the surface, and that could mean detection and detection would mean a fight. *Seawolf* had few means of protection at her disposal. Most of her torpedo tubes had been used to store potatoes. There were still some torpedoes on board, but recent tests had proved them all but useless. *Seawolf* was the loudest thing in the water, so whenever she had launched a test dummy, its sonar guidance system turned the torpedo around and sent it hurtling back toward the sub.

Seawolf's only chance was to remain hidden as she freed herself. Carefully, the crew began to blow ballast, slowly, steadily, gently, first from the bow, then from the stern. Nothing. Try again, someone ordered tensely. A little more water this time, with the anchors down to prevent an accidental flight to the surface. Again nothing.

Another try, and the submarine seemed to move slightly, but only slightly. It was like trying to get a pickup truck out of a rut, rocking back and forth, hoping sooner or later to be able to push it out. But with sand still being sucked into the machinery, the men were in a race: would they get out before their systems shut down? All through the boat, men were trying to blow the sand out, but the submarine was sucking in more than they could discard. A key reactor system was already down to less than 50 percent efficiency, maybe as low as 35 percent.

Somebody came up with the idea of cutting loose the anchors that were there to steady *Seawolf* as she sat on her skegs. Anchors might save the sub from broaching, but right now the two concrete mushrooms were also weighing her down. The order was given to cut them loose.

Seawolf began to rise. The main engines were being badly overworked, revving until it sounded as though a drill was whirring through the boat. Then there was a scratchy sound, more of a shriek really, loud enough that some of the men wondered whether their hearing would be forever affected.

The skegs remained partially buried. The gondola under the *Seawolf*'s belly, the huge "clamshell" that was built to hold missile pieces, partially ripped away. But *Seawolf* was free.

As she limped home, she was dangerously loud in the water, louder than she had ever been. There was something dangling from below, a piece of skeg, the gondola. Whatever it was, it was making a lot of noise in the water as *Seawolf* made a slow race for the Kuril Islands and out to open ocean. Crucial systems parts worn down by sand were also grinding and seemed ready to give out any moment.

Then, somewhere in the Pacific, not far from Okhotsk, she was detected. A Soviet boat, probably a trawler, began pinging with active sonar. There was no way to outrun the trawler—the submarine was too hurt—and no way to hide, because whatever she was dragging banged against her hull even when she was sitting stock still. Any speeds faster than 6 knots brought a cacophony of sound, a drum section gone wild.

The Soviet pings rang through the submarine, adding to the din. The ringing would not stop. The Soviets chased, giving up the pursuit after only about twenty-four hours—for reasons that may have been as simple as a trawler captain's whim.

When *Seawolf* finally pulled into a closed dry dock, the men could see the damage. There were dents in her superstructure and pieces torn off as if she had suffered depth charges. The bilges were still full of sand, hundreds of pounds of it, though a significant amount had been moved to the men's bunks, jars of gray, grainy souvenirs.

There were no awards given for this mission, no formal recognition of the men's brush with death. A cruise book, crafted much like a high school yearbook, mentioned the ordeal in only one cryptic cartoon memorializing the first and last leap taken by Beauregard the frog.

Back in port, the men trying to repair *Seawolf* weren't told how sand got into critical systems. Officials in Washington had far more serious fears. Following *Seawolf*'s misadventure, satellites uncovered evidence that the Soviets had found the cable tap in Okhotsk. Nobody was sure how, whether the operation had been compromised by *Seawolf*'s drop onto the cable or by a mole within the crew or, unthinkable as it seemed, among the few intelligence officers who knew about the taps in the first place.

But clearly it was crucial that someone discover how the Soviets had puzzled out one of the most secret U.S. missions.

THE CROWN JEWELS

The feeling had to have been one of disbelief. Rich Haver looked at the report on *Seawolf*'s latest patrol, then at his other intelligence reports. There was just no other way to line up the facts.

It had been easy to blame *Seawolf* and her crew for blowing one of the most important intelligence operations of the last ten years. Or so it had seemed at the time. After all, *Seawolf* had slammed tons of steel down on the Soviet cable. That had to have caused a break in communications or at least some static. Why else would the Soviets have sent a survey ship to Okhotsk? How else would they have found the cable tap?

In fact, the Soviets did more than find the tap. They reached down and lifted the large recording pods—both of them—out of the water. There was no hiding what they were—or for that matter, who had put them there. Inside of one was a part emblazoned with the words "Property of the United States Government."

Haver had checked and rechecked his time lines. There could be no mistake. None of this was *Seawolf*'s fault. The Soviet survey ship had been on its way to the area before *Seawolf* fell on the cable. It had taken a meandering route to Okhotsk, a trek that suggested camouflage, all the way from the Baltic Sea on the Atlantic side. There was, however, almost no chance that U.S. intelligence was going to miss a ship heading toward the tap site. Both in the Barents and in Okhotsk, the U.S. maintained around-the-clock surveillance with satellites, land listening stations, in short, any means possible. That was especially easy in Okhotsk. The sea was so empty any ship that went in and loitered was bound to stand out. Now, that surveillance had paid off with one horrifying realization. The search for the taps almost had to have been deliberate. And if that were the case, Haver knew there was one glaring possibility, the worst possibility—that *Seawolf* hadn't shown her hand at all. The Soviets may have been tipped. There might very well be a spy.

This was not going to go down well in the Navy or the NSA. That much was clear to Haver as he listed a spy among the reasons why the tap could have been discovered in a report dated January 30, 1982, the day that just happened to be his thirty-seventh birthday. But while Haver expected distress, what he got back was outright skepticism. Top admirals decided he was seeing ghosts again, just as they had believed a few years earlier when he had raised an alert about a possible spy or communications leak in the Atlantic. Now here he was seeing spies in the Pacific.

What Haver was saying seemed unbelievable. If he was right, there was not one but two spies. One man couldn't be responsible for the problems in both oceans. Anyone with operational knowledge of Atlantic submarine trailings in the late 1970s was almost guaranteed to be out of the loop when it came to the Pacific tapping operations. Besides, the cable taps were about the best-kept secret in all of cold war intelligence. No, top admirals concluded, Haver was seeing shadows in coincidences. The Soviets, they figured, had probably just found the Okhotsk tap on a maintenance run to the cable.

Only a few in the Navy saw Haver's report, and they gave his warnings little thought. This was a time when the United States was facing a more immediate and tangible threat. The Soviets seemed to be engineering another big change in their missile-sub strategy, one more dangerous than their move back to the bastions in the Barents in the late 1970s. They were now holding some of their missile subs even closer to their coasts, in "deep bastions" such as the White Sea and the once nearly desolate Okhotsk, and they were hiding others under a nearly impenetrable shroud, the Arctic ice.

Haver and other bright young analysts still felt sure that the Soviets were chiefly trying to protect their missile subs from attack in the early stages of a war, and the early returns from the cable-tapping in the Barents seemed to back up this idea. But if they wanted to, the Soviets also could use the Arctic cover to launch a first strike, and the United States would have less warning than ever before. A missile shot from a Delta in a Soviet bastion in the Barents could take less than thirty minutes to travel the 3,500 nautical miles to Washington, D.C. But a missile traveling from even the northern reaches of the Arctic's Baffin Bay, which sits just above Canada, could cut that time to less than twenty minutes.*

Indeed, the Soviets' shift to the Arctic was a brilliant move. After all, it had never been lost on either side that the shortest distance between the United States and the Soviet Union was over the top of the world. Both nations had already aimed their huge arsenals of land-based missiles across the North Pole. But although both had been exploring the Arctic with submarines for decades, neither the United States nor the Soviet Union had been able to develop the technology to fight in the exotic Arctic environment effectively.

---

*Naval Intelligence began to notice that the Soviets seemed to be experimenting with the idea of hiding their missile subs under the ice in 1979. USS *Gurnard* (SSN–662), under the command of Henry G. Chiles Jr., and USS *Drum* (SSN–677) helped set off a second, and much more difficult, era of trailings that year, following Soviet subs which seemed to be testing how well they could operate under ice floes. For the Soviets, a crucial moment came in the summer of 1981, when Captain Leonid Kuversky drove his Delta SSBN into the desolate Arctic Ocean to see if he could manage to rise up from the ice and calculate a workable trajectory for his sub's sixteen ballistic missiles. Kuversky succeeded beyond all expectations. For his initiative and courage, he was named "Hero of the Soviet Union," his nation's top honor. A gaggle of orders and medals went to his crew. The scientists and weapons designers who had traveled along received various state prizes in a ceremony that was held that October.

The Arctic is also the one area of the world where the prey has the distinct advantage over the hunter, where it would be hugely difficult for U.S. forces to root out the Soviet missile subs and destroy them. For one thing, there are thousands of miles of shallow ice-filled seas where the Soviets could scatter their subs. Even the most massive boats could disappear in these shallows, drift silently along with the ice, and allow the currents to decide direction. And by taking the shallow route through the Kara Sea, the Laptev Sea, and the Beaufort Sea around to the North American side, a Soviet sub could end up among the icebergs of Baffin Bay above Canada, the fjords along the west coast of Greenland, or even the channels that reach clear down to the Hudson Bay inside of Canada.

A submarine hiding motionless would be almost silent, while any attack submarine seeking it out would become the loudest and best target around. U.S. scientists had tried for years, with only limited success, to devise sonar that could compensate for conditions in these marginal ice areas where temperature and salinity layers, the din of near-constant storms, ice crunching upon ice, and the barks of seals and walruses combined to make tracking other subs nearly impossible.

No wonder an alert ran through the Navy, over to the Pentagon, and into the Oval Office when Soviet missile subs began slipping into the Arctic. At stake was nothing less than the ultimate nuclear advantage. And now the U.S. government needed to know: Was this simply another defensive move, a Soviet counterfeint in the game of deterrence? Or were the Soviets positioning for a possible first strike? Were Soviet leaders as insane and evil as President Ronald Reagan and his supporters were proclaiming? Or were the Soviets just afraid that Reagan was as hostile as his rhetoric?

Adding to these fears was the fact that the Soviet Union was building a new and powerful generation of missile subs: the Typhoons. The first was already in sea trials, and satellites had caught sight of at least three more of the subs under construction at Shipyard 402 in Severodvinsk. They were nuclear monsters, squat and bulbous and by far the largest undersea craft constructed by any nation—half again as large as the Trident missile subs, which the United States had put to sea in late 1981. While both classes of submarines stretched almost as long as two football fields, the Typhoon was twice as wide as the Trident.

The Soviets also were building four large underwater "tunnels" at a new submarine base at Gremikha near the tip of the Kola Peninsula, about 150 miles from Murmansk. Blasted out of the adjacent hillside, the granite tunnels were large enough to accommodate the Typhoons and seemed designed to give them protection from nuclear attack.

That the Typhoons would be ice-ready seemed obvious. They were protected by two pressure hulls within a third outer hull, and they had flat, retractable bow diving planes, a shielded propeller shaft, and a reinforced steel sail. Hiding in the Arctic, it would be easy enough for a Typhoon to push its massive bulk through ice cover several feet thick for an attack on the United States. A Typhoon could carry twenty SS-N-20 nuclear missiles, each 50 feet long and able to hold ten warheads programmed to hit different targets as far as 4,500 nautical miles away. This was a boat built to survive, a boat built to ensure that, in the event of nuclear war, key U.S. military centers and cities would not.

The United States needed more than ever to divine the Soviets' intentions, to get right inside their minds. And that meant the cable-tapping operation had to continue, even though the Okhotsk tap had been discovered. *Seawolf* was too old and too broken to ever send back to the Soviet coast. Future missions would be left up to *Parche*.

Meanwhile, it would be up to the rest of the sub force to keep learning about the technical capabilities of the Deltas and the Typhoons, to try to carry the crucial game of trailing to the Arctic, and to do something that had eluded the U.S. Navy for forty years—develop a true Arctic capability. And so admirals turned again to one civilian scientist who had long insisted on studying those icy waters when few others in the Navy showed much interest: Waldo K. Lyon, the director of the Navy's Arctic Submarine Laboratory in San Diego.

The Navy learned early on that Lyon's impish physical stature was hugely misleading. Partially by sheer will, partially with his ability to enlist the support of at least one top admiral or CNO every year, Lyon had kept his lab alive and working to unearth the secrets of the Arctic ice since the end of World War II, when he had first become convinced that the Soviets would ultimately learn a lesson from the Nazi captains who had taken their U-boats under the ice's edge to target Allied supply ships. He had kept the lab running despite skepticism so fierce that the CNO handbook back in 1950 included the line: "It's fantasy to think about using the Arctic Ocean."

Still, Lyon had won enough backing to inspire the sub force to send at least one sub to the Arctic almost every year since *Nautilus* traveled beneath the North Pole in the late 1950s. Lyon had been up that way more than twenty times himself, and he or someone from his lab rode along on every one of those trips, helping to map routes under the ice and to experiment with different types of sonar.

But it was only now, at sixty-seven years old, that he was being called out of relative obscurity by a bunch of admirals who were suddenly terribly interested in the Arctic. Somebody suggested sending some of the older U.S. missile boats to hide under the ice, a seemingly perfect tit-for-tat. Rickover, on the verge of being forced to retire by Secretary of the Navy Lehman, came up with his own proposal to build an experimental Arctic sub, one with a hardened hull and little more than a hump for a sail. He had tried his usual tactics to push the project through, bypassing the Navy and the Pentagon and sending Lyon and the proposal straight to the House Armed Services Committee. But all that ever came out of this effort was a letter to Lehman written by House staffers who were stunned that nearly a quarter-century of Arctic submarine expeditions hadn't left the United States ready to fight beneath the ice. Rickover had to let the fight die when Lehman finally forced him to retire at age eighty-two in January 1982.*

---

*Several previous Defense and Navy secretaries had wanted to ease Rickover out, but his supporters in Congress and presidents like Carter had always stopped them. Reagan, however, stood firmly behind his Navy secretary, even though Rickover appealed to the president forcefully in an Oval Office meeting, calling Lehman a "piss-ant" and asking Reagan, "Are you a man? Can't you make decisions for yourself?" Rickover took some revenge by hanging in his retirement office a picture of Benedict Arnold next to a portrait of Lehman.

Later, one admiral confided to Lyon that the Navy would never build an experimental Arctic sub, because doing so would show the Soviets that the U.S. Navy was unable to fight under the ice. Besides, a plan to develop an Arctic sub would compete with another proposal now before Congress: the Navy wanted funds to build a new class of super-subs, one they were claiming could do just about anything. Some in the Navy were calling the boat "Fat Albert." It was, in fact, the highly controversial Seawolf class of attack submarines, the SSN-21s, which were to follow the Los Angeles–class boats that were replacing the Sturgeon class.

Looking on, Naval Intelligence also liked the idea of a new class of submarines. Intelligence officers figured that any new technology would give the Soviets another problem to solve, another distraction. Besides, the intelligence officers believed that by announcing plans to build new and better submarines, the United States would send the message that the Soviets would never have the edge, no matter what they did.

All of this talk about new ice operations and new submarines helped distract attention from plans to send *Parche* back out to the Barents. This trip worried planners more than the return to Okhotsk had. The Barents cable carried the most sensitive information, and even if the Soviets had found the tap in Okhotsk by accident, reason might have led them to at least keep tighter watch on the Barents, especially if they suspected another tap but had been unable to find one. The round-the-clock surveillance of the tap site hadn't shown anything unusual, but it was hard to know for sure. Okhotsk was desolate; any activity was going to be pretty obvious. The waters of the Barents, on the other hand, were so active that a Soviet search for a second cable tap could have been camouflaged by the usual traffic.

There was also the possibility, though most Naval Intelligence officers thought it a long shot, that Haver was right, that there was a spy. If that was the case, the Soviets might be keeping careful track of *Parche* herself. They might even know that *Parche* had invaded the Barents through the Arctic.

But what if *Parche* were sent by a different route, a very different route, one that could confuse any efforts at surveillance? The word was put out to the crew: *Parche* was leaving earlier than usual, in April instead of late summer, and she was going to go south, on an "endurance mission," south past the Equator, away from the Arctic, away from the Soviet Union. She would travel along the U.S. Pacific coast, past Central America, and down along South America to Cape Horn.

What was held back was that *Parche* would ultimately round the Cape and head back north through the Atlantic for the Barents. She would also have to swing wide of the Falkland Islands, where Britain and Argentina were at war. It was the most indirect route anyone could have thought of, save for a trip through Antarctica. It was a feint of masterful misdirection and it would also allow *Parche* to avoid the heavy ice she would have encountered, since she was leaving so early in the year. *Parche* would have to travel more than 15,000 nautical miles each way, a round trip that would make the mission last nearly five months. She was to go entirely underwater.

"They want to see how long we can last," the men began telling one another as they unknowingly repeated their own cover story. "We are going for a record."

As *Parche* was loaded for a possible 150 days at sea, so many cans of food were hoisted aboard that the men had to cover a toilet seat with a plank in order to transform one of the heads into a pantry. After that was filled to the ceiling, the upper-level operations passageway was crammed with enough food to make it completely impassable. Anyone trying to reach the wardroom had to walk through the captain's quarters, through his bathroom to the executive officer's bathroom, and out of the XO's door, emerging to take a right at the first cleared path.

Commander Peter J. Graef was at the helm for this trip. Graef, the father of six, looked out for his crew, and they knew it. If he wasn't in the conn, Graef was probably playing cribbage in the wardroom, riding an exercise bike he had stashed in the engine room, or sitting with one of his chiefs. Rank didn't matter to him, *Parche* did. He believed every minute he was on board that he was at the high point of his career. What was to come after, he once told one of his men, "just doesn't matter, it's all downhill."

As he led his crew out for their "Odyssey 82," some of the men were reveling in their special celebrity. Others just reveled.

"Animal" was on board, so dubbed because he delighted in breaking his own record for time lapsed between showers and because he alternately entertained and tortured his mates with his "stink-off" contests. Then there was "Bumper Car," who had acquired his name because he liked to walk through the sub bouncing off walls saying, "Look at me, I'm a bumper car." There was also a quartermaster called "Big Bird." He weighed in at more than 300 pounds, and he couldn't move through any of the hatches on board without somebody shouting, "Open, shut."

As far as the crew was concerned, the best diversion of all came from one of the youngest officers, Lieutenant Timothy R. Fain. The men saw him as a "raghat" just like them. He sported a goatee and shared their disdain for officer decorum. They targeted Fain's good nature for their most daring pranks. Their favorite was "EB-Greening" him—grabbing Fain and mummifying him with the leaf-green duct tape favored by the Electric Boat company because it could withstand sea pressures. It had been developed to seal up small cracks in equipment, but on *Parche* it was used primarily to bind and gag Fain. On this trip, he would be left green-wrapped for Graef on the wardroom table, and he would be similarly bandaged and left in the tunnel on the way to the reactor compartment as a surprise for the engineer officer.

The XO, Timothy W. Oliver, had less patience for the crew's antics, especially after the door to his compartment somehow ended up beneath the engines, then in the "wine cellar," a space by the bilges, and on into other hiding places around the boat. "No movies tonight!" Oliver would shout, echoing—by all accounts, unaware—James Cagney's portrayal of a blowhard supply-ship captain in *Mr. Roberts*.

Parche might have been headed toward a mission more daring than any depicted a couple of years later in *The Hunt for Red October*, but she was manned by a crew taking its cues from *M*A*S*H*.

There was just one moment when everyone on board was certain of their position, and that was when they crossed the Equator. In a ceremony that had been repeated on many submarines, first-timers were initiated, and humiliated, as they paid homage to "King Neptune." They were forced to eat a bilious concoction off the King's belly, quite literally the stomach of one of their more-experienced mates.

There were no such celebrations when *Parche* finally entered the Barents. This time, her divers were installing a new kind of tap pod. The clamps were gone. Instead, this pod was designed to break away and remain on the sea bottom if the Soviets tried to raise the line for any reason.

Other procedures also had been changed since the Soviets found the Okhotsk tap. After *Parche*'s divers laid the pod and her spooks had listened in for about a week, the submarine pulled out for comparatively safer waters before heading back in a week later to monitor the cable again. Graef may have been giving the recorders time to accumulate extra data for short-term review. The more likely alternative is that she came back in to add a second recorder or to lay a second tap in a new spot. That's what had been done in Okhotsk. Besides, the extra recording capacity would have been needed: *Parche* was scheduled for an overhaul after this mission and wouldn't come back to the Barents for two years.

Parche finally came home after being at sea for 137 days. For this "endurance op" she won another PUC, maintaining her streak of one Presidential Unit Citation for every trip to the Barents. This PUC, her fourth in four years, was signed by Reagan, who also sent Graef a box of cigars. The certificate used the standard language about "extraordinary heroism," but then it went on to say that *Parche* had "established new standards for endurance and excellence in underwater operations." The president had immortalized the Navy's cover story.

With *Parche* scheduled to be in overhaul throughout 1983, there was no other submarine that could be trusted to service the Barents cable tap. *Seawolf* was in the shipyard, recovering from storm damage, but her days of tapping Soviet cables were clearly over. Naval Intelligence never imagined *Seawolf* clunking and banging around the Barents, and the Soviets' discovery of the Okhotsk tap had ended any tapping missions in that sea. When *Seawolf* finally did emerge from the yards, she would mainly be used to search for pieces of test missiles and other Soviet hardware in the open ocean.* It also was still just drawing up plans to convert the USS *Richard B. Russell* (SSN-687) into its fourth and final special projects sub.

So Naval Intelligence was without its best source of information during what would become one of the most tense years of the cold war since détente. The Navy was trying to learn how to trail the Soviets under the ice by following them there from their ports, but as the U.S. Navy sent more and more attack subs, the number of skirmishes with the Soviets in the Arctic increased. Not only that, trailing the Soviets under the ice was proving difficult. The Navy was most successful in the deep polar regions where the waters had sound properties most like those of the open ocean. That wasn't the case in the marginal ice zones.

Still, the Navy had no choice but to keep trying. There was enough Soviet activity that Admiral James Watkins, who had succeeded Hayward as CNO, finally told the American public that the latest front in the cold war had moved far up north. And, he said, "if there are forces in that area, we'd better know how to fight them." He added, "The ice is a beautiful place to hide."

It was now more critical than ever for Naval Intelligence to spread what it was learning about Soviet tactics and strategy throughout the sub force. The captains and spooks on regular surveillance subs were filing thicker patrol reports than ever, and even much of the information from the cable taps, once tightly guarded, was being distributed to submarine officers, although first sanitized to disguise the source. Naval Intelligence was so desperate to out-think the Soviets that it was even willing to rely on a little knowledgeable guesswork. A group of submariners and analysts were gathered and told to write up what they thought would be found in a Soviet submarine operating manual. When that was

---

*By now, the Navy also had modified its two newest mini-subs, *Turtle* and *Sea Cliff*, to go much deeper than their original maximum of 6,500 feet, and among other things they were to help recover the pieces of test missiles that *Seawolf* found and that Air Force or Navy radar had tracked through "death smacks" into the ocean. *Turtle* had been refitted in 1979 to go to 10,000 feet. *Sea Cliff* was given a titanium sphere in the early 1980s to enable it to reach 20,000 feet, making it the first Navy vessel since *Trieste I* to go as deep as John Craven had envisioned when he was dreaming of a fleet of Deep Submergence Search Vehicles in the 1960s. Still, unlike the DSSVs Craven envisioned, both submersibles had to be hauled to dive sites on surface ships.

done, they were sent to visit and brief attack-submarine commanders on what they might expect to face at sea.

By now, it was clear that no one else was going to champion Rickover's idea for a special class of Arctic subs. Instead, the Navy had decided to try to give ice capabilities to nearly two dozen remaining Los Angeles–class subs, still scheduled for construction. Conceived as open-ocean aircraft carrier escorts, the original LA-class subs lacked some of the sophisticated electronic-surveillance equipment and ice-capable sonar that had been built into *Parche* and other Sturgeon boats. That had left the nation's newest subs unable to handle what had become the most crucial spying operations as easily as the boats they were replacing.

Lyon had been asked to help research what changes were needed to allow the LA boats to do better under the ice, but his funding never seemed to come through. While under-ice operations were increasingly focused on attempts to develop torpedoes and sonar that could better distinguish between ice ridges and missile subs in the deep polar regions, Lyon kept arguing that the fleet commanders were ignoring the greatest problem— that no U.S. sub had the ability to hunt or maneuver well enough to fight within the marginal ice, where he was certain the Soviets were most likely to hide. Nobody of rank, it seemed, wanted to hear it.

Just as the Soviet sea threat was growing, relations between the superpowers were disintegrating. Yuri V. Andropov, a former director of the KGB who had succeeded Leonid Brezhnev as the Soviet leader in 1982, was spinning apocalyptic visions of a U.S. first strike that even many KGB experts saw as alarmist.

Then Reagan began stirring Soviet fears. On March 8, 1983, he outpreached the preachers at the convention of the National Association of Evangelicals, held that year in Orlando, Florida. He offered a laundry list of national and international evils: abortion, teen pregnancy, clinics providing teen birth control. After an impassioned plea for school prayer, he turned his attention to the Soviet Union.

"Yes, let us pray for the salvation of all of those who live in that totalitarian darkness, pray they will discover the joy of knowing God," Reagan intoned. "But until they do, let us be aware that while they preach the supremacy of the state, declare its omnipotence over individual man, and predict its eventual domination of all peoples on the Earth, they are the focus of evil in the modern world."

Moments later, he concluded, "So, in your discussions of the nuclear freeze proposals, I urge you to beware the temptation of pride, the temptation of blithely declaring yourselves above it all and label both sides equally at fault, to ignore the facts of history and the aggressive impulses of an evil empire, to simply call the arms race a giant misunderstanding and thereby remove yourself from the struggle between right and wrong and good and evil."

Reagan had equated the fight against Communism with the fight between good and evil before. But the phrase "evil empire" became one of those sound bites that gets repeated over and over. It definitely captured the fearful attention of the Soviets. Their concern that Reagan might consider a first strike was bolstered on March 23 when, less than two weeks after his "evil empire" speech, the president went on television to introduce the world to "Star Wars"—the strategic defense initiative (SDI).

At first, the Soviets saw this plan to orbit lasers designed to blast Soviet missiles out of the sky as impractical. But Reagan's rhetoric, as interpreted by the KGB, further convinced some Soviet officials that the president was capable of ordering a first strike.

The Soviets weren't calmed either when, shortly after the evil empire and Star Wars speeches, the U.S. Pacific Fleet began its largest maneuvers since World War II. Navy warplanes from the carriers *Midway* and *Enterprise* flew over Soviet military installations on the Kuril Islands that mark the entrance to the Sea of Okhotsk. The show of force was another step in Lehman's efforts to get the Soviets' attention.

Following that, crucial arms control talks stalled as the Soviets protested a U.S. plan to place low-flying cruise missiles and Pershing II intermediate-range ballistic missiles in West Germany and Italy. Then, on August 31, the Soviets shot down a Korean Airlines passenger plane, KAL 007, which had veered over Soviet military bases near the Sea of Okhotsk. All 269 people on board were killed.

Reagan accused the Soviets of premeditated murder, of knowingly shooting down the civilian airliner. Rather than admit that they had made a lethal mistake, the Soviets claimed that the airliner was a CIA reconnaissance plane. Following the KAL incident, Soviet students at U.S. universities were called home on the grounds that anti-Soviet sentiment put them in physical danger. By the time Lech Walesa won the Nobel Peace Prize on October 6, the KGB was convinced that the award was part of a Western-Zionist plot to destabilize Eastern Europe.

Tensions mounted further on October 26, when Reagan ordered the invasion of Grenada. The United States claimed it was rescuing American medical students. But in the process, it overthrew the infant Communist government.

As all this was going on, the KGB was actively looking for signs that NATO and the United States were considering a first strike. The search, now a top priority, had been started by Andropov when he was still heading the KGB. It was code-named "Operation RYAN" for the Russian term for nuclear missile attack, *Raketno Yadernoye Napadenie*. According to Oleg Gordievsky, a high-ranking KGB officer who later defected to England, the KGB, throughout 1983, was pressuring Soviet agents around the globe to feed RYAN, to report alarming information even if they were skeptical of it themselves.

In the wake of the KAL shoot-down, the KGB pushed RYAN agents even harder. By now, Andropov had fallen gravely ill, and one of his kidneys had been removed. He had not been seen in public since mid-August. But he was still in charge, and he still believed the world could be heading toward nuclear Armageddon.*

With Operation RYAN running wild and nearly unchecked,

---

*In the midst of all this tension, the Soviets sent a Victor III submarine to waters somewhere between the Carolinas and Bermuda. The Americans countered, sending a frigate, the USS *McCloy*, and a submarine, the USS *Philadelphia* (SSN-690), to trail the Victor. Before anyone knew it, the boats were all engaged in a tug of war, or was it a game of soccer? It happened on October 31, 1983, and the prize was some of the best sonar technology the Americans had. The Victor moved in close to the frigate and accidentally snagged the ship's towed sonar array, tearing it free from American grasp. But within moments, the Victor was on the surface and floundering—her prize wrapped around her propeller. She had been disabled by her own intelligence coup. That much made the U.S. newspapers. But what happened next has never been reported. *Philadelphia*'s crew maneuvered near the Victor, then went in tight and below to check out the sub. The next thing anyone knew the array was wrapped around the *Philadelphia*. The Americans had inadvertently snatched it back.

Gordievsky says there was a real danger of a catastrophic mistake. That was never more true, he says, than during November NATO exercises, code-named "Able Archer." From November 2 to November 11, the NATO forces were practicing release procedures for tactical nuclear weapons, moving through all of the alert stages from readiness to general alert. Because the Soviets' own contingency plans for war called for real preparations to be shrouded under similar exercises, alarmists within the KGB came to believe that the NATO forces had been placed on an actual alert.

RYAN teams were given orders to look for signs that NATO was about to start a countdown toward nuclear war: last-minute crisis negotiations between Britain and the United States; food-industry efforts to stockpile, such as mass butchering of cattle; or evacuations of political, financial, and military leaders and their families. The Soviet alerts eased after November 11, when Able Archer came to an end.

But there was little easing of the paranoia. That December, Marshal Nikolai V. Ogarkov, chief of staff of the Soviet armed forces, made a stunning public pronouncement. He said that the Soviets believed the United States "would still like to launch a decapitating nuclear first strike."

Reagan's secretary of State, George P. Shultz, met Ogarkov's announcement with outright disbelief. Shultz was certain that this had to be just more talk. But in January 1984, the Soviets followed through on a threat made during the dispute over the Pershing II missiles. Offering their own show of force, they sent some Delta missile submarines back out into the Atlantic to cruise off U.S. shores along with the Yankees that were still routinely patrolling there. The aim was to show that the Deltas could hit targets throughout the United States as easily as the Pershings in Germany could target the Soviet Union. Ironically, the Soviet move actually put the Deltas just where the U.S. Navy could track them most easily. But the implied threat was nonetheless clear. Both sides were stepping up the normal cat-and-mouse game, trailing one another more aggressively than ever.

The Reagan administration now realized that it had to try to calm things down. The incendiary rhetoric in Washington came to an abrupt halt. Shultz began talking privately with Soviet diplomats to try to dispel the tension and renew a dialogue about arms control. Reagan took the new line public in a speech on January 16, when he said, "We are determined to deal with our differences peacefully, through negotiations." He also touched again on the vision he had evoked when he made his Star Wars proposal. "As I have said before, my dream is to see the day when nuclear weapons will be banished from the face of the earth."

After a while, the Soviets began to soften as well. Andropov died that February, and his successor, Konstantin Chernenko, signaled that he might be willing to talk about arms cuts. He attached a condition, however, that Reagan wasn't willing to go for. Chernenko wanted Reagan to drop Star Wars. The Soviets feared the technology could enable the United States to launch a first strike without fear of retaliation.

Throughout, the intelligence community was struggling to keep up with these events. The CIA launched a study to try to figure out why the Soviets seemed to have gotten so edgy, and as U.S. satellites captured the first images of Soviet missile tests in the Arctic, Naval Intelligence and the NSA began anxiously planning *Parche*'s return to the Barents.

Parche left for the Barents shortly after yet another diplomatic scuffle, in which the Soviets boycotted the Olympic Games in Los Angeles, answering the U.S. boycott of the games in Moscow four years earlier. When she returned, it was clear that she had brought home far more than even the most optimistic intelligence officials had hoped for. The taps had been recording all through the alert sparked by Able Archer and had captured a detailed look at the Soviet Navy's nuclear strategy. This was an ear to the Soviet Navy's nuclear command-and-control structure as it was placing some of its missile submarines on high alert, rehearsing for war. Some former intelligence officials say this information simply confirmed the picture that had been emerging from the taps about how the Soviets planned to use their missile subs. But other former CIA, NSA, and Navy officials say that *Parche*'s take from this mission was so critical to their understanding of the Soviets that it qualified as "the big casino," or "the crown jewels."

Based on the tap data, they say, U.S. intelligence realized that some information collected by human agents had been dead wrong. The tap recordings chronicled the dispersal of key Soviet ships and submarines and offered a new picture of the state of Soviet readiness. Just as some of the younger Navy analysts had postulated years earlier, the emphasis was going to be on protecting missile subs. In the early days of a crisis, the Soviets planned to move some of their Typhoons and Deltas into safe bastions. Those bastions would be guarded by the bulk of Soviet attack subs and warships. Attack vessels would also ride shotgun as the missile subs made a dash for the safety of the Arctic ice.

This was the strategy that had so worried the Pentagon. The Soviets had engineered a way to avoid NATO forces waiting to attack at the mouth of the GIUK gap as well as any NATO sub that tried to follow Soviet boats into the Barents. Still, *Parche* had carried home confirmation of one more crucial fact that eased the Pentagon's worst fears: the Soviet Union was not preparing for a first strike from the sea. As one former intelligence official says of the tap data, both from this and other missions: "It conveyed a notion that, while preemptive war was an option, the Soviet forces were not designed to go for a first strike."

The bottom line was this: the balance of power was changing. Soviet technological advances—the increased missile ranges, the hardening of submarine sails and hulls to withstand the ice—had placed the Soviet Union on the verge of achieving nuclear parity with the United States in the last major area where it had lagged behind. Now that the Soviet Union could better protect its missile subs, it had in its grasp that all-important "strategic reserve," a nearly invulnerable second-strike force. In the Soviets' view, this would make it even less likely that the United States would ever launch a first strike against them.

President Reagan was briefed on the findings, but he left it largely to the Navy and Defense Secretary Weinberger to grapple with the strategic military implications. Lehman and Watkins had been arguing for several years that if war came, the Navy would have to go up under the ice and try to root out the Soviet missile submarines, and they now decided to make this the Navy's official strategy. Their decision was based in part on extensive war games in which U.S. officials had been asked to act as they thought Soviet commanders would. And there were assumptions made, most notably that any major crises would take months to build, giving the Navy plenty of time to flood attack subs into the Barents, pick up Soviet missile subs leaving port, and "tag" them—follow them to their patrol areas.

Heady from their successes trailing submarines in the deepest waters of the Arctic, most admirals didn't want to hear Lyon's continued warnings that it was a lot easier to play tag than hide-and-seek. He was certain that the Soviets could lose a trail easily where the U.S. subs couldn't find them, in the shallow-water marginal ice zones. The admirals were even less interested these days in his critiques of the design modifications for the new LA-class submarines. In fact, after forty years as the Navy's key Arctic expert, Lyon was inexplicably under orders to stay away from the redesign of the LA-class boats.

Navy leaders acknowledge that the sub force would have taken big losses by trying to blast into the Soviet bastions or roust their missile subs from under the ice. But they also say they had no doubt that they could have beaten many of the Soviet subs to their war positions. To test that theory, they sent more than two dozen attack subs surging from Atlantic ports toward the Soviet Union one Sunday. Every intelligence sensor was aimed at recording the Soviets' reaction, and not a single one picked up any sign that the scramble had been noticed. Besides that, Navy leaders were counting on the fact that U.S. crews were better trained than their Soviet counterparts and had spent far more time at sea given how much of the Soviet fleet was usually broken down and out of service. And if the Soviets were willing to confine themselves to the Arctic and their home waters, the U.S. subs would know roughly where to hunt their prey. They also would have prior knowledge of favorite Soviet patrol areas from surveillance ops and from the sonobuoys now peppering the marginal ice where SOSUS didn't reach.

The limits and the advantages of the U.S. strategy were voiced most bluntly by Watkins, who was the chief of Naval Operations from mid-1982 until mid-1986. He says the Soviets' strategy of pulling back their missile subs was "probably smart" and initially did make it more difficult to destroy them. But he also

believed that if the Soviets started a nuclear war with land missiles, the United States could eliminate "a very large percentage"
of the missile subs that they would have positioned to make a
second strike from the sea.

Still, any strategy that allowed for even a few enemy missile
subs to fire at U.S. targets was a far cry from the days when most
of the Soviet Yankees traveled the seas with unknown and lethal
shadows that could prevent them from shooting at all. And for
intelligence officials, it was a huge relief to realize that the
Soviets were not readying to use their improved position to start
a war.

Ironically, the 1984 run—the trip that brought home the "big
casino"—was the first of *Parche*'s five missions to the Barents
that would fail to win a Presidential Unit Citation. (Instead,
Parche was given a Navy Unit Commendation, the next highest
award.) *Parche* may have supplied the United States with an
amazing wealth of critical information, but her own role in the
ongoing cold war drama was becoming more routine.

Actually, Naval Intelligence was now hatching a plan to
access the Soviet cable in real time, without having to wait for a
submarine to travel there at all. The concept had been kicking
around NURO since the mid-1970s, when some officials envisioned linking the Okhotsk tap by cable to Japan. John Butts, the
director of Naval Intelligence, and his team were now pushing
an ambitious idea to lay 1,200 miles of cable between the
Barents taps and Greenland. He envisioned barges that would
look so perfectly innocuous that no one would ever dream that
they were involved in stretching and laying his imagined cable.
And he saw a full-time staff of linguists and cryptologists dedicated to translating and decoding the material as it came in.

The plan was grand. In fact, it was grandiose. Some of Butts's
colleagues began to joke that he was trying to take over the world.
They watched, wondering whether Butts and his aides would realize they were getting more than a little carried away. They waited
as Butts tallied up the $1 billion cost. The intelligence committees
in Congress didn't wonder or wait. They simply made it clear they
were going to sink Butts's plan, barges and all.

Throughout all of this, the two superpowers continued talking about shedding, or at least shrinking, their nuclear arsenals.

And when Chernenko died in March 1985, the old Soviet guard all but died with him. For its new leader, the Politburo reached into a younger generation to find fifty-four-year-old Mikhail Gorbachev. He had been convinced ever since the Able Archer panic that the Soviet Union had to get back to the negotiating table. Now, as he took up his post as general secretary, he seemed more willing than any of his recent predecessors to consider major changes in U.S.-Soviet relations.

Indeed, he made his first move late on the day of Chernenko's funeral. "The USSR has never intended to fight the United States and does not have such intentions now," Gorbachev flatly declared to Bush and Shultz. "There have never been such mad-men within the Soviet leadership, and there are none now."

During these first steps toward conciliation, U.S. authorities made startling discoveries that reminded the nation that the days of spies and old-style cold warriors were not over. Rich Haver, it seems, hadn't been seeing ghosts at all.

It was early in 1985 when Bill Studeman, who was about to succeed Butts as director of Naval Intelligence, walked into Haver's office with a critical piece of paper. Haver, who was now the deputy director of Naval Intelligence, took it and read through the FBI's account of an interview with a woman named Barbara Walker, who had come to report that her husband, a former Navy chief, had been spying for the Soviets. The FBI noted that Walker had been living the good life, although his only visible means of support was a failing detective business.

Haver knew instantly that he was holding the answer that he and Studeman had sought back in the late 1970s when they tried to convince admirals to investigate a possible communications break.

John A. Walker Jr. was a retired Navy submariner and communications specialist. In 1967 he had been a watch officer in Norfolk handling communications with American submarines in the Atlantic. He had access to reports on submarine operations, technical manuals, and the daily key lists that were used to unscramble all of the messages sent through the military's most widely used coding machines. If the Soviets had gotten hold of any of this, they would have known that they needed to look over their shoulders, that their missile subs were being followed by much quieter U.S. subs. They also would have known just how quiet U.S. submarines were, and just how critical submarine-quieting technology was to the balance of ocean power.

Later, Haver and Studeman learned that Walker had given all this to the Soviets, and more. Walker's espionage had given the Soviets the warning and the motivation they needed to pull off a master stroke in this cold war under the seas. They would make their subs much harder to trail by hiding them far closer to home. In fact, when Walker retired from the Navy in 1976, he had continued his espionage by drawing others into his scheme. First he recruited another Navy communications specialist, Jerry A. Whitworth, who continued Walker's access to the crucial key lists. In the early 1980s, Walker enlisted his brother Arthur, who worked for a defense contractor. And soon after that, Walker began using his son Michael, an enlisted man on the USS *Nimitz,* a nuclear-powered aircraft carrier. Walker was caught only because his ex-wife wanted to prevent him from recruiting their daughter into a spy ring that had already swallowed their son.

The news was sobering. For all the years that the United States had been eavesdropping on the Soviets through the cable taps, the Soviets had been listening in on U.S. communications, and without the years of research, investment in technology, or risk to men's lives. In fact, Walker's ring had cost the Soviets less than $1 million over eighteen years, and for that money he had almost single-handedly destroyed the U.S. nuclear advantage.

Walker was arrested on May 20. The next day, Haver was assigned to write the damage report, largely because he had written much of it ten years earlier when he first tried to raise the alarm. But the damage was worse than even Haver had predicted. Walker also had passed crucial secrets about U.S. techniques for quieting subs, such as cushioning engine equipment to prevent vibrations from resonating through hulls. Indeed, around the time Walker was caught, U.S. sonar operators were reporting that they couldn't identify some of the newest Soviet attack subs until their own boats were right on top of the Soviets—or in some cases, were surprised by them. A few of the newest Soviet subs, the Sierras and the Akulas, were, in fact, nearly as silent as the U.S. Sturgeon class. (It later turned out that the Soviets also had been helped by Japanese and Norwegian companies, including a subsidiary of Toshiba Corporation, which had surreptitiously sold them the huge, computer-guided milling machines needed to make the propeller blades on Soviet subs much smoother and quieter.)

Studeman later testified before a federal judge, saying that Walker's ring might have had "powerful war-winning implications for the Soviet side." And when Vitaly Yurchenko, a high-ranking KGB officer, defected in July 1985, he told the CIA that the Walker-Whitworth ring was the most important espionage victory in KGB history.

Walker pleaded guilty that October and agreed to help authorities assess the damage in exchange for leniency for his son. The elder Walker received a single life sentence, with eligibility for parole after ten years. The deal was approved by Defense Secretary Weinberger, but Navy Secretary Lehman was furious. In his eyes, Walker's treachery was being treated as "just another white-collar crime."

Lehman rhapsodized that if it had been up to him, he would have applied one of the penalties for treason from back in the days following the American Revolution. The essence, as Lehman quoted it, was:

> That you . . . be hanged by the neck, but not until you are dead, but that you be taken down again, and whilst you are yet alive, your bowels be taken out and burnt before your face; and that afterwards your head be severed from your body and your body divided into four quarters. . . . And may God Almighty have mercy on your soul.

A month after Walker was sentenced, Lehman had one more body for his imagined gallows and Haver had caught his second ghost. This time it was Yurchenko who offered up the Navy's second spy.

Back in January 1980, when Yurchenko was working in the Soviet embassy in Washington, he had fielded a call from a man who would only say, "I have some information to discuss with you and to give to you."

The caller visited the embassy, but Yurchenko never learned

his name or what he had to offer. Other Soviet agents had taken the case. That wasn't much to go on, but it turned out to be enough. The FBI began going through old recordings of Yurchenko's conversations that had been captured by wiretaps. Investigators found the call and played it back for some NSA employees. They recognized the voice.

Yurchenko's mystery caller turned out to be Ronald W. Pelton, a former NSA employee, who was arrested on November 25, 1985. Some of the "information" he had been offering the Soviets turned out to be about the Navy's top-secret Okhotsk cable-tapping operation. Pelton had sold out the Okhotsk taps for $35,000. In an attempt to mask his own bankruptcy, he had exposed the nation's most critical submarine spy missions and risked the lives of the men on both *Seawolf* and *Parche*. Both subs had been sent to Okhotsk during the nearly two years that elapsed before the Soviets found the tap pods. Just why it took the Soviets so long to follow up on Pelton's tip remains unclear.

After Pelton was arrested, the Navy finally turned over Haver's old report to the Senate Intelligence Committee, the one he had written in January 1982 outlining his suspicions that a spy was responsible for the loss of the Okhotsk tap. The senators were furious. At a closed hearing, they lambasted Navy representatives for withholding the report for three years. And they were indignant that the Navy had risked 140 men's lives, sending *Parche* right back to the Barents despite Haver's suspicions that there was a spy.

William Cohen, a Republican from Maine, was one of the angriest lawmakers in the room. Cohen, who would become secretary of Defense under President Bill Clinton, demanded to know who had written the report.

From the back of the room, Haver stood up.

"Sir, I wrote the report." When one of the senators wanted to know how he could be so sure that this was his work, Haver cited the report's date and noted that he wasn't about to forget his own birthday.

Cohen wanted to know why the Navy failed to react to Haver's conclusion that the Soviets probably had foreknowledge of the cable tap. He wanted to know why nobody searched for a spy.

"They didn't believe it," Haver responded.

Cohen pressed on. Was it prudent, he wanted to know, to continue to operate the cable-tapping program, push it full tilt ahead, when there may have been a spy?

All Haver could do was repeat what he had said, that nobody believed he was right, that others in Naval Intelligence had failed to reach the same conclusion. Finally, in a gesture of loyalty, he tossed in that there had been some ambiguity. He did not say that he had never had any doubt, that he had known all along there was probably only one way to add up the facts.

There was one good bit of news for the Navy and the NSA in Pelton's arrest. Now that they knew who the spy was, they also knew that the Barents tap was still secure. Pelton's job and his security clearances simply hadn't stretched that far. As long as he was in the dark, so were the Soviets.

Pelton pleaded not guilty, and his trial was scheduled for May 1986. But that created another problem. Somehow the Navy and the NSA had to keep the glare of the trial off *Parche,* away from the Barents, and clear of yet another mission.

It wasn't hard to persuade a judge to agree to keep the proceedings devoid of any real details. But Bob Woodward and other *Washington Post* reporters were already digging on their own. They had a cable-tapping story ready for the *Post*'s front page.

Navy and NSA officials were frantic. *Seawolf* was in the Mediterranean at that moment trying to tap a cable that ran from West Africa to Europe as she sought to help out in a showdown with Libyan leader Muammar el-Qaddafi. *Seawolf* was working side by side in the Mediterranean with the *NR-1* mini-submarine (though their efforts would not yield any worthwhile information). Not only that, but *Parche* was going to head back out to the Barents later in the year. She had to. The Soviets were being more aggressive than ever in the Atlantic. They had just sent a cluster of five Victor-class attack subs and for three weeks kept them so close to the East Coast of the United States that tracking them almost used up the Atlantic Fleet's store of sonobuoys.

An article now could be devastating. CIA Director William Casey threatened to prosecute the *Post* for revealing intelligence

276 BLIND MAN'S BLUFF

secrets. Reagan personally telephoned the *Post's* publisher, Katharine Graham, beseeching her not to publish, as priceless secrets were at stake.

In the end, the *Post* ran a limited story the day before Pelton's trial began. The article said little more than that Pelton had betrayed a high-tech and long-running submarine operation to intercept Soviet communications in Okhotsk. There was no mention of *Halibut, Seawolf,* or *Parche.* Not a word about the Barents or Libya. The trial disclosed no further details, and early in June, Pelton was convicted and given three consecutive life sentences plus ten years.

Their secret safe, *Parche's* crew shoved off in early September, with Commander Richard A. Buchanan at the helm. This was the sub's seventh Barents journey, the sixth trip via the Arctic route, and the second trip with Buchanan as her captain. It was a trip that would stand out from all of the rest.

Pelton's trial had left the crew nervous. By now, they would all have had to have been lobotomized not to know that they were about to replicate the very sort of operation Pelton had given away to the Soviets.

The code name from Pelton's day, "Ivy Bells," was dead. Now there were a series of new codes, including "Manta" for the overall operation and "Acetone" for the tap itself, and even those codes were being changed continuously. The men knew, however, that whatever the NSA called the operation, the Soviets had been given a look at their strategies, at their plans, at how they did business.

Crew members talked about Pelton and the man they had come to call "Johnny Walker Red," often late into the night. They thought about how much classified information each man on *Parche* had handled. How many stacks of crypto material could easily have found their way to a photocopying machine if just one of them had the itch. They also talked about how hard the Navy had tried to keep secret from them the details of their own missions. It was galling. Secrecy, the men knew, couldn't be achieved through any terrific security measures, and it couldn't be preserved by trying to keep the guys on the boat in the dark. It could only be maintained because the men themselves found the idea of selling out to the Soviets unthinkable. And it could be lost when just one of them decided that maybe selling out wasn't so unthinkable after all.

Still, as the boat made her way toward the Barents, the men also had a sense of payback and daring. The Soviets may have had Pelton and Walker, but the United States had *Parche*. And by now, her crew had the drill down cold.

The trip through the Arctic went well. *Parche* was 20 or 30 miles from where she would retrieve the tap pods and plant new ones. She had already charted the corridor, the route she would take closer to Soviet shores. Over the years, various U.S. submarines had played chicken with the sonar buoys the Soviets had set up to pop out of the water and transmit should a sub try to pass. Before *Parche* arrived at the Barents, the buoys were all mapped out—the ones that worked, the ones that were duds. All she had to do was take a path through the duds, move in a little closer, and bend to the left.

Then the message came. Hold off. Wait. Don't move. *Parche* was by now just outside the 12-mile limit. But her path in was now sealed—by presidential order. On September 19, while *Parche* was still en route, Soviet Foreign Minister Eduard Shevardnadze had delivered a letter to Reagan from Gorbachev. The general secretary had written that he wanted to push the arms negotiations along by meeting with Reagan. He gave two choices of locales, and the United States picked Reykjavík, Iceland, a quiet spot halfway between Washington and Moscow.

The meeting was set for October 11, 1986, a follow-up to the previous year's summit. At that meeting, there had been one sticking point, and that was Star Wars—Gorbachev wanted SDI eliminated. Reagan passionately insisted that SDI was the only way out of the precarious balance built on mutually assured destruction. He believed his lasers in space could forever erase the concept that peace depended on the threat that the United States and the Soviet Union could wipe each other out.

During that last meeting, discussion had often deteriorated into a shouting match, but in the heat of battle, Reagan and Gorbachev came to like and respect one another. In the end, they also came out with a joint statement saying they wanted to work toward a 50 percent reduction in strategic weapons and other arms cuts.

This second act being staged in Reykjavík promised to be the most unpredictable and remarkable superpower meeting ever. Both sides had agreed that rather than scripting everything in advance, they would just clear space for the two leaders to talk. No wonder there were such high hopes for this summit. No wonder Gorbachev unwittingly halted *Parche* in her tracks with his letter.

On board, the sense of history about to happen was lost on the men. They were certain they would be sent in to finish their task. For them, the summit just meant an uncomfortable and possibly dangerous wait.

"Let's get in, let's get out," one of the men began grumbling over and over to anyone who would listen. After a while, they were all saying it, in one way or another. They were so close to the prize, could almost see it, smell it, but their orders were to pull back, not to touch it.

It was irritating. It was worse than that. There was too much time to think, too much time to listen as one warship after another passed nearby. There was too much time to recognize that the president didn't want to be anywhere around if *Parche* was caught. The men had always known that what they were doing was illegal and that if *Parche* were ever found or forced to self-destruct, the United States would deny they had ever been there. It was just that now the message was louder than they wanted to hear.

A week passed. Then two. *Parche* was waiting, and by now, so was the rest of the world. October 11 came. Men crammed into *Parche*'s radio room all day, trying to copy the news on the radio circuits, trying to follow what was going on. But neither they nor anyone on shore was allowed to hear the details. That had been the deal. No reporters, no reports, not until it was all over.

Reagan and Gorbachev were meeting in Hofdi House, an isolated structure on the bleak edge of the North Atlantic. Shultz thought it looked haunted, and Icelanders were convinced that it was. They sat in a small room, Shultz and Shevardnadze, Reagan and Gorbachev, two translators, and two note-takers. There against a single window, looking out onto turbulent and frigid waters that would perhaps ultimately wash over to where *Parche* sat beneath the Barents, the summit began.

Compromises were offered and concessions were made. Staff negotiators agreed that they could cut ballistic-missile arsenals in half, to roughly 6,000 warheads and 1,600 delivery vehicles on each side, and that they could also slash the number of shorter-range missiles. Reagan and Gorbachev themselves were talking about making these cuts over the next five years, and then eliminating the rest of their nuclear arsenals within five years after that. It was on the table, ten years to a nuke-free world. They were actually talking about the end of the terrors that had existed since the Manhattan Project, talking about forever rendering false Robert J. Oppenheimer's horrifying 1945 prophesy, "I am become death, destroyer of worlds," a quote from the Bhagavad Gita that the physicist intoned after the first atomic bomb had been tested.

Gorbachev still wanted Reagan to give up SDI, or at least limit Star Wars research to the laboratory and to agree to refrain from testing in space for ten years. Reagan wanted to conduct space tests, at least enough of them so that SDI could be deployed in ten years. At that time, he promised, the United States would hand the entire system, all of the technology, over to the Soviets.

Gorbachev wasn't buying it, and Reagan pleaded for resolution. "I have a picture that after ten years you and I come to Iceland and bring the last two missiles in the world and we have the biggest damn party in celebration of it!" He continued, "A meeting in Iceland in ten years: I'll be so old, you won't recognize me. I'll say, 'Mikhail?' You'll say, 'Ron?' And we'll destroy the last two."

They parried. Gorbachev said he might not be alive in ten years, that he was just entering his "danger period," and that Reagan had passed through his and could now count on making it smoothly to age one hundred.

"I can't live to one hundred worrying that you'll shoot one of those missiles at me," Reagan answered.

The argument went on. Reagan insisted that he had promised

the American people he wouldn't give up SDI; Gorbachev insisted that the president would still have SDI even if he confined testing to the lab. Finally Reagan spoke the words that might have sounded like just so much lofty rhetoric in any other context: "It would be fine with me if we eliminated all nuclear weapons."

"We can do that. Let's eliminate them. We can eliminate them," Gorbachev shot back.

This could have been the defining moment. Maybe it should have been. But Hofdi House was living up to its reputation. The men were indeed haunted, by this single impasse.

"It is a question of one word," Reagan said, pleading for Gorbachev to give up his insistence that SDI proceed only in the laboratory.

"It's 'laboratory' or good-bye," Gorbachev insisted. The meeting ended on that note.

Outside, a crush of international press was learning how close the two had come to an agreement. Reporters were rushing off to wire the world their postmortems that would declare the summit a failure.

Beneath the water, another wire reached *Parche*.

Word shot through the sub as a single line was quoted throughout the boat: "You are authorized to penetrate the 12-mile line." *Parche* was going in.

She was now only six or seven hours away from her mission. Conversation on board turned to other missions, other close calls. It was how the men admitted without admitting how scared they were. They talked about tracking Yankees and the ultraquiet new Akula and Sierra attack submarines that had come out in the last couple of years. They called the Akula the "Walker sub" because the spy had inspired the Soviet move toward deadly quiet engines. In fact, Soviet technology was moving ahead so fast that more U.S. attack subs were being detected by the Soviet boats they were trying to trail. American subs were also being detected near the Soviet coasts. It was there that the spooks would hear the Soviets react in a burst of messages. The spooks had taken to calling the Soviet detection warning "stutter nine": in their code, eight bursts meant a suspected detection, nine meant one confirmed. The stutter came from repetition. The men talked about all this knowing all the while that on *Parche* detection was likely to mean self-destruction.

Maybe it was to avoid that fear that just about everyone was getting EB-Greened to the walls these days—Pharaoh's tomb under the Barents. But the mission was unfolding without a hitch. The divers went out, the spooks listened, the divers retrieved the pods and left others in place to keep collecting.

Slowly, quietly, *Parche* began the trip away from the cable to the point where she could signal the companion sub that all was well.

That's when they felt, heard, the ping, that awful sound of active sonar ringing through the hull. Someone above knew a submarine was there. Fortunately, there were two—*Parche* and her escort sub, the USS *Finback* (*SSN-670*). *Finback* quickly moved in, got the Soviets' attention, acted like this was just another game of tag under the sea. It worked. *Parche* stole away.

They were hundreds of miles from the moor when they popped up an antenna. With sonar making certain no one was around, they sent a quick message to Washington: "Mission accomplished."

It took *Parche* about a month to reach the waters outside San Diego, where she stopped briefly on her way home. Bruce DeMars, who was now the admiral in charge of submarines, came out in a small motorboat to meet her and ride back to port with the men. He was ecstatic. Casually dressed, he made it clear that nobody had to put on the spit and shine for him, not on this run anyway. DeMars carried his congratulations and videotaped copies of the New York Mets battling their way through seven games of the World Series. Baseball was the theme on the ride back to port. As usual, the men's families, wives, and girlfriends were waiting for them on the pier when they arrived.

In Washington, someone else awaited Buchanan. President Reagan wanted to meet this captain, wanted to personally congratulate the man who had earned *Parche* yet another PUC. It would be *Parche*'s fifth, on top of the three NUCs she also had won. The way the crew heard it, the brass was all there, the president, Vice President Bush, the CNO, members of the Joint Chiefs of Staff.

Buchanan stood there, commander of the Navy's most sensitive spy sub, feeling like an E-1, the lowest-ranking man on a sub. Certainly he was the lowest-ranking man in the room. Then Reagan looked him in the eye and called him a modern-day John Wayne. It was the part of the story that Buchanan's men liked best. They figured Reagan had to be sincere. He had known John Wayne.

TRUST BUT VERIFY

I f the cold war wasn't quite over, it was definitely beginning to wane. Reykjavík had been the start, and both sides seemed to sense it. Even as the U.S. Navy gave chase to a cluster of Soviet Victor III attack subs off the East Coast in 1987, and as U.S. subs continued their pace of spy missions, something was changing, something that was at first almost intangible.

To be sure, Gorbachev continued to bristle about Star Wars and blew up in frustration at nearly every meeting with Shultz, at least once because he was convinced that the American people would never forgive Soviet acts of aggression dating back to the 1960 shoot-down of Gary Powers in his U-2 spy plane. But these tirades were almost all over the failure to reach a peace soon enough, or deep enough. Just two years after the paranoid reign of Andropov, the Soviet Union was saying it had had enough.

In fact, in May 1987 the Soviets announced a formal military doctrine—one aimed simply at defending their homeland.

That December, Reagan and Gorbachev met in Washington, D.C., for the first follow-up summit to Reykjavík. They finally signed a treaty to eliminate an entire class of nuclear arms, the intermediate-range nuclear forces. It was the angry impasse over a similar INF treaty that, in 1983, had made some top Soviet officials fear that the United States was considering a first strike. Now, as both sides agreed to sign, there was only a shadow of the old hostilities.

"*Doveryai, no proveryai*—trust but verify," Reagan said, evoking an old Russian maxim at the signing.

"You repeat that at every meeting," Gorbachev teased, chuckling.

"I like it," Reagan agreed.

Who could have imagined Ronald Reagan kidding around with a Soviet leader? These two men were so ebullient that Gorbachev stopped his motorcade on the way to the White House so he could shake hands with the crowd. Reagan answered at the next summit by allowing Gorbachev to introduce him to the Soviet people milling about Red Square. Georgi Arbatov, the director of the Soviet Union's Institute for the Study of the USA and Canada, put it all into words: "We are going to do something terrible to you. We are going to deprive you of an enemy."

Still, while Gorbachev and Reagan had set the tone, it was going to take both sides some time to accept the enormity of what was happening, to believe that this friendship could last and that the cold war was really coming to an end. That much was clear as the top men in uniform began holding summits of their own.

Admiral William J. Crowe Jr., chairman of the Joint Chiefs of Staff, met Marshal Sergei Akhromeyev, the chief of staff of the Soviet armed forces. The marshal and the Joint Chiefs mixed socially. Crowe took Akhromeyev on a guided tour of a U.S. air-craft carrier. They even met in the Pentagon's "Tank," the secure room where top U.S. military men planned their moves against the Soviets. Still, as Akhromeyev sat with the Americans talking about newfound friendship, he could not disguise his frustrations over U.S. sub spying and tracking operations, which seemed unchanged from cold war days.

"You, you're the problem," he blurted out at Admiral Carlisle A. H. Trost, now the chief of Naval Operations. Not only were U.S. subs still lurking off Soviet waters, but Akhromeyev was convinced that he could track all of his own subs by simply following the American P-3 Orion sub-hunters in the air. It was a stunning revelation of just how effective U.S. antisubmarine efforts continued to be.

Trost simply tried to calm him down, saying that U.S. strategy was not intended to threaten anyone. But even as he faced Akhromeyev, Trost realized he was being given a look deep inside the Soviet psyche, and what he saw was different from what he had long believed. It had once all seemed so clear to him that Soviet forces were designed for aggression. But now Trost could see how strongly Akhromeyev believed that he had only been part of an effort to defend his country, a country surrounded by enemies, by NATO ships, submarines, and airborne sub-hunters.

Gradually, these men from such different worlds were breaking through to one another. They were connecting and realizing just what a shared experience the cold war had been. One telling moment came when Admiral Kinnaird McKee—one of the Navy's most successful sub captains, Whitey Mack's chief nemesis back in the *Lapon* days, the man who had later become Rickover's successor as the submarine force's nuclear czar—sat swapping sea stories with a top Soviet admiral at a luncheon at the Pentagon. Also there was Rich Haver. When he was introduced as a Naval Intelligence analyst, Haver heard the Soviet translator mutter to his admiral, K. A. Makarov, something about "CIA."

The tense moment seemed to pass as McKee sat with his guest of honor, blowing the old ballast tanks. McKee reminisced about his days as captain of the USS *Dace*. At the time, Makarov had his own command of a 671-project sub, the kind, he pointed out helpfully, the Americans called "Victor." Then Makarov let slip that he had been near the *Dace* on one of its patrols, that he had known it was the *Dace* even then.

"I wonder who trailed whom," Haver said, knowing quite well that it was McKee's spotting and trailing of the first Victor during its sea trials in 1968 that had helped launch the admiral's career. Makarov gave Haver an icy stare and continued staring as he offered his answer through his interpreter: "Now is not the time to discuss that."

But that look said more. It seemed to acknowledge, "I know who trailed whom, and it wasn't me." These were old wounds, and Haver had supplied the salt. He had reminded the Soviets of the long years when they were behind, when they could have been called downright inept. They may have closed the gap in the final years of the cold war, but that hadn't eased the humiliation. Haver had broken a rule of this special glasnost, of this still-new and uneasy openness among military men, and when lunch was over, Makarov made that clear. "Tell this young man that when veterans get together, it doesn't matter who won or lost," he said through his translator. "It's enough that both survived."

Although Makarov's use of the past tense may have been a bit premature, it certainly fit the Soviet perspective. After that flurry of activity off the American coast in 1986 and 1987, Soviet submarines had been pulled back home. On the U.S. side, however, it was business almost as usual. Spy subs had gotten more cautious. Improvements in sonar and the electronics-intercept gear meant they no longer had to go quite as close to Soviet subs or shore to capture intelligence. (Los Angeles subs weren't as maneuverable in tight spots anyway.) The pace of operations had not let up. For instance, Submarine Squadron 11 in San Diego alone sent eight of its ten nuclear attack submarines out on surveillance operations in 1988, keeping up with the rate set during the height of the cold war. The USS *Salt Lake City* (*SSN-716*) operated for nearly seven months in the northern Pacific, followed by the USS *Portsmouth* (*SSN-707*), the USS *Pintado* (*SSN-672*), the USS *La Jolla* (*SSN-701*), and others.

The pace of operations was fueled by signs that the Soviets had finally learned to build subs as powerful and, more important, nearly as silent as American subs. There was a colossal irony to all of this: just as the Soviets had finally learned to construct first-class submarines, they were running out of money to build and operate them. But that realization had yet to filter down through the ranks on either side.

And so, out on Mare Island the pace of special projects operations didn't let up much. *Seawolf* had been retired in 1987, and

Parche had gone into overhaul so that she could be modified to handle a wider array of potential projects. She was cut in half to fit in a 100-foot section that would hold new sophisticated equipment for cable-tapping and gear to allow her to retrieve objects from the ocean floor as *Seawolf* had. The overhaul was scheduled to take several years, but even so, the United States continued cable-tapping without pause, having readied *Parche*'s replacement, the *Richard B. Russell,* named after the senator whose name had once been synonymous with a wink and a nod and nearly blank-check acceptance of all intelligence operations.

From 1987 through 1990, *Russell* collected one award for each trip to the Barents—one Presidential Unit Citation and three Navy Unit Commendations. Her missions went on as Reagan left office in early 1989 and Bush came in, as Bush and Gorbachev picked up where Reagan and Gorbachev had left off, and even after Bush wrote privately to Gorbachev offering to help the Soviets retrieve one of their submarines that had been lost in the Norwegian Sea.*

Later that year, Trost was invited to Leningrad, the honored guest of the Soviet Navy. On this trip, a month before the Berlin Wall crumbled, he was given a firsthand look at how rapidly Soviet submarine capabilities were dwindling. The Soviets were having trouble keeping their subs at sea, paying for maintenance, and running enough operations to train their crews. Trost was stunned by the changes that had taken place since he last visited the Soviet Union in 1971, a time when he knew his room had been bugged and he and his cohorts followed, so overtly in fact, that the Navy men had stopped in their tracks to offer to tell their Soviet shadow where they were headed. Now there seemed to be no spies. Instead, there were frank discussions, admiral to admiral, about the difficulties of keeping a navy running, about the futility of nuclear warfare. Indeed, Trost got his first look at Soviet submarine construction and the problems facing Soviet commanders: they saw subs on which sometimes only the offi-

*The lost boat, the *Komsomolets*, was a 6,400-ton prototype of a new class of Soviet nuclear sub known as the "Mike," designed to dive much deeper than other full-size attack subs. It was the fourth Soviet nuclear submarine to sink during the cold war. While even more Soviet nuclear and diesel subs were crippled by reactor accidents, fires, or other mishaps, at least seven or eight sank outright.

cers spoke Russian and conscripts from the republics were so ill trained that only the officers could manage much of the critical maintenance necessary to keep the boats at sea. But perhaps the most telling moment occurred when Trost and the top Soviet admiral, Vladimir N. Chernavin, began joking, or half-joking, that their fates were linked. If either side failed to maintain an adequate-size navy, the other would have a terrible time justifying his defense expenditures. The world was changing from beneath them almost as fast as East and West Berliners had torn down the Wall with hammers, rocks, and their bare hands.

By now, top State Department officials had begun to worry about anything that could undermine Gorbachev as he continued to move toward closer relations with the United States. Their concern fell on the *Russell* cable-tapping mission that was scheduled for when Gorbachev and Bush were to meet again. In the end, the timing of *Russell*'s trip was changed.

But one changed mission was not necessarily enough. Some diplomatic officials worried that the intelligence community was adapting too slowly from its long-held views of the Soviet Union. There was no doubt that after forty years the nation's spies were reluctant to be deprived of their enemy. What would happen to the intelligence agencies when nobody cared about the measurements of weaponry, of force? What would happen in a world when the most crucial information came not from covert efforts but from the Cable News Network and its twenty-four-hour reports about the sweeping social changes?

That the submarine force faced these questions with concern and some resentment was evident when retired and current officers met at the annual convention of the Naval Submarine League in June 1990. Around the world, shards of the Berlin Wall were being sold as souvenirs, but within the convention halls at a Radisson Hotel outside Washington, D.C., it was certain that nobody would be crying out for a "peace dividend," not a single man would eye the submarine fleet with a scowl on his face, a calculator in hand, figuring the myriad social programs that could be funded even in one boat's stead. The specter of the bean counters, however, loomed large, even in their absence.

The man who was now secretary of the Navy, H. Lawrence

Garrett III, stood before the assemblage and warned that "budget-cutters are sharpening their knives, even as we speak." He failed to mention that the sharpest knife was coming from General Colin Powell, who had succeeded Crowe as chairman of the Joint Chiefs of Staff and had just announced that the military budget would probably have to be cut by 25 percent over the next several years. Garrett, taking a far harder line, went on to dismiss any effect that perestroika and glasnost might have on the game of submarine spying. "The logic of nuclear deterrence has not changed just because the Soviet leader routinely presses the flesh on Pennsylvania Avenue," he thundered.

Other speakers were more moderate but still called for prudence and skepticism when it came to the Soviet Union. William H. J. Manthorpe Jr., then deputy director of Naval Intelligence, posed the question that was quickly becoming the rallying cry of the submarine force: "What will be the intentions of the Soviet leadership of the future? Can we depend on those intentions being benign? The answer, of course, is: No, I would not bet my country's security on it."

Before long, though, something happened that convinced even the most hard-line skeptics that the Soviet Union was no longer the most likely candidate to drag the United States into a war. Almost as if he realized that there was room on center stage for a new villain, Saddam Hussein stepped forward from Iraq and overnight annexed Kuwait. The United States had a new reason to fight, and this time it stood shoulder to shoulder with the Soviet Union, issuing an unprecedented joint statement denouncing the "blatant transgression of basic norms of civilized conduct" and calling for an arms embargo against Iraq. Secretary of State James A. Baker III would later proclaim that this was "The Day the Cold War Ended."

When war finally broke out in the Persian Gulf in January 1991, submarines played only a bit part. Still, the conflict dramatized the need to refocus defense efforts on regional conflicts, and with an eye to ensuring its place in future conflicts, the submarine force highlighted the role it had played against Iraq for all it was worth. The USS *Louisville* (SSN-724) and the USS *Pittsburgh* (SSN-720) together had fired a dozen Tomahawk cruise missiles against inland targets in Iraq. Other attack submarines stood guard for cargo ships in the Mediterranean, protecting vast quantities of war supplies. A string of subs from the United States and its allies—Turkey, Greece, Spain, Britain, France, and Italy—were positioned from the Strait of Gibraltar to the Suez Canal.

The war gave the sub force a chance to show its versatility, to show that it could do more than just chase Soviet subs and shadow Soviet ports. It also gave submariners themselves a sense that they could create a new mission—a comforting realization given the fact that any lingering doubts about Soviet intentions were soon to be wiped out by one dramatic event after another. Bush and Gorbachev announced a new deal to cut strategic stockpiles by one-third. Boris Yeltsin rescued Gorbachev from a reactionary coup, signaling the last failed gasp of the Communist hard-liners. And in a richly symbolic move, Bush also grounded the Strategic Air Command bombers that had been on near-constant alert for thirty-two years.

The Pentagon began rethinking the nation's military strategy. The sub force knew it was going to have to re-create itself—just as it had been forced to do after World War II. It needed to find a new job and new enemies. There was no question that for much of the cold war submarines—missile and attack boats taken together—could stake claim to being the nation's most critical naval weapons. That made sense when the chief enemy had a fleet that was nearly as formidable. But the 1990s were bringing fundamental change, and it was already clear that the submarine was bound to fall from the pantheon. Like the clipper ships in their day, subs had been perfectly suited to their time, and they had so dominated that they defined an epoch.

For its part, the Navy started simply at first, writing new rules in mid-1991 legislating greater distances and caution for U.S. subs trailing Soviet subs. Then the Office of Naval Intelligence recommended that the number of missions off the Soviet coast be cut dramatically. No longer would the U.S. Navy try to maintain "cast-iron" coverage of the largest Soviet naval bases. No longer would one surveillance sub follow in the wake of another to Soviet waters. No longer would they keep constant watch, waiting for something—anything—interesting to happen.

Not even the vaunted special projects subs were sacred any longer. Desperate to update their fleet of spy satellites, the CIA and the Air Force began to eye the hundreds of millions of dollars still being invested in those subs. Because both *Russell* and *Parche* were in the shipyard throughout 1991, neither doing any missions, the rival agencies were able to suggest that two special projects boats might be too much of a luxury.

The process of attrition was stopped short by the surprising dissolution of the Soviet Union. On Christmas Day 1991, the Commonwealth of Independent States, a loose federation of republics, formally replaced the Soviet Union. Soon after, reports began coming out of a meeting of five thousand Russian military officers that painted a portrait of confusion, anger, and abject frustration. Members of the now-shattered Soviet Navy yanked the old hammer-and-sickle standards from their ships and began flying the flag of St. Andrew, which had marked Russian ships since the days of Peter the Great. Now U.S. Naval Intelligence desperately wanted to know who would get control of the Soviet missile subs and how they would be deployed under the new regimes.

Renewed surveillance had its price. On February 11, 1992, the USS *Baton Rouge* (*SSN-689*) collided with a Russian Sierra-class boat, among the newest and quietest to come out of the Soviet shipyards. *Baton Rouge* was tracking the Sierra near the 12-mile limit off Murmansk when the American commander lost his contact, which then struck *Baton Rouge* from below. Neither sub was damaged much, and nobody was hurt. But the incident was embarrassing.

Yeltsin quickly complained, and Baker met with him in Moscow to keep things calm. The next day, in an unprecedented move, the Pentagon publicly announced that the collision had occurred, and the Russian Navy began to complain publicly that the United States was still operating too close to its waters.

In the end, this embarrassment was what accelerated the shift in submarine surveillance away from Russia. The president's Foreign Intelligence Advisory Board, chaired by retired Admiral Bobby Ray Inman, examined the special projects program. Shortly thereafter, Naval Intelligence was told that the board had decided that there was no longer any need for more than one special projects sub and that if the Navy was going to keep tapping underwater cables, then maybe it was time to find some cables in other parts of the world.

U.S. attack subs had already handled reconnaissance off countries like Lebanon and Libya, and in the mid-1980s two old missile subs had been converted to carry SEALs. The USS *John Marshall* (*SSN-611*) had bobbed around in the Mediterranean for two months with fifty SEALs aboard during one crisis in Lebanon in 1989, waiting if needed to rescue hostages or mount a retaliatory strike.

Now as part of the Navy's new "From the Sea" military strategy, subs would ride shotgun for aircraft carriers and cruisers and take orders from task force commanders riding on those vessels. But the submarine force would also continue to lurk unseen near potential arenas of conflict and come up with the intelligence to "prepare the battlefield," before the task forces were ever called in. The term had been borrowed from the Army, but in this case it meant sending subs out two, three, four, or more years before any anticipated conflicts to learn more about nations that loomed as potential foes, to determine their weaknesses, and to pave the way for U.S. victories in conflicts that would have fewer casualties because of these undersea efforts.

Iran, for instance, had already taken delivery of the first of three "Kilo" diesel submarines—silent and highly advanced boats built in Russia. A top Iranian admiral had boasted that he intended to use these subs to gain control of the Strait of Hormuz, the entrance to Persian Gulf ports and the starting point for about one-sixth of the world's oil. That was enough to send the USS *Topeka* (*SSN-754*) to the Persian Gulf to observe the Kilo's arrival in November 1992. It was typical of the new era of reconnaissance missions.

The new spy missions raised no agonizing debates at the National Security Council or within the White House, which was still approving all sub reconnaissance operations on a monthly basis. Still, there were accusations from Capitol Hill that the sub force was merely inventing enemies to keep itself employed. The Navy's answer was simple: some of the other targets had existed for years, and it was only the collapse of the

Soviet Union that had offered the luxury of time and resources to allow subs to do a job they should have been doing all along. The enemies might be comparatively unsophisticated—an Iranian Kilo running on diesel power can't really be compared to the high-speed Akulas the Soviets sent out in the later years of the cold war. But the U.S. Navy would still need to know how the Iranians would operate the Kilos, would still need to find their blind spots. "Can you imagine the embarrassment to the U.S. Navy if the Kilos sank the USS *America*?" said one high-ranking Navy official. Pausing, he added, "Not on my watch."

The shift to these new missions was well under way when President Bill Clinton took office in early 1993. But as he and his administration laid plans for his first summit with Yeltsin, scheduled for the first week of April, they got hit by what seemed to be an anachronistic and unwelcome blast from the past.

On March 20, the USS *Grayling* (SSN-646) collided with a Soviet missile sub in the Barents Sea. *Grayling* had been shadowing the Russian sub 105 miles north of Murmansk, smack in the middle of the Northern Fleet's training range. The Russians claimed that their sub had been moving for more than an hour at a steady speed, course, and depth when *Grayling* left a huge dent in their starboard bow. Nobody was hurt.

The incident was everything the State Department had been worrying about since the final days of Reagan's tenure. Yeltsin was in the midst of a political crisis in Moscow. News that his friends within the United States were still sending submarines tooling about Russia's most sensitive ports and bases wasn't going to boost his popularity.

At first, the Pentagon said *Grayling* had been trailing one of Russia's newest missile boats, a Delta IV, but the Russians insisted that *Grayling* had been hot on the trail of a Delta III, a class of subs that dated back to the late 1970s. This provoked more than a few stinging comments from other submariners, all along the lines that the Navy already had so much information on the Delta IIIs that "we could build one from the hull up."

Clinton was furious, and so were his aides. In exasperation, one senior administration official complained of the Navy's leaders: "One wonders if they've read the newspapers."

The Russian defense ministry issued an angry statement

expressing "great concern." It was one thing to take such risks during the cold war, but now? As Rear Admiral Valery Aleksin, the chief navigator, put it, "We walk on the razor edge. Once, this hunt will end up in a disaster. I am sure today, too, that if such a practice doesn't stop, the disaster is inevitable."

Clinton offered Yeltsin a formal apology and smoothed things over with him at the start of the summit in Vancouver, British Columbia, where he also pledged $1.6 billion in aid to support Yeltsin's reforms. Declaring the collision "regrettable," Clinton said, "I don't want it to ever happen again." He ordered a review of both the incident and the policies "of which the incident happened to be an unintended part."

That last part of Clinton's promise worried the Navy. There needed to be damage control, and fast. Rear Admiral Edward D. Sheafer Jr., who was now the director of Naval Intelligence, along with the captain who coordinated the submarine reconnaissance program, prepared a detailed briefing for top officials, including Clinton's new national security adviser, Anthony Lake, and his deputy, Samuel Berger; Strobe Talbott, the deputy secretary of State; and nearly everybody, it seemed, within the office of Secretary of Defense Les Aspin. The Navy team stressed that submarine spying had indeed changed with the times. Now, only 25 percent of the missions were directed toward Russian waters. The remaining 75 percent had turned to Middle Eastern waters to spy on Iran and enforce the economic embargo against Iraq, to the Adriatic to help seal off Bosnia from Western arms shipments, to the waters off of Haiti to enforce an arms embargo there, and to monitor potential threats in the Far East. Finally the submariners marched out their new rallying cry, the one about "preparing the battlefields" around the globe.

It was a briefing as good as any offered up during the cold war, one that showed how quickly the submarine force had reinvented itself. By the time Sheafer and his staff were done, even they were astonished. Here they had thought the *Grayling* collision might sink their program, and instead, the Naval Intelligence team ended up chortling that the collision "saved our bacon." In their desperation, they did such an impressive job of touting the sub force that several administration officials were practically cheering, saying things such as, "Goddamn, it's a free ocean," and, "There's no prohibition against being outside another country's territorial waters." High administration officials who might never have focused on submarines and submarine spying were impressed that the Navy had changed so much without having to be dragged away from its old foe. The Navy even got the go-ahead to keep watching the Russians, albeit at this greatly reduced pace, as long as the reconnaissance was done more cautiously and judiciously.

Since then, the submarine force has fared relatively well under Clinton. Perhaps his biggest favor has been keeping alive the Seawolf program: Clinton agreed to build three of the mammoth $2.5 billion attack subs rather than halt the program at one, as Bush had tried to do. Clinton said he was doing that to prevent the industrial base that builds submarines from shriveling and dying altogether. There was opposition from normally hawkish Republicans, who described the Seawolf as a cold war relic.

Clinton also okayed a plan to build another new class of attack submarines, one smaller and cheaper than the Seawolf. Quieter and much more versatile than the Los Angeles subs, this new class, known first as "the New Attack Submarine," or NSSN, and now the Virginia class, is designed for the array of new missions in shallow, regional waters. Clinton agrees that the Navy will need new subs after the turn of the century to replace some of the aging Los Angeles vessels. His support has taken some of the sting out of a dramatic downsizing of the force. From a high of ninety-eight in the late 1980s, the number of attack subs fell to the low sixties in 1999 and will dwindle to fifty early in the next century and even further as the Los Angeles subs are retired. The fleet of nuclear missile subs, which are still circling quietly in the oceans, will dwindle to ten to fourteen boats from a onetime high of forty-one.

The Navy is asking Congress for the cash to build the new subs and is arguing that they will be capable of operating not only near Third World countries but also up against Russian shores. The Seawolf is said to be as much as thirty times quieter than the early Los Angeles–class subs that came out in the 1970s, and ten times quieter than even the newest LA-class subs. Both Seawolf and the Virginia class will be especially useful for the new missions closer in to shores and for assisting in conflicts on land. They will carry Tomahawk missiles, be equipped with sonar designed to be especially useful in the shallows, and be configured to carry detachments of Navy SEALs and other special forces. The Navy also has been pouring money into creating underwater drones—and even small pilotless aircraft—that could be controlled by these submarines and swim out ahead to look for mines or fly out to do surveillance.

The subs in use now are also being upgraded with new microprocessing technologies to enable them to better communicate a variety of intelligence to commanders of task force battle groups, including e-mail and photographs—even video—taken through their periscopes.* This same technology is also likely to help subs with some of the other new missions the Navy has taken on since the end of the cold war. Subs have occasionally tipped the Coast Guard to suspicious trawlers in the Caribbean that have turned out to be carrying shipments of illegal drugs. And subs have been alerting surface ships to freighters suspected of trying to make illicit shipments of arms and other cargo in violation of U.S. embargoes. In the war over Kosovo in early 1999, when the NATO allies needed to make precision strikes against sensitive Serbian targets, U.S. and British attack subs repeatedly fired Tomahawk cruise missiles from the Adriatic Sea. Subs also kept an eye out for Russian ships streaming into the region.

Still, the U.S. sub force remains most concerned with countering the threat from other submarines, including new models of both diesel and nuclear boats. Russia has been supplying advanced Kilo subs to Iran and China. Even some Western nations, such as Germany, have been exporting advanced diesel subs to Third World countries. In addition, the Russians continue to view the submarine as the most important vessel in their Navy, and they have kept improving the Akulas, their quietest and most sophisticated nuclear attack subs. (There are still significant flaws in Russian technology. According to Naval Intelligence officials, the latest Akulas are very quiet below 10 knots, but they develop audible knocks at speeds above that and become easy to detect.)

---

*When the latest class of subs, the Virginia class, begin to set out to sea in 2004, they won't even have periscopes. Instead, each will have a fiber-optic mast with a digital video system with resolution clearer than the human eye.

The Russians also have started to build an even more advanced replacement, known as the Severodvinsk class, which some U.S. officials fear could be quieter than the improved Los Angeles subs. When and if a proposed START II treaty is finally ratified by the Russian Duma, the bulk of Russian nuclear might will shift to the sea. As long as Russia still has the world's second most powerful sub force—as long as "The Bear Still Swims," as Navy briefers like to say—it needs to be watched, though now it has little money to send its subs to sea.

Clinton has agreed to continue the limited surveillance operations off of Russia, and his approvals have resulted in a few lonely sentinels lurking off Vladivostok and Murmansk, at least at times when the Navy has reason to believe the Russians might be engaging in an exercise or testing new equipment. It also is with Clinton's nod that the special projects spy program has continued, although its focus has shifted away from Russia. Government officials say that one of the special projects subs— probably *Russell* in 1992—went back to the Barents to retrieve the tap pods after the Soviet Union collapsed. *Russell* went cable-tapping in other parts of the world before she was retired in mid-1993. That's when *Parche* came back from her long overhaul, earning two more Presidential Unit Citations, in 1993 and 1994. After a string of Navy Unit Commendations in 1995, 1996, and 1997, *Parche* won another PUC in 1998. All told, *Parche* has now won eight PUCs, by far the most of any ship in Navy history. Details of exactly where *Parche* is going now have been tightly held, even more so than any of her cold war efforts, but those awards never would have been given had *Parche* not continued to pioneer new and dangerous missions. She can still tap cables, and since her refit, she can also retrieve military hardware off the ocean floor.

The Navy, it is clear, is also determined to hold on to her. When the rash of post–cold war base closings rang the end of the Mare Island Naval Shipyard in 1994, *Parche* was moved to Bangor, Washington, where she is the only attack sub to moor at a major Trident missile-sub base. The Navy has pushed her special technology forward and could even be using unmanned drones to swim out from *Parche* and handle many of the tasks of cable-tapping without risking her crew's lives.

Her targets are easy to guess at and no doubt reflect the Navy's broader intelligence concerns. Iran took possession of its third Kilo in 1997. The cover of one recent issue of *Worldwide Submarine Challenges,* a Naval Intelligence annual, pictures a Chinese submarine and crew. Inside is a running litany of nations that present a potential threat, including two Asian nations, China and North Korea. China not only used one of its Kilos in highly threatening exercises off Taiwan but fired land missiles as warning shots, forcing Clinton to send U.S. aircraft carriers to ensure that no attack took place. The Chinese are also using Russian technology to develop their own fleet of modern nuclear missile subs, and they have been testing land-based ballistic missiles with ranges long enough to reach U.S. shores. Chinese test missiles fired into the oceans would be invaluable to the United States if they were retrieved. Finally, concerns about North Korea have escalated greatly. The country repeatedly has used diesel subs to try to infiltrate commandos into South Korea.

Parche is still out there, as are other attack submarines bent on spying. The Navy has already earmarked a replacement for *Parche,* due to be retired in 2003. The third Seawolf-class submarine, USS *Jimmy Carter*, is being lengthened so that she can carry *Parche*'s unique gear and continue the sub force's most sensitive missions. The program that began with the first chill of the cold war continues.

EPILOGUE

A sub commander and his wife once made a promise: when he was at sea, they would both look at the same star at the same time of night. She would never know when he could dare bring his sub to periscope depth, dare take a peek at the sky. So she faithfully sought out their star every night at the appointed hour, even though she realized that he was probably moving silently through the darkness of the ocean. She did that in the hope that at least once they would be gazing at their star together. She did that every night until he came home.

These two were among the lucky ones. The stress caused by long months at sea and the staunch secrecy that submariners were sworn to maintain tore many other couples apart. No final analysis of the submarine war can ignore the human costs. These men traded months, years, and more to become what was for decades the country's best defense against nuclear attack from the sea.

Submariners tracked Soviet missile submarines as well as anyone could, development by development and mile by mile. Only another sub could follow a Soviet boomer, hear just what clanked, see just how its crew operated, and learn just where it would be going should the order ever come to fire. This was all intelligence that grew over time, a few facts from each mission, some of it redundant, much of it cumulative. It was intelligence that had to be collected all over again each time the Soviets put out a new class of subs, each time they came up with a new tactic.

At their best, submarines did something more: they enabled the United States to get a glimpse inside the minds of Soviet military leaders. A U.S. captain in the midst of a trail could see himself in the decisions of a Soviet commander, just as he could see how the other man was so very different.

The special fleet of submarines equipped to tap cables made it possible to listen as Soviet naval headquarters detailed day-to-day frustrations, critiqued missions, and reacted to fears of an American nuclear strike. At a point in time when both superpowers could start nuclear war with a push of a button, this was a rare and crucial look at who the adversary really was.

Human agents, satellites, and spy planes, along with subs, all got very good at collecting information about Soviet hardware—what was being built, the technical specifications. It was much harder, however, to get a glimpse into the Soviet psyche. In the end, not even the cable taps could reveal much about what the top Soviet leadership thought or show the true political and economic crises building in a country so closed. Still, the taps were often the best gauges anyone had, even when what they did record was trapped underwater for months until a sub could be sent to retrieve their tapes.

The men who serviced those cables at the bottom of the Barents and Okhotsk knew they faced immense risk. The self-destruct charges they carried on board were a grim reminder. Even men who often stood as rivals to Naval Intelligence, top officers at the CIA, acknowledge that cable-tapping was the most dangerous of any long-standing intelligence operation of the cold war. That aura of danger awarded the missions respect, just as it made them especially rare.

While satellites replaced many of the spy planes and made

intelligence-gathering safer and more antiseptic, submarines continued to confront the Soviets directly. That not only set subs apart from any other intelligence collectors, but from the rest of the military. Submariners knew they were part of the only force that practiced not simply against allies in war games, but by meeting the enemy, day in and day out.

There was always a huge risk of a destabilizing incident, even the risk that a submarine might spark real battle. Occasionally some critics worried publicly that this could have happened each time a submarine was detected in Soviet waters, each time one risked retaliation, each time there was a collision. There is no question that some skippers went too far in their quest for the big score. But when the Navy and the intelligence agencies weighed the gains against the possibility of a violent response, they relied on one simple fact: the Soviets were sending out their spies as well. As Admiral James D. Watkins, the former chief of Naval Operations and secretary of Energy, put it: "The fact that you get caught periodically is historical. So what. You know everybody's in the game." He went on to say: "As long as we're doing it, which you might say in a way that does not clearly violate agreements that we made or international laws we subscribe to, it is a fair game. We should never apologize for it. We've got to get on with it. And if we don't do it, we are not doing our job."

There's more than a bit of doublespeak in his stress on spying in ways that do "not clearly" violate laws and agreements and in his further limiting his thoughts to laws that "we subscribe to." But looking back, it's clear that even the most violent submarine encounters never sparked real crisis, just as it's clear that the Soviets were writing their rules in much the same way. Most of the time the United States was violating Soviet secrecy with the cable taps, the Soviets were getting the same kind of information—having enlisted John Walker and his spy ring to steal the codes that let them gaze right back at the U.S. Navy's soul.

The Soviet Union's efforts to keep up with the United States military, especially its efforts to create a force of missile subs that could evade U.S. attack subs during the opening salvos of a nuclear war, clearly contributed to the country's ultimate bankruptcy. The contest was costly for the United States as well, as hundreds of billions of dollars were poured into building and manning nearly two hundred nuclear subs and expanding the SOSUS net. Still, the intelligence gained also saved vast sums by helping to hone decisions about just what defense systems the United States really needed. Now that the Soviet bear is bankrupt and eviscerated and the cold war is over, the U.S. Navy's plans to build new subs have come under fire and submarine budgets have been slashed. Men will still go to sea, still brave the depths to spy on enemies of the United States, but those enemies are more likely to be found in Third World hot spots, and for now, no other country poses as big or sweeping a problem at sea as the Soviet Union did. When Congress finally gets around to cutting overall intelligence budgets, which have been only slightly reduced from cold war levels, it is likely that the sub force will be squeezed some more.

Meanwhile, both Russia and the United States are still facing other enormous costs as they decommission many of their nuclear-powered subs and are forced to find some way to dispose of the reactors that powered them. Russia has the most daunting burden—it has the enormous and perhaps impossible job of cleaning up the Barents, of undoing the damage caused by the dumping of a dozen nuclear reactors, spent cores, and radioactive parts from old submarines into the waters near the northern island of Novaya Zemlya.

Russia and the United States share something else as well. The secrecy that has been maintained on both sides about all cold war sub operations has left lingering pain, especially for the families of men lost in this cold war under the seas. For instance, neither navy has yet offered conclusive answers about the disappearance of the subs they lost in 1968: not the Americans about *Scorpion* and not the Russians about the Golf.

Soviet officials simply marked the Golf's men as missing and were so determined to bury their embarrassing secret that they refused to bestow the honors and pensions that normally went to loved ones of those who suffered a military death, a death that occurred, in Soviet parlance, "while executing the combat task." Instead, wives were given a onetime payment of 1,500 rubles and an annual pension of 58 rubles for each child and disabled relative of the dead men.

Irina Zhuravina, who lost her husband on the Golf, refused to spend those rubles because she thought that would be reconciling to her husband's death on her government's terms. After the Golf was lost, she was working at the customs office at an airport, where foreign newspapers and magazines were collected, censored, or confiscated outright, and she began reading the forbidden pages, risking imprisonment as she did so. Year after year, she kept at it, hoping that news from another country could tell her how her husband had died.

It wasn't until seven years after *Halibut* found the Golf that Zhuravina came across the account of the *Glomar* recovery attempt in a Western magazine. That's how she learned that her husband's submarine had gone down, that the Americans had found it, tried to raise it, and brought up at least six bodies, six men who were prevented by politics from coming home. But when she asked, her government refused to acknowledge any of this.

Andrei Kobzar, who was the captain's son, got the same kind of evasive answers when he wrote to several directorates about his father, Vladimir Ivanovich Kobzar. Finally, he went to the U.S. embassy in Moscow. Surely someone there could tell him something. But the U.S. diplomats held firm to their nondisclosure agreement with the Kremlin—held firm to their conspiracy of silence.

Then, two years after the Soviet Union disappeared, Robert M. Gates decided to make what he considered "a dramatic gesture" as he prepared to become the first CIA director to visit the Kremlin. Somebody at the CIA mentioned that the crew of the *Glomar* had videotaped the burial at sea they had given the six recovered Golf submariners. Gates fought for and won permission to bring the tape with him to his first meeting with Boris Yeltsin. Two weeks later, the tape aired on Soviet national television. The Golf families got to see American sailors standing at attention as both national anthems were played and as the Americans added Russian prayers to the naval service for the dead. Kobzar, Zhuravina, and the rest were astonished and moved that Americans, their enemies for so long, would treat their men with such respect. Still, the tape wasn't enough, any more than the declassified pictures of *Scorpion*'s remains were enough to appease the families who lost men on that sub.

In the United States and in Russia, families of the dead—and of the living—have been calling for more. They have wanted their governments to give up their remaining secrets. Some want simply to lay their men to rest; others want the answers to all of those questions that have been so long forbidden. They want to know: was it all worth it?

Perhaps the entire nuclear arms race was insane, but once it existed, spy subs became a crucial part of dealing with that insanity. That subs were lost to technological failures and in a rush to the sea is horrible. But once nuclear missiles were put on submarines, there had to be a way to track them, to threaten them, to ensure that neither country felt safe enough to use them. For the Soviet Union, that meant trying to keep the United States from knowing just how many failures their nuclear subs were suffering. For the United States, it meant trying to keep the Soviets from knowing just how truly vulnerable their subs were.

With stakes this high, there were valid reasons for secrecy. But obsessive secrecy tends to feed on itself, obscuring critical lessons from the past—lessons that are being lost forever as generations of men who lived that past are dying. Now, with the end of the cold war and a new phase in submarine espionage beginning, it's time to look back, time to assess what has so long been hidden.

AFTERWORD

"If your father can find a route home, he will. You'll have to listen hard, though. Submarines are awfully quiet, but they are always there."

That's how we ended an inscription on one of our books to a ten-year-old boy whose father, a submariner, had recently died. His buddy had come to one of our book signings, and he wanted us to tell the boy that his dad was a hero.

He wanted us to tell the boy all the things that his dad never could tell him when he was alive, and now never will.

There have been many moments like this as we have toured the country. The tour was meant to be a promotion for the hardcover edition of *Blind Man's Bluff*, the first detailed look at America's submarine spy operations. But it quickly turned into something else. We realized right away that our book had given voice to a generation of men who had taken huge risks in silence. It was on tour that we discovered that breaking that secrecy has not only given the public a chance to read one of the last great tales of the cold war, but it has provided catharsis for tens of thousands of men who went out on submarines and to many others still going out, unable to speak even to one another of all they have faced.

When we met these men, some wanted reassurance that we had taken care not to harm ongoing submarine operations. Mostly, though, they wanted to say thanks. And they wanted us to write one more thing for them in their copies of *Blind Man's Bluff,* something personal, something they could then show to their wives, their parents, their closest friends. See, they asked us to say, this is what he—many he's—can't say. This is what he faced, this is why he was gone, this is who he is.

The lines at many of our book signings have been hours long. As one signing stretched past five hours, our hosts began serving coffee and cookies to the intrepid who waited throughout while we began time-stamping our inscriptions. At midnight, we dutifully changed the dates. That was the night that a sailor on *Parche,* the most decorated of all subs for her cable-tapping missions, came and asked us to write a letter to his eighteen-month-old son, believing that even when the boy was eighteen years old, his oath of secrecy would still be in place and he would still not be able to explain. And so we tried, writing as best we could, to say what this man could not: why Daddy hasn't been there to tuck the boy in at night, to watch his first steps. We wrote that his father was with him in another way all along, and that Dad would never have gone away if the mission weren't so profoundly important.

We met many men like this man, this submariner and dad. They were the ones who answered with tears when we asked, "How old are your children?" We came to understand that the question had an unintended echo, one that whispered, "How many years did you miss?"

In California, one veteran of *Halibut,* the first sub to dare an undersea cable tap, sat down to say that the silence wasn't too awful, that he and his wife had learned to build a relationship around and on top of all of the walls the Navy had installed between them. Now, she was reading *Blind Man's Bluff*—pages, she told us, she would only turn when her husband was at home. She recalled all those years she would insist to the curious that her man was just out guarding the Golden Gate Bridge. But as she read about the self-destruct charges on board his sub, about the storms he faced in a Soviet sea, she finally felt the reality, and the fear. It would be a while before she could relax enough to be impressed.

The submarine force learned something within the pages of *Blind Man's Bluff* as well. Shortly after the book's publication, a team of investigators was assembled to review all documents related to *Scorpion*'s loss in 1968. We had uncovered evidence that *Scorpion* may have been primed for disaster before she ever left port, evidence that the massive batteries that powered some of her torpedoes suffered from a defective design and might have blown up, causing a low-order detonation of a warhead. Now the Navy is searching its own archives for any indication of the warning that predicted just that kind of tragedy, a warning that quality assurance engineers sent to the ordnance command, but that the ordnance command never forwarded to investigators looking into *Scorpion*'s loss.

The book also has stirred up emotions over another submarine lost that year, this one sent out from the Soviet Union. In Russia, President Boris Yeltsin recently awarded the Order of Valour posthumously to the ninety-seven men who went down with the Golf-class sub that the CIA later tried to raise.

As we researched this cold war under the seas, there was one story that was harder to get than almost any of the others, one that left us wondering how the men involved would react when the details were finally made public. It was the 1981 tale of *Seawolf*, another cable-tapping sub, as she became the victim of a typhoon so fierce it forced her to rock until her ski-like legs became buried so deep into a Soviet seabed that sand came in through the water intake valves in her belly and threatened to kill the cooling system of her aging, always-ailing reactor. The men had so resented their brush with death, so resented their officially imposed silence, that their resentment had turned inside out until they began to hold on to their near-death experience with a vehemence even greater than that created by the usual secrecy oaths. Their silence almost defined them as they bore it all with survivors' pride, pride built on what they could not say.

Sherry was in Silverdale, Washington, when a *Seawolf* submariner approached her.

"I never thought I'd see it in my lifetime," he said once, then said it again. He was wearing a *Seawolf* cap, like so many of the men who came that night. These men had served through different years, different times. But there was a look in his eyes, one that set him apart, a look that made her just say it, "You were there for the storm, weren't you?"

He nodded, then stepped forward as she held her breath wondering how he would react. He leaned down and took both her hands in his.

"Thank you," he said. "Thank you for finally telling our story."

Appendix A

SUBMARINE COLLISIONS

Throughout the cold war, there were dozens of submarine accidents as boats that relied on sound for sight came as close as they dared to the enemy—sometimes too close. None of these accidents were as severe as *Tautog's* collision with *Black Lila*, but even a relatively minor bump by a four-thousand-ton vessel is enough to send men and their craft reeling. Here are some of the other incidents caused when submarines sent on spec ops by the United States and Great Britain slammed into or were hit by Soviet subs and ships or other vessels.

This list includes collisions that were confirmed and others considered probable. Some have never been disclosed before.

1960–1961: USS *Swordfish*

While *Swordfish* (SSN-579) was on a surveillance mission off the Soviet Pacific coast, a Soviet sub apparently attempted to surface—from directly below. The American boat was at periscope depth when it suddenly shook from an impact. One crew member recalls that the officer at the conn looked through the scope and saw "running lights"—lights along port and starboard that a sub might turn on as it surfaced. By the time *Swordfish* itself came to the surface, the ocean was clear; the crew assumed that the Soviet sub had dived back down.

Early 1960s: Unidentified Sub, Possibly USS *Skipjack*

One former Navy intelligence official clearly remembers an incident in which a U.S. sub got tangled up with a Soviet destroyer in the Barents Sea. He wasn't sure, but believed that the sub was *Skipjack* (SSN-585). He was certain, however, that the American boat came home with "a propeller gouge on the sail." This may be one of the incidents that Seymour M. Hersh mentioned in the *New York Times* in May 1975, when he described an unnamed Holystone sub that was damaged when it surfaced underneath a Soviet ship in the midst of a Soviet fleet naval exercise. Hersh also reported that the sub suffered damage to its conning tower and escaped despite a search by Soviet vessels.

July 1965: USS *Medregal*

Medregal (SS-480) smashed into, and crippled, a Greek cargo freighter that was under surveillance because it was suspected of carrying supplies to enemy forces in Vietnam. The accident happened in the Gulf of Tonkin when the diesel sub was being driven by a temporary commander. *Medregal*'s regular skipper had broken his neck diving into a swimming pool during a port stop in the Philippines.

March 1966: USS *Barbel*

Barbel (SS-580), one of the last diesel subs the Navy built, collided with a freighter suspected of carrying arms near a port on Hainan Island, China, across the Gulf of Tonkin from North Vietnam. The force of the collision tore the sail planes from the sub, probably lodging parts of them in the ship's hull. The collision was hard enough that *Barbel* was forced down, hitting bottom about one hundred feet underwater. The Vietnamese later reported that the freighter had sunk when it hit a submerged object.

Indeed, the *Barbel* collision was especially upsetting to Defense Secretary Robert McNamara because he had earlier instructed Navy leaders to keep U.S. subs out of the area to avoid inflaming tensions. *Barbel* remained submerged, backed away from the freighter, and left without checking what happened to the sailors on the ship.

December 1967: USS *George C. Marshall*

Marshall (*SSBN-654*), a Polaris missile sub, was clipped by a Soviet sub in the Mediterranean Sea. The Americans knew the Soviet sub was there but couldn't move their massive boat away fast enough. Crewmen say the collision was "a glancing blow" but noted that it still left a gash in *Marshall*'s forward starboard ballast tank.

October 9, 1968: Unidentified American or British Attack Sub

Russian Navy officials say this was the first collision involving a NATO surveillance sub and a Soviet nuclear boat in the Barents Sea. They told our Russian researcher, Alexander Mozgovoy, that the Soviet sub was operating normally when suddenly it began listing starboard, its hull shaking. The crew quickly surfaced and through the periscope sighted another submarine's silhouette. With the conning tower hatch now jammed, the Soviets used a sledgehammer to open it, and it was several minutes before the commander could climb outside to the bridge. By then, the waters were clear. Back at base, repair crews discovered a hole in the outer hull so large that one of the sub's officers said "a three-ton truck could easily" have driven through. Judging from small bits of red and green glass and metal fragments stuck in the wreckage, the Soviets concluded that they had been hit by a foreign sub. Soviet intelligence later discovered that a British diesel sub had pulled into Norway with a damaged sail around that time. However, the Soviets also believe they could have been hit by a U.S. sub.

November 1969: USS *Gato*

Gato's (*SSN-615*) sail was scraped by the hull of the Soviet Hotel-class missile sub known as *Hiroshima* when *Hiroshima* passed over the American boat. The men on *Gato* heard a dull grind as the subs bumped. Despite Soviet Admiral Gorshkov's wish that *Gato*'s corpse be recovered, the sub escaped and nobody on board was hurt (see Chapter 7).

March 14, 1970: USS *Sturgeon*

As *Sturgeon* (SSN-637) passed over a Soviet sub in the Barents Sea the men on board could hear crunching. *Sturgeon*'s sonar dome had grazed the top of the Soviet sub's sail, scraping off pieces of steel. The pieces became lodged in the grating under *Sturgeon*'s ballast tanks.

June 1970: USS *Tautog*

In one of the most violent collisions of the cold war, *Tautog* (SSN-639) was rammed by the Soviet Echo II submarine *Black Lila* off Petropavlovsk. President Nixon was briefed that taped sonar sounds indicated the Soviet sub had sunk, though now her captain has come forward to say that his sub survived (see Chapter 7).

March 1971: Unidentified Sub

On March 31, 1971, another Holystone sub collided with a Soviet boat, according to Hersh's May 1975 story in the *New York Times*. Hersh cited a memo addressed to CIA Director Richard M. Helms that put the collision seventeen nautical miles off the Soviet coast.

Mid-1971: USS *Dace*

After *Dace* (SSN-607) hit something that rolled her to one side, her men were almost certain they had bumped a Soviet submarine in the Mediterranean. Indeed, Naval Intelligence later learned that a Soviet sub pulled into a port soon afterward with the kind of damage that would have been expected from an impact with another sub.

Late 1971 or Early 1972: USS *Puffer*

Puffer (SSN-652) collided with a Soviet diesel sub in waters near Petropavlovsk when the Soviet boat took an unexpected dive just as *Puffer* was making one last surveillance pass. Both subs were moving at slow speed, and crewmen on *Puffer* say it was almost as if the Soviet boat sank on top of them and bumped.

May 1974: USS *Pintado*

Pintado (SSN-672) collided with a Soviet sub inside Soviet waters in the approaches to Petropavlovsk, according to a story in the *San Diego Evening Tribune* in July 1975. Both subs were about two hundred feet deep at impact. Crewmen said the collision smashed much of *Pintado*'s detection sonar, jammed a torpedo tube hatch, and damaged a diving control fin. The Soviet sub, a Yankee-class ballistic missile boat, surfaced soon after the crash. The crewmen said that they believed *Pintado* had gone close to the Soviet harbor to check Soviet undersea defense systems. After the collision, *Pintado* raced from the scene.

November 3, 1974: USS *James Madison*

Madison (SSBN-627) was leaving the U.S. submarine base at Holy Loch, Scotland, when she collided with a Soviet attack sub in the North Sea, according to reports by the columnist Jack Anderson and the *Norwich* (Connecticut) *Bulletin* in 1975. *Madison* dove onto the Soviet boat, which was shrouded by the noise of her baffles. One former *Madison* crew member noted that the Soviet sub was probably one of the Victor class.

Late 1981: HMS *Sceptre* of Great Britain's Royal Navy

This nuclear-powered British attack submarine collided with a Soviet nuclear sub that she was trailing in northern waters close to the Arctic, according to reports a decade later in the British media. One officer said *Sceptre* had lost contact with the Soviet boat for as long as thirty minutes before his boat shook. "There was a huge noise," he said, adding, "Everybody went white."

October 1986: USS *Augusta*

In an especially embarrassing moment, *Augusta* (SSN-710) bumped into a Soviet missile sub in the Atlantic while testing a new, highly computerized sonar system that had promised to make it easier to detect other vessels. The accident happened a few days after a Soviet Yankee-class missile sub caught fire and sank off

Bermuda, owing to problems with one of its missile tubes. But contrary to the story told in *Hostile Waters,* a 1997 Home Box Office movie, *Augusta* crew members and Naval Intelligence officials say *Augusta* did not hit the Yankee. Instead, the *Augusta* collided with a Delta I–class sub. The lingering confusion is the ultimate irony for *Augusta*'s captain, who had once been so confident of his own abilities that he tacked a plaque on his stateroom door endowing himself with the lofty title "Augusta Caesar."

December 24, 1986: HMS *Splendid* of Great Britain's Royal Navy

According to Russian Navy officials, *Splendid* was surveying a Soviet sub in the Northern Fleet's training range in the Barents Sea when the Soviets noticed and tried to get away. The Russians say that at that point commanders of both subs made maneuvering mistakes, and the Soviet submarine brushed against *Splendid,* snagging its towed sonar array. The Soviet sub, possibly one of the huge Typhoon missile boats, made her way back to base, still entwined in the array.

February 11, 1992: USS *Baton Rouge*

Baton Rouge (SSN-689) collided with a Russian Sierra-class sub near Murmansk. In an unprecedented move, and in response to Yeltsin's complaints, the Pentagon publicly announced that the collision had occurred (see Chapter 12).

March 20, 1993: USS *Grayling*

Grayling (SSN-646) collided with a Russian Delta III missile sub in the Barents Sea. Nobody was hurt, but Clinton was furious that the Navy was still taking such risks (see Chapter 12).

Appendix B

FROM THE SOVIET SIDE

The U.S. Navy spent decades spying on Soviet submarines but never really knew much about what went on inside those boats, who their men were, or what they were going through. Periodically, word would come of horrible radiation accidents. The Pentagon was willing enough to share those incidents with the American public, along with constant and seemingly contradictory warnings about how big and dangerous the Soviet sub fleet was becoming. Now, with the end of the cold war, the Russian Navy has opened up and has been willing to offer some of the details about the tense days back when the Soviet Navy scrambled to catch up to the Americans. Former Soviet submariners feel free to say what they never could before—that their commands put more emphasis on numbers and deadlines than on submarine safety. As a result, the Soviets suffered some of the most horrific accidents of the cold war.

A Lethal Beginning

In the early stages of the arms race in the mid-1950s, Khrushchev called for the Soviet Union "to catch up with and pass America." And so a fleet of nuclear submarines was designed and constructed, all in a hurry, all haphazardly. The work was so bad that in 1959 Commander Vladimir N. Chernavin (who would ultimately succeed Admiral Gorshkov as commander in chief of the Soviet Navy) refused to take one of the first Soviet nuclear attack submarines out of the yard for her first sea trials. He stood firm when his command was threatened, and he stood firm until his sub was repaired.

While Chernavin stood his ground, another submarine, the K-19, had already been sent to sea with the swing of a champagne bottle. That the bottle failed to break was one of those omens that every submariner, no matter what his rank, rate, or nationality, knew to be ominous. It was an inauspicious beginning for the first Soviet nuclear-powered submarine to carry ballistic missiles.

In the summer of 1961, K-19 was setting out for exercises in the North Atlantic, exercises code-named "Arctic Circle." She was to play the role of an American sub, hide beneath the surface, and make her way through Soviet antisubmarine forces. After that she was going to leave the rest of the fleet and find a *polynya*, a break in the ice. She would surface at the edge of the Arctic and conduct a practice launch of a ballistic missile.

The rest of the fleet stayed behind to continue their exercises as K-19 broke away to make a submerged transit through the Norwegian Sea. The waters were calm. There were no storms. Her crew was already counting down to the end of this cruise and their homecoming.

On July 4, at 4:15 in the morning, just as the sub reached a point about one hundred miles off of Jan Mayen, the small Norwegian island above Iceland, K-19's radiation detection equipment came to life. A reactor scrammed, shutting down. The fuel rods in her nuclear core continued to heat. The primary cooling circuit had failed. A pipe had burst, pumps had broken, leaving nothing to control the chain reaction, nothing to stop the rods from heating up, nothing to prevent them from getting so hot that they would melt through the reactor itself. As the fuel rods climbed past one thousand degrees, the paint began burning on the reactor's outer plating. There should have been a backup cooling system, something to stop catastrophe. But K-19 was an early design, a first attempt.

Captain Yuri Posetiev gave the order to surface. He tried to radio for help, but communications had failed. Meanwhile, engineers on board began desperately trying to improvise a new cooling system from the sub's drinking water reserves. They came up with a desperate plan. Several men were going to have to walk into the now highly radioactive reactor compartment and climb inside "the Boa's Mouth."

Lieutenant Boris Korchilov was on his first submarine cruise, and he was the first to volunteer. Others from the reactor team followed. These men, still boys really, made their way into the compartment. There they stood, a team of eight, welding pipes, connecting them to pumps and valves. They remained in the compartment for two hours, braving the heat and the invisible particles that shot through their bodies. Each received one hundred times the lethal dose of radiation.

Ivan Kulakov, a twenty-two-year-old chief petty officer, watched as they came out of the compartment, each man barely able to move, unable to speak, their faces changed beyond recognition. He watched horrified as the first team's efforts failed. As the cooling pumps came apart, it became clear that someone had to jury-rig the jury-rig. Kulakov volunteered. He was certain that he could do the work fastest. And he was just as certain that he was going to die trying.

Kulakov's mind played back the faces of those first eight men, a running loop that wouldn't stop as he walked through a lake of radioactive water, ankle deep. As the water soaked through his leather shoes, as the radiation began to burn his feet, he thought he saw the walls and water shine, perhaps glow.

His hands were burned as he opened valves to draw steam from the reactor. He could barely see. He could barely breathe. All he could do was pray that he could finish, make his way out without falling headlong into the horrible, painful, radioactive lake that was already destroying his feet.

Finally, he did get out, only to watch another valve fail, only to know he had to go back in. He had already taken on five times the lethal dose of radiation. Outside the compartment were the living dead. Back inside, he was more certain than ever that he was one of them.

Then, just as the fuel rods reached 1,470 degrees, the pipes held, the valves held. The makeshift cooling system began to do its work. Kulakov stumbled out of the Boa's Mouth, and Captain Posetiev turned K-19 around in a run toward the fleet they had left still conducting exercises a lifetime ago, at least eight men's lifetimes ago. He knew he couldn't try for home. His entire crew would be fatally irradiated if he didn't get them off the sub fast.

The team of eight, those first men into the compartment during the crisis, died before the week was out. They were buried in lead coffins.

Posetiev lingered longer: three weeks. Other crewmen who had come too close to the outer door of the reactor compartment lasted a month, some a little longer, before they too succumbed. Kulakov, whose feet and hands were irreparably burned, managed to survive with transfusions and bone marrow transplants. He would always be crippled.

Even with all this, Moscow wasn't willing to let go of one of its few nuclear subs. Khrushchev was still racing the Americans. Men would one day be sent back into K-19, back into that reactor compartment. Only now, K-19 would bear a new name. She would be known as the *Hiroshima*.

The Missile That Was Never Launched

In 1962 the Soviet Navy wanted very much to appease Khrushchev, who wanted very much to see a nuclear submarine launch a ballistic missile from underwater. His naval leaders came forward with a sub that they told him would give him just what he demanded, another success to herald in the *Krasnaya Zvezda* newspaper.

Khrushchev witnessed just such a test and was so delighted that he declared a reward for a perfect missile firing to the crew of the nuclear sub on display, the K-3, which had also just made a successful transit to the North Pole. Nobody would ever dare tell him he had just offered up an award for a clever illusion.

The Soviet Navy was still having too many problems getting its nukes to shoot, much less shoot straight, to risk yet another failure with Khrushchev looking on. So, instead of letting K-3 even make the attempt, commanders strategically positioned a Golf diesel sub near the nuke. Hidden and in anonymity, it was the diesel boat that made the perfect shot.

And so Soviet naval history marched on, intermingling the heroic, the tragic, and the comic.

The Race to the Mediterranean

It was June 1967, the eve of the Arab-Israeli War, and the K-131 had been sent to the Adriatic Sea, outside the Mediterranean, to await orders from command. Those orders came as the first shots were fired. Captain Vadim Kulinchenko was given fifteen hours to bring his sub in position to aim nuclear missiles at Tel Aviv.

The captain was flabbergasted. He knew he didn't want to fire nuclear weapons at Israel, but he also knew he wouldn't have to. In order to make it from the Adriatic to the Mediterranean, in order to race past Greece, past Crete, and arrive within reach of Israel's coast, K-131 would have to somehow reach speeds of fifty-seven knots. Her normal transit speed was twenty knots.

He had to make a show of trying, but when the war ended six days later, Kulinchenko, K-131, and her nuclear weapons were still in transit.

Eventually he met up with his battle group in the Med, forty surface ships and ten diesel subs from the Black Sea fleet. The K-131 didn't belong with this group, she wasn't from the Black Sea. But for their show of force in the Med, the Soviets wanted one of their new Northern Fleet nuclear submarines. It was a beginning. Soon the Med would be the new battleground in the submarine wars.

For now, however, most of the Soviet Navy had little idea of what nuclear subs couldn't do, or for that matter, what they could. Indeed, before the war, when K-131 was on her way to the Adriatic, a supply ship helpfully offered fuel and water—although, the supply ship noted, those were two commodities it was running low on.

"We have fresh water, as much as you like," came the answer from the submarine. "We've just cooked it and are ready to give it to you." The Black Sea fleet didn't have nuclear subs, and the astonished supply crew had no idea that water and fuel were two of the things any nuclear boat can produce for itself.

Disaster Strikes Again

One of the next Soviet subs to travel to the Mediterranean was the K-3, the same sub that Khrushchev had rewarded for the nonexistent missile launch. Only this time, one of her officers, Lev Kamorkin, had a bad feeling.

Two days before embarking from a port in the Barents, he walked with his five-year-old daughter and a friend, who recalls him confiding: "I don't know why, but I don't want at all to go to this voyage."

The feeling was so strong, the urge not to leave so powerful, that Kamorkin swore that this would be his very last trip on a submarine. Sadly for the little girl who listened as her father talked of his misgivings, Kamorkin was right.

On September 8, 1967, at 1:52 A.M., a fire broke out in one of K-3's oxygen generators. She was returning from that run to the Mediterranean and was near home, just off the North Cape of Norway, just about where *Cochino* had suffered her first explosion.

Showing much of the honor of *Cochino*'s Rafael C. Benitez, Kamorkin raced to prevent the fires from blowing the torpedoes and sinking his boat. He ordered everyone out of the weapons compartment and stayed behind to let the ocean in and flood the room. As he watched the waters rise to cover the torpedoes, he knew that he had engineered his own death. He drowned alongside the weapons.

He would never know that forty of the men he had tried so valiantly to save would succumb to carbon monoxide poisoning and die moments after he did.

The *Hiroshima* Makes a Final Appearance

The sub already known as *Hiroshima* continued to cause problems for the Soviet sub command. In November 1969, she ran into the USS *Gato* with a blow that forced her into a steep bow-first dive, sending the huge volume of *Navigational Astronomy* tumbling down off a bookshelf and onto Captain Valentin Anatolievich Shabanov, who had been dozing. The collision also knocked out the sub's forward sonar and crushed the doors of her torpedo tubes.

Still, *Hiroshima* continued to operate long enough for one final disaster. In 1972 fire broke out on the sub when she was about six hundred miles northeast of Newfoundland. This time, twenty-six officers and crewmen were killed. There were twelve others who expected to die, men who were entombed inside the sub's stern compartment, unable to make it through the gassed portions of the sub. They stayed there for twenty-three days until *Hiroshima* limped home.

That those twelve men lived is the only happy ending ever written for *Hiroshima*. She is remembered and memorialized as the submarine that earned her name for fire, radiation, and death.

Trawlers and Spies

The Soviets added a twist to the at-sea espionage routine by supplementing their fleets of subs with surface trawlers (specially equipped to eavesdrop), known as AGIs. There was a certain genius in this since it was the cheapest and easiest way for the Soviet Union to post a sentry off all the major U.S. bases, both here and abroad. U.S. missile boats went to great lengths to avoid these trawlers. One sub even grounded in the late 1960s while trying to keep from being detected by an AGI lurking off of Holy Loch, Scotland.

Mostly, the trawlers just sat there, but sometimes they were downright brazen. That was the case in 1979 when the crew of one trawler operating near Guam reached out and grabbed a torpedo fired in a practice round by a U.S. missile sub, USS *Sam Houston* (*SSBN-609*). The trawler just rushed up, made the snatch, then began heading in a slow crawl back to the Soviet Union. Operational commanders were dumbstruck. They were also at a loss at just what to do. After some debate, they decided that sometimes there is no alternative to sending an obvious message, a show of military force to make sure no other Soviet vessel ever tried anything this audacious again.

Within twelve hours, two aircraft carrier battle groups were sent from Yokosuka and the Philippines to corner the trawler. A day or two later, the trawler was boxed in outside of Okinawa. By now, the Navy had gotten the State Department involved, and messages were flying back and forth between U.S. diplomats and high-ranking Soviets. Finally, the trawler captain, who had stared down the American ships, dropped the torpedo over the side. Attached was a note, written in English, deft and to the point. The captain simply said the torpedo had come alongside his ship. To Naval Intelligence officers looking on, it seemed as though the Soviet was saying "look what I found," as if he had just landed a big fish and it was the most natural and innocent thing in the world.

Death in the Norwegian Sea

In the late summer of 1985, the USS *Baltimore* (SSN-704) was sent to watch a Soviet Zulu IV sub in waters just above Norway. The U.S. Navy knew that the 1950s-vintage diesel sub was a research boat, one that had been seen loitering in the area before. *Baltimore* prepared to make a pass beneath the Zulu when the American submariners saw a cable, about as wide as a man's arm, dangling from the Soviet sub. Then, through a murky underwater periscope view, they saw the Soviets lowering an open underwater sled with ballast tanks on either side. On the sled were one or more divers wearing suits reminiscent of those designed for outer space, with air hoses connected back up to the submarine. Silence was ordered on board *Baltimore* as the Soviet sled moved toward the ocean floor. Men were ordered to wear their rubber shoes, not to slam doors. The ice machine was turned off. So was the bug juice machine. The only thing left running in *Baltimore*'s mess was the coffee-maker.

Soon, sonar reported the sound of what seemed to be digging in the sand, three hundred feet below the surface. Listening in on the Zulu's own onboard intercom, the *Baltimore*'s crew realized that the Soviets were looking for an underwater communications cable.

Naval Intelligence officials knew that there was such a cable there, one running from Murmansk to northern England that had been laid in the days of the czar. It wasn't used anymore, and the Soviets had to have known that. Perhaps the Soviets were practicing. Perhaps they were preparing to try to match the U.S. cable-tapping feat that had been exposed a few years earlier. Or perhaps they were practicing to disrupt the cables that connected the U.S. SOSUS nets.

The oceans were rough, with swells reaching as high as thirty feet. Still the Zulu loitered, and still *Baltimore*'s crew watched from one day to the next. On the third day, all sounds of digging, all noise in fact, stopped. *Baltimore* was inched closer and her men realized that there was now a cable dangling from the Zulu, with no sled attached. It had been lost, presumably with its divers.

A stunned silence reigned on *Baltimore*. "I remember that everyone in the conn turned around and looked at each other," one crew member said, adding that it no longer seemed to matter which side anybody was on. "It was more like we realized a submariner was dead."

Appendix C

U.S. SUBMARINE AWARDS

DIESEL AND NUCLEAR FAST-ATTACK SUBMARINES:
AWARDS FOR SURVEILLANCE MISSIONS
AND OTHER ACHIEVEMENTS

Like the rest of the military, the Navy loves to give awards to boost morale and honor achievements, especially for highly secret missions where there can be no public recognition and the men cannot even tell their families what they did. So for nuclear attack submarines, a list of the major awards provides a terrific guide to which boats and crews brought home the best intelligence during the cold war and the years since it ended.

Some of the awards were for other bits of daring, such as the *Nautilus* sneaking under the Arctic ice to reach the North Pole in 1958. And only a few diesel boats are represented here. In the early days of the cold war, admirals who had been shot at in World War II weren't willing to hand out the kind of awards that old friends had gotten—often posthumously—for facing Japanese depth-charge attacks.

But in general, the awards have gone to the top boats in each era of submarine spying, for the full array of missions as they evolved: from surveillance runs right off the Soviet coast to trailing Soviet missile subs and tapping undersea communications cables. Since the mid-1980s, the awards also have reflected the changing focus of submarine spying. The cluster of prizes in the spring of 1986, for instance, went to submarines involved in a showdown with Libya. In the 1990s, many subs won for surveillance during wars in the Middle East and Bosnia and for watching other hotspots far from Russia.

The highest award for individual ships, given only for exceptional bravery, is the Presidential Unit Citation (PUC), signed by the president himself. Next is the Navy Unit Commendation (NUC), followed by the Meritorious Unit Commendation (MUC). Now that many subs are assigned to broader military task forces, some also are winning the Joint Unit Commendation (JUC). What follows is a comprehensive list, drawn from Navy records, of all the subs that have taken top prizes and the time periods for which they were honored:

1958

Nautilus, SSN-571, PUC, Jul. 22–Aug. 5
Seawolf, SSN-575, NUC, Aug. 7–Oct. 6
Skate, SSN-578, NUC, Aug. 9–12

1959

Skate, SSN-578, NUC, Mar. 4–Apr. 6
Greenfish, SS-351, NUC, Sep. 23, 1959–Jan. 11, 1960

1960

Sargo, SSN-583, NUC, Jan. 18–Feb. 26
Triton, SSN-586, PUC, Feb. 16–May 10
Skipjack, SSN-585, NUC, May 1–Jul. 31
Seadragon, SSN-584, NUC, Aug. 1–Sep. 14

1962

Scorpion, SSN-589, NUC
Sargo, SSN-583, NUC, Feb. 22–May 22

1963

Sargo, SSN-583, one NUC for three missions:
Jul. 17–Sep. 15, 1963
May 17–Jul. 13, 1964
Apr. 19–Jun. 19, 1965
Swordfish, SSN-579, one NUC for three missions:
Oct. 8–Dec. 3, 1963
Sep. 22–Nov. 25, 1964
May 20–Aug. 23, 1965

1964

Shark, SSN-591, NUC, Apr. 5–May 9
Sculpin, SSN-590, NUC, Summer

1965

Pollack, SSN-603, NUC
Snook, SSN-592, NUC, Spring
Wahoo, SS-565, MUC, Fall 1965–Spring 1966

1966

Haddo, SSN-604, NUC
Shark, SSN-591, NUC
Triton, SSN-586, NUC
Barb, SSN-596, NUC, Spring 1966
Permit, SSN-594, NUC, Summer 1966
Plunger, SSN-595, NUC, Winter 1966
Sculpin, SSN-590, NUC, Dec. 1, 1966–Sep. 1, 1967

1967

Dace, SSN-607, NUC
Haddo, SSN-604, MUC
Ray, SSN-653, NUC
Triton, SSN-586, NUC
Flasher, SSN-613, MUC, Mar. 1, 1967–Aug. 31, 1968
Remora, SS-487, NUC, Summer and Fall 1967
Queenfish, SSN-651, one NUC for two periods:
Winter 1967 and Spring to Fall 1968

1968

Halibut, SSN-587, PUC, for three missions in 1967 and 1968
Dace, SSN-607, NUC
Greenling, SSN-614, NUC
Lapon, SSN-661, MUC
Sturgeon, SSN-637, MUC
Permit, SSN-594, NUC, Apr. 1, 1968–Mar. 1, 1969
Ray, SSN-653, MUC, Apr. 8–Jun. 9
Sargo, SSN-583, one NUC for three periods:
  Summer 1968, Spring 1969, Winter 1970
Plunger, SSN-595, one NUC for three periods:
  Fall 1968, Winter 1969, Fall 1970

1969

Lapon, SSN-661, PUC, Sep. to Nov.
Lapon, SSN-661, MUC, Spring
Hammerhead, SSN-663, MUC
Pollack, SSN-603, MUC
Ray, SSN-653, NUC
Sturgeon, SSN-637, MUC
Whale, SSN-638, MUC, Mar. 18–Apr. 25
Skate, SSN-578, MUC, Mar. 24–Apr. 25
Pargo, SSN-650, NUC, Mar. 24–May 17
Shark, SSN-591, MUC, May 3–11
Tautog, SSN-639, NUC, Summer
Swordfish, SSN-579, MUC, Summer and Fall
Barbel, SS-580, Jul. 1–Nov. 1
Bergall, SSN-667, NUC, Jun. 13, 1969–May 31, 1972
Gato, SSN-615, MUC, Sep. 5, 1969–Jun. 30, 1970
Greenling, SSN-614, NUC, Sep. 5, 1969–Jun. 30, 1970
Jack, SSN-605, MUC, Sep. 5, 1969–Jun. 30, 1970
Pargo, SSN-650, NUC, Sep. 5, 1969–Jun. 30, 1970
Bonefish, SS-582, MUC, Dec. 4, 1969–May 26, 1970
Queenfish, SSN-651, NUC, Winter 1969 to Summer 1970

1970

Flasher, SSN-613, PUC
Greenling, SSN-614, MUC
Greenling, SSN-614, NUC

Ray, SSN-653, MUC
Spadefish, SSN-668, MUC
Sturgeon, SSN-637, MUC
Sunfish, SSN-649, MUC
Tullibee, SSN-597, MUC, Sep. 9–Oct. 31
Whale, SSN-638, MUC, Oct. 2–30
Gato, SSN-615, MUC, Oct. 8–31
Aspro, SSN-648, NUC, Fall 1970
Ronquil, SS-396, NUC, Fall 1970
Blueback, SS-581, MUC, Apr. 1, 1970–Jul. 1, 1972
Pargo, SSN-650, MUC, Jul. 1, 1970–Mar. 31, 1971
Clamagore, SS-343, MUC, Sep. 9–Oct. 1
Tautog, SSN-639, MUC, Oct. 1, 1970–Apr. 1, 1971
Grayling, SSN-646, MUC, Oct. 9, 1970–Jun. 4, 1971
Hammerhead, SSN-663, NUC, Oct. 12, 1970–Dec. 7, 1970
Skate, SSN-578, MUC, Oct. 12, 1970–Nov. 18, 1970
Swordfish, SSN-579, NUC, Nov. 1, 1970–Sep. 26, 1971

1971

Halibut, SSN-587, NUC
Finback, SSN-670, NUC
Flying Fish, SSN-673, MUC
Hammerhead, SSN-663, NUC
Narwhal, SSN-671, MUC
Sea Devil, SSN-664, MUC
Spadefish, SSN-668, NUC
Whale, SSN-638, MUC
Skate, SSN-578, MUC, Feb. 26–Mar. 9
Trepang, SSN-674, MUC, Feb. 26–Mar. 9
Aspro, SSN-648, MUC, Jul. 6–20
Seahorse, SSN-669, MUC, Summer
Queenfish, SSN-651, NUC, Summer to Fall 1971
Gurnard, SSN-662, MUC, Jan. 1, 1971–Jan. 1, 1972
Grayling, SSN-646, MUC, Oct. 13, 1971–Dec. 16, 1972
Sargo, SSN-583, MUC, Dec. 11, 1971–Jan. 16, 1972
Flasher, SSN-613, NUC, Winter 1971 and Spring 1972
Scamp, SSN-588, MUC, periods in 1971 and 1972

1972

Halibut, SSN-587, PUC
Flying Fish, SSN-673, NUC
Seahorse, SSN-669, NUC
Trepang, SSN-674, MUC
Sculpin, SSN-590, MUC, Apr. 8–24
Guardfish, SSN-612, NUC, Spring
Pogy, SSN-647, MUC, May 1–Nov. 30
Dace, SSN-607, NUC, May 12–Aug. 7
Barb, SSN-596, MUC, Jul. 8–9
Gurnard, SSN-662, MUC, Jul. 8–10
Tautog, SSN-639, NUC, Summer
Tinosa, SSN-606, MUC, Summer
Sea Devil, SSN-664, NUC, Fall and Winter 1972
Puffer, SSN-652, MUC, Fall 1972 and Winter 1973

1973

Flying Fish, SSN-673, NUC
Pargo, SSN-650, NUC
Archerfish, SSN-678, NUC, Jan. 15–Jun. 20
Barb, SSN-596, MUC, Spring
Pintado, SSN-672, MUC, May 1–31
Trepang, SSN-674, NUC, Jun. 20–Nov. 22
Lapon, SSN-661, NUC, Jun. 21–Dec. 1
Haddock, SSN-621, MUC, Summer and Fall
Blueback, SS-581, MUC, Summer and Fall
Narwhal, SSN-671, NUC, Fall
Sea Devil, SSN-664, NUC, Oct. 23–Dec. 12
Silversides, SSN-679, MUC, Aug. 12, 1973–Jan. 27, 1974
Bluefish, SSN-675, MUC, Sep. 15, 1973–Mar. 10, 1974
Shark, SSN-591, MUC, Nov. 4, 1973–Apr. 20, 1974
Gato, SSN-615, MUC, Dec. 1, 1973–May 11, 1974
Billfish, SSN-676, MUC, Winter 1973 to Spring 1974
Pogy, SSN-647, NUC, Winter 1973 to Winter 1974

1974

Halibut, SSN-587, NUC
Seawolf, SSN-575, NUC
Bluefish, SSN-675, NUC

Ray, SSN-653, NUC
Whale, SSN-638, MUC
Greenling, SSN-614, Jul. 4–28
Archerfish, SSN-678, NUC, Winter 1974
William H. Bates, SSN-680, NUC, periods in 1974 and 1975

1975

Halibut, SSN-587, NUC
Archerfish, SSN-678, MUC, Jan. 1–Mar. 31
Archerfish, SSN-678, NUC
Flying Fish, SSN-673, MUC
Hammerhead, SSN-663, NUC
Ray, SSN-653, NUC
Pargo, SSN-650, NUC, Jun.
Greenling, SSN-614, MUC, Jun. 1–Jul. 16
Spadefish, SSN-668, MUC, Jun. 1–Jul. 16
Tunny, SSN-682, MUC, Jun. 1–Jul. 16
Seadragon, SSN-584, MUC, Jul. 27–Sep. 8
Gurnard, SSN-662, MUC, Jul. 28–Aug. 13
Batfish, SSN-681, NUC, Jul. 25, 1975–Jan. 24, 1976
Puffer, SSN-652, NUC, Aug. 28, 1975–Jan. 15, 1976

1976

Seawolf, SSN-575, NUC
Flying Fish, SSN-673, MUC
Hawkbill, SSN-666, NUC
William H. Bates, SSN-680, NUC, Jan. 1–Aug. 31
Gurnard, SSN-662, NUC, Mar. 8–May 8
Sunfish, SSN-649, MUC, Mar. 30–May 11
Queenfish, SSN-651, NUC, Apr. 19–May 15 and Jul. 3–Aug. 6
Plunger, SSN-596, MUC, Aug. 6–Dec. 11
Drum, SSN-677, MUC, Sep. 6–Oct. 22
Tautog, SSN-639, MUC, Nov. 1, 1976–Jul. 5, 1977

1977

Seawolf, SSN-575, NUC
Hawkbill, SSN-666, NUC
Narwhal, SSN-671, MUC
Flying Fish, SSN-673, NUC, Mar. 26–May 26

Batfish, SSN-681, NUC, May to Aug.
Dace, SSN-607, MUC, Jun. 1977–Jul. 1977
William H. Bates, SSN-680, MUC, Aug. 4–Nov. 10
Queenfish, SSN-651, NUC, Aug. 31–Nov. 12

1978

Parche, SSN-683, NUC
Guardfish, SSN-612, MUC
Tunny, SSN-682, NUC
Richard B. Russell, SSN-687, NUC
Batfish, SSN-681, NUC, Mar. 2–May 17
L. Mendel Rivers, SSN-686, NUC, Aug. to Nov.
Pintado, SSN-672, MUC, Sep. 12–Nov. 8
Trepang, SSN-674, NUC, Nov. to Dec.
Guitarro, SSN-665, MUC, May 1978–Jul. 1981

1979

Parche, SSN-683, PUC
Drum, SSN-677, MUC
Gurnard, SSN-662, NUC
Haddock, SSN-621, NUC
Plunger, SSN-595, NUC
Queenfish, SSN-651, MUC
Sand Lance, SSN-660, NUC, Feb. 12–Apr. 28
Archerfish, SSN-678, NUC, Mar. 14–May 11
Narwhal, SSN-671, MUC, Mar. 26–May 26
Ray, SSN-653, MUC, Apr. to Oct.
Lapon, SSN-661, MUC, May 3–Jul. 5
L. Mendel Rivers, SSN-686, NUC, Nov. to Dec.
Pintado, SSN-672, MUC, Nov. 13, 1979–Feb. 8, 1980

1980

Parche, SSN-683, PUC
Guardfish, SSN-612, MUC
Omaha, SSN-692, MUC
Permit, SSN-594, MUC
Puffer, SSN-652, NUC
Queenfish, SSN-651, MUC
Baton Rouge, SSN-689, NUC, Mar. to Jul.

Seahorse, SSN-669, MUC, Mar. 7–May 12

Flasher, SSN-613, MUC, Spring

Glenard P. Lipscomb, SSN-685, NUC, Apr. to Jun.

Groton, SSN-694, NUC, Apr. to Aug.

Archerfish, SSN-678, NUC, Jun. to Aug.

Tautog, SSN-639, MUC, Summer

Flying Fish, SSN-673, MUC, Jul. 21–Nov. 22

Birmingham, SSN-695, NUC, Aug. 8, 1980–Jan. 24, 1981

Bergall, SSN-667, MUC, Sep. 12, 1980–Jan. 26, 1981

Memphis, SSN-691, NUC, Dec. 1980–Jan. 1981

1981

Parche, SSN-683, PUC

Baton Rouge, SSN-689, MUC

Groton, SSN-694, MUC, periods in 1981 and 1982

Los Angeles, SSN-688, MUC

New York City, SSN-696, MUC

Cavalla, SSN-684, NUC, Feb. to Jun.

Pargo, SSN-650, MUC, Feb. to Apr.

Archerfish, SSN-678, NUC, Mar. 16–Jun. 11

Pintado, SSN-672, NUC, Mar. to Aug.

Bergall, SSN-667, MUC, Apr. 20–May 11

Birmingham, SSN-695, MUC, Apr. 24–May 18

Bluefish, SSN-675, MUC, Spring

Spadefish, SSN-668, NUC, Jun. to Aug.

Jack, SSN-605, NUC, Jun. 7–Jul. 16

Sea Devil, SSN-664, NUC, Jun. 12–Jul. 15

Ray, SSN-653, NUC, Sep. to Oct.

Memphis, SSN-691, MUC, Oct. 10–Nov. 12

Silversides, SSN-679, Sep. 9–Nov. 17

Guitarro, SSN-665, MUC, Jul. 1981–Dec. 1982

Sunfish, SSN-649, NUC, Aug. 21, 1981–Jan. 8, 1982

Aspro, SSN-648, MUC, Fall 1981–Winter 1982

Lapon, SSN-661, MUC, Dec. 11, 1981–Apr. 24, 1982

Groton, SSN-694, MUC, periods in 1981 and 1982

1982

Parche, SSN-683, PUC

New York City, SSN-696, MUC

Grayling, SSN-646, MUC, Feb. to Apr.

Hammerhead, SSN-663, MUC, Mar. to Jul.

Spadefish, SSN-668, NUC, Mar. 18–Jul. 2

Tunny, SSN-682, MUC, Apr. 3–May 12

Gurnard, SSN-662, MUC, May 28–Jul. 5

Permit, SSN-594, NUC, Jun. to Sep.

Bergall, SSN-667, MUC, Jul. 24–Dec. 1

Batfish, SSN-681, NUC, Aug. to Sep.

Cavalla, SSN-684, NUC, Aug. 1, 1982–Dec. 12, 1983

Birmingham, SSN-695, MUC, Dec. 1982–Feb. 1983

Puffer, SSN-652, NUC, period in 1982 and 1983

1983

Atlanta, SSN-712, MUC

Pogy, SSN-647, NUC

Puffer, SSN-652, NUC

Lapon, SSN-661, MUC, Feb. to Apr.

Spadefish, SSN-668, MUC, Feb. to Apr.

Cincinnati, SSN-693, MUC, Feb. 2–Mar. 17

Jacksonville, SSN-699, MUC, Mar. to Apr.

Birmingham, SSN-695, MUC, Apr. 15–Jun. 20

Philadelphia, SSN-690, NUC, Oct. to Dec.

Boston, SSN-703, MUC, Mar. 28, 1983–Sep. 28, 1984

Sand Lance, SSN-660, MUC, Jun. 1983–Mar. 1984

Norfolk, SSN-714, MUC, Sep. 1983–Jun. 1985

1984

Parche, SSN-683, NUC

Bremerton, SSN-698, NUC

Cavalla, SSN-684, MUC

Memphis, SSN-691, MUC

Finback, SSN-670, MUC, Spring

Snook, SSN-592, MUC, Spring

Gurnard, SSN-662, MUC, Sep. to Nov.

Pintado, SSN-672, MUC, Sep. to Nov.

Aspro, SSN-648, NUC, Oct. to Nov.

City of Corpus Christi, SSN-705, MUC, Mar. 31, 1984–Sep. 30, 1985

Albuquerque, SSN-706, MUC, Oct. 1984–Jul. 1985

Lapon, SSN-661, MUC, Oct. 1984–Dec. 1985
Gato, SSN-615, MUC, Oct. 1, 1984–Apr. 30, 1986
Pollack, SSN-603, NUC, Nov. 1984–Jan. 1985
Pogy, SSN-647, MUC, Nov. 10, 1984–May 7, 1985
Seahorse, SSN-669, MUC, late 1984–early 1985

1985

Parche, SSN-683, NUC
Seawolf, SSN-575, MUC
Boston, SSN-703, MUC
Sunfish, SSN-649, MUC
Tunny, SSN-682, NUC
Trepang, SSN-674, MUC, Spring 1985
Finback, SSN-670, MUC, Apr.
Minneapolis–Saint Paul, SSN-708, MUC, Apr. 25–Jul. 7
Hyman G. Rickover, SSN-709, MUC, May 1, 1985–Mar.
   31, 1987
L. Mendel Rivers, SSN-686, MUC, Jul. 10, 1985–Aug. 18,
   1985
Phoenix, SSN-702, NUC, Feb. 1985–Feb. 1986
Snook, SSN-592, MUC, Feb. 1985–Apr. 1986

1986

Parche, SSN-683, PUC
Seawolf, SSN-575, NUC, Mar. 1–Apr. 23
Finback, SSN-670, NUC
Grayling, SSN-646, MUC
Guardfish, SSN-612, NUC
Plunger, SSN-595, MUC
Minneapolis–Saint Paul, SSN-708, MUC
Sam Houston, SSN-609, MUC
   (converted from missile sub to carry Navy SEALs)
Sea Devil, SSN-664, MUC
Sunfish, SSN-649, MUC
Bremerton, SSN-698, NUC, Jan. to Jun.
Salt Lake City, SSN-716, NUC, Apr. to Oct.
Dace, SSN-607, NUC, Mar. 23–Apr. 17
Dallas, SSN-700, NUC, Mar. 23–Apr. 17
Jack, SSN-605, NUC, Mar. 23–Apr. 17

Tullibee, SSN-597, NUC, Mar. 23–Apr. 3
Spadefish, SSN-668, NUC, Apr. 13–17
La Jolla, SSN-701, MUC, May to Sep.
City of Corpus Christi, SSN-705, NUC, Mar. 10, 1986–Mar. 31, 1987
Pittsburgh, SSN-720, MUC, Jun. 1, 1986–Jun. 2, 1988
San Francisco, SSN-711, NUC, Oct. 1986–Jan. 1987
Philadelphia, SSN-690, MUC, Oct. 17, 1986–Mar. 1, 1987
Olympia, SSN-717, MUC, Nov. 1986–May 1987

1987

Richard B. Russell, SSN-687, PUC
Bremerton, SSN-698, MUC
Permit, SSN-594, MUC
Queenfish, SSN-651, MUC, Jan. to Jul.
Sturgeon, SSN-637, MUC, Jan. to Jul.
Scamp, SSN-588, MUC, Feb.
Sea Devil, SSN-664, NUC, Apr. 1–Sep. 1
Portsmouth, SSN-707, MUC, May to Jul.
Guitarro, SSN-665, NUC, Jul. 1–Dec. 1
Silversides, SSN-679, MUC, Aug. 1–Oct. 1
Providence, SSN-719, MUC, Jan. 1, 1987–Nov. 23, 1988
Trepang, SSN-674, MUC, Feb. 1, 1987–Mar. 1, 1989
William H. Bates, SSN-680, NUC, Sep. 1, 1987–Mar. 31, 1988
Sam Houston, SSN-609, MUC, Sep. 1, 1987–Oct. 1, 1989 (converted from missile sub to carry Navy SEALs)
Minneapolis–Saint Paul, SSN-708, MUC, Dec. 1, 1987–May 24, 1988

1988

Richard B. Russell, SSN-687, NUC
Salt Lake City, SSN-716, NUC, Jan. to Jul.
Silversides, SSN-679, NUC, Jan. to Dec.
L. Mendel Rivers, SSN-686, MUC, Feb. 1–Apr. 30
Hawkbill, SSN-666, MUC, Mar. 1–May 1
Dallas, SSN-700, MUC, May to Jun.
Drum, SSN-677, MUC, Aug. to Oct.
Ray, SSN-653, MUC, Sep. 1–Nov. 1

Buffalo, SSN-715, NUC, Apr. 1988–Apr. 1989
Los Angeles, SSN-688, MUC, Aug. 1, 1988–Aug. 1, 1989
Sea Devil, SSN-664, MUC, Aug. 1988–Oct. 1990

1989

Richard B. Russell, SSN-687, NUC
Honolulu, SSN-718, MUC
New York City, SSN-696, MUC, Apr. to Aug.
Chicago, SSN-721, MUC, May to Jun.
Providence, SSN-719, MUC, May 1–Aug. 1
Philadelphia, SSN-690, MUC, Jun. 1–Oct. 1
Drum, SSN-677, NUC, Jul. 1–Aug. 1
Portsmouth, SSN-707, MUC, Jul. 1–Sep. 1
Houston, SSN-713, NUC, Jul. 26–Sep. 12
Olympia, SSN-717, NUC, Jul. 26–Sep. 12
Key West, SSN-722, MUC, Jul. 1, 1989–Sep. 1, 1990
Pittsburgh, SSN-720, MUC, Sep. 1, 1989–May 31, 1990

1990

Richard B. Russell, SSN-687, NUC, Feb. 1–Apr. 1
Gurnard, SSN-662, MUC, Mar. 1–Jun. 30
Hammerhead, SSN-663, MUC, Mar. 1–Jun. 1
Oklahoma City, SSN-723, MUC, Mar. 1–Aug. 1
Omaha, SSN-692, MUC, Jan. 1, 1990–Aug. 1, 1991
Baltimore, SSN-704, MUC, May 1, 1990–Feb. 1, 1993
San Juan, SSN-751, MUC, Apr. 1, 1990–May 1, 1991
Dallas, SSN-700, MUC, Aug. 1, 1990–Jan. 21, 1991
Drum, SSN-677, MUC, Sep. 1, 1990–Feb. 28, 1991
Chicago, SSN-721, MUC, Oct. 1, 1990–Mar. 1, 1991
Pittsburgh, SSN-720, NUC, Nov. 1, 1990–Feb. 1, 1991
Louisville, SSN-724, NUC, Dec. 1, 1990–Apr. 1, 1991

1991

Ray, SSN-653, MUC
Tinosa, SSN-606, MUC
New York City, SSN-696, MUC, Jan. 1–Jun. 30
Hammerhead, SSN-663, MUC, Feb. 1–Jul. 1
Flying Fish, SSN-673, MUC, Mar. 1–Jun. 1
Pargo, SSN-650, MUC, Mar. 9–Jul. 27

Flasher, SSN-613, MUC, Apr. 1–Jun. 1
Sturgeon, SSN-637, MUC, May 1–Jun. 1
Honolulu, SSN-718, MUC, Jun. 1–Nov. 30
La Jolla, SSN-701, MUC, Jun. 1–Nov. 30
Boston, SSN-793, MUC, Jul. 15–Sep. 7
Seahorse, SSN-669, MUC, Mar. 20, 1991–Apr. 30, 1993
Puffer, SSN-652, MUC, Sep. 1, 1991–Jan. 1, 1992

1992

Richard B. Russell, SSN-687, NUC, May 1–Sep. 1
Chicago, SSN-721, MUC
Bergall, SSN-667, MUC, Jan. 1–Apr. 30
Topeka, SSN-754, MUC, Jan. 1–Dec. 31
Albany, SSN-753, MUC, Jul. 1–Dec. 24
Drum, SSN-677, MUC, Mar. 30, 1992–Mar. 30, 1995
Pogy, SSN-647, MUC, Mar. 30, 1992–Mar. 30, 1995
Portsmouth, SSN-707, MUC, Mar. 30, 1992–Mar. 30, 1995
Puffer, SSN-652, MUC, Mar. 30, 1992–Mar. 30, 1995
Salt Lake City, SSN-716, Mar. 30, 1992–Mar. 30, 1995
Silversides, SSN-679, MUC, Aug. 1, 1992–Oct. 31, 1993
Bergall, SSN-667, NUC, Oct. 1, 1992–Mar. 1, 1993
Louisville, SSN-724, JUC, Dec. 5, 1992–May 4, 1993

1993

Parche, SSN-683, PUC, May 1–Aug. 1
Richard B. Russell, SSN-687, NUC
San Francisco, SSN-711, MUC
Jacksonville, SSN-699, MUC, Jan. 1–Jun. 30
Pogy, SSN-647, MUC, Feb. 1–Jul. 31
Norfolk, SSN-714, MUC, Mar. 11–Sep. 10
Pargo, SSN-650, MUC, Mar. 25, 1993–Sep. 22, 1994
Dallas, SSN-700, MUC, Jun. 1, 1993–Nov. 30, 1994
Gato, SSN-615, MUC, Jun. 2, 1993–Jun. 2, 1994
Kamehameha, SSN-642, MUC, Jul. 18, 1993–Apr. 6, 1995
   (converted from missile sub to carry Navy SEALs)

1994

Parche, SSN-683, PUC
San Juan, SSN-751, NUC, Mar. 16–Jul. 1

Aspro, SSN-648, May 1–Jul. 1
Hyman G. Rickover, SSN-709, MUC, Jun. 11–Nov. 5
Newport News, SSN-750, MUC, Jun. 11–Nov. 5
Jefferson City, SSN-759, MUC, Jul. 9–Dec. 9
Phoenix, SSN-702, MUC, Jan. 1, 1994–Mar. 31, 1995
Honolulu, SSN-718, MUC, Jun. 1, 1994–Feb. 28, 1996

1995

Parche, SSN-683, NUC
Buffalo, SSN-715, MUC
Tunny, SSN-682, MUC
Atlanta, SSN-712, NUC, Jan. 1–Sep. 30
Cavalla, SSN-684, MUC, Mar. 8–Jun. 8
Archerfish, SSN-678, NUC, Apr. 5–Sep. 12
Batfish, SSN-681, NUC, Apr. 5–Sep. 12
Billfish, SSN-676, NUC, Apr. 5–Sep. 12
Finback, SSN-670, NUC, Apr. 5–Sep. 12
Montpelier, SSN-765, NUC, Apr. 5–Sep. 12
Key West, SSN-722, NUC, Apr. 5–Sep. 12
Providence, SSN-719, NUC, Apr. 5–Sep. 12
Minneapolis–Saint Paul, SSN-708, MUC, May 1,
    1995–Jul. 31, 1997
Boston, SSN-703, MUC, Nov. 1, 1995–Dec. 1, 1996
Birmingham, SSN-695, MUC, Dec. 1, 1995–Jun. 30, 1996
Portsmouth, SSN-707, MUC, Dec. 13, 1995–May 3, 1996

1996

Parche, SSN-683, NUC
Houston, SSN-713, NUC
Cavalla, SSN-684, MUC, May 1–Nov. 1
Providence, SSN-719, MUC, Jun. 1–Sep. 30
San Francisco, SSN-711, MUC, Jun. 1–Oct. 1
Spadefish, SSN-668, NUC, Jun. 1–Oct. 31
Jefferson City, SSN-759, MUC, Jul. 10–Sep. 4
Albuquerque, SSN-706, MUC, Feb. 1, 1996–Jun. 1, 1997
Phoenix, SSN-702, MUC, Jul. 1, 1996–Apr. 1, 1997
Batfish, SSN-681, MUC, Nov. 1, 1996–Jul. 1, 1997
Miami, SSN-755, MUC, Nov. 1, 1996–Sep. 1, 1997
Archerfish, SSN-678, MUC, Dec. 1, 1996–Oct. 1, 1997

1997

Parche, SSN-683, NUC
San Juan, SSN-751, MUC, Jan. to Jul.
Boston, SSN-703, JUC, Jan. 1–Dec. 31
Trepang, SSN-674, JUC, Jan. 1–Dec. 31
Los Angeles, SSN-688, MUC, Feb. 1–Jul. 1
Indianapolis, SSN-697, NUC, Apr. 1–Sep. 1
Key West, SSN-722, MUC, Apr. 1–Sep. 1
Annapolis, SSN-760, NUC, Oct. 1, 1997–Apr. 30, 1998
Charlotte, SSN-766, NUC, Oct. 1, 1997–Apr. 30, 1998
Olympia, SSN-717, NUC, Oct. 1, 1997–Apr. 30, 1998
Providence, SSN-719, NUC, Oct. 1, 1997–Apr. 30, 1998
Hyman G. Rickover, SSN-709, MUC, Dec. 1, 1997–Mar. 1,
    1998

1998

Parche, SSN-683, PUC
Batfish, SSN-681, NUC, Mar. 1–Sep. 1
L. Mendel Rivers, SSN-686, NUC, Mar. to May
Tucson, SSN-770, NUC, Mar. to May
    (The records show that a SEAL team won a NUC
    along with the *L. Mendel Rivers* and the *Tucson* for an
    unspecified mission in this same time period.)

DEEP-DIVING SUBMERSIBLES: AWARDS FOR INTELLI-GENCE GATHERING, SEARCHING FOR LOST SUBMARINES AND OCEAN RESEARCH

Dolphin, AGSS-555, MUC, Aug. 17–Nov. 24, 1968
NR–1, NUC, Feb. 18–Apr. 17, 1986
Sea Cliff, DSV 4, MUC, Jun. 10–Sep. 21, 1974
    MUC, Jun. 4–Nov. 30, 1984
Trieste R/V, NUC, Apr. 1–Sep. 1, 1963
Trieste II, NUC, Feb. 3–Oct. 7, 1969
    MUC, Sep. 1, 1971–May 23, 1972
Trieste II, DSV I, MUC, May 31–Nov. 17, 1977
Turtle, DSV 3, MUC, Aug. 30–Nov. 5, 1982

BALLISTIC MISSILE SUBMARINES: AWARDS FOR DEPLOYMENTS TO NEW PATROL AREAS OR CONVERSIONS TO NEW TYPES OF MISSILES AND OTHER EQUIPMENT

1950s

George Washington, SSBN-598, NUC, Jun. 9, 1959–Jul. 20, 1960

1960s

Daniel Boone, SSBN-629, Dec. 1, 1964–Feb. 29, 1968

Benjamin Franklin, SSBN-640, MUC, Oct. 1, 1965–Sep. 30, 1968

Lafayette, SSBN-616, MUC, Oct. 1, 1967–Aug. 1, 1969

Von Steuben, SSBN-632, MUC, Dec. 7, 1967–Jun. 20, 1969

Ethan Allen, SSBN-608, MUC, period in 1968

Benjamin Franklin, SSBN-640, MUC, Jul. 1, 1968–Oct. 1, 1970

Daniel Boone, SSBN-629, MUC, Jul. 1, 1968–Apr. 19, 1969

Kamehameha, SSBN-642, MUC, Jul. 1, 1968–Jun. 5, 1970

Mariano G. Vallejo, SSBN-658, MUC, Jul. 1, 1968–Apr. 1, 1970

Tecumseh, SSBN-628, MUC, Jul. 1, 1968–Oct. 27, 1969

Stonewall Jackson, SSBN-634, MUC, Jul. 1, 1968–May 8, 1970

Ulysses S. Grant, SSBN-631, MUC, Jul. 1, 1968–Sep. 24, 1969

Sam Houston, SSBN-609, MUC, period in 1969

James Madison, SSBN-627, MUC, Feb. 3, 1969–Aug. 3, 1970

Robert E. Lee, SSBN-601, MUC, Oct. 10–29, 1969

Nathan Hale, SSBN-623, MUC, Oct. 27, 1969–Oct. 1, 1970

Woodrow Wilson, SSBN-624, MUC, Nov. 4, 1969–Oct. 1, 1970

John Adams, SSBN-620, MUC, Dec. 28, 1969–Oct. 1, 1970

1970s

Simon Bolivar, SSBN-641, MUC, period in 1970

James Monroe, SSBN-622, MUC, Jan. 1–Oct. 1, 1970

Daniel Webster, SSBN-629, MUC, Mar. 7–Oct. 1, 1970

Ethan Allen, SSBN-608, MUC, Apr. 9–30, 1970
Francis Scott Key, SSBN-657, MUC, May 1–31, 1970
Henry Clay, SSBN-625, MUC, Jun. 29–Oct. 1, 1970
Daniel Boone, SSBN-629, MUC, Aug. 12, 1970–Apr. 25, 1971
Thomas Jefferson, SSBN-618, MUC, Aug. 17–Sep. 8, 1970
Henry L. Stimson, SSBN-655, Aug. 19–Sep. 9, 1970
Benjamin Franklin, SSBN-640, MUC, Oct. 2–Nov. 9, 1970
James Monroe, SSBN-622, MUC, Oct. 2, 1970–Dec. 31, 1971
Daniel Webster, SSBN-629, MUC, Dec. 1, 1970–Dec. 31, 1971
Andrew Jackson, SSBN-619, MUC, Jan. 1, 1971–Aug. 1, 1972
George Bancroft, SSBN-643, MUC, Mar. 1–31, 1971
John Marshall, SSBN-611, MUC, Mar. 3–31, 1971
Thomas Jefferson, SSBN-618, MUC, Aug. 1–31, 1971
Lafayette, SSBN-616, MUC, Sep. 1–30, 1971
Mariano G. Vallejo, SSBN-658, MUC, Jan. 1–Dec. 31, 1974
James Madison, SSBN-627, MUC, Sep. 1–Nov. 10, 1974
Francis Scott Key, SSBN-657, MUC, Sep. 1978–Oct. 1979

1980s

James Monroe, SSBN-622, MUC, Oct. 1, 1980–Sep. 30, 1983
Tecumseh, SSBN-628, MUC, Oct. 1, 1981–Sep. 30, 1982
John C. Calhoun, SSBN-630, MUC, Oct. 1, 1982–May 31, 1984
Ohio, SSBN-726, MUC, Gold crew, Sep. 6, 1983–Apr. 28, 1986
George Bancroft, SSBN-643, MUC, Oct. 1, 1983–Oct. 1, 1984
Kamehameha, SSBN-642, MUC, Oct. 1, 1983–Sep. 30, 1985
Ohio, SSBN-726, MUC, Blue crew, Jun. 3, 1984
Michigan, SSBN-727, Blue crew, MUC, Jul. 2–3, 1984
Florida, SSBN-728, Gold crew, MUC, Sep. 12, 1984
Woodrow Wilson, SSBN-624, MUC, Jan. 1, 1985–Jan. 28, 1987
Michigan, SSBN-727, Gold crew, MUC, Apr. 22, 1985
Georgia, SSBN-729, Gold crew, MUC, May 26, 1985
Georgia, SSBN-729, Blue crew, MUC, Sep. 12–13, 1985
Georgia, SSBN-729, MUC, Feb. 1986–Aug. 1986
John C. Calhoun, SSBN-630, MUC, Jun. 27, 1986–Oct. 1, 1988

Nevada, SSBN-733, MUC, Apr. to Aug. 1988

Henry L. Stimson, SSBN-655, MUC, Apr. 5–Aug. 6, 1988

Michigan, SSBN-727, Blue crew, MUC, Jul. 1, 1992–Dec. 31, 1993

Tennessee, SSBN-734, MUC, Jan. 1, 1993–Dec. 31, 1995

Nebraska, SSBN-739, MUC, Aug. 18, 1994–Jan. 1, 1997

NOTES

This book is based primarily on several hundred interviews we conducted with submariners, government officials, and intelligence officials, most of whom we cannot name. We do use names where we can. We also relied on many sources of public information to verify our facts and put them into historical context. Among other things, we consulted declassified patrol schedules of the subs in Navy archives, dug up published Naval Intelligence reports, and read numerous articles and books.

Throughout the book, we relied on several standard reference works for basic information about the history, size, and capabilities of different classes of submarines. Among them were various editions of *Guide to the Soviet Navy* and *Ships and Aircraft of the U.S. Fleet,* both written by the well-known naval analyst Norman Polmar and published by the Naval Institute Press in Annapolis, Maryland. We also consulted various editions of *Jane's Fighting Ships* and other publications of the authoritative British company Jane's Information Group Limited.

For a more detailed understanding of submarine tactics and technology, we also relied on Norman Friedman, *Submarine Design and Development* (Annapolis, Md.: Naval Institute Press, 1984); Richard Compton-Hall, *Sub Versus Sub: The Tactics and Technology of Underwater Warfare* (New York: Orion Books, 1988); and Norman Polmar, *The American Submarine* (Annapolis, Md.: Nautical and Aviation Publishing Company of America, 1983). Handy resources for most submarine hull numbers were the *United States Submarine Data Book,* prepared by the Submarine Force Library and Museum in Groton, Connecticut, and a list of all nuclear-powered submarines distributed by Electric Boat Company, a division of General Dynamics Corporation. We obtained records of the awards granted to individual submarines from the official Navy awards office at the Navy Yard in Washington, D.C.

Prologue

Much of the history of submarines we cite came from *The Ultimate Naval Weapon—Its Past, Present, and Future* by Drew Middleton (Chicago: Playboy Press, 1976). Chapters 1–4 were invaluable for their insight into the history of submarines, as was Friedman's book and Polmar's *The American Submarine.*

Chapter 1: A Deadly Beginning

Main interviews: Rafael C. Benitez, Harris M. "Red" Austin, and other crew members of USS *Cochino.*

In various parts of this chapter, we also drew on the following government documents, articles, books, and other sources:

Jan Breemer's *Soviet Submarines: Design, Development, and Tactics* (London: Jane's Information Group Limited, 1989) provides a good description of the advanced German snorkel submarines and how they were divided among the Soviet Union and the Western Allies after World War II. The changes involved in converting America's fleet submarines into snorkel boats such as the *Cochino* and the *Tusk* are described in Polmar's *The American Submarine* and in a "Welcome Aboard" brochure, USS *Tusk,* in the *Tusk* file at the Ships History Branch of the Naval Historical Center, Washington, D.C.

The U.S. Navy's early fears that the Soviets would build a large fleet of advanced snorkel subs are chronicled in an article by Breemer entitled "The Submarine Gap: Intelligence Estimates 1945–1955," in *Navy International* 91, no. 2 (February 1986): 100–105. Breemer notes that U.S. intelligence began receiving reports as early as 1948 about Soviet test launches of missiles from the decks of submarines (*Soviet Submarines,* pp. 88–89). Some of this information comes from declassified issues of the *ONI Review,* a fascinating internal magazine published each month by the Office of Naval Intelligence from 1945 through 1962. These publications are available at the Operational Archives Branch, Naval Historical Center.

Information about Operation Kayo comes from "The Reminiscences of Rear Admiral Roy S. Benson," an oral history set down in 1984 and quoted with the permission of Paul Stillwell, the director of history (reference and preservation) at the U.S. Naval Institute, Annapolis, Maryland. It is part of a large collection of oral histories of former naval officers that Stillwell and others have put together. Retired Admiral Robert L. J. Long, a former vice chief of Naval Operations and commander in chief of U.S. forces in the Pacific, first mentioned Operation Kayo to us. As a young officer, he served on the USS *Corsair* and was detached before it accompanied *Cochino* on the ill-fated mission.

Deck logs for the USS *Sea Dog* and the USS *Blackfin,* on file at the National Archives, Suitland Records Center, Suitland, Maryland, show that both made deployments from Pearl Harbor to areas off Alaska's Aleutian Islands in May and June of 1948. Lawrence Savadkin, a World War II submarine hero who was the executive officer of the *Sea Dog,* described the intelligence goals of their missions in an interview.

In addition to extensive interviews with Benitez and Austin, we drew parts of our account of the *Cochino*'s final mission and sinking from several documentary sources. The most comprehensive was the declassified version of the *Cochino* patrol report filed by Commander Benitez on September 8, 1949, which is available at the Operational Archives Branch of the Naval Historical Center. Excerpts from the report also were included in "The Loss of the *Cochino*," *ONI Review* (February 1950): 57–66. The *Cochino*'s daily deck logs were lost when it sank, but the logs from the *Tusk,* the *Corsair,* and the USS *Toro* are on file at the Suitland Records Center.

The loss of the *Cochino* made front-page headlines in most large American newspapers in 1949. One of the most detailed articles we reviewed was James D. Cunningham, "Tears and Smiles Greet *Cochino* and *Tusk* Survivors at Sub Base; Officers Give Details on Tragedy," *New London* (Connecticut) *Day,* September 8, 1949. And a Navy public relations officer, Commander William J. Lederer, interviewed some of the surviving crew members for a dramatic article, "Miracle Under the Arctic Sea" (*Saturday Evening Post,* January 14, 1950), and for a book, *The Last Cruise* (New York: William Sloane Associates, 1950). We have drawn only a few details from Lederer's book that seemed to come directly from the survivors' recollections. But our chapter differs in several crucial respects because both Austin and Benitez said Lederer's account was overdramatized and included information that was purposely altered by the Navy. In fact, Austin wrote a letter to the *Saturday Evening Post* to complain about these changes, and he saved the responses that he got from both Benitez and Lederer. Benitez wrote to Austin on February 3, 1950, that Lederer's "story as originally written was very far-fetched and what actually appeared was a compromise." Lederer acknowledged in a letter to Austin on March 2, 1950, that the Navy had reviewed his manuscript and that there were "certain things which I 'fixed.' For example, I altered the timing of the piece because I didn't want the Russians to be able to measure back and estimate where the *Cochino* sank; I made small changes in such parts where the truth might make the relatives of men feel bad; and I left out certain things which might give clues to confidential means of communicating."

One fact that Lederer did not reveal, of course, was Austin's true mission. Lederer described Austin simply as a "communications technician." Austin's background as an electronic-intercept specialist was first disclosed in "USS *Cochino*,"

Cryptolog (Fall 1983); *Cryptolog* is a publication of the Naval Cryptologic Veterans Association, a group that includes some of the spooks who rode submarines. But that article did not discuss what Austin was trying to accomplish on the *Cochino,* and our account is the first that reveals the *Cochino*'s role in helping to set off a new era of submarine spying.

Lederer's article and book also omitted any mention of the faulty foul-weather gear and boots that dragged some of the *Tusk* crew members to their deaths. This problem was documented in the *Tusk* log for August 25, 1949. Retired Rear Admiral Eugene B. Fluckey, who was the Atlantic submarine fleet's legal officer at that time, also confirmed in an interview that the foul-weather gear given to the men on the *Tusk* was "an experimental suit that nobody had tested. But the only thing is when you're in the water, it turns you upside down. And they got hung with their boots up."

On the Soviet side, we drew our description of the Soviet naval bases near Murmansk from "Kola Inlet and Its Facilities," *ONI Review* (September 1949). And the Soviets' suspicions that the *Cochino* was on a spy mission were cited in Associated Press articles that appeared on September 3 and 19, 1949, in the *New London Day* and on September 21, 1949, in the *New York Herald Tribune.*

Chapter 2: Whiskey A-Go-Go

Main interviews: Former crew members of the USS *Gudgeon* and other diesel submarines and former top officials from the U.S. submarine force, the Office of Naval Intelligence, and the Naval Security Group, which employed the Russian linguists and other spooks who rode on the subs.

Government documents, articles, books, and other sources: The dates of the *Gudgeon*'s deployment in the summer of 1957 come from its daily deck logs on file at the National Archives, Suitland Records Center. The logs show how many miles the *Gudgeon* steamed each day and other basic facts, but they give no hint that it was on an intelligence mission.

A listing of all of the diesel submarines that made surveillance deployments during the Korean War—and descriptions of the difficulties some encountered with icy weather and primitive reconnaissance equipment—are included in the interim evaluation reports that were prepared every six months during the Korean War by the commander in chief of the U.S. Pacific Fleet. They are in the files of the Operational Archives Branch at the Naval Historical Center.

U.S. surface ships probably sank a Soviet sub that came close to an aircraft carrier attack force in December 1950, early in the Korean War, according to two former intelligence officers. The United States was so concerned that the Soviet Navy would try to help the North Koreans that surface ships were under orders to protect U.S. warships by depth-charging any possible hostile submarines, and in this case, three destroyers, led by USS *McKean* (*DD-784*), depth-charged a suspected Soviet sub and then saw no signs that it had survived. Asked about this, current Russian Navy officials said they knew of no sub losses around the time of the Korean War, and then said it would be too difficult to check navy archives or reach a definitive answer.

The U.S. Navy itself used one sub in a direct combat role during the Korean conflict, sending the diesel boat, USS *Perch* (*SS-313*), to the shores of North Korea in 1950. On board were U.S. troops and sixty-three British Royal marines. Although *Perch* was detected, commandos managed to board rubber rafts and make their way to shore. A bombing raid staged by the United States that night helped draw fire away, while the men landed, blew up a culvert, mined a tunnel, and destroyed a train. One British marine was killed by enemy troops. This tale is well recounted in *Submarines at War: The History of the American Silent Service* by Edwin P. Hoyt (New York: Stein and Day Publishers, 1983), pp. 299–303.

The monthly issues of the *ONI Review* provided an excellent source for tracking the rapid growth of the Soviet submarine fleet throughout the 1950s. The information about the Soviet Whiskey crew that was ravaged by gases on a 30-day test came from retired Soviet Navy Captain First Rank Boris Bagdasaryan, who served on that sub and was interviewed by a Russian military reporter, Alexander Mozgovoy, whom we hired to do research for us. The unconfirmed intelligence reports that the Soviets were modifying some of their Zulu-class subs to carry missiles were mentioned in

"Developments and Trends in the Soviet Fleet During 1956," *ONI Review* [secret supplement] (Spring-Summer 1957): 9–10.

The encouragement of regular Navy officers to receive intelligence training and thus engage in the world's "second-oldest profession," one with "even fewer morals than the first," appeared in the article "Postgraduate Intelligence Training: An Avenue to Rewarding Service," *ONI Review* (August 1957): 337.

President Eisenhower's hesitancy about approving U-2 flights in the mid-1950s is described in Chapter 2 of Graham Yost's *Spies in the Skies* (New York: Facts on File, 1989), a book about the evolution of U.S. spy satellites.

We drew some background details about the *Gudgeon*'s captain, Norman G. Bessac, from his official biography on file in the Operational Archives Branch at the Naval Historical Center.

The Soviet version of "Hansel and Gretel" was cited in "Trends in Communist Propaganda," *ONI Review* (May 1955): 226. The Soviet offers to American pen pals to swap pictures were mentioned in "Security Control of Technical Data," *ONI Review* (April 1951): 127.

The first nuclear-powered submarine, the USS *Nautilus*, was commissioned on September 30, 1954, and sent out its historic message, "Underway on nuclear power," at the start of its first training deployment on January 17, 1955. The USS *Seawolf* became the second nuclear-powered sub to go into service when it was commissioned on March 30, 1957. The personal background and political savvy of Admiral Hyman Rickover is well covered in two excellent books: *Rickover: Controversy and Genius,* a full-scale biography by Norman Polmar and Thomas B. Allen (New York: Simon and Schuster, 1982), and *The Rickover Effect: How One Man Made a Difference,* a memoir by one of Rickover's former associates, Theodore Rockwell (Annapolis, Md.: Naval Institute Press, 1992). The adventures of the *Nautilus* in becoming the first submarine to reach the North Pole are chronicled in *Nautilus 90 North,* a book written by its second captain, Commander William R. Anderson, with Clay Blair Jr. (New York: Harper & Row, 1959).

Middleton's *The Ultimate Naval Weapon* notes that the World War II fleet boat named the USS *Gudgeon* (SS-211) also had a

major success: it was credited with the first American kill of a
Japanese U-boat.

The Soviets' August 26, 1957, announcement of their first suc-
cessful intercontinental ballistic missile test is mentioned in
"Soviet Scientific and Technical Developments, 1957," *ONI
Review* (May 1958): 214. It also is discussed in Peter Pringle and
William Arkin, *SIOP: The Secret U.S. Plan for Nuclear War* (New
York: W. W. Norton, 1983).

A series of Navy press releases about *Gudgeon*'s trip to circum-
navigate the globe and take part in Eisenhower's "People to
People" program are in the file on the *Gudgeon* at the USS *Bowfin*
Submarine Museum and Park in Honolulu.

One of the young officers on the USS *Wahoo* when it was
caught near a Soviet beach in 1958 was William J. Crowe Jr., who
rose to become an admiral and the chairman of the Joint Chiefs of
Staff under Presidents Ronald Reagan and George Bush. He
described the *Wahoo*'s perilous encounter with the Soviets in his
memoir *The Line of Fire: From Washington to the Gulf, the
Politics and Battles of the New Military* (New York: Simon and
Schuster, 1993).

Russian military officials now say there were several reasons
they showed greater restraint in dealing with spy subs than spy
planes. Soviet warships dropped low-capacity "drill bombs"
instead of full depth charges, officials told our researcher, Alexander
Mozgovoy, in case American subs like *Gudgeon* had made navigational errors and found themselves in Soviet territory accidentally. The Russian officials also said that the smaller, grenadelike
charges were used in keeping with their regulations for warning
foreign submarines encroaching upon their territorial waters,
rules that included this method of signaling them to leave.

Some of the hysteria about the possibility that Soviet subs were
coming close to American shores in the late 1950s was fueled by
U.S. Representative Carl Durham, a Democrat from North
Carolina who chaired a joint House-Senate committee on atomic
energy. He was quoted in an Associated Press dispatch on April
14, 1958, as saying that 184 Russian submarines had been sighted
off the U.S. Atlantic coast in 1957 alone. Mrs. Gilkinson's sharp
eye for foreign submarines was reported in the "Monthly Box
Score of Submarine Contacts," *ONI Review* (January 1961): 38.

The man from Texas was mentioned in "Monthly Box Score of Submarine Contacts," *ONI Review* (January 1962): 27.

In describing the expansion of SOSUS in this and subsequent chapters, we drew on an excellent declassified history of many of the Navy's antisubmarine warfare programs, "*Sea-Based Airborne Antisubmarine Warfare 1940–1977*," vols. 1–3, prepared by a Navy consultant, R. F. Cross Associates, Ltd., Alexandria, Virginia, in 1978. It is available at the Operational Archives Branch of the Naval Historical Center.

Admiral Jerauld Wright's proclamation, the case of whiskey he offered as a prize, and USS *Grenadier's* surfacing of the Soviet Zulu are described in "The Wright Stuff," *U.S. Naval Institute Proceedings* (December 1984): 74–76. The article was written by retired Navy Captain Theodore F. "Ted" Davis, who was the *Grenadier's* captain during the chase. In an interview, Davis said he saved one bottle of Jack Daniels as a souvenir and divided the rest among his crew. He kept the sealed bottle on a shelf in his study until a housekeeper helped herself to a taste one day in the late 1970s. Not long after that, retired Navy Captain William L. "Bo" Bohannan, who had been the *Grenadier's* engineer, came to visit. Recalled Davis, "I said, 'Well, now that it's open, we may as well drink the whole damn thing.' So we sat down and drank it all."

The July 1959 issue of the *ONI Review* also discussed the *Grenadier's* feat and its importance in confirming the intelligence reports that some Zulus had been converted to carry missiles. This article, "Soviet Submarine Surfaced by U.S. Forces Off Iceland" (292–295), was accompanied by four photographs of the Zulu taken by *Grenadier.* The article also noted that as soon as the Zulu surfaced, crew members scurried up onto the deck to paint over the sub's identifying number (82) and rig a canvas over the top rear of the sail. Naval Intelligence suspected that this part of the sail housed two vertical missile-launching tubes, and the article said that an analysis of the photographs indicated that the tubes "may be larger than previously estimated," meaning that the missiles also may have been slightly larger than the United States had expected.

The diary of George B. Kistiakowsky was published as *A Scientist at the White House: The Private Diary of President Eisenhower's Special Assistant for Science and Technology*

(Cambridge, Mass.: Harvard University Press, 1976). The entry we quote (p. 153) describes a special intelligence briefing that Kistiakowsky received on November 12, 1959.

The dates of all forty-one deterrent patrols made by Regulus missile subs from September 1959 through July 1964 are listed in the July 1997 issue of the *Submarine Review,* an excellent quarterly published by the Naval Submarine League, a nonprofit group made up of current and former submariners and other people who support the submarine force. That article drew information from *Regulus: The Forgotten Weapon* (Paducah, Ky: Turner Publishing Company, 1996), By David K. Stumpf, Ph.D. The four diesel subs that carried the guided missiles (the "G" in the standard submarine number designations stands for "guided") were the USS *Grayback* (*SSG-574*), the USS *Tunny* (*SSG-282*), the USS *Growler* (*SSG-577*), and the USS *Barbero* (*SSG-317*). One nuclear-powered sub, the USS *Halibut* (*SSGN-587*), made seven Regulus patrols from February 1961 through July 1964. Retired Navy Commander Herbert E. Tibbets, who served on the USS *Growler,* showed us the S-M-F pin designed for members of the "Northern Pacific Yacht Club."

In describing the pervasive safety problems with Soviet nuclear subs, we drew on research by Mozgovoy, our Russian stringer; Joshua Handler, a former research coordinator for Greenpeace, the international environmental group; and a large body of articles that have appeared in the Russian press since the end of the cold war. We recount the reactor accident on the *Hiroshima* and other similar incidents more fully in Appendix B.

The scrambling of the early Polaris subs during the Cuban Missile Crisis was described to us in interviews with retired Vice Admiral Philip A. Beshany and other former submarine officers. President Kennedy's fears about encountering Soviet subs early in the crisis were quoted by his brother, Robert F. Kennedy, in his book *Thirteen Days* (New York: Signet Books, 1969), p. 70. For information about the U.S. Navy's surfacing of Soviet diesel subs during the crisis, we drew on "Cordon of Steel: The U.S. Navy and the Cuban Missile Crisis" by Curtis A. Utz, a historian at the Naval Historical Center's Contemporary History Branch. His 48-page study was published by the Naval Historical Center in 1993 as the first in a series of reports on "The U.S. Navy in the Modern World."

Chapter 3: Turn to the Deep

Main interviews: John P. Craven; former submarine, Naval Intelligence, and Naval Security Group officials; former crew members of the USS *Halibut.*

Government documents, articles, books, and other sources: In describing the Navy's general lack of enthusiasm for deep-sea exploration and how that attitude changed after the *Thresher*'s sinking, we drew on several news and magazine articles. The June 1964 issue of *National Geographic* was particularly intriguing, with articles such as "*Thresher:* Lesson and Challenge" by James H. Wakelin Jr., and "Tomorrow on the Deep Frontier" by Edwin A. Link. We also relied on two books. One, *Mud, Muscle, and Miracles: Marine Salvage in the United States Navy* (Washington, D.C.: Naval Historical Center/Naval Sea Systems Command, 1990), was written by Captain C. A. Bartholomew, a top Navy salvage engineer. The other, *The Universe Below: Discovering the Secrets of the Deep Sea* (New York: Simon and Schuster, 1997), was written by William J. Broad, a science reporter for the *New York Times.*

The full sequence of events that caused the USS *Thresher* disaster has never been conclusively determined. Just a few minutes before *Thresher* sank, a Navy salvage ship monitoring the tests received a sonar-type message from *Thresher* saying it was experiencing minor problems and was trying to blow ballast, or release high-pressure air to force water out of its ballast tanks and propel itself to the surface. Officers on the salvage ship then heard the sounds of air under high pressure, followed only, as that maneuver failed, by sounds of the *Thresher* breaking apart. A Navy court of inquiry later concluded that a piping system probably had failed in the engine room, letting loose a violent spray of water that damaged electrical circuits and caused a loss of power.

Rickover always denied that his reactor controls and procedures were to blame. But in *Death of the* Thresher (Philadelphia: Chilton Books, 1964), Norman Polmar has suggested that an unexpected reactor scram, or shutdown, may have been a crucial factor in the *Thresher*'s demise. Polmar and his coauthor, Thomas B. Allen, also make this point in *Rickover: Controversy and Genius,* in which Rear Admiral Ralph K. James, chief of the Bureau of Ships during the *Thresher*'s construction, is quoted as saying: "I feel from what I know of the inquiry in which I participated, what I know of the ship itself, and events that occurred up to that time, that a failure of a silver soldered pipe fitting somewhere in the boat caused a discharge of a stream of water on the nuclear control board and 'scrammed' the power plant." Then, according to James, "because of inadequate design of the nuclear controls for the plant, power on the boat was lost at a time where [*sic*] the depth of water in which the submarine was operating forced enough water into the hull that prevented her from rising again because they couldn't get the power back on the boat" (p. 433). While Rickover never acknowledged any blame, he did shorten the time that operators had to wait to restart the reactor after a scram—from ten seconds to six.

The Soviets' hold-down of USS *Ronquil*, in late 1963 or early 1964, was nearly as dramatic as the *Gudgeon* incident. Caught by five Soviet surface ships, "we didn't know if they were going to unload on us" with depth charges, one *Ronquil* crew member recalls. "It was touch-and-go." *Ronquil*'s men tried to drive away, but accomplished nothing more than running down her battery. Finally, XO Lloyd Bucher realized that the Soviets were creating a blind spot as they periodically rotated their positions. He and Peter F. Block, the CO, waited until the ships began the maneuver again, then summoned up all the energy left in the sub's ailing batteries. *Ronquil* slipped through before the Soviets realized what was happening. Bucher's luck ran out the next time he was out on a ship that was caught: he was in command of the surface spy ship, USS *Pueblo*, when she was captured off North Korea in 1968.

The plans to create Deep Submergence Search Vehicles, minisubs capable of retrieving objects from the ocean floor, were detailed in Navy fact sheets in the 1960s, some of which are available in the files at the USS *Bowfin* Submarine Museum and Park in Honolulu. The dates of each stage in the *Halibut*'s conversion to a special projects submarine come from official histories of the ship and articles in the *Mare Island Grapevine,* a newspaper that covered the Mare Island Naval Shipyard and base near San Francisco, and from the files of the *Vallejo* (California) *Times-Herald.*

Rickover's drive to create the small, nuclear-powered *NR-1* submarine also is recounted in Polmar and Allen, *Rickover: Controversy and Genius* (pp. 435–443). Polmar and Allen devote a chapter (pp. 269–293) to Rickover's idiosyncratic techniques for interviewing applicants for his nuclear-powered submarine program and the worst horror stories that came out of it. Many of the people we interviewed told similar tales. Bartholomew, *Mud, Muscle, and Miracles,* and Broad, *The Universe Below,* also describe the efforts to recover the nuclear bomb off Palomares, Spain.

The fact that Rickover always wanted to know what was going on in the submarine intelligence programs—and was insulted at the thought that he should have to sign a secrecy oath like everyone else—came from interviews with two former high-level Naval Intelligence officials. As one of them put it, "Rickover wanted to know everything the reconnaissance programs were producing, what they were doing, where they were operating, and he refused to ever sign a security oath. He absolutely wouldn't sign it." Referring to several men who served as directors of Naval Intelligence in the 1960s, this source added: "There were legendary stories of Rickover shouting and screaming at them, summoning them, demanding to know what was going on and refusing to sign," and they were all "reluctant to cross" him.

Chapter 4: Velvet Fist

Main interviews: Former top Pentagon, submarine, Naval Intelligence, and CIA officials; John P. Craven; and former crew members of the USS *Halibut.*

Government documents, articles, books, and other sources: The code name "Operation Winterwind" is mentioned in the *Halibut*'s official command history for 1967. The documents do not disclose that *Halibut* was trying to locate parts of a Soviet ballistic missile or give any hint about the nature of her "assigned special project." They do, however, give the dates for what crew members say were two "test search operations"— practice runs off Hawaii—and the first attempt to locate the Soviet nose cone. The first test occurred from March 16 to April 4, 1967, and crew members say it was on this run that the *Halibut* found the boxlike object that had floated before crew members on the surface ship could weigh it down with anchor chains. *Halibut* made a second brief test run, July 10–20, 1967, to check the cameras on its fish. Crew members say the first attempt to find the Soviet missile parts took place on what the command history describes as "a 57-day special mission," from August 28 through October 24, 1967. Crew members say the second deployment to look for missile pieces—the one during which Charlie Hammonds fell overboard—took place from mid-January to April 11, 1968.

A series of six articles by Christopher Drew, Michael L. Millenson, and Robert Becker, published January 6–11, 1991, in the *Chicago Tribune* and the *Newport News Daily Press*, contained the first public disclosure of *Halibut*'s role in locating the Golf submarine. Craven described her search for the Golf in very general terms in a letter to a subcommittee of the U.S. Senate Energy and Natural Resources Committee in early 1994, and William J. Broad followed with an article in the *New York Times* on February 7, 1994. Roger C. Dunham, who was a reactor officer on the *Halibut* in the late 1960s, has written a fictionalized account of the search for the Golf in *Spy Sub: A Top Secret Mission to the Bottom of the Pacific* (Annapolis, Md.: Naval Institute Press, 1996). The Navy required Dunham to change the boat's name—the star of his book is a submarine called the USS *Viperfish*—and modify crucial technical details.

The split in opinions over the CIA's plan to build the *Glomar Explorer* and try to recover the Golf submarine was evident in several interviews with former high-level Navy and Pentagon officials. In an interview that took place a few months before he died in 1993, Frederick J. "Fritz" Harlfinger II, the former director of Naval Intelligence, said the CIA "did the craziest things. The CIA always got in our way."

But Admiral Thomas H. Moorer, the chief of Naval Operations in the late 1960s, said that along with the skeleton of the Soviet sailor, his most vivid memory of the Velvet Fist photos was that the Golf "was intact enough to make the judgment that we could raise it." Moorer dismissed Craven's and Bradley's idea of just blasting open parts of the Golf and sending a mini-submarine to try to retrieve the missile warheads and coded-communications gear. "Yeah, but there's no way you could be sure you got all the crypto stuff—I mean, how they thought you were going to get inside of it and make a thorough search. And so, if we were going to do anything, we might as well go all the way," Moorer said, adding with obvious irritation: "There's always some son-of-a-bitch can figure out a better way to do, but he don't have to do it."

Melvin Laird, President Nixon's secretary of Defense, acknowledged in an interview that "some people thought you didn't have to try to recover the whole thing just to get the important pieces like missiles and crypto." And in recommending construction of the *Glomar Explorer* just a year or so after the USS *Scorpion* had sunk, he added: "I felt that the technology was important because we might be able to use it with one of our submarines if we got in a problem. That really had more to do with it as far as I was concerned because I was always worried about crews getting trapped. So that had a lot to do with it. You didn't have to do that much as far as the Russians were concerned. But I was thinking about it in a different way. This idea that it was just done for that one submarine is a mistake."

Laird also added one other interesting historical note. Some critics have questioned whether Howard Hughes, the paranoid and reclusive billionaire, ever knew that his companies were involved in an effort to raise a sunken Soviet submarine. But, Laird said, "I remember talking to Howard Hughes about it too."

Chapter Five: Death of a Submarine

Main interviews: John P. Craven, former top submarine and Naval Intelligence officials, and torpedo experts who asked not to be identified.

Government documents, articles, and other sources: The safety concerns of former *Scorpion* crew member Dan Rogers were first disclosed, and are explored in more detail, in Stephen Johnson, "A Long and Deep Mystery: Scorpion Crewman Says Sub's '68 Sinking Was Preventable," *Houston Chronicle,* May 23, 1993. We also interviewed Rogers. Johnson's article includes the quote from the letter that *Scorpion* Machinist's Mate David Burton Stone wrote to his parents about the poor condition of the ship's equipment. Johnson was also extraordinarily generous in sharing many other aspects of his extensive research with us.

The Navy's difficulties in tracking Soviet subs in the Mediterranean Sea in the late 1960s are discussed in R. F. Cross Associates, Ltd., *Sea-Based Airborne Antisubmarine Warfare 1940–1977*, vol. 2. More details of the collision between the USS *George C. Marshall* and the Soviet sub are in Appendix A. Retired Navy Commander Herbert E. Tibbets, the former skipper of the USS *Cutlass*, described in an interview the game of chicken involving the *Scorpion* and the Soviet destroyer.

The main concerns fueling the notion that *Scorpion* was destroyed by Soviet forces were disclosed in an article by Ed Offley: "Game of 'Chicken' Led to Loss of *Scorpion* 25 Years Ago," that ran both in the *New London Day*, May 23, 1993; and as "Remembering the *Scorpion*—Evidence Points to an Underwater Dogfight as the Sub's Demise," in the *Virginian-Pilot* and *Ledger-Star* (Norfolk, Virginia), May 30, 1993. Offley quotes Jerry Hall, an enlisted man who worked as an aide at the Atlantic Fleet submarine command in 1968, as saying he heard talk among more senior officers that on its way home from the Med, *Scorpion* had been diverted to "brush off" a Soviet attack sub that was trying to trail a Polaris missile sub leaving the port at Rota, Spain. But our sources who had top Navy jobs flatly denied that in interviews. They acknowledged that *Scorpion* had been diverted, but they said its real mission—checking into the Soviets' baffling balloon activities—was much less provocative. And in recounting details of *Scorpion*'s final radio communications, which indicated that it had collected a few photographs of the balloon activity and then cleared that area, these officials said there was no reason to suspect that it was engaged with any Soviet vessels when it sank.

In one recent article in the May 21, 1998, *Seattle Post-Intelligencer* titled "Navy Says Sinking of the *Scorpion* Was an Accident, Revelations Suggest a Darker Scenario," Offley suggested that *Scorpion* may still have been close to Soviet vessels when she sank. But no one who examined the wreckage found any evidence of an attack, and search teams back in 1968 were told all Soviet vessels had been far from the scene.

The information that we attribute to "declassified Navy documents" at various points in the chapter comes from more than seventy pages that the Navy released to the *Chicago Tribune* and other news organizations under the Freedom of Information Act on October 25, 1993. The most important document was the final report of the findings of the Navy's court of inquiry that investigated the *Scorpion* disaster in 1968 and 1969. Citing cold war secrecy, the Navy did not make the report public at that time. Instead, the Navy and the Defense Department simply issued summaries in news releases, dated January 31, 1969, saying that the "certain cause" of *Scorpion*'s loss could not be determined. The news releases—which are masterful examples of government obfuscation—did not disclose that the court of inquiry had concluded that the most likely cause of the *Scorpion*'s loss was some type of torpedo accident; indeed, the releases included several misleading statements that made that possibility seem improbable. The Navy did not declassify the court of inquiry's report until 1984, when Ed Offley, then a reporter at the Norfolk papers, petitioned for the documents and wrote the first comprehensive story examining how the court had come to believe that a hot-running torpedo was the most likely culprit. That article, "Mystery of Sub's Sinking Unravels," was published on the front page of the *Virginian-Pilot* and the *Ledger-Star* on December 16, 1984, and included the first interview with John Craven on his role in finding the *Scorpion*'s wreckage. Christopher Drew also described the hot-running torpedo theory in "How *Scorpion* Killed Itself: Navy Discloses Sub Sunk by Own Torpedo 25 Years Ago," *Chicago Tribune*, October 26, 1993.

Our own reconstruction—and the disturbing new information about how torpedoes were being rushed out to the fleet despite rampant safety failures—is based largely on extensive interviews with John Craven and various torpedo experts and weapons engineers. Early in May 1998, we attempted several times to reach Rear Admiral Arthur Gralla, who headed the Naval Ordnance Command when *Scorpion* was lost and to whom the safety engineer's alert about the torpedo battery failures was addressed. He was traveling abroad and did not return messages. He died a few weeks later.

The 1970 examination of the *Trieste* photos of *Scorpion*'s wreckage was analyzed and written up in the Navy's "Evaluation of data and artifacts related to USS *Scorpion* (*SSN-589*)" prepared by the *Scorpion* advisory group and released in 1998. Among the people we called upon to help us evaluate that report were Ross E. Saxon, who dove down to the wreckage on *Trieste*; Robert S. Price, who re-analyzed the acoustic data after Craven retired; several submarine officers who served in *Scorpion*'s era; and various weapons safety experts. The review of the work of the first Technical Advisory Group set up to help find *Scorpion* in 1968 under John Craven was also released in 1998, "The *Scorpion* Search 1968, An Analysis of the Operation for the CNO Technical Advisory Group (TAG)." The letter summarizing the Jason's findings was released in the same group of documents, "*Scorpion* Artifacts," January 14, 1987, signed by Peter M. Palermo.

Robert Price, research engineer at the Naval Ordnance Laboratory, which was at White Oak, Maryland, and separate from the Naval Ordnance Command, says that when his team went back in 1969 or 1970 and examined the original acoustic data, their read on it was far different than Craven's. For one thing, Price and his team believed that the first sound that registered at the Canary Islands' hydrophone was not the sound of an explosion of either a torpedo or the main battery that powered *Scorpion*. "The acoustic evidence we examined does not indicate why the sub went down," Price says. "All we know is that it wasn't a full-scale outside-the-hull type explosion which would be very loud."

Instead, he says, the first sound recorded was the implosion. The subsequent sounds that began 91 seconds later, he says, were likely caused by the tail of the submarine rattling around inside the auxiliary machine space after two sections had telescoped. Further, he says that a model submarine sent down in a one-hundred-foot tank began to spiral on the way to the bottom almost immediately, suggesting that there was no predicting the direction *Scorpion* would have fallen.

His data does not shed light on why *Scorpion* went down. He also does not know why *Scorpion* was found just where Craven had predicted, using his very different interpretation of the data. That, Price says, may have been coincidence, or luck.

Though he did not know about the malfunctioning torpedo batteries, Mark A. Bradley provided the best published analysis of the newly released documents in "Why They Called the *Scorpion* 'Scrap Iron,'" U.S. Naval Institute Proceedings, July 1998, pp. 30–38.

In describing the months of searching for the *Scorpion*'s wreckage, we owe a large debt of thanks to Jack W. Davis Jr., the president and publisher of the *Newport News* (Virginia) *Daily Press*, who granted us access to the newspaper's voluminous files of news stories on the *Scorpion*. Many of the articles provided helpful background. One that we relied on in describing the *Mizar*'s role in the search was Alexander C. Brown, "The Cruise of the *Mizar* in Quest of the *Scorpion*," *Newport News Daily Press*, December 15, 1968. The *Daily Press* files also included copies of the original press releases about the court of inquiry's findings, and we quoted from the one issued by the Office of the Assistant Secretary of Defense (Public Affairs), "Navy Reports Findings of the Court of Inquiry on the Loss of the USS *Scorpion*," January 31, 1969, no. 80–69. We also interviewed retired Rear Admiral Robert R. Fountain, the former *Scorpion* executive officer who helped with Craven's tests in the submarine simulator.

The bitterness among the survivors of *Scorpion* crew members at the Navy's failure to tell them the truth about the possible reasons for the boat's sinking came through clearly in several news articles. Barbara Baar Gillum expressed her disappointment in a sidebar story by Stephen Johnson, "The Explanation That Never Came," *Houston Chronicle*, May 23, 1993; William H. McMichael, "What Happened on the *Scorpion*?" *Newport News Daily Press*, October 31, 1993, and Mike Knepler, "Families Mark 30th Anniversary of the Loss of Norfolk Sub *Scorpion*," *Norfolk Virginian-Pilot*, May 26, 1998, also brought home the poignant suffering that the families have endured.

Chapter 6: "The Ballad of Whitey Mack"

Main interviews: Former crew members of the USS *Lapon*, the USS *Dace*, the USS *Ray,* and the USS *Greenling,* and former top submarine and Naval Intelligence officials.

Government documents and other sources: George T. "Tommy" Cox, the singing spook, copyrighted and pressed 3,500 copies of his own album of 13 submarine songs, *Take Her Deep,* in 1978 and easily sold his entire supply at stores near Navy bases. Other songs had titles like "Big Black Submarine,"

"Diesel Boats Forever," and "Sailor's Prayer." There also was a poignant ode called "Scorpion." Recently Cox rereleased his album as a CD. Information on how to obtain copies is available at *www.sontagdrew.com.*

Among the subs to do some of the early experimental work that showed it possible to execute a long trail was USS *Pollack.* She slipped behind a noisy Soviet HEN up near the Kola Peninsula in 1965 and followed it all the way down into the Mediterranean. This early trail, led by *Pollack* captain Harvey E. Lyon, lasted nearly three weeks.

The dates of some of the deployments mentioned in this chapter come from annual command histories for the *Lapon, Dace, Ray,* and *Greenling,* some of which are in files for each of those subs at the USS *Bowfin* Submarine Museum & Park in Honolulu and at the Submarine Force Library & Museum at the Naval Submarine Base in Groton, Connecticut. An unclassified excerpt from Vice Admiral Arnold F. Schade's congratulatory message to the *Lapon* on October 13, 1969, is in a file on the *Lapon* at the Groton museum. That file also contains an unclassified excerpt from a message sent to the *Lapon* on October 22 by Admiral Ephraim P. Holmes, the commander of the Atlantic Fleet: "FOR C.O. I HAVE SEEN THE RESULTS OF THE LAPON'S EXPLOITS ON TWO PREVIOUS MISSIONS, BUT THIS HAS TO BE THE BEST. THE PERFORMANCE OF YOU AND YOUR FINE CREW IN THIS MOST DEMANDING TASK HAS BEEN SUPERB." Both messages were originally coded top-secret. In an interview, Admiral Schade said the significance of the *Lapon*'s feat was easy to see: "That we were able to do it, trail them, that was it. In fact, that was about all we wanted to know. What were the weak spots? If we had to go after them, how would we find them, detect them, and destroy them?"

Chapter 7: "Here She Comes..."

Main interviews: Former crew members of the USS *Tautog,* former top Pentagon and Navy officials, retired Soviet Navy Captain First-Rank Boris Bagdasaryan, and Rear Admiral Valery Aleksin, the former chief navigator of the Russian Navy.

Government documents and other sources: The fact that two U.S. attack subs were fooled by Soviet missile drills and radioed warnings in the early days of trailing the Yankees was disclosed to us in an interview with a former high-level U.S. submarine official. He said: "Our submarine in trail was always alert to any activity of the Soviet that indicated he was getting ready to launch. Like the opening of the outer doors of the missile tube, fourteen or sixteen of those things banging open, like flooding the tube, this is a critical indication that he's getting ready to launch. We would then be instructed to, the hell with security, get up and get the word out with as much early warning as possible.

"We did discover they were conducting a drill a couple of times. Instead of opening sixteen tubes, they opened two. Instead of flooding sixteen, they'd flood two. This, of course, was critical to their own training, to do that, and so we, the first couple of times, panicked everybody, but we learned to live with it." In those two instances, he said, the trailing American subs quickly rose to periscope depth, stuck up their radio antennas, and sent warnings back to military command authorities. "But luckily it was a thing where they'd get up and transmit and then they very soon thereafter would be in a position to say, 'Cancel, it is a drill,' and within three or four minutes we'd be in a position to follow up and take away the urgency of this thing." He said some of the first subs involved in these trailings taped the sounds of the Soviet drills so other attack sub captains could listen to them and know what to look for. After that, he said, "It was a waiting thing. It was just that one period in the beginning that everybody got a little goosey."

This official and several other former senior Navy officers said that, to avoid mistakes, U.S. attack subs involved in such trailings did not have the authority during the cold war to attack Soviet missile subs on their own; even if they radioed in an alert that the Soviet sub's missile doors were opening, they had to wait to receive orders from shore before taking further action. But if hostilities had broken out, that would have changed. "A sub captain's orders would depend on whether it was peacetime, we were already at war, or we were on heightened alert because of the possibility of war," one retired admiral said. He added that there normally would be "a range of orders, with the most aggressive coming, of course, if we were at war."

The reaction of Soviet Navy Commander-in-Chief Sergei G. Gorshkov to the collision between the USS *Gato* and the Soviet Hotel-class sub K-19 was described to our researcher Alexander Mozgovoy by two Russian naval officers. They are Rear Admiral Vladimir Georgievich Lebedko and Captain Second-Rank Valentin Anatolievich Shabanov. Shabanov was the captain of the K-19 in November 1969, and Lebedko was a deputy submarine division commander. Both were on the K-19 at the time of the crash.

The information that *Gato* was armed and ready to fight after the collision, and that its captain prepared false mission reports showing his boat had broken off her patrol two days before the accident, comes from a front-page article in the *New York Times* on July 6, 1975, by Seymour M. Hersh. Former *Gato* crew members told Hersh that, immediately after the crash, *Gato*'s weapons officer ran two decks below and prepared for orders to arm the sub's torpedoes, including some with nuclear warheads. "Only one authentication—either from the ship's captain or her executive officer—was needed to prepare the torpedoes for launching," Hersh wrote. "No order came from the *Gato*'s captain because the Soviet vessel—obviously confused—made no attempt to pursue the *Gato*." Hersh also quoted crew members as saying that the *Gato*'s captain was ordered by the Navy's Atlantic Fleet command to prepare twenty-five copies of a top-secret after-action report alleging that the sub had broken off her patrols two days before the date of the collision because of a propeller shaft malfunction. He also was told to prepare six accurate reports describing the collision and the events right after it and to deliver those by hand to a unit of the Atlantic Fleet command. Navy officials acknowledged both the collision and that some falsified reports were prepared.

Part of the background sketch of *Tautog*'s captain, the late Commander Buele G. Balderston, is taken from his official Navy biography. Other information comes from an interview with his widow, Irene Balderston. The dates of *Tautog*'s deployment to the western Pacific—June 8 through July 1, 1970—come from the sub's official command history for that year. The history, prepared by Balderston, lists the deployment simply as a "Training Cruise." Just like in the Atlantic, there also was a competition among sub captains in the Pacific. And when Balderston took *Tautog* out in mid-1970, USS *Flasher* (*SSN-*

613), under CO Emsley Cobb, had just won a Presidential Unit Citation for the first long trailing in the Pacific—after following a Hotel II–class missile sub for more than twenty days. Spec-ops in the late 1960s led by star commanders had also helped set the pace in the Pacific. Among the best were Jackson B. Richard of USS *Queenfish* (*SSN–651*) and Nils R. Thunman of USS *Plunger* (*SSN–595*). Richard went on in the mid-1970s to coordinate much of sub spying, while Thunman later became a vice admiral and the head of submarine warfare.

In describing the threat posed by Soviet Echo II submarines to U.S. aircraft carriers operating off Vietnam, we drew on R. F. Cross Associates, Ltd.'s declassified study *Sea-Based Airborne Antisubmarine Warfare 1940–1977,* pp. 2, 68–70.

Now that the Soviets had so many nuclear subs, the Pacific Fleet followed the earlier lead of the Atlantic command and quit sending diesel boats to spy off the Soviet coast. It was the end of a swashbuckling era, and diesel vets coined a romantic phrase— "Diesel Boats Forever"—to try to keep them alive, at least in their memories. Some diesel subs still did surveillance ops in less hazardous areas, such as in the Med and off Cuba, where Spanish-speaking spooks rode diesels in 1969 and 1970 to check on Soviet efforts to build a port for Russian subs in Cuba. The Navy later transferred many of the diesel subs to various allies with small navies and retired the rest.

The *Tautog*'s collision with the Echo II was first revealed publicly on January 6, 1991, in the submarine series by Drew, Millenson, and Becker published January 6–11, 1991, by the *Chicago Tribune* and the *Newport News Daily Press*. Based on interviews with Admiral Thomas H. Moorer, who was about to be promoted from chief of Naval Operations to chairman of the Joint Chiefs of Staff at the time of the collision, Rear Admiral Walter L. Small Jr., who was commander of submarines in the Pacific in 1970, and several *Tautog* crew members, that series reported the conclusion of U.S. officials that the Echo II had sunk. Both Moorer and Small said in the interviews that they were told verbally that the Echo had sunk. In an interview for this book, former Defense Secretary Melvin Laird said that he had been given the same tragic news, and that he immediately passed it on to President Nixon. "I briefed the president. The president knew." Asked whether he recalled Nixon's reaction, Laird said: "No, you never knew what kind of reaction he had. He was glad to get the information."

Before the series was published, the Soviet Navy did not respond to repeated requests by the *Tribune* and the *Daily Press* for comment on the incident. But in the spring of 1992, Alexander Mozgovoy located Boris Bagdasaryan, a former Soviet submarine commander who announced that he was the captain of the Echo that had collided with *Tautog*. Mozgovoy published Bagdasaryan's assertions in a Russian newspaper in 1992. He since has asked Bagdasaryan numerous questions on our behalf. Though there are a few discrepancies between what Bagdasaryan and the *Tautog* crew members recall, there seems to be little reason to doubt that they are talking about the same collision.

Chapter 8: "Oshkosh B'Gosh"

Main interviews: Former top Navy, Naval Intelligence, CIA, and NSA officials and crew members of the USS *Halibut*.

Government documents, articles, books, and other sources: We based our description of Petropavlovsk and the Kamchatka Peninsula on information and photographs provided by Joshua Handler after a visit there.

The most comprehensive history of the Navy's development of saturation diving techniques is *Papa Topside: The SeaLab Chronicles of Captain George F. Bond, USN,* ed. Helen A. Siiteri (Annapolis, Md.: Naval Institute Press, 1993). Bond, who died in 1983, was a Navy medical doctor who pioneered ways for divers to live and work at much greater depths. Reporting to John Craven, he supervised the experiments with the Navy's SeaLab habitats in the 1960s. For technical information, we also relied on the *NOAA Diving Manual: Diving for Science and Technology,* 2d ed. (Washington, D.C.: U.S. Department of Commerce/National Oceanic and Atmospheric Administration, December 1979); we found it in the library at the Navy Yard in Washington, D.C. The divers involved in the cable-tapping were neither Navy SEALs nor the regular Navy divers who helped perform maintenance on ships and subs. They were instead a special group of saturation divers who worked for Submarine Development Group One, a Navy detachment that included the *Halibut*. SUBDEVGRU 1 was cre-

ated in August 1967, according to a Navy brochure, "to operate as a permanent Naval command with deep ocean search,
location, recovery, and rescue capability." By the early 1970s,
the detachment included *Halibut; Trieste II; Turtle* and *Sea
Cliff,* two new mini-subs that initially could go as deep as 6,500
feet to recover objects or do ocean research; surface ships
equipped to assist in submarine rescue operations; and one
Deep Submergence Rescue Vehicle. The development group was
headquartered in San Diego and had an office at the Mare
Island Navy base, where *Halibut* was docked.

Our discussion of the "40 Committee" draws mainly on two
sources: Seymour M. Hersh, *The Price of Power: Kissinger in
the Nixon White House* (New York: Summit Books, 1983); and
the final report of a special House intelligence committee,
chaired by Rep. Otis G. Pike, as reprinted in the *Village Voice,*
February 16, 1976.

One example of the local headlines that publicized the Navy's
cover story for *Halibut* was "Navy Bares Secret Role of M.I.
[Mare Island] Sub," *Vallejo Times-Herald,* September 25, 1969.
The article said that the *Halibut* "will be the lead mother submarine for the development, installation and evaluation of a rescue
system which has been determined to be necessary to cover the
potential loss of submarines on the continental shelf. The system
will include a completely self-contained navigation, search, location and personnel rescue capability, using a deep submergence
rescue vehicle which will be carried aboard *Halibut.*"

In describing NSA headquarters, we relied predominantly on
James Bamford's groundbreaking study *The Puzzle Palace: A
Report on NSA, America's Most Secret Agency* (Boston: Houghton
Mifflin, 1982). Former CIA officials have said the operation to tap
car-phone conversations of Soviet leaders ended after the
Washington columnist Jack Anderson disclosed it in a news article
in the early 1970s. Anderson has said that his government sources
told him the operation had ended before he wrote about it. One
other deal reached with the Soviets in 1972 was the Incidents at Sea
agreement, which was meant to put an end to the games of chicken
and other harassment between U.S. and Soviet surface vessels. At
the U.S. Navy's insistence, the agreement did not place any restric-
tions on submarines operating below the surface.

We drew our accounts of arms control negotiations mainly from three books: Gerard Smith, *Doubletalk: The Story of SALT I* (Garden City, N.Y.: Doubleday, 1980); Paul H. Nitze, *From Hiroshima to Glasnost: At the Center of Decision—A Memoir* (New York: Grove Weidenfeld, 1989); and Hersh, *The Price of Power*. Hersh's book and Elmo R. Zumwalt Jr., *On Watch: A Memoir* (New York: Quadrangle/New York Times Book Co., 1976), give detailed accounts of the tensions between Kissinger and Zumwalt.

Former *Halibut* Chief John White made his comments about leaving the sub's crew in an interview with us. "There's not too many people who got away with what I did and who didn't get busted for it," he said. He acknowledged that he and the chiefs were drinking beer the night he decided not to go back aboard *Halibut,* although he denies anyone drank too much. "I wouldn't say I was sober as a judge," he added. He insisted that his decision to leave the sub in the middle of the deployment was "totally unrelated" to the nature of its mission and was not meant to be any type of protest. But he declined to say what his motivation was.

Chapter 9: The $500 Million Sand Castle

Main interviews: Seymour M. Hersh; William E. Colby; Otis Pike; Aaron Donner, Edward Roeder III, and other former staff members of the Pike Committee; John P. Craven; former crew members of the *Glomar-Explorer;* and former top Navy, CIA, and Naval Intelligence officials.

Government documents, articles, books, and other sources: Some of the difficulties that Hersh faced in researching the *Glomar* story are described in Harrison E. Salisbury, *Without Fear or Favor: The New York Times and Its Times* (New York: Times Books, 1980). William Colby's memoir, *Honorable Men: My Life in the CIA* (New York: Simon and Schuster, 1978), also provided excellent background, particularly on his fencing with Hersh over Hersh's article on the CIA's domestic spying.

We interviewed Hersh several times, and interviewed Colby once before he died in 1996. Colby said that when he heard that Hersh had gotten a tip about the *Glomar* operation, "it scared the living daylights out of me. I didn't ask any more. I knew we had a problem." Asked whether he was worried that the *Glomar* operation could have threatened détente, Colby said: "We always knew we had a hot potato on our hands." Still, he said, Kissinger was always "fully supportive. Kissinger's idea was that it was my business . . . it was my problem, it was my money." And Colby remained adamant that the gamble to recover the Golf was worth taking: "The answer I give to that is: What would the Russians have given to have a full American submarine in their hands? The nuclear weapons. The command and control system. The communications system. The war planning. All of it." He also dismissed Craven and Bradley's idea of making a more limited recovery attempt with a deep-diving mini-sub by saying: "On any engineering job, you have different ways of proceeding."

We drew our description of the location of the patrol areas of the Soviet Yankees and the continued expansion of SOSUS from R. F. Cross Associates, Ltd., *Sea-Based Airborne Antisubmarine Warfare 1940–1977,* volume 2. Several submarine force officials described in interviews how they kept track of Soviet submarines during the Yom Kippur War.

In the interview with us, Colby said he thought the "real genius" in the planning of the *Glomar* operation was in the choice to use the secretive Howard Hughes and the manganese cover story. Colby also was blunt in saying that no matter what legal justifications the CIA lawyers might have drafted, "obviously we were secretly trying to steal this submarine. If they had known we were after that, it would have been legitimate for them to be able to try to stop us." Colby also said it was obvious that the CIA was sending *Glomar* into a potential *Pueblo*-like situation. Asked what *Glomar*'s crew would have done if the Soviets had tried to board her, he said: "Probably dodge and weave." He added: "We had some protection. . . . We had a deal with the Navy. They were just down at Pearl Harbor," where Naval Intelligence was assiduously monitoring every Soviet communications frequency possible while the *Glomar* was at sea.

We drew most of our technical description of the *Glomar* and how it used Clementine, its steel arm and claw, in trying to lift up the Golf from Roy Varner and Wayne Collier, *A Matter of Risk: The Incredible Inside Story of the CIA's Hughes* Glomar Explorer *Mission to Raise a Russian Submarine* (New York: Random House, 1978). Collier helped recruit many of the oil-field roughnecks who operated the *Glomar*'s huge machinery, and he and Varner later interviewed them and some government officials to piece together a detailed account of what happened on the ship. Another book, Clyde Burleson's *The Jennifer Project* (Englewood Cliffs, N.J.: Prentice-Hall, 1977), also provided helpful background information, particularly about the *Glomar*'s design and technical capabilities. Because almost everything written about the heavily shrouded *Glomar* operation contains some mistakes, we went through both of these books carefully with our intelligence sources to avoid picking up any errors.

Hersh's story on the CIA's domestic spying led the *New York Times* on December 22, 1974, with a headline spread over three columns at the top of page 1: "Huge CIA Operation Reported in U.S. Against Anti-War Forces, Other Dissidents in Nixon Years." Charging the CIA with "directly violating its charter," Hersh wrote that the agency had "conducted a massive illegal domestic intelligence operation" and compiled dossiers on ten thousand or more American citizens. CIA operatives, the story said, had been shadowing war protesters and infiltrating antiwar organizations. Colby always insisted—and repeated again in our interview—that Hersh "blew it all out of proportion" by using the word *massive*. Colby added in the interview: "We were engaged in a few things we shouldn't have done." But, he said, "if he had left the word *massive* out, it would have been very hard to contest." Colby also said he attacked the Hersh story publicly at that time because "there was a good chance the agency was going to be destroyed. I was fighting for its survival."

Colby's campaign to try to keep news organizations from breaking the *Glomar* story was described in Salisbury, *Without Fear or Favor*, and in two news articles that drew on declassified CIA documents: George Lardner Jr. and William Claiborne, "CIA's *Glomar* 'Game Plan,'" *Washington Post*, October 23, 1977; and William Claiborne and George Lardner Jr., "Colby Called *Glomar* Case 'Weirdest Conspiracy,'" *Washington Post*, November 5, 1977. The quote from Jack Anderson about why he went ahead and broke the *Glomar* story on his radio show comes from Martin Arnold, "C.I.A. Tried to Get Press to Hold Up Salvage Story," the *New York Times*, March 20, 1975.

The best analysis of the lack of success of the *Glomar* operation remains the first detailed one—Hersh's first article, "C.I.A. Salvage Ship Brought Up Part of Soviet Sub Lost in 1968, Failed to Raise Atom Missiles," on the front page of the *New York Times,* March 19, 1975. Hersh also interviewed Wayne Collier extensively for a follow-up article: "Human Error Is Cited in '74 *Glomar* Failure," the *New York Times,* December 9, 1976. Hersh made some errors, such as initially overstating the number of bodies recovered with part of the Golf. But in describing how little of value was gained through the *Glomar* operation, he was right on the mark, while the *Washington Post* consistently wrote that the operation was relatively successful, and *Time* magazine published an article stating that it was a total success and the entire Golf submarine had been recovered. In our interview, Colby, who had previously declined to say much about the *Glomar* operation, finally confirmed that only part of the Golf was recovered. And while he said that some of the information gleaned from it was "useful," the sub "was not raised."

Hersh's story on the Holystone operations—"Submarines of U.S. Stage Spy Missions Inside Soviet Waters"—appeared on the front page of the *New York Times,* May 25, 1975. His follow-up on the *Gato* collision appeared in the *Times* on July 6, 1975.

Our description of the Pike Committee's conclusions comes from its final report, as reprinted in the *Village Voice* on February 16, 1976. After the full House voted not to release the report, it was leaked to the *Voice* by the veteran CBS newsman Daniel Schorr, who describes what happened in his book *Clearing the Air* (Boston: Houghton Mifflin, 1977).

Chapter 10: Triumph and Crisis

Main interviews: Former top Navy, intelligence, and White House officials and crew members of the USS *Seawolf* and USS *Parche.*

Government documents, articles, books, and other sources: For President Jimmy Carter's background as a submarine officer and his general defense policies as president, we reviewed two of his books, *Why Not the Best?* (Nashville: Broadman Press, 1975); and *Keeping Faith: Memoirs of a President* (New York: Bantam Books, 1982). Our description of the briefing for him on the activities of the special projects subs is based on interviews with former high-level officials who were familiar with it. Because of the sensitivity of the decision to tap Soviet cables in a second location, we should note that Richard Haver did not discuss the Barents taps with us in any fashion. In fact, we deliberately avoided describing as characters in this chapter or the next anyone who did talk to us about the operation.

The pulling back of Soviet missile subs to the bastions was discussed in general terms in a number of articles in trade journals such as the *U.S. Naval Institute Proceedings* and the *Submarine Review* during the 1980s. An excellent discussion of the initial differences in opinion among Navy leaders and analysts about what this Soviet move meant appeared in Gregory L. Vistica, *Fall from Glory: The Men Who Sank the U.S. Navy* (New York: Simon and Schuster, 1995). Vistica, a former reporter for the *San Diego Union-Tribune* who now works for *Newsweek,* set out to chronicle the Tailhook sex scandal and some of the problems with the Navy's leadership that seemed inevitably to lead to it. But he also delved into how Naval Intelligence formed its views of the Soviet threat, including the discussion about what to make of the satellite evidence in November 1980 that the Soviets might be building an aircraft carrier. Vistica's book also gave the first public description of the briefing on submarine spying that was given to President Ronald Reagan on Friday, March 6, 1981. We also interviewed officials who attended that briefing, as well as crew members of the USS *Besugo (SS-321)*—the diesel submarine used in filming *Hellcats of the Navy*—who watched Reagan closely as he practiced barking out his orders and who saw the pier break.

Information about drug use among *Seawolf* and *Parche* crew members came from crewmen on those boats. Frederick H. Hartmann's book *Naval Renaissance: The U.S. Navy in the 1980s* (Annapolis, Md.: Naval Institute Press, 1990) provides good background on how pervasive this problem once was in the Navy as a whole. He cited a Department of Defense drug-use survey in 1980 in which 47 percent of the respondents in the Navy and the Marines acknowledged using marijuana, compared to 40 percent in the Army and 20 percent in the Air Force. Only 2 percent of the Air Force respondents reported using cocaine, compared to 6 percent for the Army and 11 percent for the Navy. Alarmed by these and other similar findings, Admiral Thomas B. Hayward, the chief of Naval Operations, released a videotape in December 1981 to be shown to every man and woman in the Navy. Hartmann recounts how in this message Hayward announced a new "pride and professionalism" program and delivered a stern warning to the people who were using drugs: "Not here, not on my watch, not in my division, not on my ship or in my squadron, not in my Navy." This program, enforced with huge numbers of random drug tests, sharply reduced the amount of illicit drug use in the Navy.

The dates of the missions by the *Seawolf* and the *Parche* are derived from official command and other histories for the ships found in Navy archives. Also helpful was the "cruise book"—an album of photographs, inside jokes, and crew rosters put together by *Seawolf* crew members and given to everyone who was on the 1981 mission. For information about the massive storm system that assaulted the Sea of Okhotsk and imperiled the *Seawolf,* see the *Mariners Weather Log* (published by the U.S. Department of Commerce/National Oceanic and Atmospheric Administration) 26, no. 2 (Spring 1982): 89; this volume gives the weather reports for October, November, and December 1981.

Chapter 11: The Crown Jewels

Main interviews: Former officials of U.S. intelligence agencies and former members of the crew of the USS *Parche.*

Government documents, articles, books, and other sources: After the cold war ended, the KGB placed a photograph of one of the two cable-tap pods that it had recovered—along with some of the data-recording equipment that had been inside—on display in the Russian Ministry of Security's museum at the notorious Lubyanka Prison. On a visit there, our Russian researcher, Alexander Mozgovoy, was shown a small plate on the data-recording equipment that identified it as belonging to the U.S. government. Russian officials told Mozgovoy that the tap pods had been recovered about 60 kilometers, or roughly 38 miles, off of Kamchatka in the Sea of Okhotsk. They also said that one of the pods was clearly newer than the other and had more sophisticated recording equipment that made extensive use of microprocessing technology. The Russians confirmed that the devices were nuclear-powered and could work for about 125 days. Mozgovoy also obtained the picture of the tap pod that we have included with the photographs in this book.

Waldo K. Lyon helped us in interviews with the portion of this chapter that fell within his amazing area of expertise: the scientific properties of Arctic sea ice and their troubling implications for submarine warfare. Lyon fought tirelessly throughout the 1980s to try to persuade Navy officials to take more account of his views. Born in 1914, he had long operated with the energy and vigor of two men. He continued to work at the Arctic lab—and also was a national senior badminton champion—in his seventies. In his eighties, he was still fighting a 1997 order to raze the building that houses one of the few giant pools in the world where scientists can "grow" Arctic sea ice and conduct experiments. Lyon, who died in May 1998, wanted the lab mothballed intact so that study could be revived quickly should there be a war, and he found it hard to believe that the submarine force had not recognized the importance of saving the facility. He believed that the lesson from German tactics in World War II and the Soviets' shift to the ice proved that potential enemies will again use the almost impenetrable cover to attack U.S. targets on shore or at sea. He noted that even a simple diesel sub could easily hide in the ice and that, without further study, the United States would remain vulnerable.

Another good source on Lyon's early work (the first two or three decades of it) is *The Reminiscences of Dr. Waldo K. Lyon*, a 297-page oral history in the collection at the U.S. Naval Institute, Annapolis, Maryland.

The stunning scene when Admiral Rickover appealed to President Reagan to block Lehman's efforts to retire him is recounted in full detail in the introduction to John F. Lehman Jr., *Command of the Seas: Building the 600-Ship Navy* (New York: Charles Scribner's Sons, 1988). Rickover's retaliation—putting up the picture of Benedict Arnold near John Lehman's—was recounted in Rockwell, *The Rickover Effect*, (p. 364).

Rickover was still an icon, but even some veteran submariners thought it was time for him to go—and that the demands of his reactor safety bureaucracy had gotten out of hand. In 1981, one sub captain, Commander Ed Linz, resigned his command of the USS *Kamehameha* (*SSBN-642*) to protest the management of the sub program. He said some officers had so little time to focus on seamanship skills that he feared a nuclear sub might run aground "due to total incompetence in basic navigation and ship handling, but the reactor-control division records would be perfect as it hit." Rickover died in July 1986.

Odyssey 82 was the name of a cruise book put together by crew members on *Parche* that year.

Admiral Watkins's quote on the Arctic ice as "a beautiful place to hide" for Soviet submarines was cited by Compton-Hall, *Sub Versus Sub*, p. 97. In a lengthy interview, Admiral Watkins also explained to us why he thought the U.S. sub force still could have countered the Soviets under the ice, as well as some of the moves he and others made to intimidate the Soviets psychologically. One of the most fascinating involved Watkins's decision to allow the U.S. Naval Institute—a private, nonprofit organization that works closely with the Navy—to publish the first edition of Tom Clancy's submarine novel *The Hunt for Red October* in 1984 even though some admirals believed it would enable the Soviets to learn more about U.S. submarine capabilities.

Watkins told us that about two-thirds of the technical information in Clancy's novel is on target and the rest is wrong, and that it typically overstates U.S. abilities. Rather than blocking publication of the book, or attempting to correct the misperceptions, when Clancy submitted his manuscript to the Navy for clearance, Watkins said he decided to let the book go forward as it was. "*The Hunt for Red October* did us a service," he said. "The Soviets kind of believed it, and we won the battle, and therefore it was a significant part of the noncostly deterrence of submarines."

Along the same lines, Watkins said that he was "sending a signal" to the Soviets by allowing detailed papers on the new forward U.S. maritime strategy to be published in the *U.S. Naval Institute Proceedings* in 1986. While some in Congress questioned his move, he testified that the public declarations told the Soviets: "Don't risk either conflict or serious conventional war with the United States, because you are going to run into a hornets' nest and one of those is going to be at sea and you're not going to win that one." Publication of both the novel and the strategy, he added, demonstrated that "we had the resolve, we had the plan."

Another former official said the Navy also funded undersea expert Robert D. Ballard's search for the wreckage of the *Titanic* as part of this game of psychological warfare against the Soviets. Ballard found the *Titanic* in 1985 and explored its wreckage with the mini-sub *Alvin* in 1986. This official said the Navy's aim in supporting Ballard's highly publicized missions was to show the Soviets that "we could find things underwater and look inside" so that they would think "we were not merely 10 feet tall but 20 feet tall." He said all these efforts to intimidate the Soviets—and make them think they could not compete with the United States—were encouraged by the late CIA Director William Casey.

Much of the information about the tumultuous year in U.S.-Soviet relations in 1983 comes from George Shultz, *Turmoil and Triumph: My Years as Secretary of State: The Memoirs of George P. Shultz* (New York: Charles Scribner's Sons, 1993). The sense of paranoia among Andropov and other KGB officials is vividly described in Chapter 13 of Christopher Andrew and Oleg Gordievsky, *KGB: The Inside Story* (New York: HarperCollins, 1990).

In explaining the importance of hiding a second-strike capability on submarines, Admiral Watkins also said: "The mission of the strategic deterrent at sea is not first strike. It is called war termination strategy. That's where it fits. So the first strike was the intercontinental ballistic missiles, obviously. The land-based missiles were the potential first strike and probably the most destabilizing of the elements of the deterrent.

"The maritime forces, while they were large in numbers of warheads, were there for the war termination strategy, which said: How do you win such a thing? Who wins? Well, we both know that nobody really wins. But who wins the battle is going to be largely a function of how much you have left after the first exchange. And while this is an insidious game, and I'm not trying to say I love the game, that's the reality of when you get into offensive weaponry on both sides as a strategic deterrent, as opposed to strategic defense."

Watkins also said he believed very strongly that the Soviets weren't going to launch a first strike. "We briefed the Joint Chiefs, we briefed the president on what we thought we could do, why we thought we could do it, and I think we felt very comfortable, and I believe that that self-confidence was transmitted to the Russians in a variety of ways—by the strength of our resolve at our incidents-at-sea agreements, our discussions, by the maritime strategy publication itself, by their intelligence-gathering network on the sophistication and ability and capability of our submarine force, by a variety of publications and unclassified speculation and so forth, over a long time.

"Their intelligence sources were good, and we wanted them to know how self-confident we were. That's the role it plays. It's not a matter of charging up there and shooting up a lot of ballistic missile submarines as being the goal to prevent them from even launching first strike. No. That's not the way they would deploy their submarine force, and not the way that we would deploy ours.

"It was far deeper than that. These were the backup forces necessary to—you might say—undergird a nuclear exchange, and our job, of course, was to set up a deterrent that would make it unwise to do that, and we did it. And I believe it was one of the reasons that we were able to bring the Russians to their knees in the cold war. Because they could not win that battle, and therefore, why continue?"

Bob Woodward first described Admiral Butts's proposal to lay cables in the Barents and relay information from taps on Soviet lines in real time in *Veil: The Secret Wars of the CIA 1981–1987* (New York: Simon and Schuster, 1987). *Veil* also gives the best previously published description of how the Soviets found the taps in the Sea of Okhotsk and how the White House and the intelligence community sought to keep the *Washington Post* from publishing what it knew about the tap operations in 1986. But even though *Veil* outlines Butts's costly proposal, neither Woodward's stories in the *Post* nor his book say that the Navy already was tapping Soviet cables in the Barents.

The only public indications that the Navy was involved in tapping cables in the Barents have come in brief statements in three other books that also mention Butts's proposal: Angelo Codevilla, a former Senate staff member who reviewed intelligence budgets from 1977 to 1985, notes in *Informing Statecraft: Intelligence for a New Century* (New York: Free Press, 1992) that the Sea of Okhotsk taps had been so valuable that "by the early 1980s the U.S. government had begun a multibillion-dollar project to make the flow simple and instantaneous. It involved tapping a Soviet undersea cable near the northwestern city of Murmansk with an American cable, buried under the sands of the Arctic Ocean's floor, and reaching all the way to Greenland. This intrusion into Soviet communications would have provided foolproof, timely warning of any Soviet decision to go to war." Still, Codevilla added that this idea eventually fell victim to "a classic bureaucratic coup de grace. Powerful factions within both CIA and NSA had opposed the direct-cable tap because it would have been expensive and would have taken money from current programs" (pp. 163–164). In *Fall from Glory*, Greg Vistica cites an unnamed defense source who said that the Navy had experimented with, and then abandoned, plans for an undersea plow that could "lay a cable from Greenland directly to the pods on the north coast of the Soviet Union, thus eliminating the submarine's work" (p. 72). And in *The Universe Below*, Bill Broad states that in addition to the Sea of Okhotsk, the cable-tapping "feats were repeated" in the Barents. He cites an interview with Codevilla where he added that the cables to Greenland would have been made of fiber optics and would have been so long that they would have needed special devices to boost the signals. He also stated that the project—"a massive industrial undertaking on the seafloor, the likes of which had never before been attempted"—became the most expensive item in the intelligence budget before "the plug was pulled" (pp. 82–83). Before *Blind Man's Bluff*, nobody has ever written any more about how the Navy was tapping cables in the Barents, and nobody has identified *Parche* as the sub that laid the taps, or described how extensive and hazardous these operations were.

Two books give the full history of John Walker and his spy ring: John Barron, *Breaking the Ring: The Bizarre Case of the Walker Family Spy Ring* (Boston: Houghton Mifflin, 1987); and Pete Earley, *Family of Spies: Inside the John Walker Spy Ring* (New York: Bantam Books, 1988). John Lehman offers his ghoulish advice on what kind of punishment Walker should have received in *Command of the Seas* (pp. 133–34). Studeman's assessment of the damage that Walker did was included in an affidavit he wrote as part of the criminal case against Jerry Whitworth. It is on file in the U.S. District Court for the Northern District of California, and a copy is included in Senate Select Committee on Intelligence, "Meeting the Espionage Challenge: A Review of United States Counterintelligence and Security Programs," September 23, 1986. The tale of Toshiba's treachery in selling the advanced propeller-milling equipment to the Soviets is well summarized in Ralph Kinney Bennett, "The Toshiba Scandal: Anatomy of a Betrayal," *Reader's Digest* (December 1987). In the case of Ronald Pelton, we drew mainly on the coverage of his trial by Woodward, Patrick Tyler, Susan Schmidt, and Paul W. Valentine in the *Washington Post* and Stephen Engelberg and Philip Shenon in the *New York Times*. Rich Haver's appearance before the Senate Intelligence Committee and a summary of the contents of his report about the Soviets' discovery of the taps in Okhotsk were described to us by former government officials familiar with them.

Our quotations from what Reagan and Gorbachev said to each other in Reykjavík all come from Shultz, *Turmoil and Triumph*, Ch. 36 ("What Really Happened at Reykjavík"). Shultz notes in that book that he usually kept careful notes of his meetings with key leaders and/or contemporaneous notes taken by others.

Interestingly enough, Shultz told us in an interview that while he supported risky, "military-oriented" intelligence missions like the cable-tapping, he also thought much clandestine intelligence was overrated. "The most important information—people have to keep reminding themselves—is what you get by just common observation," he said. "I always felt—I don't want to distinguish among newspapers—but I always felt that the dispatches of Bill Keller, who wrote for the *New York Times,* were about as rewarding reading about anything that was going on as anything I read. And he didn't have any clandestine sources or what not. He was just a smart guy who got around.

"And I think that as a general proposition, the basic State Department reporting, using open sources, and observation, and talking to people, give you the basic picture. Sometimes you can be even misled by what you pick up in some clandestine way. Because there is a feeling that if you got it by some secret means, it must be very important." Laughing, he added: "And it may be that it's not anywhere near as important as things that are just obviously there."

Chapter 12: Trust but Verify

Main interviews: Admiral Carl Trost and other current and former top Navy officials.

Government documents, books, articles, and other sources: Admiral Crowe describes Marshal Akhromeyev's visits in detail in Chapter 16 of *The Line of Fire.* Admiral Trost, in an interview, described the meeting with Akhromeyev in the Joint Chiefs' "Tank" as well as his own travels to Russia and conclusions about the Soviet Navy. Akhromeyev committed suicide after the failed coup against Gorbachev in 1991.

The activity of the submarines in Squadron 11 was included in its official command history for 1988.

Bush wrote to Gorbachev to offer the Soviets help after their prototype for an advanced "Mike"-class nuclear attack submarine sank in 8,400 feet of water 270 miles north of Norway. It sank after a fire broke out on board, and 42 crew members were killed.

Transcripts of speeches from the Naval Submarine League's convention in 1990 were reprinted in the organization's quarterly magazine, the *Submarine Review,* later that year. The role of U.S. attack submarines in the Persian Gulf War and details of the Navy's new "From the Sea" maritime strategy have been described in numerous news articles and in brochures prepared by the Navy. The Navy publicly released a report of an investigation into the collision involving the USS *Baton Rouge,* and we also drew from news articles about both that and the *Grayling* collision in the *New York Times* and the *Washington Post,* which published the quote from the unnamed senior administration official wondering whether top Navy officials "read the newspapers" before undertaking such missions.

There also have been numerous articles in the major daily newspapers, the *U.S. Naval Institute Proceedings,* and the *Submarine Review* on the plans for, and capabilities of, both the new *Seawolf* and the proposed NSSN attack submarines, as well as extensive coverage on how much the submarine force is being cut back from cold war levels. The *Submarine Review*'s practice of reprinting Sub League convention speeches from top Navy officials has made it easy to keep track of all the changes in the sub force, from new technology to the new roles and missions. One recent article in the general press—Richard J. Newman, "Breaking the Surface," *U.S. News & World Report*, April 6, 1998, pp. 28–42—also provides a comprehensive look at what the sub force is focusing on now.

Two articles noted the USS *Parche*'s move from Mare Island to a new port in Washington State: Ed Offley, "Secret Nuclear Navy Submarine Finds New Home," *Seattle Post-Intelligencer* [the article title as it appeared in the *Times-Picayune* (New Orleans), November 24, 1994]; and Lloyd Pritchett, "Will Top-Secret Sub Be Able to Slip into Area Quietly?" *Bremerton Sun*, August 8, 1994.

Both Offley's and Newman's stories suggest that Iran and China would be good targets for cable-tapping by the *Parche*. The Navy's plans to lengthen the USS *Jimmy Carter* and make her a replacement for *Parche* in 2003 were disclosed by a trade publication, "Inside the Navy," on February 1, 1999.

Epilogue

Gates's decision to bring the videotape of the funeral held for the men on the Golf was ultimately motivated by the fact that the United States wanted to inspire Russia to offer up information on missing American servicemen in Vietnam. Before that, "We had never confirmed anything to the Russians except in various vague senses," he said in an interview. "Shortly after the USSR collapsed, the Bush administration had told the Russians through an intermediary that we couldn't tell them any more about what had happened on Golf/*Glomar*. But then when we started asking the Russians about what had happened to U.S. pilots shot down over Vietnam, and if any U.S. POWs had been transferred to Russia and held there, they came back and said, 'What about our guys in the submarine?'"

At the time, the administration told the Russians only that there were no survivors and that there were only scattered remains. Later, Gates says, "It seemed to me, as I was getting ready for the trip, that there would be symbolic value in terms of assuring the Russians that, from the CIA's standpoint, the cold war was over." It was then that he decided to give them information about the *Glomar*. He planned the move as a surprise, he says. "We didn't tell the Russians what I was bringing. We told them I was bringing a gift for Yeltsin of historic and symbolic importance. They were dying to know what it was. For once, we kept a secret. I guess Aldrich Ames was not brought into the picture."

Appendix A: Submarine Collisions

Main sources: U.S. and Russian submariners and navy officials, Joshua Handler, Alexander Mozgovoy, and news articles cited in the text.

Appendix B: From the Soviet Side

Main sources: U.S. and Russian submariners and navy officials, and articles in Russian newspapers and magazines. The most detailed account of the reactor accident on the *Hiroshima* came from the May 1991 issue of *Soviet Soldier,* in an article titled "Ivan Kulakov Versus a Nuclear Reactor," pp. 28–31.

Since the end of the cold war, the Russian Navy has been much more open about what went on than the U.S. Navy, and numerous articles have appeared in the Russian press detailing submarine disasters and disclosing other problems. Our researcher, Alexander Mozgovoy, wrote some of these articles for various publications. Several articles have described the travails of the K-19 and the drama of the reactor accident that killed eight of its crew members in 1961. (An additional twenty-two men ultimately died from radiation poisoning.) The episode involving the USS *Baltimore* and the Soviet Zulu IV sub was first reported in the series in the *Chicago Tribune* and the *Newport News* (Va.) *Daily Press* in 1991.

ACKNOWLEDGMENTS

Most of the submariners and intelligence officials who have helped us with this book have done so only under the condition of anonymity and took great risk in speaking to us. We were surprised at first at just how warm a welcome many gave us, letting us inside their lives and sharing their secrets. Looking back, we have come to realize that our book gave them their first opportunity to share what had been, for many of them, at once the best and most harrowing days of their lives. They needed to talk as much as we wanted to shine a light on an extraordinary era that had gone largely unexamined and unheralded.

Some people were able to help us openly, and it is with great pride we name them here. We hired a top Russian military reporter, Alexander Mozgovoy, to interview Russian Navy leaders and submariners to help us understand their side of the story. Joshua Handler, who traveled all over Russia investigating Soviet submarine accidents and their environmental damage, made this possible by introducing us to Mozgovoy, and Josh's wife, Sada Aksartova, translated his report. Mozgovoy's son, Vasily, also helped. On the American side, John Craven made us smile with his volumes of maxims and elfin wit, then helped us understand the most daunting technical topics, sharing his vision of the deep and of the men who agreed with him and the men who scoffed. We would also like to thank Rafael C. Benitez and Harris M. "Red" Austin of the USS *Cochino* for bringing us back in time to the days the submarine wars began. Otis G. Pike, Aaron Donner, and Seymour M. Hersh shared with us what they went through when they tried, twenty years ago, to take the first serious look at the hidden realm of cold war submarine operations. Waldo K. Lyon patiently explained the daunting properties of Arctic ice. There were also a number of people who went out of their way to help us who belong to veterans groups such as the Naval Submarine League, United States Submarine Veterans, Naval Intelligence Professionals, U.S. Naval Cryptologic Veterans Association, and the Association of Former Intelligence Officers.

Finally we would like to thank Harry Disch of the Scientists Institute for Public Information, who helped us get around the Navy's reluctance to give us an outing on a submarine by including us in a tour of the 6th Fleet that he had arranged for military writers. We would also like to thank Diane Wilderman, whose husband Alvin B. Wilderman, captain of the USS *Plunger* (*SSN-595*), was pulled overboard by severe waves and killed while passing near the Golden Gate Bridge in 1973. She and many other submariners' wives gave us an invaluable understanding of how the families were affected by the risks their men took every time they went out on a submarine.

Even with such assistance, there were times over the past five years that we were nearly overwhelmed by the task of telling four decades of hidden history while trying to navigate a publishing world undergoing its own confused metamorphosis. We could never have done that without Esther Newberg, our agent at ICM. With her behind us, we knew we could focus on what was most important—getting this book written. We succeeded in wrestling with the silence and secrecy because we knew we could count on her to take on any and all comers on shore. She

grew up outside of New London, Connecticut, watching submarines come and go and wondering what they did, and she
came to help us find our way through publishers' row in
Manhattan. She is one of the strongest, most caring, and best
women we know, and we are awfully glad she is on our side. In
her office, first Amanda Beesley and then Jack Horner were
always there to cheer us on. John De Laney, ICM's attorney,
also has been a remarkable ally and a good friend. Helen
Shabason, an ICM film and documentary agent, has also
worked tirelessly on our behalf. We would also like to thank
Robert Asahina, who early on saw the potential of this project.

It was Esther who first brought us to Peter Osnos, publisher
and chief executive of PublicAffairs. Peter created PublicAffairs
because he believed that there could be books beyond the topic
du jour, that journalists and historians deserved to be heard,
that there could be and should be "good books about things
that matter." We are very proud to be among the first of his
offerings. It was Peter who put us in the hands of Geoff
Shandler, who, as our editor, proved himself to be a throwback
in the best sense of the word. He believes that editors and
authors can still work together, that there is more to an editor's
job than making deals for manuscripts and watching sales
charts. It is that conviction, along with his considerable talent,
that helped us through the final hurdles of completing this project. We couldn't have been in better hands. He and Robert
Kimzey, PublicAffairs' managing editor, helped give this book
its design and flair, and Lisa Kaufman, Mary-Claire Flynn, Erica
Brown, Kate Darnton, and Gene Taft also helped enormously.

HarperCollins Publishers adopted us next, publishing the paperback. Susan Weinberg, publishing director of HarperPerennial and
Gail Winston, senior editor, did more than we ever could have
asked to ensure this book's place in publishing history. Bridget
Sweeney, Tom Finnegan, and Kyoko Watanabe labored hard to
guarantee the paperback carried all the style and flair of the original hardcover release.

When a book takes over your life, someone, many someones,
have to pick up the slack. All three of us also want to thank the people who stood behind us and for us.

From Sherry Sontag:

First I want to thank my parents, Marvin and Sandra Sontag. When I write, I am really speaking to them. I would also like to thank my sisters and their husbands, Lauren Sontag Davitz and Michael Davitz; and Aviva and Yedidiah Ghatan; and my brother and his wife, Avi and Freyda Sontag. They never flagged in their support despite the fact that my work on the book often meant my absence from them and from the offshoots of the Sontag clan: Tova, Josh, Shoshana, Shira, Matt, Ariella, Gabriel, and Zachary.

Doreen Weisenhaus of the *New York Times* encouraged me to find my voice as a writer when I was at the *National Law Journal* and ever since has been my best mentor and a close friend. James Finkelstein, my publisher at the *Law Journal,* never let me forget that there would be life after this book. Along with Deidre Leipziger and Claudia Payne of the *New York Times,* they have all been unfailing supporters and terrific teachers.

Holly, Bob, Emily, and Anya Carter were always there to listen to submarine tales and anything else as were Jon Stewart; Alexis Thomason; Julianne, Greg, and Peter Genua; and Joe Gallant. Bethany Birkett and Larry Howard guided me through all of the rough spots with great love and wisdom. Michael Dalby; Lima Kim; Shirley Loci; Mala Feit; Manfred Fulda; Martin Weidner and his sons Chris and Josh; Carlos and Marina Trovar; Mark Peterson; Chris DeMarco; Michael Whitlow; and Joan Yager stepped in whenever they were needed, which was often. I couldn't have gotten through without any of them.

Edgar Ievins gave endless time and support, fostered my cat all the months I spent on the road doing research, and handled much of the paperwork of running life and a business. Julie Whitney forced me to relax and celebrate as small pieces of this book got finished and kindly ignored all the work that still had to be done.

Tim Sheetz and Gary Leib at AT&T Global Information Solutions kept the laptop computer we used on the road functioning long past its natural life. Barry Sears, a fellow author, and his brother Doug Sears offered reams of advice and crucial help.

There are other people who have been terrific friends and who have picked up the slack wherever and whenever. Some of them are Leah Dilworth, Rick Birkett, Debra Strell, Carol Neal, Carl Allocco, Ruth Stone, Jane and Emily Hall, Jeanie Walsh, James O'Conner, Jodi Lambert, Mike Taranto, Jeremy Lampel, Steve Darling, Rob Wolfson, Larry Vedilago, Walt Bogdanich, David Millman, Paula Lovejoy, Brian Hoffman, Judith Spindler, Cara Hogue, Ann Day, Greg (Tauron) Mitchell, Lissie Mitchell, Mike Mullen, Kim Brewer, Randy Cooper, Bruce Harlan Boll, Ernie Foster, Tom Hruby, Josh Mills, Harvey Goldschmid, James M. Milligan, Dominick Oliveri, Martin Baskin, Robert From, Richard Klein, Julie Mitnick, Lila Nachtigal, Donald Rubell, Adriana Semnicka, Anna Sposej, Maria and Juaquin Valdez, Gene Andre, the gang at Muffin, and the folks at Marin Management. I would especially like to thank Maggie Hopp and Ché Graham for shooting the author photos for the publisher's catalogue and the book.

Finally I would like to thank Mary O'Conner Spinner and my grandparents, Sydell and Abraham Bockstein and Harry and Dora Sontag. I wish they could have read this book. I will miss them forever.

From Christopher Drew and Annette Lawrence Drew:

We also would like first and foremost to thank our parents, brothers and sisters, and other relatives. Chris's parents, Leon and Helen Drew; his sisters, Cynthia Drew and Laura Bussey; Laura's husband, David, and daughter, Chelsea; and Jane Stevens provided constant love and support. Annette's mother, Maxine S. Lawrence, a gifted researcher in her own right, showed her enormous love and patience—and was always ready to sympathize and offer encouragement. Annette's brothers and sisters and their spouses, Mark and Catherine Lawrence, John and Priscilla Lawrence, Paul and Mary-Elise Lawrence Soniat, and Betsy Lawrence all offered support and encouragement throughout this long process, and one of Annette's aunts, Irma M. Stiegler, cheerfully volunteered to spend days microfilming old news articles for us in a public library. And a note of thanks to my deceased father, John W. Lawrence, who strived for excellence in all things; he set a wonderful example.

Chris also would particularly like to thank top editors at the *New York Times*—Joseph Lelyveld, Bill Keller, John M. Geddes,

Allan M. Siegal, Soma Golden Behr, Dean Baquet, Andy Rosenthal, Glenn Kramon, Joyce Purnick, Matt Purdy, and Stephen Engelberg—for providing the flexibility he needed at crucial moments. Others at the *Times*—Jeff Gerth, Michael Wines, Steven Erlanger, Philip Shenon, Don Van Natta, Lizette Alvarez, Lora Korbut, Timothy L. O'Brien, Nancy Weinstock, and Adam Liptak—were helpful as well.

Chris and Sherry first got interested in submarine spying when Chris coordinated the reporting on a series of articles for the *Chicago Tribune* that began to peel away the secrecy surrounding these missions. That series was published jointly in January 1991 by the *Tribune* and its sister paper, the *Newport News Daily Press*, which had ample interest in the subject given its proximity to Newport News Shipbuilding, one of the country's largest submarine construction yards. Michael L. Millenson, then a *Tribune* reporter, and Robert Becker, then the Washington correspondent of the *Daily Press* and now a *Tribune* reporter, also devoted themselves to the project, and Jill Olmsted, Ruth Lopez, Mary Ann Akers, and Linda Harrington handled some of the research. Nicholas M. Horrock, then the *Tribune*'s assistant managing editor for Washington news, and Jack W. Davis Jr., who has been editor, president, and publisher of the *Daily Press*—and is now president of a Tribune Internet company—oversaw the effort, both as wonderful friends and two of America's finest teachers of investigative reporting. Jack and his wife, Mimi, opened their home, as well as the library and photography archives of the *Daily Press*, to us in the long process of giving birth to this book. Will Corbin, the editor of the *Daily Press*, also graciously helped.

Several other friends took us in off the road or otherwise helped out: Curt and Sharon Hearn, Leonard and Rhoda Dreyfus, Richard F. Hoefer, Annie Tin, Cindy Lerner and her sons Elliot and Austin, Eric and Gaby Shilakis, Jeff and Sarah Kestner, Terry Atlas, Peter and Kate Goelz, Mimi Read, Charlie Burke, and George Wallace. Robert Becker and his wife, Karen Heller, remained steadfast, as did Michael Tackett and Julie Carey, Husein and Carol Jafferjee, Mike Karras and Kathy Macor, Ulf and Suzanne Ghosh, Don and Meryl McCusker, Brian and Eileen

Machler, James T. High Jr., and Jeffrey T. Werner, who has no peer in his enthusiasm for learning every last fact about the submarine force.

From All of Us:

All three of us also would like to thank several military and political analysts who were always ready to help: William M. Arkin, Bruce G. Blair, Richard J. Boyle, retired Navy Captain James T. Bush, Dr. Michael Gold-Biss, Chuck Hansen, Hans M. Kristensen, Barry M. Posen, Jeffrey Richelson, Richard Russell, and Zong-Yee Willson Yang.

To all the people at the Naval Historical Center in Washington, D.C., who gave us their interest, support, and professional expertise we express much gratitude: Kathleen Lloyd, Operational Archives Division; Bernard F. Cavalcante, Operational Archives Division; John C. Reilly Jr., Ships' History Branch, and the members of his staff; the staff of the library at the Naval Historical Center. We also thank the library staff at the Submarine Force Library & Museum at the Naval Submarine Base in Groton, Connecticut, and Arlyn Danielson and Aldona Sendzikas of the USS *Bowfin* Submarine Museum & Park in Honolulu. For all their help in providing access to the extensive holdings of the Naval Institute, particularly their superb oral histories, we would like to thank Paul Stillwell and Linda O'Doughda. Sue Lemmon, Mare Island historian, was invaluable in saving historical materials when that naval base was shut down amid all the recent base closings. We owe special gratitude to Kathy Vinson and the staff of the Defense Visual Information Center and to Bill Tiernan of the *Norfolk Virginian-Pilot*.

For help in checking various submarine subjects, we would like to thank Rhonda Coleman, the *Vallejo Times-Herald*; Alex S. Weinbaum III, John M. Pfeffer, The Free Library of Philadelphia; Wendy Sheanin, *San Francisco Chronicle*; Stephen Johnson of the *Houston Chronicle*; Dorothy Marsden, Tom Lucy, The Vallejo Naval and Historical Museum; Axel Graumann, National Climatic Data Center, U.S. Department of Commerce, National Oceanic and Atmospheric Administration; T. J. Tucker, Naval Safety Center, Norfolk, Virginia; Dennis Filgren, The Harry S.

Truman Presidential Library; Michelle Dzyak, Penn State University; the staff of the Martha Washington Library in Fairfax County, Virginia; and the staff of the Research Correspondence Division of the National Geographic Society.

There were dozens of people who came forward to help us get through our long months on tour when *Blind Man's Bluff* was published. They are far too many to list here, but a few must be named. They are George and Patty Knudtzon, Les Honda, Marge Thorne, and Max Monningh.

We also owe a special debt to some of the wonderful men we met along the way who helped us ensure that this history got told before it was lost forever. Among them were several fine submarine and intelligence officers who died over the last several years, such as Bernard A. "Chick" Clarey, Frederick J. "Fritz" Harlfinger II, Roy S. Benson, Levering Smith, Ray S. Cline, and scientist Waldo K. Lyon. Sadly, in early 1999, after the hardcover edition of this book was published, two heroes of the *Cochino* chapter also died: the courtly captain, Rafael C. Benitez, and the sub's hulking spook, Harris M. "Red" Austin. Most recently, we lost Charles Thorne— the man who stepped forward to give the Navy what may become the key to solving *Scorpion*'s loss. We feel very fortunate that we got to hear their stories.

PHOTOGRAPHIC CREDITS

In 1900, the Navy purchased . . . : U.S. Navy photo

Almost one hundred years later . . . : Electric Boat Co.

The last picture of Cochino . . . : photo courtesy of Harris M. Austin

Cochino's *commander* . . . : U.S. Navy photo, courtesy of Rafael C. Benitez

Red Austin, 1939 . . . : courtesy of Richard M. Austin

Cochino's *men survived* . . . : photo and back note courtesy of Harris M. Austin's son, Richard M. Austin

Tusk *traveled with* . . . : U.S. Naval Historical Center

Gudgeon *(top):* courtesy of a Gudgeon crew member

Gudgeon (bottom): U.S. Naval Historical Center

With the undying belief . . . : Electric Boat Co.

Nautilus *was the first* . . . : Electric Boat Co.

If the president could have Air Force One . . . : U.S. Navy photo

John Craven dreamed . . . : U.S. Navy Photographic Center, R. P. Allan, 1969

Even before the Navy sent . . . : U.S. Navy photo taken by crew of *Trieste II*

Halibut *had a mammoth* . . . : U.S. Navy photo

Halibut *patch:* U.S. Navy photo

Commander C. Edward Moore . . . : U.S. Navy photo

Scorpion *was outside of Naples, 1969* . . . : U.S. Naval Historical Center, courtesy of H. John R. Holland

Craven (left), Harry Jackson, and . . . : U.S. Navy photo

Scorpion's *shattered hull, 1969* . . . : U.S. Navy photo

Commander Whitey Mack . . . : *Newport News* (Va.) *Daily Press*

Lapon *and Mack were immortalized* . . . : photographs of original album cover taken for this book

INDEX

SHERRY SONTAG is a former staff writer for the *National Law Journal* and has written for the *New York Times*.

CHRISTOPHER DREW is a special projects editor at the *New York Times* and has won numerous awards for his investigative reporting.

ANNETTE LAWRENCE DREW, the book's researcher, has a PhD from Princeton.

PublicAffairs is a publishing house founded in 1997. It is a tribute to the standards, values, and flair of three persons who have served as mentors to countless reporters, writers, editors, and book people of all kinds, including me.

I. F. STONE, proprietor of *I. F. Stone's Weekly*, combined a commitment to the First Amendment with entrepreneurial zeal and reporting skill and became one of the great independent journalists in American history. At the age of eighty, Izzy published *The Trial of Socrates*, which was a national bestseller. He wrote the book after he taught himself ancient Greek.

BENJAMIN C. BRADLEE was for nearly thirty years the charismatic editorial leader of *The Washington Post*. It was Ben who gave the *Post* the range and courage to pursue such historic issues as Watergate. He supported his reporters with a tenacity that made them fearless and it is no accident that so many became authors of influential, best-selling books.

ROBERT L. BERNSTEIN, the chief executive of Random House for more than a quarter century, guided one of the nation's premier publishing houses. Bob was personally responsible for many books of political dissent and argument that challenged tyranny around the globe. He is also the founder and longtime chair of Human Rights Watch, one of the most respected human rights organizations in the world.

•   •   •

For fifty years, the banner of Public Affairs Press was carried by its owner Morris B. Schnapper, who published Gandhi, Nasser, Toynbee, Truman, and about 1,500 other authors. In 1983, Schnapper was described by *The Washington Post* as "a redoubtable gadfly." His legacy will endure in the books to come.

[signature]

Peter Osnos, *Founder and Editor-at-Large*